Vorhergehende Doppelseite:
Der Greifensee im leuchtenden Morgenlicht.
Doppelseite am Schluss des Buches:
Torfriet am Pfäffikersee.

Previous double-page:
The Greifensee in luminescent morning light.
Double-page at the end of the book:
Torfriet near the Pfäffikersee.

ZÜRCHER LANDSCHAFTEN

Natur- und Kulturlandschaften
des Kantons Zürich

ZURICH LANDSCAPES

Natural and Cultural Landscapes
in the Canton of Zurich

Herausgeber · Editor **Heinz von Arx**
Fotos · Photos **Roth + Schmid**
Texte · Texts **Hans Weiss, Bernhard Nievergelt**
Bildlegenden · Captions **Bernhard Nievergelt**

AS Verlag

Wir danken dem Lotteriefonds des Kantons Zürich,
der mit seiner Unterstützung die Realisierung
dieses Buches ermöglicht hat.

We want to sincerely thank the Lottery Fund
of the Canton of Zurich for its generous support;
it made this book possible.

www.as-verlag.ch

© AS Verlag & Buchkonzept AG, Zürich 2016
Gestaltung und Herstellung / Design and Production:
AS Verlag, Heinz von Arx, Urs Bolz, Zürich
Lektorat und Korrektorat / Editing / Proofreading:
Andres Betschart, bürobetschart, Winterthur
Übersetzung / Translation: Beverly Zumbühl, WordsWork, Zürich
Druck / Printing: B&K Offsetdruck GmbH, Ottersweier
Einband / Cover: Grossbuchbinderei Josef Spinner GmbH, Ottersweier
ISBN 978-3-906055-54-1

Inhalt

Hans Weiss
9 **Natur und Landschaft im Kanton Zürich**
Im Spannungsfeld zwischen Stadt und Land · 11
Von tropischen Korallenriffen zu
kalbenden Gletschern · 12
Was ist eine Landschaft? · 16
Landschaft als Heimat · 18
Bedrohung und Verlust der Landschaft · 21
Vom Wandel der Agrarwirtschaft und den
Folgen für die Landschaft · 22
Die ökonomische Einäugigkeit · 24
Der Kanton Zürich als Vorreiter für einen
raumgreifenden Naturschutz · 26
Wo die Not ist, wächst auch das Rettende · 28
Ausblick · 29

Bernhard Nievergelt
63 **Voralpin geprägte Landschaften**
119 **Seen- und Flusslandschaften**
163 **Landschaften der Auen und Moore**
205 **Waldlandschaften**
241 **Parkanlagen und Stadtwälder**

260 Übersichtskarte
262 Literaturverzeichnis
263 Biografien der Autoren
264 Nachwort und Dank des Herausgebers

Contents

Hans Weiss
9 **Nature and Landscape in the Canton of Zurich**
Caught between city and countryside · 11
From tropical coral reefs to calving glaciers · 12
What is a landscape? · 16
A landscape as 'home' · 18
Threats and the loss of landscapes · 20
On changes in the agricultural economy and the
consequences for the landscape · 22
Turning a blind eye to economic conditions · 24
The Canton of Zurich as a pioneer for
nature protection · 26
Where there is a need, a rescue
arises as well · 28
Outlook · 29

Bernhard Nievergelt
63 **Characteristic Prealpine Landscapes**
119 **Lake and River Landscapes**
163 **Water Meadows and Moor Landscapes**
205 **Forest Landscapes**
241 **Parks and Municipal Forests**

260 Overview Map
262 Bibliography
263 Biographies of the Authors
264 Epilogue and Acknowledgements

Natur und Landschaft im Kanton Zürich

Nature and Landscape in the Canton of Zurich

«Am richtigen Ort nicht bauen ist auch ein Qualitätsmerkmal.»

'Not building in the right place is also an indication that quality matters.'

Immer mehr gelangt zum Bewusstsein, wie knapp und kostbar die unvermehrbaren Güter Boden und Landschaft sind. In den letzten 60 Jahren hat unsere Gesellschaft mehr natürlichen Boden verbaut und damit irreversibel zerstört als alle Generationen zuvor. Am 17. Juni 2012 hat das Stimmvolk eine kantonale Initiative angenommen, die einen strengen Schutz des landwirtschaftlichen Kulturlandes verlangt.

We are becoming more and more aware of just how scarce and precious these non-renewable goods of land and landscape are. In the last 60 years, our society has built on more natural ground, thus irreversibly destroying it, than all previous generations put together. On June 17, 2012, voters approved a cantonal initiative that requires the strict protection of agricultural land.

Zürich! Für die meisten Touristen aus dem Ausland verbirgt sich hinter diesem Namen vor allem eine Stadt, und einige verbinden damit noch einen interkontinentalen Flughafen. Auch viele Schweizer, die nicht Zürcher sind, setzen Zürich einfach mit der grössten Stadt und der finanzstärksten Wirtschaftsmetropole der Schweiz gleich. Natürlich ist Zürich historisch und verkehrsgeographisch der Mittelpunkt des gleichnamigen Kantons. Aber dass dieser auch der viertgrösste Agrarkanton unseres Landes ist und überdies auf seinem Territorium eine aussergewöhnliche Vielfalt von Landschaftstypen sowie natürliche oder naturnahe Gebiete birgt, ist viel weniger bekannt. Diesen kostbaren Lebensräumen ist dieses Buch gewidmet.

Im Spannungsfeld zwischen Stadt und Land
Nun ist das Bild von der Wirtschaftsmetropole und vom volksreichsten Schweizer Kanton nicht falsch. Wie ein prall gefüllter Kartoffelsack sieht der Kanton auf einer Karte der Schweiz aus, die nicht die Fläche des Areals, sondern die Einwohnerzahl als Kriterium für die Grösse beizieht.[1] Auf dieser Karte nehmen sich etwa die Kantone Graubünden, Wallis oder Tessin, deren Territorium sehr viel grösser ist, wie kleine und etwas verschrumpelte Anhängsel aus. Der Kanton Zürich weist nicht nur die höchste Einwohnerzahl, sondern auch das umfangreichste überbaute Areal aus. Ein Amerikaner, der auf seiner Europareise zum ersten Mal nach Zürich kam, soll gesagt haben, er habe nicht gewusst, dass die Stadt rund um einen See herum gebaut sei. Dementsprechend ist, in absoluten Zahlen, auch das Steueraufkommen des Kantons am höchsten. Dass Zürich sowohl wirtschaftlich als auch verkehrsgeographisch den Mittelpunkt des Kantons und ein Zentrum der ganzen östlichen Landeshälfte ist, kann nicht bestritten werden. Im Raumkonzept des Bundes, der Kantone und der Gemeinden figuriert der Grossraum Zürich als Metropolitanraum, der weit über die Kantonsgrenzen hinausgreift.[2]

Zurich! For most tourists from abroad, this name usually means the city, although some simply connect the name to another intercontinental airport. In fact, many Swiss who are not 'Zurchers', think of Zurich as the nation's largest city and its economically strongest metropolis. However, the City of Zurich is also the historical, geographical and strategic middle point of the canton of the same name. And, even less well known is that the Canton of Zurich is the fourth largest agricultural canton in our country; moreover, its territory contains an extraordinary diversity of landscapes and natural habitats. This book is dedicated to those invaluable living spaces.

Caught between city and countryside
Now, the image of Zurich as an economic metropolis and the most populated Swiss canton is not wrong. But, on a map of Switzerland that indicates the population rather than surface area, it does look rather like a bulging potato sack.[1] On such a map, for example, the Cantons of Graubünden, Wallis, or Ticino, which are very much larger, look small and sort of shrivelled compared to Zurich because of their lower population. The Canton of Zurich not only has the highest resident numbers, it also has the most extensive built-up area. An American on his European travels visited Zurich for the first time and afterwards said that he had not realised that the city had been built around a lake. Accordingly, in absolute numbers, the tax revenue of this canton is also the highest. That Zurich is both economically and geographically the middle point of the canton and indeed the centre of the entire eastern half of the country, cannot be denied. In the spatial development concept of the federal government, the cantons and communities of the Greater Zurich Area form a metropolitan space that extends far beyond the cantonal borders.[2]

However, as with all generalised statistics and cartographic representations that are limited to a single or a few criteria, this map also conveys an im-

Doch wie alle verallgemeinernden Statistiken und kartographischen Darstellungen, die sich nur auf ein einzelnes oder wenige Kriterien beschränken, vermittelt auch diese Karte ein Bild, das der Wirklichkeit nicht entspricht oder sie nur verzerrt wiedergibt. Im Gegensatz zu Basel ist Zürich kein Stadtkanton. Das Bild vom einzigen grossen Zentrum stimmt schon aus kultureller Sicht nicht. Man sage einmal einem Winterthurer, Zürich sei das Kulturzentrum des Kantons. Er wird einen mit verächtlich strafendem Blick als Ignorant einstufen oder auf einer Führung durch diese Garten- und Museumsstadt eines Besseren belehren.

Die Vorstellung vom Kanton mit der grössten Einwohnerzahl und der stärksten Wirtschaft weckt zumal in den Nachbarkantonen, aber auch innerhalb des Kantons selber jene Mischung aus Bewunderung und leisem Neid, den man gegenüber dem erfolgreichen Bruder oder dem reichen Onkel hegt. Gepaart ist dieses Gefühl durchaus mit einem gewissen Stolz, der das Eigene und die Andersartigkeit betont. Vor nicht manchen Jahren unterbreitete der Vorstand einer Zürichsee-Gemeinde ihren Einwohnerinnen und Einwohnern ein grosszügiges Projekt für eine umfassende Erneuerung des Dorfzentrums mit neuer Verkehrsführung samt unterirdischen Parkplätzen, Einkaufsmöglichkeiten mit Supermarkt und allem, was dazugehört. Das Projekt schien ziemlich unbestritten oder jedenfalls mehrheitsfähig zu sein, bis sich gegen Ende der Gemeindeversammlung, die den Kredit zu bewilligen hatte, ein alteingesessener Einwohner erhob und sagte, man wisse ja die Vorteile der nahen Stadt durchaus zu schätzen, aber man wolle doch selber nicht zur Stadt werden. Der Votant erntete lauten Beifall, das Projekt wurde mit überwältigendem Mehr bachab geschickt.

Das Beispiel zeigt, dass gerade im dicht besiedelten Raum bei aller Bejahung der Urbanität das Bedürfnis nach Bewahrung der einstigen Ländlichkeit wächst. Es sind die natürliche und die naturnahe Landschaft, die eine räumliche Identität stiften, und nicht grosse Bauwerke, ob es sich nun um Zeugen vergangener Zeiten handelt oder um moderne und postmoderne Architektur. Richten wir also unser Augenmerk vorerst auf den weiterum unbekannten Kanton Zürich, auf jenen Teil, der weder zugebaut noch zersiedelt ist: seine Natur und Landschaft.

**Von tropischen Korallenriffen
zu kalbenden Gletschern**

Die naturräumliche Vielfalt des Kantons Zürich ist gross. Sie umfasst eine Entstehungsgeschichte von vielen Millionen Jahren. Geologische Ereignisse und mannigfaltige Prozesse von der globalen Vereisung über sich abwechselnde Warm- und Kaltzeiten prägten hier wie anderswo die Gestalt und die Formenwelt

age that does not reflect the reality or perhaps even distorts it. In contrast to Basel, with its two cantons, Basel Land and Basel City, the City of Zurich is not a canton on its own. In fact, from a cultural point of view, even the image of a single large centre is not correct. Try telling that to a man from Winterthur who said that Zurich was the cultural centre of the canton! He got a contemptuous, punishing look, judged to be ignorant and perhaps taken on a tour of the Garden and Museum City of Winterthur to be taught a lesson.

The idea of a canton with the largest number of residents and the strongest economy awakens, especially in neighbouring cantons, but also within the canton itself, a mixture of admiration and light envy, such as one might bear towards a successful brother or a rich uncle. This feeling is paired with a certain pride that emphasises 'our own' and the 'others'. Not many years ago, the executive committee of a Zurich lake community submitted a proposal to its residents to fund a major project for a comprehensive renovation of the village centre with a new traffic management scheme, including underground parking, shopping opportunities with a supermarket, and everything that goes with it. The project appeared to be mostly unopposed, or at least capable of raising a majority, until the moment came near the end of the community general assembly to approve the loan, when an older local resident stood up and said that although one could certainly appreciate the advantages of a nearby city, one does not necessarily want to become part of a city themselves. The speaker reaped great acclamation and the project was sent packing by an overwhelming majority.

This example shows that precisely in those densely settled spaces with all the affirmatives to urbanity, the need for protecting rural areas is growing. It is the natural and the near-to-natural landscapes that endow an area with a spatial identity and not large, impressive structures, whether they are witnesses to past times or modern and post-modern architecture. Thus, we turn our attention now to the generally unknown Canton of Zurich, to those parts that are neither built-up nor sprawled-out: its nature and its landscapes.

**From tropical coral reefs
to calving glaciers**

The natural spatial diversity of the Canton of Zurich is quite broad. It encompasses a genesis story of many millions of years. Geological events and multi-faceted processes from global ice ages to the alternating warm and cold periods have left their mark here, as on other places, in the gestalt and forms of its territory, the 'Face of the Earth', as the well-known Swiss geographer, Emil Egli, so memorably formulated it.

Die heute auf Höhen von über 2000 Meter beschränkten Alpengletscher nahmen zur Zeit der letzten Vereisung, der Würm-Eiszeit, ungeheure Dimensionen an und wiesen Eismächtigkeiten von über 1000 Meter auf. Im Kanton Zürich (weisse Umrandung) ragten nur gerade die Lägern, der Irchel, die höchsten Gipfel des Zürcher Oberlandes und im Süden die Albiskette und der Aeugsterberg aus dem Eisstrom des Linthgletschers.

The Alpine glaciers, which are now limited to an altitude of over 2000 metres ASL, were at the time of the last glaciation, the Würm Ice Age, of immense proportions and had a thickness of over 1000 metres. In the Canton of Zurich (white outline), only the Lägern Mountains, the Irchel Elevation, and the highest mountain peaks of the Zurich Oberland managed to rise above the ice stream of the Linth Glacier, while in the south, the Albis mountain range and the Aeugsterberg rose proudly through it as well.

des Territoriums, das «Antlitz der Erde», wie es der bekannte Schweizer Geograph Emil Egli einprägsam formulierte. Beginnen wir mit der Lägern, der ältesten Formation von kompakten Gesteinsschichten im Kanton Zürich, die im Lauf der Zeit an die heute sichtbare Erdoberfläche auftauchten. Geologisch gehört die Lägern zum Jura, jenem langgestreckten Gebirgsbogen, der von Genf bis Schaffhausen weit ausholend das schweizerische Mittelland gegen Frankreich und Süddeutschland begrenzt. Es sind Meeresablagerungen der Jurazeit, die in einer späten Phase der Alpenbildung vor etwa 100 Millionen Jahren aufgefaltet und aus der Tiefe emporgehoben wurden. Gipsgruben an der Lägern stammen aus der noch weiter zurückliegenden Keuperzeit (Trias) und sind demnach rund 200 Millionen Jahre alt. Aus diesen Sedimenten ist die Lägern, dieser östlichste Ausläufer des Jura, aufgebaut.

Es folgt im Uhrzeigersinn das regenarme Unterland, das landschaftlich sehr reizvolle, noch durchaus ländlich anmutende Zürcher Weinland und weiter im Osten dann das Zürcher Oberland, dessen stark bewegte Topographie ebenfalls, aber in einer späteren Phase, der Hebung der Alpen geschuldet ist, sowohl hinsichtlich des Inhalts der Gesteinsschichten als auch ihrer Bauart (Tektonik). Die Schichten bestehen aus bunten Abfolgen von Ton, Sand und Geröll, welche die Flüsse aus den sich langsam hebenden Alpen ins Vorland hinunterschwemmten, wo sie sich zu mächtigen Paketen aus Mergel, Sandstein und Nagelfluh verfestigten. Dem Druck der nachstossenden alpinen Decken mit ihren mächtigen Gesteinsmassen

We begin with the Lägern, the oldest formation of compacted rock layers in the Canton of Zurich, which rose up over the course of time to be visible on today's earth surface. Geologically, the Lägern belongs to the Jura Mountains, a long arc of mountains that stretch from Geneva to Schaffhausen, its broad sweep thus separating Central Switzerland from France and southern Germany. Ocean deposits from the Jurassic Period, which unfolded in a later phase of alpine formation about 100 million years ago, were raised up from the depths here. Gypsum mines on the Lägern stem from the still earlier Keuper Age (Triassic) and are therefore around 200 million years old. This sediment layer formed the Lägern, the most eastern branch of the Jura Mountains.

What follows, in clockwise fashion, are the rather dry lowlands, which are very scenic throughout Zurich's pastoral wine country (Weinland). Further to the east is the Zurich Oberland (uplands), whose rough topography is due to the lifting of the Alps at a later phase, especially in regard to the contents of the rock layers and their formation (tectonic). The strata are made of a colourful sequence of clay, sand and rubble that the rivers from the slowly rising Alps washed into the floodplain where they solidified into abundant packets of marlite, sandstone and molasse conglomerate. However, these packets could not withstand the pressure of the advancing alpine mantle with its powerful rock masses. As the strata had relatively thin layers, they did not react plastically like the deeper sediment layers from the much ear-

hielten sie aber nicht stand. Sie reagierten wegen der relativ geringen Überdeckung nicht plastisch wie die tiefer liegenden Sedimentschichten aus viel früheren Meeresablagerungen der Jura- und Kreidezeit, sondern spröde. Deshalb zerbrachen sie, wurden schräg gestellt oder teilweise überschoben. Zum Vergleich kann man sich auf dem Tisch liegende Spielkarten vorstellen, die seitlich gegen einen Stapel anderer Karten geschoben werden. Unter dem wachsenden Druck verbiegen sie sich, werden geknickt, oder sie schieben sich übereinander.

Südlich und westlich des vom eiszeitlichen Linthgletscher ausgehobelten Zürichseebeckens zieht sich sanft geschwungen die Albiskette hin. Ihr Kamm mit dem Uetliberg ragte während der letzten Eiszeit wie ein grönländischer Nunatak (Berginsel) aus dem umgebenden Eismeer auf. Von diesem Kamm aus blickten die eiszeitlichen Menschen vor 20 000 und mehr Jahren auf die riesigen Eisströme des Linth-, Rhein- und Reussgletschers, die ins Vorland und weit nach Norden vorstiessen. Auch sie formten das Mittelland und gaben ihm die heutigen klein- und grossräumigen Oberflächenformen, in die sich während und nach dem allmählichen Abschmelzen der Gletscher die Flüsse und Bäche eingruben oder einschnitten und je nach den topographischen Höhenunterschieden breite Flusstäler oder enge Bachtobel schufen. Auch die sogenannten Drumlins sind das Ergebnis der eiszeitlichen Gletscherströme, die das darunterliegende Terrain modellierten. Zurückgeblieben sind diese heute zum Teil bewaldeten Hügel, die, vergleichbar den Rücken einer nach Nordwesten ziehenden Schafherde, die Topographie des oberen Glatttals bestimmen.[3]

Äusserst anschaulich hat der Naturwissenschafter Oswald Heer, seines Zeichens Paläobotaniker und Insektenforscher, sein in den Grundzügen noch heute gültiges Werk «Urwelt der Schweiz» 1865 mit leicht kolorierten Kupferstichen illustriert.[4] Diese sind gleichsam Momentaufnahmen der damaligen Landschaften, sehr detailgetreu ausgeführt. Man fühlt sich in fremde Erdteile versetzt. Da ist beispielsweise ein Bild von Koralleninseln im heutigen Jura, es könnte der Ort sein, wo vor mehr als 100 Millionen Jahren die Kalkablagerungen entstanden, die heute die Lägern bilden. Man fühlt sich in die tropischen Meere von Indonesien versetzt. Oder dann gibt es in diesem in Leder gebundenen Buch ein Bild von Dürnten am Fuss des Bachtels im Zürcher Oberland aus der geologischen Neuzeit. Grasende Auerochsen, Urnashörner und Waldelefanten bevölkern eine von Sümpfen, Seen und Nadelbäumen geprägte Landschaft aus einer warmen Zwischeneiszeit, über die der Blick bis zu den vertrauten Alpengipfeln schweift. Auf noch einer anderen Tafel tummeln sich etwa dort, wo sich heute das Limmatquai und der Bürkliplatz befinden, Rentierherden

lier ocean deposits of the Jurassic and Cretaceous Periods, they were brittle and fragile. Therefore, they broke and snapped, ended up in skewed positions or were partially thrust forward. To compare this process, one can imagine playing cards lying on a table that are slid sideways against a pile of other cards; under the growing pressure they bend, some buckle or they slide in one above the other.

South and west of Lake Zurich, which the Linth Glacier gouged out during the Ice Age, the Albis mountain chain extends in a gentle curve. Its crest, including the Üetliberg, rose during the last Ice Age like a Greenland Nunatak (mountain island) out of the surrounding sea of ice. 20,000 or more years ago, Ice Age people standing on this crest glimpsed the enormous ice streams of the Linth, Rhein and Reuss glaciers that thrust forward into the flood plain and pushed their way farther north. These glaciers also formed the Central Swiss Plain and gave it today's small and large surface forms, in which the rivers and streams dug or cut their way, during and after the gradual melting of the glaciers, and, depending on the topographical height differences, created broad river valleys or narrow ravines. The Drumlins are also the result of Ice Age glacier currents, which shaped the terrain lying beneath it. What remains today (in part) are forested hills that, resembling a herd of sheep moving northwest, determine the topography of the upper Glatt Valley.[3]

The natural scientist, Oswald Heer, who made his mark as a paleobotanist and insect researcher, illustrated his book, *Urwelt der Schweiz* (1865), which is still a valid work in its main features, with extremely descriptive, lightly coloured copper engravings.[4] These 'snapshots' of the then existing landscapes are very clear and accurate in every detail. One feels as if suddenly relocated to a foreign part of the earth. There is, for example, a picture of coral islands in today's Jura; this could be the place where 100 million years ago the calcium deposits formed that today compose the Lägern. One could find suddenly find himself in the tropical seas of Indonesia. This leather-bound book contains a picture of Dürnten at the foot of the Bachtel in the Zurich Oberland from the geological Quaternary Period (our current period). Grazing aurochs, early rhinoceros and forest elephants populate a dramatic landscape of swamps, lakes and conifers from a warm interglacial period, behind which the view sweeps up to the familiar alpine summits.

On yet another print, herds of reindeer and mammoths tromp around on what is today the Limmatquai and Bürkliplatz in Zurich. The eye is drawn in the direction of the Alps, where the Albis and Pfannenstiel stand today. Here, the enormous ice sheet of the Linth

Die Gegend der heutigen Lägern in der geologischen Zeit des Jura vor rund 200 Millionen Jahren: Ein flaches tropisches Meer mit Koralleninseln prägte weite Teile des heutigen Mitteleuropa (links).
Die Gegend von Dürnten mit Ur-Nashörnern und Ur-Rindern zur Zeit des Tertiärs, das vor 65 Millionen Jahren begann und vor 2,6 Millionen Jahren endete. Es folgte mit einem Wechsel von Kalt- und Warmzeiten das Quartär, auch Eiszeitalter genannt. (aus O. Heer, «Urwelt der Schweiz», 1865)

In the geological Jurassic Period, approximately 200 million years ago, a shallow tropical sea with coral islands filled the area of today's Lägern Mts. and shaped large parts of today's central Europe (left).
The area of Dürnten as it would have looked in the Tertiary Period with prehistoric rhinoceroses and aurochs. The Tertiary began 65 million years ago and ended 2.6 million years ago. It was followed by the Quaternary, an exchange of cold and warm periods, also called the Ice Age (O. Heer, *Urwelt der Schweiz*, 1865).

und Mammuts. Der Blick geht alpenwärts. Der riesige Eisstrom des Linthgletschers trägt dort, wo sich heute Albis und Pfannenstiel befinden, Seitenmoränen, die wie schwärzliche Bänder von den Glarner Alpen herunterkommen und später beim Schmelzen erratische Felsblöcke, manche mehr als hausgross, deponierten. Das zerklüftete Ende des Gletschers gleicht den Gletschern, die man heute im südlichen Alaska oder in Patagonien noch bestaunen kann. Die einstigen Tropen sind innerhalb von Zeiträumen, gegenüber denen die Geschichte der Menschheit nur eine Episode und ein Menschenleben ein Wimpernschlag ist, zu arktischen Gefilden mutiert. Denken wir uns eine geologische Skala, auf der ein Jahr auf eine Sekunde verkürzt wird, dann ist die Erde etwa 1870 entstanden. Um 1997 hinterliessen die ersten Säugetiere ihre Zähnchen im schaffhausischen Hallau, und der erste Primat, ein eichhorngrosser Halbaffe, erschien 2001. Vor drei Stunden kalbten beim heutigen Bürkliplatz die Eisberge des Linthgletschers ins Wasser, vor gut zwei Stunden fand mit der Einführung von Ackerbau und Viehzucht der grösste soziale Fortschritt statt, und vor 1 ½ Stunden begann die geschriebene Weltgeschichte im Zweistromland, dem heutigen Irak.[5]

Wir können uns an diesen Bildern aus der Vergangenheit im bequemen Lehnstuhl erbauen. Max Frisch aber erinnert uns daran, wie mächtig und gleichzeitig empfindlich die scheinbar übermächtige Natur gegenüber kleinsten Schwankungen ist. Nach einem Alpenflug schreibt er in sein Tagebuch:

«Zum Bewusstsein kommt, wie gering eigentlich die Zone ist, die den Menschen ernährt und gestaltet; schon kommen die letzten Matten, schon beginnt die

Glacier carried along side moraines that came down like black ribbons from the Glarner Alps, later during melting, the glacier deposited erratic boulders, some larger than a house. The ragged end of the glacier resembles the glaciers that can still astound one today in southern Alaska or Patagonia. The erstwhile tropics mutated into an arctic region within a timeframe that is almost inconceivable when we realise that the history of mankind is just one episode and a human life is just the blink of an eye.

If we think of a geological scale in which one year is shortened to one second, then the Earth was created around 1870. Around 1997, the first mammals left their teeth behind in Schaffhausen's Hallau district, and the first primate, a pro-simian the size of a squirrel, appeared in 2001. Three hours ago, the icebergs of the Linth Glacier started to calve into the water near today's Bürkliplatz in Zurich, while a good two hours ago, the introduction of agriculture and animal husbandry fostered the largest social advance of humankind and about one and a half hours ago, the written history of the world began in Mesopotamia, today's Iraq.[5]

We can edify ourselves on these images from the past in a comfortable reclining chair. Max Frisch, however, reminds us how powerful and, at the same time, how sensitive the apparently all-powerful Nature is to the smallest fluctuation. After an alpine flight, he wrote in his diary:

'It comes to mind how limited the zone is that humans actually feed off and design; already comes the last meadow, already begins the next icy area. Two thousand or three thousand metres are enough and

Vereisung. Zweitausend oder dreitausend Meter genügen, und unsere Weltgeschichte ist aus. Gewisse Kessel, die wir sehen, könnten auch auf dem Mond sein. Die vielleicht einzig vorkommende Gunst von Umständen, die irgendwo im Weltall ein menschliches Geschlecht ermöglicht hat, liegt als ganz dünner Hauch in den Mulden, und es genügt die geringste Schwankung der Umstände; eine Vermehrung des Wassers, eine Verdünnung der Luft, eine Veränderung der Wärme. Unser Spielraum ist nicht gross. Wir nisten in einem Zufall, dessen empfindliche Zuspitzung, wenn sie uns manchmal zum Bewusstsein kommt, beklemmend wird und zugleich begeisternd.»[6]

Hier liegt vor uns eines der schönsten modernen literarischen Zeugnisse zum Thema Mensch und Umwelt, das angesichts einer menschgemachten globalen Klimaänderung mit unabsehbaren Folgen für die Menschheit und unsere Zivilisation nichts an Aktualität verloren hat.

Was ist eine Landschaft?
Dieser erdgeschichtliche Überflug gibt von den Zeiträumen, mit denen wir es zu tun haben, nicht mehr als eine Ahnung. Bevor wir zu unserem Hauptthema zurückkehren, nämlich der heutigen Natur und Landschaft des Kantons Zürich, seien ein paar Gedanken der scheinbar simplen Frage gewidmet: Was ist überhaupt eine Landschaft? Wissenschaftler haben sich darüber schon den Kopf zerbrochen, und es gibt wohl mehr als ein Dutzend verschiedene Definitionen, von denen, die nur die nicht oder wenig bebaute Landschaft als solche anerkennen, bis zu jenen, die auch die Siedlungen und Städte einbeziehen. Man kann tatsächlich auch von einer Stadtlandschaft sprechen

our world history is over. Certain basins that we see could also be on the moon. The perhaps only naturally occurring benefit of circumstances that somewhere in the universe had made a human race possible, lies as a very thin skin in the depressions and it suffices as the smallest variation of the circumstances; an increase of water, a thinning of the atmosphere, a change in temperature. Our margin is not large. We nest in a fluke of nature, whose sensitive culmination, when it sometimes comes to our awareness, will be oppressive and, at the same time, inspiring.'[6]

Here before us is one of the finest modern literary testimonies on the theme of man and his environment that, seen from the perspective of a man-made global climate change with unforeseen consequences for humanity and our civilisation, has not lost any of its topicality.

What is a landscape?
This flyover of Earth's history offers no more than an inkling of the timeframes that concern us here as the origins of our topic. Before we return to our main theme, namely, today's nature and landscapes of the Canton of Zurich, here are a couple of thoughts dedicated to the seemingly simple question: What is a landscape really? Scientists have already racked their brains on this question and there are certainly more than a dozen various definitions, including those that only recognise undisturbed or minimally cultivated landscapes up to those that also include settlements and cities. One can, in fact, also speak of an urban landscape and distinguish it from rural agricultural landscapes and these again from untouched natural landscapes. What immediately comes to mind is that

Gegen Ende der letzten Eiszeit reichte der Linthgletscher noch bis zur heutigen Quaibrücke und zum Bürkliplatz in Zürich. Diese Eiszeit begann vor 115 000 Jahren und endete vor 12 500 bis 10 000 Jahren. Die Menschen waren Jäger und Sammler.
(aus O. Heer, Urwelt der Schweiz, 1865)

Towards the end of the last Ice Age, the Linth Glacier extended up to today's Quaibrücke and Bürkliplatz in Zurich. This Ice Age began 115,000 years ago and ended around 12,500 to 10,000 years ago. The people were hunters and gatherers (O. Heer, *Urwelt der Schweiz*, 1865).

und sie von der bäuerlich geprägten Agrarlandschaft und diese wiederum von der unberührten Naturlandschaft abgrenzen. Wobei sofort zu bedenken ist, dass es auf unserem Territorium schon seit langem keine vom Menschen völlig unberührten Naturräume mehr gibt. Selbst steile, abgelegene Wälder wurden einst von Menschenhand genutzt, die einstigen Moore zu über 90 Prozent ihrer Ausdehnung entwässert, Flüsse und Bäche begradigt, und schliesslich gibt es keinen Kubikzentimeter Boden mehr, der unbeeinflusst wäre von den Nitraten und anderen künstlichen Stoffen, die, verursacht durch die Immissionen aus Motorfahrzeugverkehr, Industrie und Heizungen, mit den Niederschlägen ausgeregnet werden. Wir wollen uns hier aber weder mit den Spitzfindigkeiten eines wissenschaftlichen Landschaftsbegriffs noch mit den mannigfaltigen Problemen des wissenschaftlichen und technologischen Umweltschutzes abgeben. Für unsere Betrachtung sollen drei Feststellungen genügen.

Erstens liegt der Landschaft kein naturwissenschaftlich strenger Begriff zu Grunde. Landschaft kann so wenig mit einem eindeutigen Begriff umschrieben werden, wie man etwa den Ausdruck Seele durch eine chemische Formel oder die Beschreibung eines neurobiologischen Systems ersetzen kann. Landschaft ist auch nicht ein Stück Erdoberfläche. Landschaft ist sowieso nie eine Fläche, auch wenn sie topfeben ist. Zur Landschaft gehören nicht nur die Oberfläche und die darauf gedeihenden Pflanzen, sondern auch der Boden darunter mit Eigenschaften, die von geologischen Prozessen bestimmt werden sowie den Milliarden von Lebewesen, die am Prozess der Bodenbildung und den Kreisläufen in der Natur beteiligt sind.

Zweitens kann Landschaft nie losgelöst gesehen werden von unserem eigenen Empfinden und unserer durch viele subjektive Umstände beeinflussten Wahrnehmung. Landschaft hat immer eine objektive und eine subjektive Komponente.

Und drittens können in der Landschaft Natur und Kultur nie gänzlich voneinander getrennt werden. Es beginnt schon bei einer gewöhnlichen Wiese oder einem Acker. Für den Landwirt sind diese eine zu bewirtschaftende Parzelle, für den Bodenkundler und Biologen ein Areal samt Untergrund, bestehend aus Mineralien, Humus und Milliarden von Lebewesen, für den Geomorphologen ein von der Eiszeit geformtes Stück Erdoberfläche und für einen Städter, der sich in der Landschaft spazierend, wandernd, joggend oder bikend erholt, sind sie einfach ein Stück freie Natur, im besten Fall eine beim angestrengten Pedalen flüchtig wahrgenommene Kulisse, zu welcher vielleicht noch ein Waldrand, der Blick auf einen See oder die Alpen gehören. Wenn schon ein Acker so unterschiedlich wahrgenommen wird, um wie viel grösser muss der Unterschied für eine ganze Landschaft sein! Auch blos-

in our territory there have not been any fully natural spaces for quite a long time. Even steep isolated forests were once used by human hands; earlier, moorlands were drained by over 90 %; rivers and streams were straightened and, finally, there is not one cubic centimetre of land that has not been influenced by nitrates and other artificial materials caused by emissions from motorised vehicles, industry and heating that rain down along with the precipitation. However, here we neither want to deal with the subtleness of a scientific landscape terminology nor with the multiplicity of problems of scientific and technological environmental protection. For our examination, the following three statements should be enough.

First, 'landscape' does not have a scientifically rigorous definition. Landscape cannot be described with a less ambiguous term. Much like the word soul cannot be replaced by a chemical formula or the description of a neurobiological system. Landscape is also not a piece of the earth's surface. A landscape is never a flat surface anyway, even when it is flat as a pancake. The word 'landscape' includes not only the surface and its flourishing plants, it also includes the ground lying beneath the surface with characteristics that were determined through geological processes and all the billions of animals that are involved in the process of forming the ground and participating in the cycles of nature.

Second, landscape can never be separated from our own feelings and perceptions or our awareness, which has been influenced through many subjective situations. Landscape always has an objective and a subjective component.

And, third, landscape, nature and culture can never be completely separated from one another. Starting with a common meadow or a field as an example, for the farmer, these are parcels to be cultivated; for the soil scientist or biologist, it is an area that has an underground made up of minerals, humus, and billions of creatures; for the geo-morphologists, it's one of the fragments of the earth's surface shaped by an Ice Age, and for city dwellers who walk, hike, jog and bike through the landscape for recreation, landscapes are simply a piece of free nature, in the best case, where strenuous pedalling brings a fleeting awareness of the backdrop, part of which is perhaps a forest edge, a glimpse of a lake or the Alps.

When such varied perceptions arise for a single field, then how many more must come up for an entire landscape! Indeed, a sheer cliff or a snow-capped mountain that one can see from Lake Zurich and from the surrounding mountain ridges, are not just physical phenomenon, they are part of our cultural history. Think of the legend behind Vrenelisgärtli (Verena's Garden), which gave its name to the

se Fels- oder Firngipfel, die man vom Zürichsee und von den umliegenden Höhenzügen sehen kann, sind nicht nur physische Phänomene, sondern Teil unserer Kulturgeschichte. Denken wir an die Sage vom Vrenelisgärtli, die dem nordöstlichen Gipfel in der Gruppe des Glärnisch seinen Namen gab. Oder an das «weisse Spitzchen», das man mit geübtem Auge hinter viel näher gelegenen Bergketten an klaren Tagen hervorlugen sieht. Als begeisterter Bergwanderer wusste der Zürcher Dichter Conrad Ferdinand Meyer, dass es sich um den weit weg im Unterengadin stehenden Gipfel Piz Linard handelt. Oder lesen wir wieder einmal den Zürcher Schriftsteller Kurt Guggenheim, dessen bedeutendstes Werk «Alles in Allem» dem Leben in der damaligen Stadt Zürich gewidmet ist. Im Roman «Riedland» beschreibt er den Mürtschenstock mit folgenden Worten: «Im Hintergrund stand mit seinen zwei Zacken, gross und grau, der Mürtschenstock und glich der doppelten Gebottafel, die Moses den Juden vom Sinai herabgebracht hatte.» Natürlich wissen wir, dass der Mürtschenstock nicht im Kanton Zürich steht. Aber als unverkennbarer Berg gehört er genauso zur heimatlichen Landschaft wie irgendein sogenanntes Kulturobjekt, und sei es nur eine ohne Mörtel aus den Ackersteinen aufgeschichtete Mauer, der Dorfbrunnen oder ein Wirtshausschild. Die Landschaft ist nicht bloss Natur und auch nie nur ein von Menschen geschaffenes Werk und somit Kultur. Sie ist immer beides, und zwar in einer wechselseitig verschlungenen Beziehung.

Nehmen wir als vierte Dimension zum Raum noch die Zeit hinzu, könnten wir sagen, die Landschaft sei ein natur- und kulturgeschichtlich geprägtes Gebilde, in dem frühere Lebensformen und Gewohnheiten, aber auch geistige Errungenschaften der Gesellschaften, die vor uns gelebt haben, eine auch heute noch unser Leben mitbestimmende Realität sind. Diese Umschreibung würde nicht mehr gelten, wenn wir dereinst nur noch in künstlichen Systemen lebten und von Robotern versorgt und gelenkt würden. Ob wir das wollen, sei hier nicht diskutiert. Aber wie auch immer, auf die gewachsene Landschaft im oben beschriebenen Sinn wollen wir nicht verzichten, umso weniger, je stärker unser Alltag von der modernen Technik bestimmt ist.

Landschaft als Heimat
Vielleicht kann man anstelle umständlicher Umschreibungen für Landschaft einfach das Wort Heimat nehmen. Zwar ist es belastet, weil man es bis in die Nachkriegsjahrzehnte hinein immer wieder mit einer fragwürdigen Einheit von Abstammung und Territorium in Verbindung brachte, womit der Begriff immer anfällig war und ist für nationalistische und gefährliche Rassentheorien. Der Heimatschutz wird – auch in der Politik – zu Unrecht immer wieder mit einer musealen und nur rückwärtsgewandten Einstellung gleichge-

northeasternmost peak in the Glärnisch group. Or, of the small white tip of a mountain that pops out – but only to the practised eye – from behind a much closer mountain chain on a clear day. As an enthusiastic mountain hiker, the Zurich poet, Conrad Ferdinand Meyer, knew that the faraway peak was the Piz Linard in the Unterengadin,

We can also read the words of the Zurich author Kurt Guggenheim once again. His most important work, *Alles in Allem* (novel in 4 volumes, 1952–1955), is dedicated to life in 1950s Zurich. In his novel *Riedland* (1938), he describes the Mürtschenstock massif in Glarus in the following words: 'In the background stood the Mürtschenstock with its two jagged peaks, large and grey, like the two commandment tablets that Moses brought down to the Jews from Mount Sinai.' Of course, we know that the Mürtschenstock is not in the Canton of Zurich, however, as an unmistakeable mountain, it is part of the native landscape just like any other cultural object, such as a stone wall built without mortar, the village well or the distinctive sign of a restaurant. The landscape is not just nature and it is also not just one of the works created by man and therefore culture. It is always both and, in fact, it is an intricate reciprocal relationship.

If we take Time as a fourth dimension to Space, we could say that 'landscape' is a natural, cultural and historically shaped construct in which earlier life forms and habits, as well as the spiritual attainments of societies that lived before us, are a reality that even today co-determine our lives. This description would no longer be true if one day we live in artificial systems and are provided for and managed by robots. Whether we want that will not be discussed here. However, as always, we do not want to dispense with the natural landscape in the above-described sense, and even less the more our everyday lives become more heavily determined by modern technology.

A landscape as 'home'
Perhaps one can, instead of using lengthy descriptions for landscape, simply use the word 'home'. Certainly, the word was contaminated in the post-war decades; the questionable unity of lineage and territory was connected again and again, which made the term susceptible to nationalistic and dangerous racist theories. Home or heritage protection was, also in politics, wrongly put on a level with an attitude of looking backward that was considered to belong in a museum. However, if we want to free 'home' from such misuse, the word is actually an expression of a vital essential circumstance, which geographer Emil Egli brought home in a simple sentence: 'To be sure, we live in a time, however, at home we are in a space.'[7]

setzt. Wenn wir aber Heimat vor solchem Missbrauch befreien, meint der Ausdruck einen lebenswichtigen Sachverhalt, den der Geograph Emil Egli mit einem einfachen Satz auf den Punkt brachte: «Wohl leben wir in einer Zeit, aber zuhause sind wir in einem Raum.»[7] Bezeichnend ist auch, dass das Wort Heimat keine Mehrzahl kennt, man hat letztlich nur eine Heimat, sie ist nicht austauschbar, und das gilt wohl erst recht für eine Zeit, in der immer mehr Menschen unterwegs sind, auf der Flucht vor existenziellen Problemen oder als Globetrotter, die sich Reisen in andere Länder und Kontinente leisten können. Auch diese sind irgendwie auf einer Flucht, und sei es nur vor dem Trott eines durchorganisierten Alltags, und vergessen dabei, dass sie Natur und Landschaft praktisch auch vor der Haustüre intensiv erleben könnten.

Der moderne Alltag hat zumindest in unseren Breitengraden die Landschaft allein in den letzten 50 Jahren grossflächiger und radikaler umgestaltet als alle Generationen, die vor uns gelebt haben. Auch unsere in Hüttendörfern auf Pfählen lebenden Vorfahren, die vor vielleicht 8000 Jahren begannen, die nacheiszeitliche Landschaft nutzbar zu machen, griffen stark in die vorgefundene Natur ein. Das Ergebnis war eine allmählich gewachsene Kulturlandschaft, deren Gesicht – bis auf zeitweise überschwemmte Flussauenwälder, Sümpfe, Hochmoore oder schwer zugängliche Bachtobel – nicht mehr der einstigen Naturlandschaft glich. Aber es war immer noch eine naturnahe Kulturlandschaft. Denn die Menschen hatten ihre auf Viehzucht und Ackerbau ausgerichtete Wirtschaftsweise und ihre Arbeitsmethoden gleichsam der Natur entliehen. Es gab keine Zufuhr fremder Energie über grössere Distanzen, die grossen Kreisläufe der Natur wurden nicht unterbrochen, sondern höchstens geringfügig erweitert. Man konnte etwa Getreide, Gemüse oder Obst so konservieren und lagern, dass diese Nahrungsmittel auch in der kalten Jahreszeit zur Verfügung standen. Oder dass Milchprodukte, auch wenn es draussen heiss war, frisch blieben. Gegenüber dem Naturzustand entwickelte sich in der kultivierten Landschaft sogar eine grössere Artenvielfalt. Beispielsweise die Kornblume, manche lichtbedürftige Orchideen wie der Frauenschuh, die Hummel-Ophrys oder die Küchenschelle und auch viele Sträucher, wie zum Beispiel der Färberginster, sind in wärmeren Klimaperioden aus Südeuropa und den Steppengebieten Vorderasiens eingewandert. Sie wurden dank der kultivierenden Tätigkeit des Menschen als «Unkräuter» behandelt, aber eben nicht ausgerottet, sondern als Begleitflora an Ackerrändern, auf zeitweilig brachliegenden Parzellen, ungedüngten Wiesen, extensiven Weiden und in lichten Wäldern heimisch. Aus anderen Arten entstanden durch intelligente Zucht und Kreuzung Nutzpflanzen und Haustiere, die der Umwelt optimal angepasst

Also indicative is that the word 'home' does not have a plural, ultimately, one has just one birthplace, you can't change it or exchange it and it holds true even more in a time in which more and more people are underway, fleeing from existential problems, or as globetrotters who have the means to travel to other countries and continents. It seems that these travellers are somehow also fleeing something, perhaps a thoroughly organised daily routine, forgetting that they can also intensively experience nature and landscape practically outside their own front door.

In the last 50 years alone, modern daily life has, at least in our latitude, made the landscape larger and redesigned it more radically than all the generations that lived before us. Even our forefathers living in pile dwellings some 8000 years ago, made strong interventions in the nature around them in order to make the post-ice age landscape useful. The result was the gradual growth of a cultural landscape, whose face, apart from the regularly flooded alluvial meadows, swamps, high moors or hard to access streams, was no longer the once totally natural landscape. But, the landscape was then definitely still very close to a natural landscape. The people had borrowed their animal husbandry and agricultural economy and work methods from nature. There was no supply of foreign energy over a great distance; the grand cycle of nature was not interrupted, at the most, perhaps slightly expanded. One could conserve some grains, vegetables or fruit and store them so that these foodstuffs would also be available in the winter season, or develop milk products that would stay fresh even when it is hot outside.

Vis-a-vis the natural state, in the cultivated landscape, our forefathers actually developed a much wider range of plants. For example, the cornflower, some of the orchids that need more light, such as the lady's slipper, the Hummel Ophrys and the pasque flower or meadow anemone, as well as many shrubs, for example, dyer's greenwood, 'immigrated' from southern Europe and the steppes of the Near East during warmer periods. They were, thanks to the cultivation activities of people, treated as weeds, but were not completely eradicated, but used instead as companion plants at the edges of cultivated fields, or in rotation planting, fallow fields, unfertilised meadows, extensive pastures and in light forests. Through intelligent breeding and crossbreeding, crop plants and domesticated animals were developed from other species to be optimally suitable and sustainable, i.e. deliver stable gains over long periods of time. Today, this race and species variety is endangered through competition, often only for maximising profits from targeted plants and animal breeding, and this competition is just as acute as that of wild plants and animals.

sind und nachhaltige, das heisst über lange Zeiten stabile Erträge lieferten. Heute ist diese Rassen- und Sortenvielfalt durch die Konkurrenz einer oft nur auf eine Maximierung des Ertrags zielenden Pflanzen- und Tierzucht ebenso akut gefährdet wie wildlebende Pflanzen- und Tierarten.

Nun ist die von uns beanspruchte Erholungslandschaft, in der Natur und Kultur in einzigartiger Weise miteinander verwoben sind, sicher kein beabsichtigtes Produkt unserer bäuerlichen Vorfahren. Aber das ändert nichts daran, dass dieses Gut kostbar und knapp ist. Wir alle zehren davon, ohne dass es den meisten von uns im Alltag zum Bewusstsein käme. Schlagzeilen in den Medien machen nicht der stille Schwund an natürlichen Lebensgrundlagen und biologischer Vielfalt, sondern eine neue Grippeepidemie, ein Flugzeugabsturz, technische Pannen oder sichtbare Umweltverschmutzungen, die aber nur die Spitze eines Eisberges sind.

Was macht es aus, dass uns das natürliche und kulturelle Erbe in einem grösseren Raum als typische, wertvolle oder gar einmalige Landschaft erscheint? Es sind nicht die in der Tourismuswerbung oder in Kunstführern abgebildeten und beschriebenen Sehenswürdigkeiten, sozusagen die Rosinen im Kuchen. Nein, es ist etwas anderes, nämlich das unauflösbare Gewebe aus dem, was wir als natürlich empfinden und dem, was die Menschen allmählich in die Natur hineingearbeitet haben, und zwar so, dass uns die Natur nicht mehr fremd, sondern vertraut und die Kultur nicht mehr künstlich erscheint. Naturnahe Kulturlandschaften sind alle auf ihre je eigene Weise typisch, aber nicht so, wie ein künstliches Produkt das typische Markenzeichen seines Herstellers trägt, sondern indem sie einem grösseren Naturraum mit seinem Klima, seiner Topographie und seinen Gewässern wie eine unverkennbare Handschrift eingeschrieben sind. Die kulturellen Erscheinungsformen der Landschaft sind unverwechselbare Variationen und Abwandlungen einer vorgegebenen Natur. Heimat beinhaltet somit das Typische und das Einmalige zugleich. Aus diesem Grunde ist es letzten Endes falsch, Landschaften nach einem objektiven Schönheitsgrad, nach Seltenheit oder, gemäss einem neuen Fachausdruck, nach einem «Alleinstellungsmerkmal» einteilen und bewerten zu wollen. Was wir als schöne Landschaft empfinden, ist immer auch mit subjektiven Wertungen verbunden, die untrennbar auch mit Prägungen aus unserer Kindheit zu tun haben. Es wäre allerdings falsch, aus dieser Subjektivität zu schliessen, der Schutz überkommener Landschaften entspreche nicht einem objektiven und erstrangigen öffentlichen Interesse. Denn schliesslich trägt jeder Mensch, ob es ihm nun zum Bewusstsein kommt oder nicht, solche subjektiven Vor-Bilder der Landschaft in sich.

The recreational landscape that we demand today, in which nature and culture are interwoven in a unique way, is surely not something our farming forefathers intended to leave us. However, that does not change the fact that this asset is precious and in short supply. We all live in it, although most of us are not conscious of it everyday. Headlines in the media do not cover the silent disappearance of the foundations of natural life and biological diversity, they are rather about a new epidemic, an aeroplane crash, technical failures or obvious environmental pollution; all these, however, are only the tip of the iceberg.

What is it that makes the natural and cultural heritage in a larger space appear to us as a typical, valuable, or even a unique landscape? It is not the pictures and descriptions of places of interest in tourism ads or an art guide, like the 'raisins in the cake'. No, it is something else, namely, the indissoluble tissue from what we feel is natural and what people have gradually worked into nature, so that we no longer find nature foreign, rather it is trusted and culture no longer appears to be artificial. Cultural landscapes that are close to their natural state are all in their own way typical, but not in the way an artificial product carries the typical label of its producer, rather in the way that they are a larger natural space with their own climate, topography and bodies of water, unique, the way an unmistakeable handwriting is recognised.

The cultural manifestations of the landscape are unmistakeable variations and modifications of a given nature. 'Home' contains as well the typical and the unique at the same time. For this reason, it is wrong in the end to want to classify and evaluate landscapes according to an objective degree of beauty or rareness, or a new special term, a 'unique feature'. What we see as a beautiful landscape is always connected with a subjective evaluation that is also inseparable from the imprinting from our childhood. However, it would be wrong to conclude from this subjectivity that the protection of threatened landscapes does not correspond to an objective and top-priority public interest. Finally, whether he is conscious of it or not, every person carries such subjective models of the landscape inside them.

Threats and the loss of landscapes

The industrial-technical transformation of the landscape in the above-described sense had already started at the beginning of the 19th century with the razing of old city walls, construction of railways and factories, or building villas and hotels, which showed, from today's perspective, little respect for the scenic value of the banks of Lake Zurich or the Limmat and Töss Rivers, with the exception of those places where nature had forced action. However, it remained

Bedrohung und Verlust der Landschaft

Die technisch-industrielle Umformung der Landschaft im oben beschriebenen Sinn begann schon zu Beginn des vorletzten Jahrhunderts mit der Schleifung der alten Stadtmauern, dem Bau der Eisenbahnen und Fabriken, Villen und Hotels. Ausser dort, wo die Natur es erzwungen hat, wurden sie – aus heutiger Perspektive – mit wenig Rücksicht auf landschaftliche Werte gebaut, so etwa an den Ufern des Zürichsees, an der Limmat oder Töss. Aber es blieb den Generationen, die seit etwa 1950 aktiv sind, vorbehalten, die Kulturlandschaft grossflächig zu uniformieren und Naturlandschaften bis auf sehr kleine Relikte zu dezimieren. Lebensräume wie Streueriede, Ackersäume, stufige Waldränder, Torfmoore, Magerwiesen, Bach- und Feldgehölze wurden ausgemerzt oder bis auf winzige Reste ihrer einstigen Ausdehnung zurückgedrängt. Die Ursachen sind bekannt. An erster Stelle war es das im Verhältnis zur Wohnbevölkerung weit überproportionale Wachstum der Agglomeration im Grossraum Zürich, aber auch das Siedlungswachstum in den Gemeinden links und rechts des Zürichsees, im Glatttal, um Winterthur und in der Form der sogenannten Speckgürtel rund um viele kleinere Zentren und Dörfer. Treiber dieser Entwicklung waren nicht nur die Zunahme der Wohnbevölkerung, sondern auch die Steigerung des Wohlstandes mit gewaltig gestiegenen Raumansprüchen für Wohnen und Arbeiten und, nicht zu vergessen, der rasanten Zunahme der Mobilität. Die disperse Besiedelung ging und geht Hand in Hand mit einem Ausbau der Strassen, der sich zu ersterer wie das Huhn zum Ei verhält: Die explosionsartige Motorisierung der Gesellschaft bald nach dem Zweiten Weltkrieg erforderte in- und ausserhalb der Dörfer und Städte einen rasanten Ausbau eines Strassennetzes, das nicht für den Autoverkehr gebaut war. Dieser Ausbau förderte wiederum die Besiedelung, indem er eine immer grössere Entfernung zwischen dem Arbeitsort und dem Wohnen im Grünen ermöglichte. Im Planerjargon nannte man dies Entmischung. Die während langer Zeit ungeordnete Besiedelung in die Fläche hinaus bewirkte ein grösseres Verkehrsaufkommen, namentlich durch tägliche Pendlerströme, und dieses wiederum rief nach einem weiteren Ausbau der Strassennetze. So entwickelte das Wachstum seine Eigengesetzlichkeit. Der sich ausbreitende Siedlungsteppich eilte der Infrastruktur davon und war mit dem öffentlichen Verkehr nicht mehr oder nur ungenügend zu erschliessen. Einen weiteren Schub erhielt die Besiedelung bis weit an die Peripherie hinaus durch den Bau der S-Bahn, der nicht mit einer verbindlichen interkommunalen und überregionalen Raumplanung koordiniert war. So wurde nicht nur im Kanton Zürich, sondern auch in allen anderen Landesteilen und Kantonen zwischen 1950 und der Jahrtausendwende mehr Land verbaut und

the reserve of the 'active' generations between 1950 and today to create uniform cultural landscapes over large areas and decimate natural landscapes down to the very smallest relic. Habitats such as litter meadows, field borders, gradual forest edges, peat bogs, rough pastures, shoreline trees and hedgerows were culled out or pushed back to tiny remnants of their former expanse.

The causes are known. For one, in relationship to the resident population, the growth of the agglomeration in the greater Zurich area was by far over-proportional. In addition, settlement growth expanded in the communities left and right of Lake Zurich, in the Glattal, around Winterthur and in the form of the so-called 'stockbroker belt' around many small centres and villages. This development was not only driven by the increase in resident populations, it was also the increase of affluence with increased demands for living and working space and, not to be forgotten, the rapid increase in mobility.

Dispersed settlements go hand-in-hand with road construction, which is like the perennial question about the hen and the egg. The explosive motorisation of society soon after the Second World War required a quick build-up of the road network inside and outside of the villages and cities. The old roads had not been built for auto traffic so the new construction fostered in turn new settlements, which made it possible to have a longer distance between the workplace and the home 'in the green'. In planner jargon, this is called segregation. For a long time, the settlements in the lowlands were unregulated and caused a larger traffic volume, mainly through daily commuter flows, and these in turn called for a further build-up of the road network. This is how growth develops into a law unto itself. The expanding settlements pushed the infrastructure to catch up and public transport could not sufficiently close the gap. The construction of the S-Bahn (the suburban railway that serves the Zurich agglomeration) added possibilities for settlements well into peripheral areas, however, this was not coordinated by any inter-communal or intra-regional spatial planning office or indeed any binding regulations. The effect, not only in the Canton of Zurich, but also in all other regions and cantons between 1950 and the end of millennium, was that more land was built over and more agricultural land was covered with concrete or sealed over than in all the human generations that had gone before.

In 1969, the economical treatment of land and regulations for orderly settlements were defined and established in the constitution along with all the applicable requirements for the public authorities. But, we did not manage to achieve these goals, not even

mehr Kulturland zubetoniert oder versiegelt als in allen Menschengenerationen zuvor.

Der haushälterische Umgang mit dem Boden und die geordnete Besiedelung sind zwar seit 1969 als für alle Behörden geltende Vorgaben in der Verfassung festgeschrieben. Aber wir haben diese Ziele nicht erreicht, auch im fortschrittlichen Kanton Zürich nicht. Was man gemeinhin Verstädterung nennt, erzeugte oft nicht eine neue Stadtqualität oder Urbanität, sondern nur ein lockeres Durcheinander, das weder Stadt noch Land ist. Wir wurden von dieser Entwicklung aber nicht überrollt, wie man gerne sagt. Weitsichtige Architekten wie Armin Meili, der Erbauer der Landi 1939, oder der an der ETH lehrende Bauernsohn und Geograph Ernst Winkler erkannten die Gefahren einer räumlich ungeordneten oder zufälligen Entwicklung frühzeitig. Nur wurden ihre Mahnungen und ihre Vorschläge kaum gehört. Wer etwa den schon 1944 von der kantonalen Baudirektion durch die Architekten und Planer Walter Custer, Rudolf Steiger, Rolf Meyer-von Gonzenbach und den damaligen Kantonsbaumeister Heinrich Peter erstellten Bericht über den Landschaftsschutz am Zürichsee betrachtet, kommt nicht ohne Wehmut zum Schluss, dass hier Chancen, die bis in die 1970er- und 80er-Jahre hinein noch bestanden, ohne Not vertan wurden. Bei gleicher Zunahme der Bevölkerung und gleichem Bauvolumen hätten – notabene ohne zusätzliche Wohnhochhäuser und hässliche Wohnblöcke – nicht nur in den Seegemeinden die Landschaft, gewachsene Ortsbilder und die Natur viel besser geschützt werden können.

Diese Entwicklung beschrieben 1955 die Autoren Lucius Burckhardt, Markus Kutter und Max Frisch, der nicht nur als Schriftsteller, sondern auch als sensibler Architekt ein Auge für die Landschaft hatte, wie folgt:

«Und also wuchern Städte wie's halt kommt geschwürartig, dabei sehr hygienisch. Man fährt eine halbe Stunde mit einem blanken Trolleybus und sieht das Erstaunliche, dass die Vergrösserung unserer Städte zwar unaufhörlich stattfindet, aber keineswegs zum Ausdruck kommt. Es geht einfach weiter, Serie um Serie, wie die Vergrösserung einer Kaninchenfarm. Fährt man weiter, zeigt sich, dass das schweizerische Mittelland aufgehört hat, eine Landschaft zu sein. […] Was wir wollen: die Schweizerstadt und das Schweizerland, und was wir nicht wollen: das unselige Durcheinander, wie es rings um unsere jetzigen Städte zu finden ist, halb verstädtertes Dorf und halb dörflerische Stadt.»[8]

Vom Wandel der Agrarwirtschaft und den Folgen für die Landschaft
Eine weitere und vielleicht die grösste Ursache des Schwundes an naturnahen Lebensräumen und ihrer Artenvielfalt ist im Wandel der Agrarwirtschaft und der Agrarpolitik zu suchen. Diese erfuhr mit dem Druck

in the progressive Canton of Zurich. What one commonly calls urbanisation often does not create a new urban quality or urbanity, rather just an informal confusion that is neither city nor country. We were not overrun by this development, as people like to claim. The dangers of spatially unregulated or random development were recognised early on by far-sighted architects such as Armin Meili, the architect and director of the Swiss National Exhibition in 1939, or the farmer's son and geographer Ernst Winkler, who taught at ETH. However, their warnings and suggestions fell on deaf ears.

Anyone who reads the 1944 report on landscape protection for Lake Zurich, issued by the Cantonal Building Department and written by the architects and planners Walter Custer, Rudolf Steiger, Rolf Meyer-von Gonzenbach and Canton Master Builder, Heinrich Peter, comes away feeling melancholy or even sad about the conclusion that now the opportunities, which lasted well into the 1970s and 1980s without any emergencies, are now lost forever. With the same increase in population and the same construction volume and, by the way, without additional high-rise apartment buildings and ugly housing blocks, the landscape, emergent townscapes and nature – and not only in the lakeside communities – could have been much better protected.

The authors Lucius Burckardt, Markus Kutter and Max Frisch (who was not only a writer, but also a sensitive architect with an eye for the landscape), described this development in 1955 as follows:

'And the cities proliferate in the landscape, like cancer throughout the body, distorting the landscape even if they are well built. If you ride a half-hour on a bright trolley bus, you will notice something astounding: our cities are growing constantly, but no one is saying anything about it. It simply continues, run-by-run, row-by-row, much like the expansion of a rabbit farm. And, if you travel further, you will see that the Swiss Central Plain has ceased to be a landscape. […] What we want: a Swiss city and a Swiss countryside; and what we do not want: the disastrous chaos that can be found around our current cities; half an urbanised village and half a village-city.'[8]

On changes in the agricultural economy and the consequences for the landscape
Another and perhaps the largest cause of the disappearance of natural living spaces and their biological diversity is the changes in the agricultural economy and agricultural politics. This happened with the pressure from foreign trade partners and the gradual sinking of agricultural prices at the beginning of the 1990s, which is another fundamental change. Previously, there were performance improvements

durch die Aussenhandelspartner und der schrittweisen Senkung der Agrarpreise zu Beginn der 90er-Jahre eine weitere grundlegende Änderung. Vorher waren Leistungssteigerungen durch den Produktivitätsfortschritt die hauptsächlichsten Resultate der Agrarpolitik. Erreicht wurden diese durch die Schaffung grosser, geometrisch geformter Nutzflächen, die den Einsatz immer grösserer Maschinen ermöglichten. Bauernhöfe in den Dörfern wurden ausgesiedelt, das heisst durch moderne, farmähnliche Betriebe an der Peripherie ersetzt. Dies und die Leistungssteigerungen in der Pflanzen- und Tierproduktion sowie der gesteigerte Einsatz von Dünge- und Schädlingsvertilgungsmitteln bewirkten eine gewaltige Ertragssteigerung, auch wenn das offizielle Ziel der Agrarpolitik des Bundes schon gegen Ende der 70er-Jahre nicht mehr Ertragssteigerung, sondern Strukturverbesserung durch Rationalisierung lautete. Die damit erreichte Produktivitätssteigerung machte den Verlust von Kulturland und den Rückgang der in der Landwirtschaft tätigen Bevölkerung zwar mehr als wett. Aber die Kehrseite der einseitig nur nach betriebswirtschaftlichen Kriterien durchgeführten Aussiedlungen war die soziale und ökologische Entmischung. Der soziale Austausch zwischen bäuerlicher und nicht bäuerlicher Bevölkerung wurde praktisch unterbunden. Das abwechslungsreiche Muster von Ackerfluren, Brachlandstreifen, Gehölzen und Wiesen mit hochstämmigen Obstbäumen wich monotonen, mit Strassen erschlossenen Anbauflächen und eingezäunten Umtriebsweiden. Man spricht von «ausgeräumten Landschaften». Ökonomisch gesprochen, wurden bei allen diesen Massnahmen zur Strukturverbesserung die sozialen und ökologischen Kosten nicht in Rechnung gestellt.

Der Gerechtigkeit halber muss hier gesagt werden, dass der massive Verlust an naturnaher Kulturlandschaft und damit der Artenvielfalt dennoch nicht einfach Ausfluss eines blinden Fortschrittsglaubens war. Die Schaffung zusammenhängender, rationell zu bewirtschaftender Nutzflächen erwies sich als wirksames Mittel gegen eine weitere Zersiedelung des Landes. Unter der damaligen Annahme, dass die Wohnbevölkerung im Kanton Zürich gegen zwei Millionen und in der Schweiz auf zehn oder gar zwölf Millionen ansteigen würde und dass der Verfassungsauftrag befolgt würde, wonach die Landwirtschaft einen hohen Selbstversorgungsauftrag erfüllen muss, hatten Massnahmen wie Güterzusammenlegungen und Meliorationen mit ihren Entwässerungen und der Begradigung von Bach- und Flussläufen durchaus ihre Logik. Diese Politik, welche die Landschaft des Mittellandes, aber auch alpine Regionen weitgehend prägte, war eine lineare Fortsetzung der «Anbauschlacht», des kriegswirtschaftlichen «Plans Wahlen» während des Zweiten Weltkrieges und der schon in frühen Jahrzehnten des

through the advancements in productivity, mainly the result of agricultural politics.

This was achieved through the creation of larger geometrically shaped areas of cultivation, which made the use of ever-larger machines possible. Farmsteads in the villages were evacuated and replaced by modern farm-similar operations on the periphery. That and the performance improvement in plant and animal production as well as the increasing use of fertilizer and pesticides brought about a huge increase in profits, even though the official goal of federal agricultural politics in the 1970s was no longer profit increases, but focused on structural improvements through rationalisation instead. The productivity increases achieved by this change actually made the loss of agricultural land and the decline of the agricultural population more than even.

However, the reverse of this one-sided resettlement programme, conducted on operational management criteria, was social and ecological segregation. The social exchange between the farming and non-farming populations was practically prohibited. The varied pattern of agricultural fields, fallow lands, woods and meadows with sturdy fruit trees gave way to monotonous cultivation areas accessed by roads and fenced-in cyclical meadows. One speaks of 'cleared landscapes'. Economically speaking, for all these structural improvement measures, none of the social and ecological costs were presented in the balance sheet.

To be fair, it must be said here that the massive loss of near-natural cultural landscapes and with them biological diversity, was not simply the result of a blind belief in progress. The creation of contiguous agricultural areas that could be cultivated efficiently, proved to be an effective means against further sprawl. Assuming that the housing population in the Canton of Zurich was approximately two million and the national estimate was expected to increase to 10 million, under the rule of compliance with the constitution, the various measures definitely had their own logic: agriculture had to fulfil a high self-sufficiency goal, goods and freight transport had to be consolidated, and improvements made to solve water problems with drainage programmes and the 'straightening' of streams and rivers.

These policies affected not only the landscape of the Swiss Central Plateau, alpine regions were also extensively affected, which was a linear continuation of the famous *Anbauschlacht*, Switzerland's approach to farming in the wartime economy of the Second World War *(Plan Wahlen)*, some of which had already been carried out in the early decades of the past century. At that time, it was about offering the resident population an alternative to burdensome

vergangenen Jahrhunderts durchgeführten Meliorationen. Damals ging es in erster Linie darum, der ansässigen Bevölkerung eine Alternative zu drückender Armut oder dem Los der Auswanderung zu bieten. Bezeichnenderweise wurde dafür das Wort «Innenkolonisation» geschaffen. Sümpfe und Flussmäander mit zeitweilig überschwemmten flachen Kiesufern sowie Steilufer, in denen Schwalben nisteten, nahm man damals als «Fehler» war, die es zu korrigieren galt. Von da kommt der Begriff der Flusskorrektion. Diese Begradigungen wurden zusammen mit dem Bau von Entwässerungskanälen zum hauptsächlichsten Mittel der grossflächigen Entsumpfung und Urbarisierung (Nutzbarmachung) von «Ödland», wie damals nicht oder nur ganz extensiv genutztes Land genannt wurde.

Nicht zu vergessen ist auch, dass der bäuerlichen Bevölkerung alle diese Massnahmen zur Ertragssteigerung auf Kosten der Natur aufgezwungen wurden – und zwar weniger durch Gesetze oder die Politiker und die ausführenden technischen Organe, sondern durch eine Gesellschaft, die ihr Volkseinkommen seit Beginn des letzten Jahrhunderts real um mehr als das Achtfache steigern konnte, ihre Siedlungsfläche mehr als verdoppelt und die durchschnittliche Arbeitszeit halbiert hat und heute anteilmässig weniger als je für Nahrungsmittel ausgibt. Wer Bauer bleiben und eine Familie ernähren wollte, musste entweder alles auf eine Steigerung des Ertrags und eine Senkung der Kosten setzen oder aufgeben. Es ist sozialpolitisch weder erwünscht noch möglich, dass ein heute sehr kleiner Teil der Bevölkerung im vorindustriellen Zeitalter verharrt, während sich die von ihr weitgehend ernährte Mehrheit rücksichtslos den Zielen der Konsum- und Freizeitgesellschaft verschreibt.

Die ökonomische Einäugigkeit
Wir haben die treibenden Kräfte des gesellschaftlichen und ökonomischen Wandels etwas näher beschrieben, weil sie verantwortlich sind für den dramatischen Rückgang der Natur und unverbauten Landschaft, dem Thema dieses Buches, und weil der Kanton Zürich auch hier eine gewisse Vorreiterrolle innehatte. Wir haben es dabei mit einem weltweit anzutreffenden Phänomen zu tun, das man als eine «ökonomische Einäugigkeit» umschreiben könnte. Unsere gesamte Wirtschaftsordnung ist weitgehend blind für die Umweltkosten, die wir mit unserem Konsumverhalten verursachen. Dabei werben gerade Vereinigungen zur Förderung der Wirtschaft mit der hohen Umweltqualität und der landschaftlichen Schönheit und Vielfalt der Umgebung. In Umfragen nennen erfolgreiche Unternehmen neben guten Ausbildungsmöglichkeiten und lange vor günstigen Steuerbedingungen die intakte Landschaft und eine saubere Umwelt als wichtigstes Kriterium für die Wahl des Standorts ihres Firmensit-

poverty, including the opportunity to emigrate. The term 'internal colonisation' was created and is indicative of the plan. Swamps and river meanderings with intermittent flooding over flat gravel banks, as well as steep banks in which swallows nest, were at that time perceived as 'mistakes' that should be corrected. Out of this came the notion of river 'correction'. This was, together with the construction of drainage canals, the primary means of draining large swamp areas and the reclamation of wastelands, as land was called that was not used or used only to a small extent.

One thing to remember is that all of these measures to raise profits at the cost of nature was forced on the farming population and, indeed, less through laws or politicians or technical executive organs, but through society, which managed to increase its national income eight times over since the beginning of the last century. In addition, the settlement area was more than doubled, the average work-time was halved and on average, one paid proportionately less than ever before for food. Anyone who wanted to remain a farmer and feed their family, had to believe in an increase in profits or a decrease in costs, or, they had to give up. It is neither socially or politically desired nor possible that today a very small part of the population would still live in a pre-industrial state, and provide food for a majority that pursues the goals of a consumer and leisure society without any reservations.

Turning a blind eye to economic conditions
We have somewhat more closely described the driving power of the social and economic changes because they are responsible for the dramatic reduction of nature and unspoilt landscapes, the theme of this book, and because the Canton of Zurich also had a part in leading the way. We have here a worldwide phenomenon that one could describe as economic blindness. Our entire economic system is completely blind to the environmental costs that we have created with our consumer behaviour. And yet, associations for promoting the economy often use the high environmental quality, scenic landscapes and a diversity of surroundings as advertising material.

In surveys, successful companies name, next to good educational opportunities, and way ahead of favourable tax conditions, intact landscapes and a clean environment as important criteria for their choice of location as a company headquarters or production facility. They perceive the landscape as if it is a God-given matter and therefore, of course, it is available for nothing, which, as we have seen, does not correspond to reality. Someone who constructs a pretentious new building on a piece of land,

zes oder ihrer Produktionsstätte. Dabei nehmen sie die Landschaft wahr, als handle es sich um eine gottgegebene Selbstverständlichkeit, die hier zum Nulltarif zur Verfügung steht, was, wie wir gesehen haben, der Wirklichkeit nicht entspricht. Wer auf einem Grundstück einen protzigen Neubau erstellen lässt und dabei einen Mehrwert erzielt, berücksichtigt in seiner Kostenrechnung nicht, dass die Seesicht für alle anderen, die es sich nicht leisten können dort zu wohnen, verbaut wird. Er konsumiert ein nicht vermehrbares öffentliches Gut, ohne dafür zu bezahlen.

Nun kann es nicht darum gehen, dass man für einen Waldspaziergang oder das Bad an einem nicht verbauten öffentlichen Fluss- oder Seeufer Eintritt zahlen muss. Aber der Wert der Landschaft für das Gedeihen von Gesellschaft und Wirtschaft erscheint nicht in der Kosten-Nutzenrechnung der privaten und der öffentlichen Haushalte. Das ist mit eine Ursache, weshalb bei politischen Entscheiden über Bauvorhaben die Werte der Landschaft, die in Mitleidenschaft gezogen oder gar zerstört werden, in der Regel nicht beachtet werden. Im Klartext gesagt: Landschaft und Natur werden als wertvoll eingestuft, aber nicht in Rechnung gezogen. Man verwechselt ihren Wert mit dem Preis, der nicht wie bei jedem Konsumgut samt Gewinnmarge berechnet und auf dem Preisschild angeschrieben steht. Ergo, so der falsche Schluss, ist diese Landschaft nichts wert oder man erkennt ihren Wert erst, wen es sie nicht mehr gibt und wir immer weiter reisen müssen, um unverdorbene Landschaft und Natur überhaupt noch anzutreffen.

Zwar haben wir seit Jahrzehnten Verfassungsartikel und Gesetze, die der Natur und der heimatlichen Landschaft einen Eigenwert zuordnen. Sie verpflichten die Behörden zu ihrer Schonung und dort, wo das allgemeine Interesse überwiegt, zu ihrer ungeschmälerten Erhaltung. Diese Formulierung ist zugegebenermassen offen für Interpretationen, aber es ist unzulässig, sich darum zu foutieren mit der Ausrede, man wisse im Einzelfall nicht, wie dieses «allgemeine Interesse» zu gewichten sei.

Von Zeit zu Zeit schafft ein Referendum oder eine Volksinitiative Klarheit. In der Schweiz gelten Moore und Moorlandschaften ohne Wenn und Aber als geschützt, und zwar auf Verfassungsstufe. Das haben das Volk und alle Stände 1987 in einer denkwürdigen Abstimmung so beschlossen. Das hinderte den Regierungsrat des Kantons Zürich nicht daran, die Projektierung einer Autobahn in das Zürcher Oberland voranzutreiben, obschon dieses Bauwerk Moore und eine ganze Moorlandschaft schwer beeinträchtigt und beschnitten hätte. Zum Glück gab es Kläger, und so musste das Bundesgericht entscheiden, dass die Autobahn wegen dem verfassungsrechtlichen Moorschutz dort nicht gebaut werden kann. Wie immer in

produces added value. However, in his cost calculation, he did not consider that the lake view would be obstructed for all those who cannot manage to live there. He consumes a non-renewable public good – without having to pay for it.

Now, this does not mean that if one goes for a walk in the woods or to a swimming area on a public river or lakeshore, one must pay to enter. But, the value of the landscape for the success of society and the economy does not appear in the cost-benefit calculations of the private and the public 'household'. This is one reason, among others, why the value of the landscape that will be affected or even destroyed, generally draws the short straw during political decisions about building plans. In plain English: Landscape and nature are classified as valuable, but are not included in the accounting. One confuses their value with a price, and this is not the same as consumer goods where the price is calculated, including the profit margin, and written on the price tag. This kind of thinking leads to a false conclusion: this landscape has no value. As often happens, we only recognise its value when it is no longer there and we must travel ever further to find a still unspoiled landscape and nature.

Indeed, for decades, we have had constitutional articles and laws that assign an intrinsic value to nature and the native landscape as well as officials to protect it. And, if general interest prevails, we commit ourselves to its unconditional preservation. Admittedly, the formulation is interpreted for each case, but it is inadmissible to ignore it with the excuse one doesn't know in individual cases how this 'general interest' is to be measured.

From time to time, a referendum or initiative manages to bring clarity. In Switzerland, moors and moor landscapes are automatically protected, without any 'if or when' and this is on a constitutional level. The people and all cantons decided this in 1987 in a memorable vote. However, that did not hinder the Cantonal Council in Zurich from pushing through the project planning for a highway in Zurich's Oberland, although this construction would have heavily impacted the moors and reduced them in size, and included an entire moor landscape. Luckily, there were those who objected so the Federal Supreme Court had to rule that the highway could not be built there because of the constitutional moor protection. As always in such cases, there was also criticism of the last instance decision, although the highest court actually only confirmed that the valid law had to be upheld.

This example is not an isolated instance, it shows that the enforcement of the rights of nature and landscape, among others, is not self-evident, exactly

solchen Fällen gab es auch Kritik am letztinstanzlichen Entscheid, obwohl das höchste Gericht eigentlich nichts anderes entschieden hatte, als dass geltendes Recht befolgt werden muss.

Das Beispiel ist kein Einzelfall. Es zeigt, dass die Durchsetzung des Rechtes der Natur und Landschaft gerade auch wegen der erwähnten ökonomischen Einäugigkeit nicht selbstverständlich ist. Der Anwendung geltenden Rechts im Landschafts- und Naturschutz muss immer wieder mit dem Rechtsmittel der Einsprachen und Beschwerden nachgeholfen werden. Das ist nicht populär. Jene, die dafür kämpfen, müssen sich oft den Vorwurf der Wirtschaftsfeindlichkeit gefallen lassen, obschon sie wesentlich mithelfen, nichtmaterielle Güter, die für die Wirtschaft und die gesamte Gesellschaft von unschätzbarem Wert sind, vor dem endgültigen Untergang zu retten.

Der Kanton Zürich als Vorreiter für einen raumgreifenden Naturschutz
Das Beispiel der Oberlandautobahn wirft kein gutes Licht auf den Kanton Zürich. Es muss aber auch gesagt sein, dass es auch und gerade hier Gegenkräfte gab und gibt, ohne die vieles, was wir in der Natur draussen noch bewundern können, nicht mehr da wäre. In manchen Gemeinden hat die meist private Initiative von Natur- und Heimatschutzvereinen immer wieder beispielhaft die Rettung einzelner wertvoller oder besonders typischer Gebäude, Biotope oder Naturschönheiten bewerkstelligt, die später zum staatlichen Inventar und sozusagen zum behördlichen Aushängeschild für den Kulturkanton wurden. Auch die Regierung selbst hat beispielsweise per Dekret den Greifensee und den Pfäffikersee samt seinen Ufern durch eine umfassende Verordnung mit Datum vom 27. Juni 1941 geschützt – zu einer Zeit, als Landschaftsschutz und Raumplanung noch kaum ein öffentliches Thema waren. Ohne diese weitsichtige Weichenstellung wäre diesen Seeufern das unrühmliche Schicksal so mancher anderen Seelandschaft nicht erspart geblieben.

In den Nachkriegsjahren wurde es dann immer offensichtlicher, dass einzelne Schutzverordnungen nicht mehr genügten, wenn Natur- und Landschaftsschutz nicht zum hoffnungslosen Flickwerk verkommen sollten. Der freisinnige Zürcher Politiker und spätere Bundesrat Fritz Honegger bewirkte mit einem Vorstoss im Kantonsrat in den 1960er-Jahren einen Stopp der weiteren Zersiedelung, indem er die Ergänzung des damaligen Wasserbaugesetzes forderte: Bauten, die nicht aufgrund ihrer Zweckbestimmung auf einen Standort ausserhalb von Bauzonen angewiesen waren, durften ausserhalb des für die Kanalisation der Abwässer geltenden Perimeters nicht mehr bewilligt werden – und zwar auch dort, wo Bauzonen noch gar nicht bestanden. Der primäre Beweggrund für diesen

because of this kind of thinking; one could call it a blind spot. The implementation of valid rights must be assisted again and again, especially in the area of landscape and nature protection, by applying the legal instruments of objections and complaints. This is not popular. Each person who fights for such issues often has to put up with the accusation of being hostile to the economy, although they are essentially helping to save areas that are of inestimable worth to the economy, and indeed to the entire society, from their final demise.

The Canton of Zurich as a pioneer for nature protection
We should not be misled by the example of the Oberland autobahn into thinking the Canton of Zurich is not supportive of nature protection. It must also be said that there were and still are active counter-forces in the canton. Without them, much of what we can still admire outside in nature would no longer be there. In some communities, the mainly private initiatives on nature and heritage protection again and again managed in an exemplary fashion to rescue individual valuable or particularly typical buildings, biotopes or areas of natural beauty. Many were later added to the national inventory and led to the canton becoming, as it were, an official figurehead as the 'culture canton'. The government had, for example, protected the Greifensee and Pfäffikersee, including the shores, by issuing a comprehensive decree dated 27 June 1941, a time when landscape protection and spatial planning were only just becoming public issues. Without these far-sighted decisions, these lakeshores would not have been spared the inglorious fate that so many other lake landscapes suffered.

In the post-war years, it became more obvious that individual protection regulations were no longer enough if nature and landscape protection were not to become a hopeless patchwork. The liberal Zurich politician and later Federal Councillor, Fritz Honegger provoked an effective stop to further sprawl with a campaign in the cantonal parliament in the 1960s for an amendment of the then current hydraulic engineering law. Any construction that was not reliant on a location outside the building zones, due to a specific function or purpose, would no longer be permitted outside the valid perimeters for wastewater canalisation, and even anywhere that building zones do not yet exist.

The primary motivation for this initiative was perhaps not landscape protection, probably more the insight that the development of settlements without a spatial reduction of this rampant building spree would deteriorate to a literally endless Sisyphus task. That was, as a pre-runner of the federal law about

Vorstoss war vielleicht nicht der Landschaftsschutz, wohl aber die Einsicht, dass die Erschliessung der Siedlungen ohne räumliche Beschränkung der Bauerei zur Sisyphusarbeit verkommt. Das war als Vorläufer des Bundesgesetzes über die Raumplanung, das 1980 in Kraft trat, eine landesplanerische Tat, dank der manche Landschaften im volksreichsten Kanton der Schweiz nicht zersiedelt wurden oder jedenfalls mit geringeren Schäden «über die Strecke» kamen.

Als erster hat der Kanton Zürich 1995 ein Naturschutz-Gesamtkonzept verabschiedet. Auch dies geschah aus einer ganzheitlichen Betrachtungsweise. Wenn es schon Gesamtkonzepte für den Verkehr oder die Energie gab, musste der Natur- und Landschaftsschutz als Querschnittsaufgabe auf die gleiche Ebene gehoben werden. Mit dem Naturschutzkonzept wurde eine nur anthropozentrische Betrachtungsweise endlich ergänzt durch eine Schau, die Natur als einen übergreifenden Zusammenhang erkennt, von dem wir Menschen nur ein Teil sind. Deshalb sollte eigentlich – auch wenn das heute politisch unmöglich scheint – ein räumliches Konzept für den Naturschutz dem Verkehrs- und Energiekonzept sogar übergeordnet werden, aus dem einfachen Grund, weil Bauten und Anlagen an verschiedenen Orten erstellt werden können, im Unterschied zu Natur und Landschaft. Diese können nicht verpflanzt werden.

Das Naturschutzkonzept des Kantons Zürich bezieht sich nicht nur auf Restflächen, wo die Landschaft noch einigermassen intakt ist, sondern es umfasst auch Siedlungs- und Verkehrsräume. Eine tragende Rolle kommt den Pärken und Gärten der Städte zu. Aber auch so unscheinbare Elemente wie Strassenborde, Areale mit Bahngeleisen, Hinterhöfe oder nicht mit Chemie behandelte Plätze sind sehr wichtig für die Flora und Fauna. Der weit über die Landesgrenzen hinaus bekannte Zürcher Botaniker Elias Landolt hat in seiner auf der Basis eines Quadratkilometernetzes erstellten Flora der Stadt Zürich nicht weniger als 2000 Pflanzenarten auf dem Boden der politischen Gemeinde Zürich ermittelt.[9] Die Artenzahl pro Quadratkilometer beträgt im Mittel 451. Sie variiert zwischen 294 und 607. Ein Drittel der Arten wächst aber nur auf etwa sechs Prozent der Gesamtfläche. Besonders viele Arten enthalten das Gebiet der Chatzenseen mit viel Sumpf- und Teichflächen, ferner ausgedehnte Bahnareale sowie die Steilhänge des Uetlibergs. Das darf aber nicht als Entwarnung gelten. Die Anzahl der ausgestorbenen Arten beläuft sich auf 188 (14 %), jene der neu eingewanderten und eingeschleppten Arten auf 294 (21 %). Nach neueren Erhebungen sind in Städten und Siedlungen nur etwa 15 Prozent der privaten Gärten in einem naturnahen Zustand: Der grösste Teil ist mit seinen Kunstrasen und immergrünen bodenbedeckenden und meist fremdländischen Sträuchern

spatial planning that came into effect in 1980, a national planning act, thanks to which many landscapes in the most populous canton in Switzerland were not lost to sprawl or, at least, managed to come through it with limited damage.

In 1995, the Canton of Zurich was the first to adopt an overall concept for a nature protection plan. Once more, this came out of an integrated approach. If the canton had already had an overall concept for traffic or energy, then nature and landscape protection, as a cross-sectional task, would have to be raised to the same level. With the nature protection concept, a purely anthropocentric approach was finally complemented by a view that recognises nature as a comprehensive interrelationship, of which we humans are only a part. Therefore, even if today it seems to be politically impossible, a spatial concept for the protection of nature should actually have overriding importance over traffic and energy concepts, for the simple reason that constructions and compounds can be erected in various places, in contrast to nature and landscapes: these cannot be transplanted.

The nature protection concept of the Canton of Zurich covers not only the remaining areas where the landscape is to a certain degree still intact, it also includes settlement areas and traffic zones. The parks and gardens of the city play a strong supporting role. And even such unprepossessing elements as street and road borders, areas with railroad tracks, back yards or courts that have not been treated with chemicals are very important for the flora and fauna. The well-known Zurich botanist, Elias Landolt, determined that there were no less than 2,000 plant species on the ground within the political boundaries of the city of Zurich, using a square kilometre network as the basis for the count.[9] The number of species per square kilometre averaged out to 451. They ranged between 294 and 607. Nevertheless, a third of all plants grew on only about 6 % of the total area. In particular, many types were found in the area of the Chatzenseen with its many marsh and pond areas, and in long stretches of railway lands as well as on the steep bluffs of the Uetliberg. However, this does not serve as an all-clear signal. The number of extinct plants runs to 188 (14 %), while those of the immigrated and introduced species is 294 (21 %).

According to new surveys, only about 15 % of the private gardens in cities and settlements are in a near-nature state: The largest part is covered with artificial turf and evergreen groundcovers with mostly foreign bushes. These are life threatening for the native flora and fauna and are sterile. The use of chemicals against so-called weeds and vermin or pests is an additional threat.

für die heimische Flora und Fauna lebensfeindlich und somit ökologisch steril. Hinzu kommt der Einsatz von Chemie gegen sogenanntes Unkraut und sogenannte Schädlinge.

Wo die Not ist, wächst auch das Rettende
Das Sprichwort nach Friedrich Hölderlin trifft auch für den Umgang mit den Fliessgewässern zu. Und auch hier spielte der Kanton Zürich eine Pionierrolle, denn im Jahr 1989 genehmigte der Kantonsrat einen Fonds zur Wiederbelebung der Fliessgewässer. Die Idee dahinter ist eine doppelte: Gewässer sind nicht nur eine Rinne, durch die Wasser möglichst schadlos abfliessen soll, sondern sie sind Lebensräume mit vielen Organismen, die am oder im Wasser leben und deren Leben von ganz spezifischen Bedingungen und Nahrungsketten des jeweiligen Gewässers abhängt. Nach einer alten Weisheit ist die Natur geduldig, sie gibt immer Kredit, aber sie vergisst nie Rechnung zu stellen. Verheerende Überschwemmungen und grosse Dammbrüche an der Thur und an vielen anderen Flüssen der Schweiz öffneten 1978 vielen Menschen die Augen. Man hatte den Flüssen und Bächen in Zeiten des Landhungers und oft auch im Zeichen eines einseitigen Nützlichkeitsdenkens sehr viel Lebensraum weggenommen. Nun kommt es immer wieder zu Starkniederschlägen, nach denen die Gewässer über die Ufer treten. Man spricht dann häufig von Naturereignissen oder gar Naturkatastrophen. In Wirklichkeit ist es aber so, dass sich die Bäche und Flüsse nur das ihnen einst geraubte Land zurückholen – und zwar umso heftiger und unkontrollierter, je enger das Korsett ist, in das man sie einst gezwängt hat. Seit sich diese Erkenntnis als ein neues Paradigma des Gewässer- und des Hochwasserschutzes durchgesetzt hat, werden dort, wo sich die Gelegenheit bietet, etwa im Rahmen von neuen Meliorationen, beim Bau von Nationalstrassen, bei der Erneuerung von Infrastrukturanlagen oder zum besseren Schutz der unterliegenden Siedlungen Dämme abgetragen und weiträumig verlegt. Flusssohlen und Bachbette werden erweitert. Man gibt dem Gewässer wieder Raum, um sich dort auszutoben und Schlamm oder Schutt abzulagern, wo der Schaden an bestehenden Nutzflächen und Bauten nicht zu gross ist. Damit macht man das, was man früher mit dem irreführenden Begriff Fluss- und Bachkorrektion eigentlich nicht verbessert, sondern verschlechtert hatte, wenigstens teilweise wieder rückgängig. Dass dies nicht immer ohne Opfer geht, liegt auf der Hand. An manchen Orten müssen auch Menschen ihre oft übertriebenen Ansprüche aufgeben – dort nämlich, wo man geglaubt hatte, einen Bach oder Fluss endgültig gezähmt zu haben und landwirtschaftliche Nutzflächen und sogar einzelne Bauten zu nah am Wasser errichtete. Diese müssen nun dem neu geschaffenen

Where there is a need, a rescue arises as well
(Wo die Not ist, wächst auch das Rettende)
This well-known poetic expression from Friedrich Hölderlin also appears in association with flowing water. Here the Canton of Zurich also played a pioneering role: In 1989, the Cantonal Council approved an endowment fund for the revitalisation of flowing water. The idea held a double goal: Waters are not just the channel through which water should flow, most preferably without damage, they are also a living space with many organisms that live in or on the water and their lives are dependent on very specific conditions and a food chain in the respective waters. According to a wise old saying; Nature is very patient, she always gives credit; but she never forgets to send the invoice either. Devastating floods and huge dam breaks on the Thur River in 1978, as well as on many other rivers in Switzerland, caused many people to open their eyes. In the period when owning land was a high priority for many and a kind of one-sided utilitarian thinking held sway, a great many water-based living spaces were removed. Now, heavy rainfall is becoming more and more frequent and afterwards the waters overflow their banks. One often speaks of natural events or even of natural catastrophes. However, the truth is that the streams and rivers are only taking back the land that was stolen from them in the first place and indeed the level of reaction is stronger and more uncontrolled based on how tight the corset was that we gave them.

This knowledge has become accepted as a new paradigm for the protection of bodies of water, watercourses and floodwaters. If an opportunity arises, for example, as part of improvements in the construction of national highways, during the renewal of infrastructure sites or the installation of better protection for settlements underlying a dam, then dams are removed and carefully relocated, stream- and riverbeds are widened. Water has room to flow freely and deposit mud, silt and rubble in places where the damage to existing useful areas and buildings is not too great. These measures are intended to reverse, at least partially, what man did earlier under the misleading concept of river and stream correction, which actually did not improve things at all, and, in fact, made the situation worse. It is probably obvious that this cannot always be accomplished without sacrifices.

Sometimes people must also give up their often excessive demands, not with life and limb, but in existing agricultural land and individual constructions where one believes he has finally tamed the stream or the river, but has actually set these up too close to the water. These must now yield to the newly

Gewässerraum weichen. Durch die Aufweitungen des Flussbettes wird die Flut des Wassers mit seinem Geschiebe und Schlamm verlangsamt und die Gefahr für unterliegende bewohnte Gebiete verringert. Nicht zuletzt profitieren von den Massnahmen auch manche Lebewesen, etwa Vögel wie der Regenpfeifer und der Strandläufer, die hier wieder Brutplätze und Nahrung finden. Forscher gehen davon aus, dass sich als Folge des Klimawandels Hochwasser und Überschwemmungen häufen und deshalb der Wiederbelebung von Gewässern künftig noch wesentlich mehr Bedeutung zukommt.

Ausblick

Im Kanton Zürich erkennt man in verdichteter Form den räumlichen, wirtschaftlichen und gesellschaftlichen Wandel, der die ganze Schweiz erfasst hat. Angesichts der beschleunigten Entwicklung sind die in den letzten Abschnitten unvollständig beschriebenen Leistungen des Kantons für den Natur- und Landschaftsschutz beachtlich. Aber sie geben keinen Anlass für eine Entwarnung. Nach wie vor sind viele Arten bedroht, die Biodiversität nimmt ab, Naturnetze werden durch Netze der Infrastruktur zerschnitten oder ausgedünnt – oder sie schrumpfen zu Inseln, die zu klein oder zu weit voneinander entfernt sind, um den notwendigen Austausch unter den heimischen Tier- und Pflanzenvorkommen zu gewährleisten.

Auch in der Raumplanung besteht immer noch ein Vollzugsdefizit. Neue Herausforderungen verlangen nach neuen Lösungen, wobei es dazu nicht jedes Mal neue Gesetze oder neue Regelungen braucht. Die wesentlichen Grundsätze der Raumplanung und des Umwelt- und Naturschutzes sind in den Gesetzen von Kanton und Bund schon längst festgeschrieben, man muss sie bloss befolgen. Sie sind nämlich so formuliert, dass sie auch die kreativen Lösungen von gewandelten Problemen erlauben. Zu Hoffnung Anlass geben sehr gute Beispiele, wo es gelungen ist, die Verdichtung von bestehenden Wohnbauten und Siedlungen mit einer ökologischen Aufwertung zu verbinden. Mehr Natur muss die Losung sein, sowohl in den Siedlungen als auch draussen in der Agrarlandschaft. Und die verbliebenen Juwelen, die wirklich naturnahen Gebiete, dürfen nicht mehr verkleinert werden, sondern sie sollen dort, wo es die Raumverhältnisse erlauben, erweitert werden.

Ob der Kanton Zürich diese Spannung zwischen grossstädtischer Urbanität und Natur, zwischen Agglomeration und ländlichem Raum auffangen und gestalten kann oder ob sich mit der Zeit alles im Einerlei eines heranwachsenden Weltdorfes auflöst, ist ungewiss. Dies hängt primär nicht mehr von neuen Gesetzesparagraphen und hochtrabenden Raumentwicklungsprogrammen ab. Und vielleicht auch nicht

created water spaces. Through widening the riverbed, the flow of the water with its rubble and mud will be slower and the danger for underlying inhabited areas will be limited. Not least, some living organisms might profit from the measures as well, such as birds like the plover and the sandpiper that will be able to find brood sites and food again. Researchers assume that high water and flooding are happening more often as a result of climate change and therefore the revitalisation of water will receive essentially more importance in future.

Outlook

The Canton of Zurich united spatial, economic and social change in a concentrated form that has captured all of Switzerland. In view of this accelerated development, the previous sections have substantially incompletely described the remarkable performance of the canton for the protection of nature and landscape. But, this is no reason to assume there is an all-clear signal. Now, as before, many species are threatened, biodiversity is dwindling, nature's networks are cut into pieces by our network of infrastructures, thinned out or shrunk to islands that are too small or too far away from one another to be able to manage the required exchange among the native plants and animals.

An implementation deficit also still exists in spatial planning. New challenges require new solutions, however, it does not need another new law or regulation every time. The essential foundations of spatial planning and the protection of the environment and nature are already long established in the laws of the cantons and federal government; one must simply follow them. They are formulated in such a way that they also allow creative solutions to problems that have been altered. To bring hope, there are some very good examples of places where they have managed to combine the density of existing residential buildings and settlements with an ecological upgrade. In the settlements as well as outside in the agricultural landscape, the solution must be bringing in more nature. And, the remaining jewels in current nature areas must not be allowed to shrink; they should be expanded in places where the spatial conditions allow it.

Whether the Canton of Zurich can absorb this tension between large city urbanity and nature, between agglomeration and rural spaces and then shape and redesign it, or whether all this will dissolve over time into the monotony of a growing world village is unknown. This no longer depends primarily on new legal paragraphs and grandiose spatial development programmes. And perhaps not on visionary designs either, especially when they remain on paper.

von visionären Entwürfen, die dann doch nur auf dem Papier bleiben. Nötig sind vielmehr neue Allianzen zwischen bewahrenden und erneuernden Kräften. «Erhalten ist progressiv», lautete schon vor Jahren ein Slogan, der radikal tönt, aber in seiner Stossrichtung noch genauso aktuell ist. Ein rastloser Umbruch, dem das Gewachsene geopfert wird, wirkt zerstörend. Aber das blosse Festhalten am Alten führt zur Erstarrung und deshalb ebenfalls zum Untergang. Vielleicht ist es auch eine Frage des Tempos. Wenn der sogenannte Wandel einfach dem radikalen Umbruch gleichgesetzt wird, dann bleibt keine Zeit zur sorgfältigen Synthese von Bewährtem und Neuem.

Wie geht es weiter? Die Zukunft ist immer ungewiss, was uns nicht hindern soll, die Schritte zu unternehmen, von denen wir heute annehmen können, dass sie uns wenigstens nicht immer näher an eine nie dagewesene ökologische Krise heranführen. Eine solche wird je unausweichlicher, desto länger wir auf dem quantitativen Wachstumskurs weiterfahren. Eine kantonale Volksinitiative für einen umfassenden Schutz von gutem Ackerland gab dem weitverbreiteten Unbehagen über das sich flächenhaft ausdehnende Siedlungswachstum Ausdruck. Sie wurde in einer Abstimmung 2012 zur Überraschung der bürgerlichen Parteien und der politischen Behörden deutlich angenommen. Letztere müssen sich nun damit befassen, wie das Begehren auf Gesetzesstufe strikt und verbindlich umgesetzt wird.

Sicher, der Umweltschutz, der die Erhaltung der Artenvielfalt und den Schutz von Boden, Luft, Wasser und Landschaft umfasst, hängt von globalen Entwicklungen ab, auf die wir gesamthaft nur einen beschränkten Einfluss haben. Aber das Gute kommt nicht nur von oben und vor allem nicht von alleine! Es beginnt auch im Kleinen. Natur und Landschaft vor der eigenen Haustüre können uns einen Zugang zu einem bewussteren, sorgsameren und kreativeren Umgang mit den begrenzten Ressourcen inspirieren. Wie Landschaft und Natur in Zukunft aussehen werden, hängt nicht nur von äusseren Umständen ab, sondern auch davon, ob wir als Bürgerinnen und Bürger Verantwortung dafür übernehmen, nachdem wir zu lange für fast alles den Staat oder die Politiker verantwortlich gemacht haben. Es kommt mit anderen Worten auch darauf an, ob wir selber etwas beitragen zu jener Umwelt und Landschaft, die wir uns wünschen.

What is needed are new alliances between reliable, proven and forward-looking methods. 'Preservation is progressive' proclaimed a slogan some years back, which sounded radical then, but its orientation is still current. Any hasty change or decision that sacrifices the natural development gained through experience will have a destructive effect. However, a mere adherence to the old has a numbing effect and inclines toward destruction. Perhaps it is also a question of tempo. When the so-called transformation is simply equated with radical change, then there is no time for a careful synthesis of proven and innovative methods.

What's next? The future is always unknown, but that should not hinder us from taking the steps that we can take today, so that at least we are not moving closer to an unprecedented ecological crisis. One such crisis is inevitable if we continue on the road to quantitative growth. A cantonal voter's initiative for the comprehensive protection of good arable land offered an opportunity to express the widespread unease about the rapid settlement expansion that was taking place. This unease found a positive expression in a cantonal voters' initiative for the comprehensive protection of good farmland. In a vote in 2012, to the surprise of the centre and right-wing parties and the political authorities, it was clearly accepted. Now, they must decide how the demand can be implemented on the legal level as valid and binding.

Surely, environmental protection, which includes the preservation of species diversity and the protection of land, air, water and landscape, also depends on global developments, where in general, we have limited influence. However, 'Good' doesn't just come from above – and especially not by itself! It can also begin small. Having nature and landscape right in front of your door could awaken a more conscious, more careful and more creative approach and inspire how we deal with our limited resources. How landscape and nature will look in future depends not only on external circumstances, but also on whether we as citizens take up the responsibility ourselves for what we want and, after quite a long time, stop holding the state or the politicians responsible. In other words, the future depends on whether we contribute something to that environment and to the landscape that we want for ourselves.

Eine Klimanachhersage: Das Bild des späteren Zürich während der grossen Riss-Eiszeit vor rund 200 000 Jahren. Der Mast signalisiert den Uetliberg.

A climate 'post-cast': An image of Zurich's future location during the great Riss Glaciation approximately 200,000 years ago. The mast marks the Uetliberg.

Alles Zürich? Der Blick vom Uetliberg zeigt die auf beiden Seeseiten nahtlos zusammengewachsenen Dörfer der Gemeinden Kilchberg – Rüschlikon – Thalwil und Zollikon – Küsnacht – Erlenbach – Herrliberg. Diese Gemeinden verstehen sich aber keineswegs als zusammengehörig. Aus landschaftlicher Sicht hat mit dem Zusammenwachsen der Dörfer ein Umkehrprozess stattgefunden, indem der Siedlungsraum an Stelle des Grünraumes zum landschaftsverbindenden Element geworden ist.

Is it really all Zurich? The view from the Uetliberg shows the seamlessly merged villages on both sides of the lake: Kilchberg – Rüschlikon – Thalwil and Zollikon – Küsnacht – Erlenbach – Herrliberg. However, these communities do not seem to have any feeling of belonging together. From a scenic point of view, the merging of the villages has actually caused a reverse process to take place in that the settlement space has become the landscape-connecting element instead of the green space.

Blick vom Uetlibergturm auf die Albiskette mit ihrer von der Stadt Zürich bis nach Sihlbrugg durchgehenden Wanderstrecke. Hier wächst der grösste zusammenhängende Laubmischwald der Schweiz, der weitere Raum des «Wildnispark Zürich Sihlwald». Die offene Verbindung bis in die Voralpen und Alpen trägt zur hohen biologischen Vielfalt im Park bei (vorhergehende Doppelseite).

View from Uetliberg Tower towards the Albis mountain range, which has a continuous hiking trail from Zurich City up to Sihlbrugg. The largest continuous mixed deciduous forest in Switzerland grows here; an additional open space of the Wilderness Park Zurich Sihlwald. The open connection to the foothills and the Alps contributes to the high biodiversity in the park (previous double-page).

Sanft modellierte Moränenlandschaft südöstlich von Hirzel. Das Tobel eines Seitenbachs der Sihl ist vom Wald abgeschirmt. Mit einer Linde auf einem Hügel zeigt sich dahinter die zusammenhängende charakteristische Moränenlandschaft.

A softly molded moraine landscape southeast of Hirzel. The ravine of a tributary stream of the Sihl River is shielded by the forest. A linden tree on a hill shows off a characteristic continuous moraine landscape behind it.

Die Moränenlandschaft im Raum Hirzel-Schönenberg ist bergseitig durch die Höhronen begrenzt, die über den Schindellegi-Sattel mit dem Etzel verbunden ist. In der sanft modellierten Landschaft hat die junge Sihl ihren Weg entlang der Höhronen gefunden, wird dann aber durch Moränen des Reussgletschers nordwärts umgelenkt. Die bewaldeten Tobel im Vordergrund erodieren weiter und trennen die Landschaft. Säntis, Speer und die Glarner Alpen zeichnen den Horizont (folgende Doppelseite).

The moraine landscape in the Hirzel-Schönenberg area is restricted by the Höhronen mountain range, which is connected via the Schindellegi saddle with Etzel Mountain. In the gently rolling landscape, the young Sihl River has found its way along the Höhronen Mountains, but is then diverted northwards by the moraines of the Reuss Glacier. In the foreground, the wooded ravines erode further and separate the landscape. The Säntis, Speer and the Glarus Alps on the left mark the horizon (following double-page).

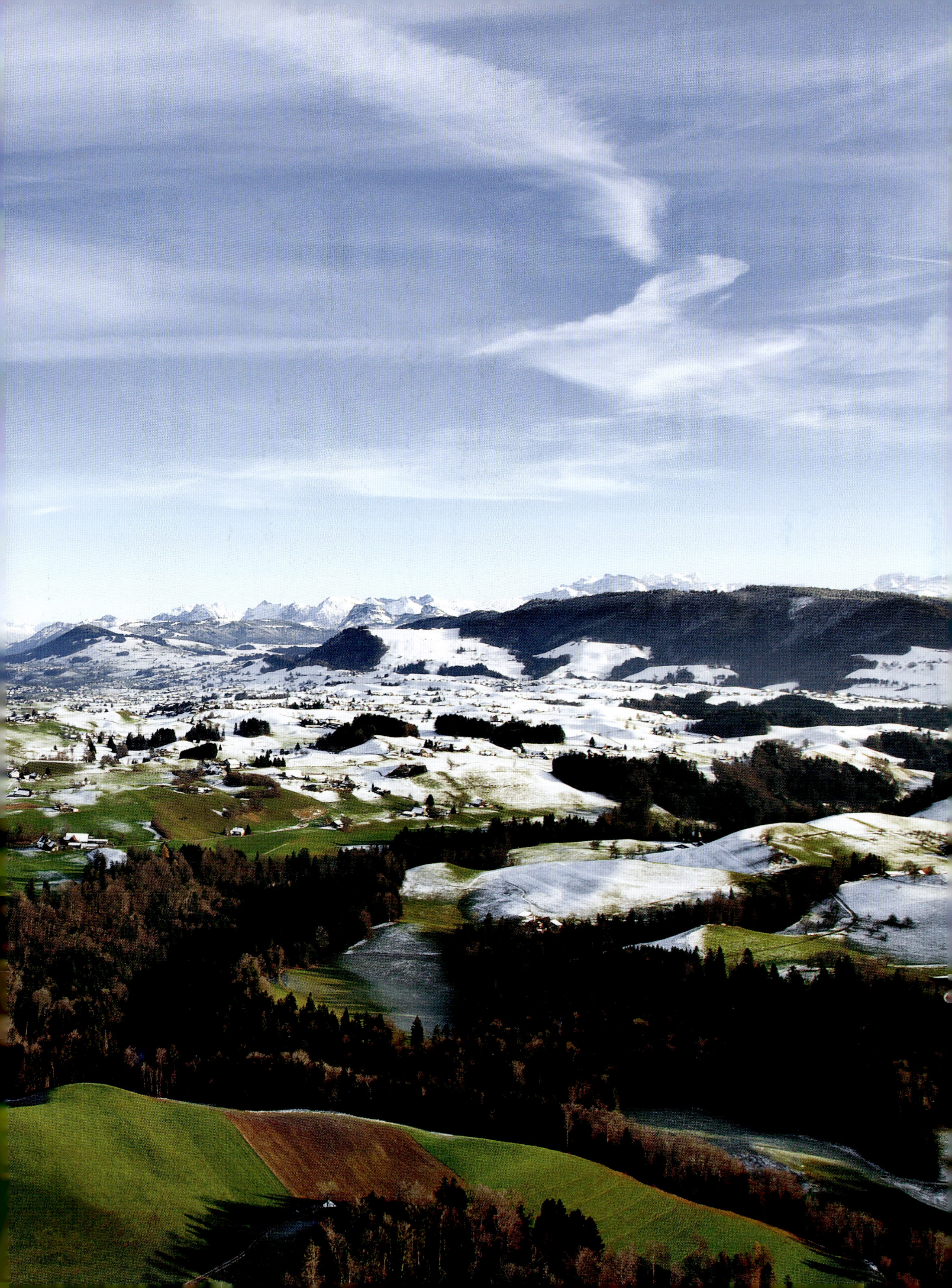

Blick über die Kantonsgrenze am oberen Zürichsee. Der Frauenwinkel mit dem im ruhigen Wasser spiegelnden Uferstreifen ist das wichtigste Stück natürlicher Uferlandschaft, das noch erhalten ist (links).
Gemäss einer urkundlich belegten Schenkung gehört die Ufenau, die grösste Insel der Schweiz, mit weiteren Gütern dem Kloster Einsiedeln. Die zusammenhängende Ried-, Ufer-, Wasser und Insellandschaft ist als intakte, auch von einer reichen Vogelwelt genutzte Naturlandschaft am Zürichsee einmalig (rechts).

View across the cantonal border at the Rapperswil end of Lake Zurich. The Frauenwinkel, with its shoreline reflecting in the calm water, is the most important piece of natural shoreline landscape that is still preserved (left). According to a documented donation, the Ufenau, the largest island in Switzerland, together with other goods, belongs to the monastery at Einsiedeln. The continuous marsh shore, water and island landscape is an intact and unique natural landscape of Lake Zurich, and is used by a rich and varied bird population (right).

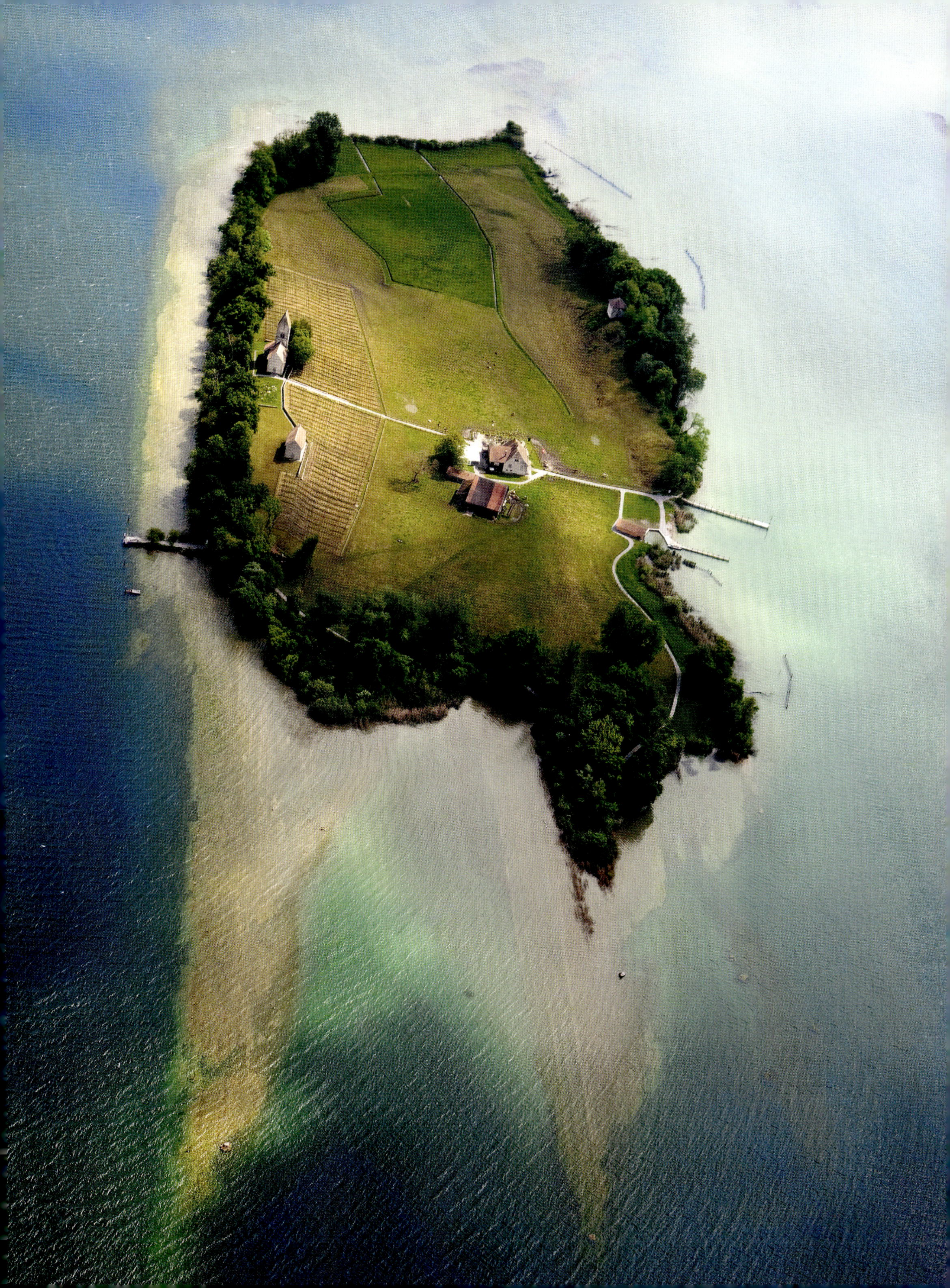

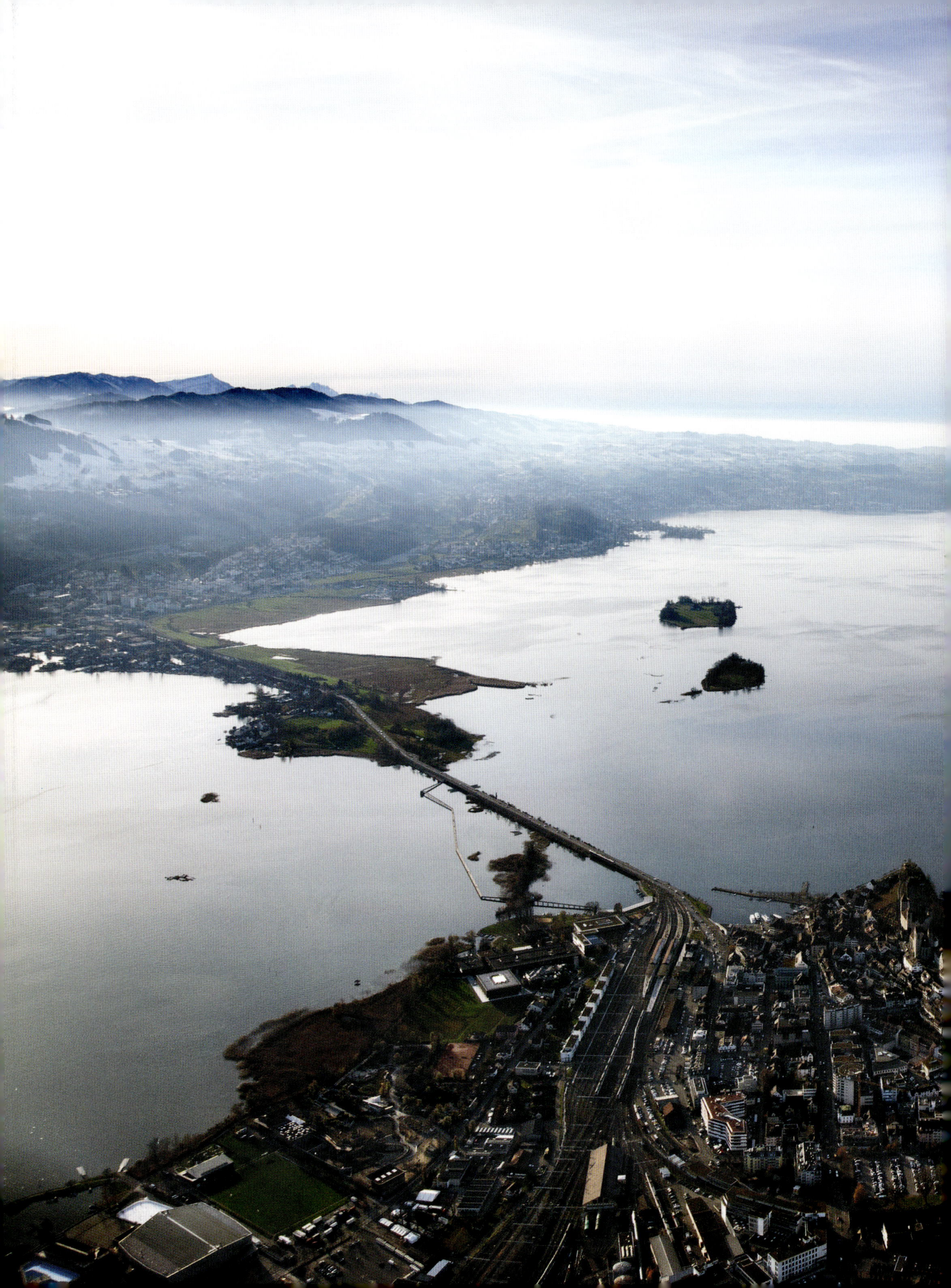

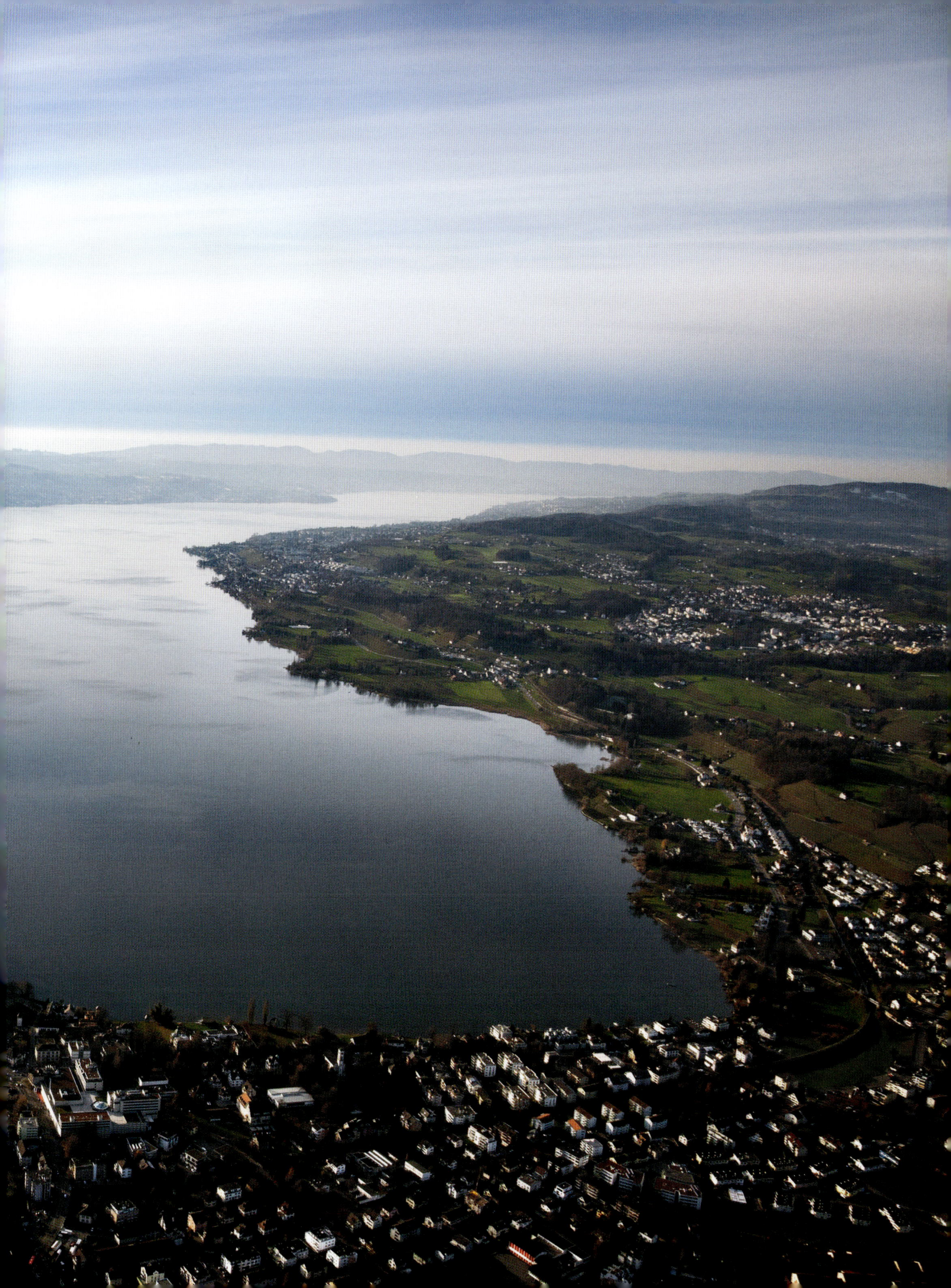

Blick über Rapperswil seeabwärts. Links im Bild ist das Schutzgebiet Frauenwinkel mit den Inseln Lützelau und Ufenau zu sehen, neben dem Seedamm der im April 2001 eröffnete, 841 Meter lange Holzsteg. Er wurde in Anlehnung an den historischen Holzsteg als Wanderweg zwischen Rapperswil und Hurden errichtet. Rechts im Bild erkennt man die naturnahen Seeufer von Schirmensee und Feldbach (vorhergehende Doppelseite).

Das Tössbergland zeigt oberhalb Gibswil seinen grundlegenden Charakter: zahlreiche Hügel, Täler, Wiesen, Weiden und Waldtypen, tief eingeschnittene Bachläufe, Quellmoore, kleine Siedlungen und Einzelhöfe mit Viehwirtschaft.

View from Rapperswil down the lake. On the left in the photo is the nature reserve of the Frauenwinkel with its islands Lützelau and Ufenau, next to the Seedam, an 841 m boardwalk that opened in April 2001. It was built in the style of the historic boardwalk and is used as a hiking trail between Rapperswil and Hurden. On the right, one can recognise the natural lakeshore of Schirmensee and Feldbach (previous double-page).

Just above Gibswil, the Töss mountain area shows its fundamental character: Numerous hills, valleys, meadows, pastures and various kinds of forests, deeply incised streams, spring moors, small villages and isolated farms with livestock.

Im Blick vom Irchel über Neftenbach und weite offene Wiesen Richtung Winterthur zeichnen bewaldete Hügelkuppen im Siedlungsraum die besondere landschaftliche Grundstruktur der Stadt Winterthur. Der Ruf als «Schweizer Gartenstadt» hängt mit dem grossen Baumbestand auch ausserhalb der Wälder zusammen (folgende Doppelseite).

The view from Irchel across the wide-open meadows to Neftenbach and on towards Winterthur draws the eye from wooded hilltops into the settled area, the special landscape structure of the City of Winterthur. Winterthur's reputation as a Swiss Garden City is also because of its large tree population, much of which is outside the forested areas (following double-page).

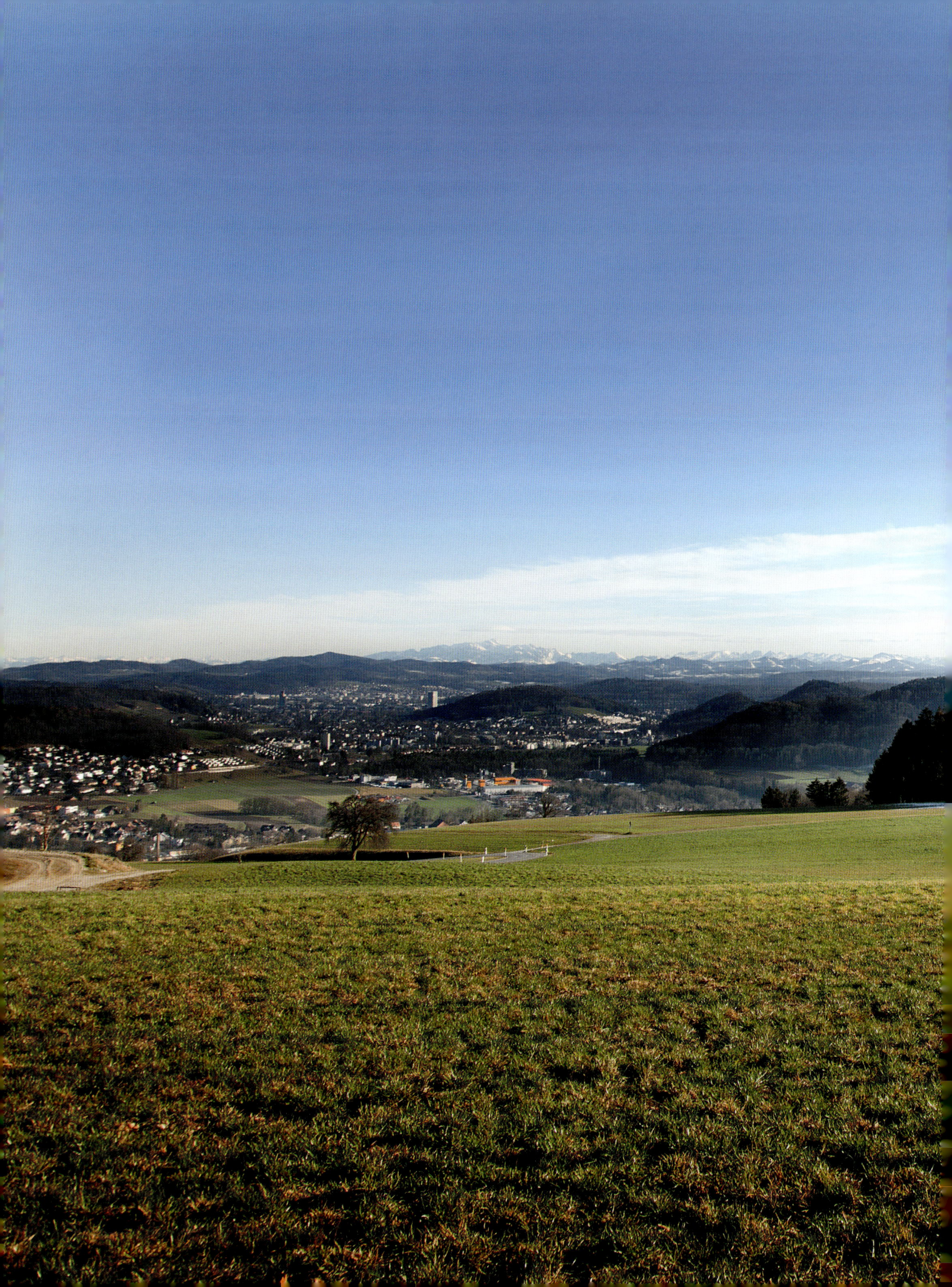

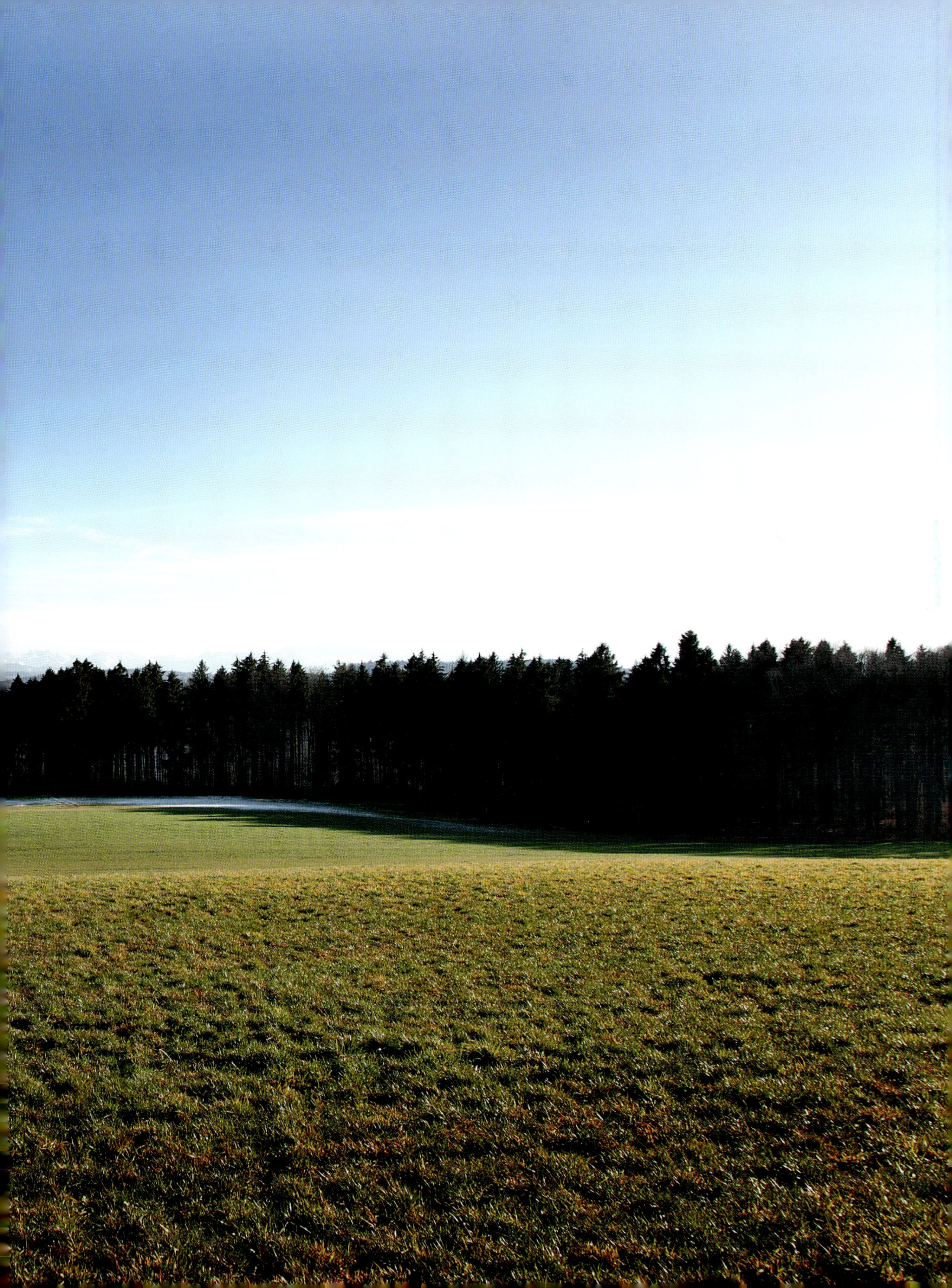

Weinlese in Eglisau (rechts). Der Weinbau hat im Kanton Zürich Tradition: 1881 produzierten zwei Drittel aller Grundbesitzer eigenen Wein. Mit dem Einschleppen des Falschen Mehltaus und der Reblaus aus Amerika brach der Rebbau aber europaweit ein. Vielfältige Rettungsversuche führten zur gängigen Praxis, die europäischen Kultursorten auf amerikanische Wurzeln aufzupfropfen. Heute lebt die Zürcher Weinbautradition in den trocken-warmen Lagen des Weinlandes und des Unterlandes sowie an den sonnigen rechtsseitigen Ufern von Thur, Rhein, Limmat und dem Zürichsee fort.
Schloss Schwandegg thront über dem Rebberg bei Waltalingen; die hübsche Winzerhütte bezeugt Stolz und Bodenverbundenheit (links).

Grape harvest in Eglisau (right). Wine growing has a long tradition in the Canton of Zurich: in 1881 two-thirds of all landowners produced their own wine. With the arrival of the downy mildew and the grape phylloxera from America, viniculture and viticulture collapsed all over Europe. Various rescue attempts led to the common practice of grafting European cultured varieties onto American roots. Today, the Zurich winegrowing tradition lives on in the dry, warm localities of the wine country and the Zurich lowlands, as well as on the sunny shores on the right side of the Thur, Rhine, and Limmat Rivers and Lake Zurich.
Castle Schwandegg presides over the vineyards of Waltalingen; the pretty little winegrower's cottages testify to their pride and solid bond with nature (left).

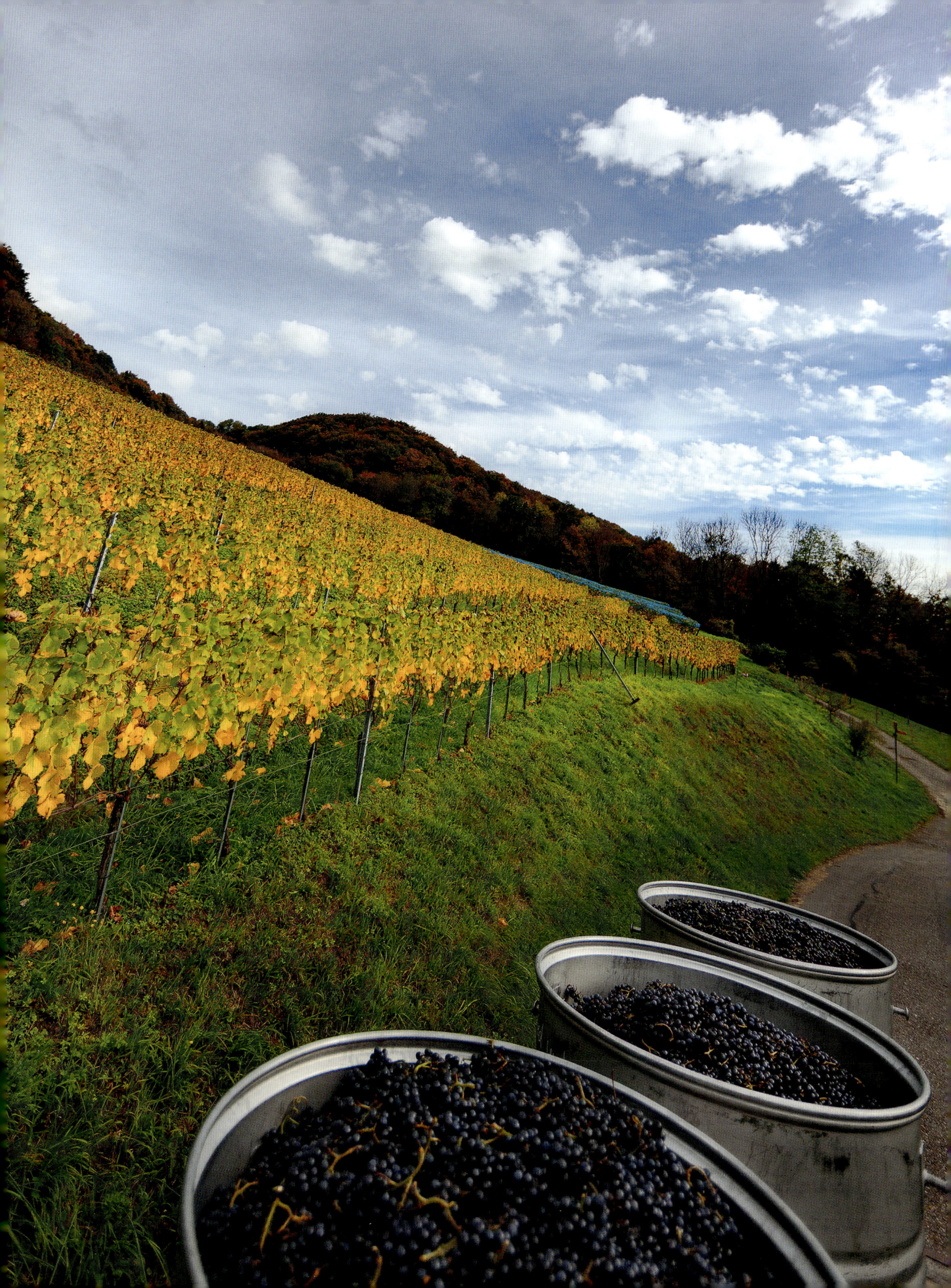

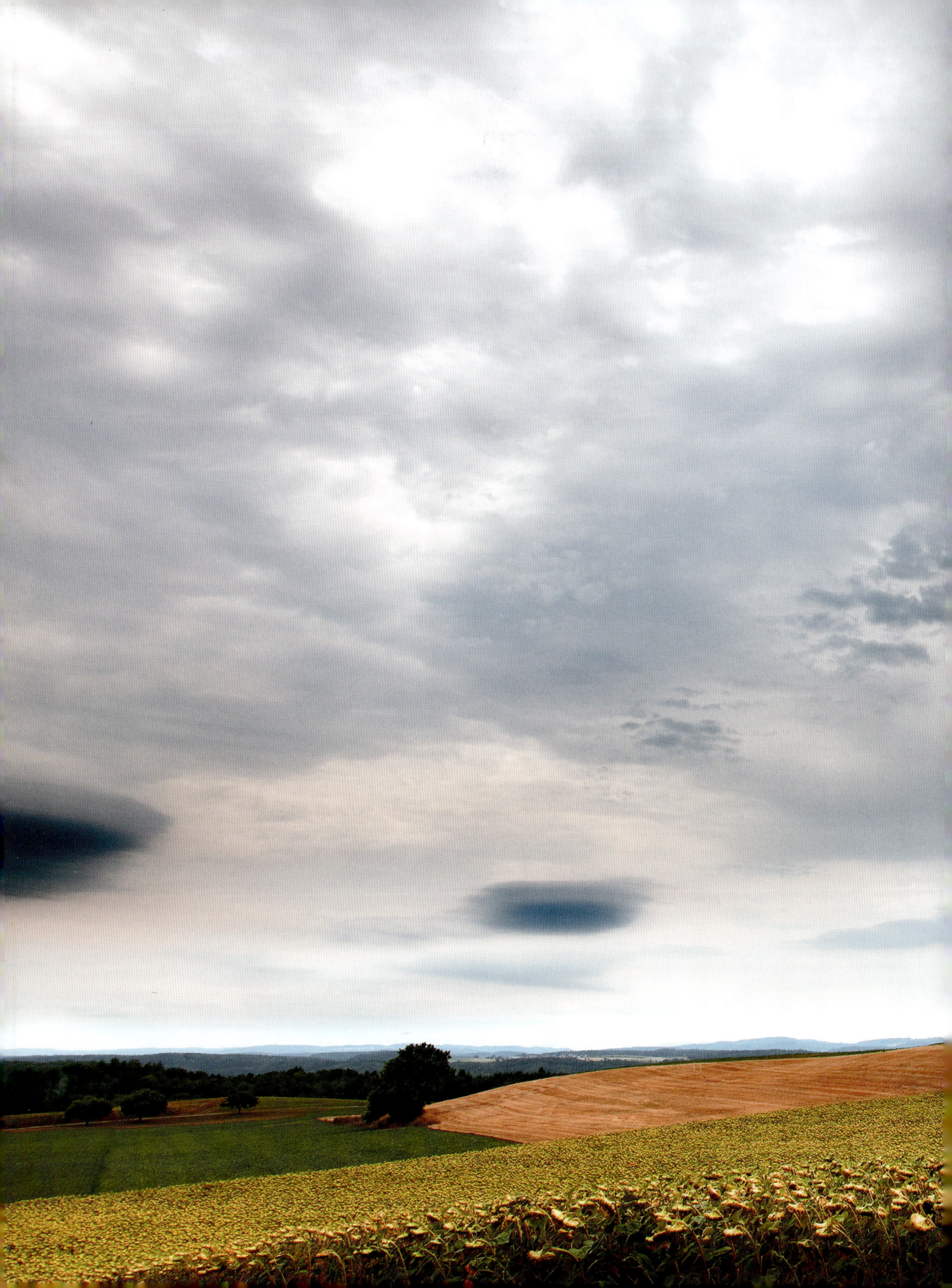

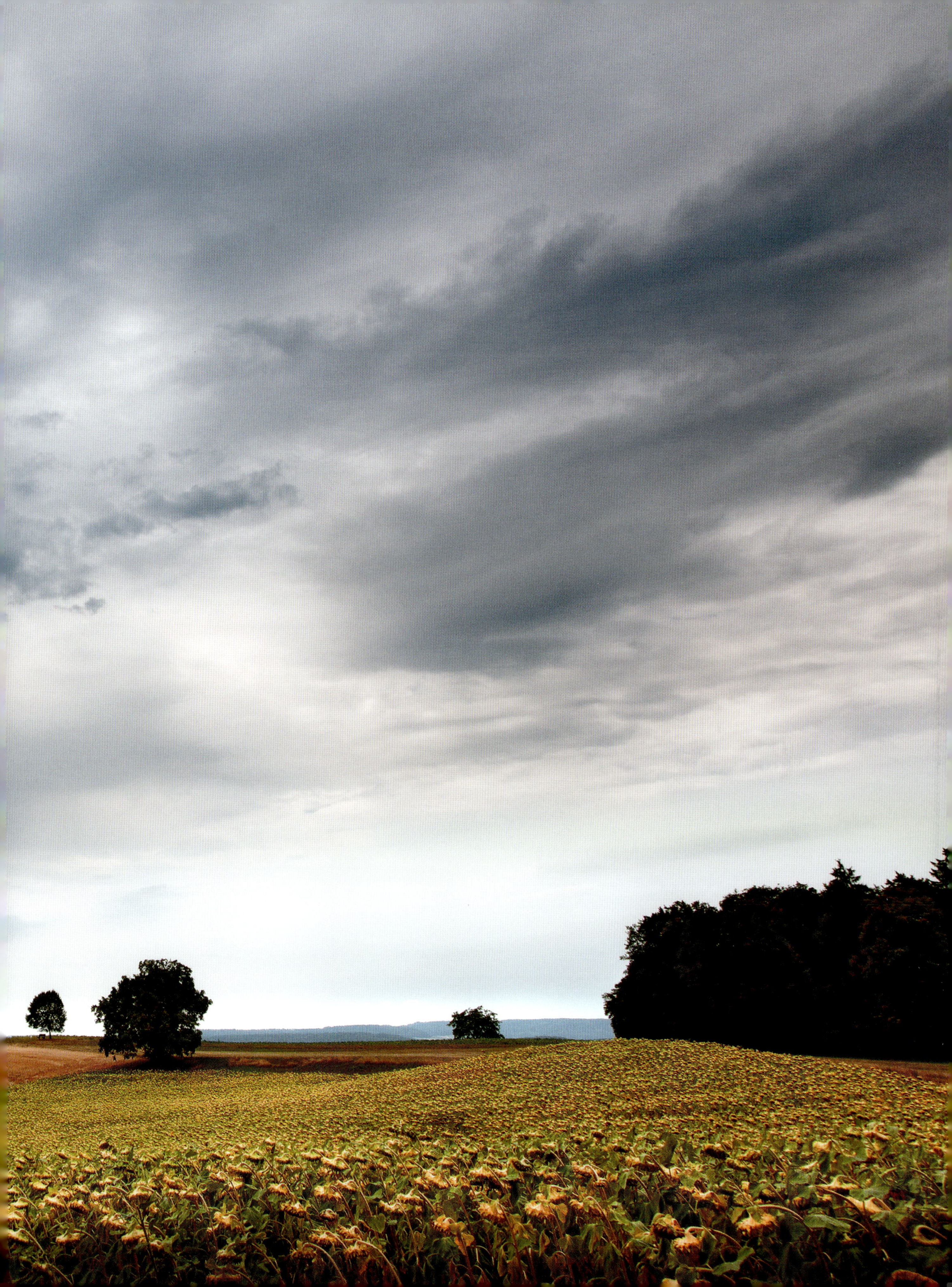

Weite ist der Grundcharakter der offenen Landschaften im Weinland. Einzelne Fruchtbäume, Ackerbegleitflora oder eigentliche Ackerrandstreifen in den Gemüse- und Getreidefeldern fördern die Biodiversität und wirken als stabilisierendes Element gegen unerwünschte Krankheiten. Die Sonnenblumenfelder sind Ausdruck der Klimagunst und der Bereitschaft, die Produkte dem Markt anzupassen (vorhergehende Doppelseite).

In den ebenen Lagen im Weinland sind auch Ackerbauprodukte wie Hopfen und Zuckerrüben begünstigt (links).
Blick auf die harmonische Dachlandschaft in Oberstammheim. Die im Weinland charakteristischen, oft barocken Fachwerkbauten sind Zeugen einer stolzen ländlichen Baukultur (rechts).

The basic character of open landscapes in the wine country is their size. Individual fruit trees, companion flora for arable fields or characteristic strips on the edges of vegetable and grain fields promote biodiversity and act as a stabilizing element against unwanted diseases. The sunflower fields are an expression of a favourable climate and the willingness to adapt to market demands (previous double-page).

In level areas of the wine country, agricultural products, such as hops and sugar beets, are also preferred (left).
View overlooking the harmonious roof landscape of Oberstammheim. The characteristic, often baroque half-timbered constructions of the wine country are witness to a proud rural building culture (right).

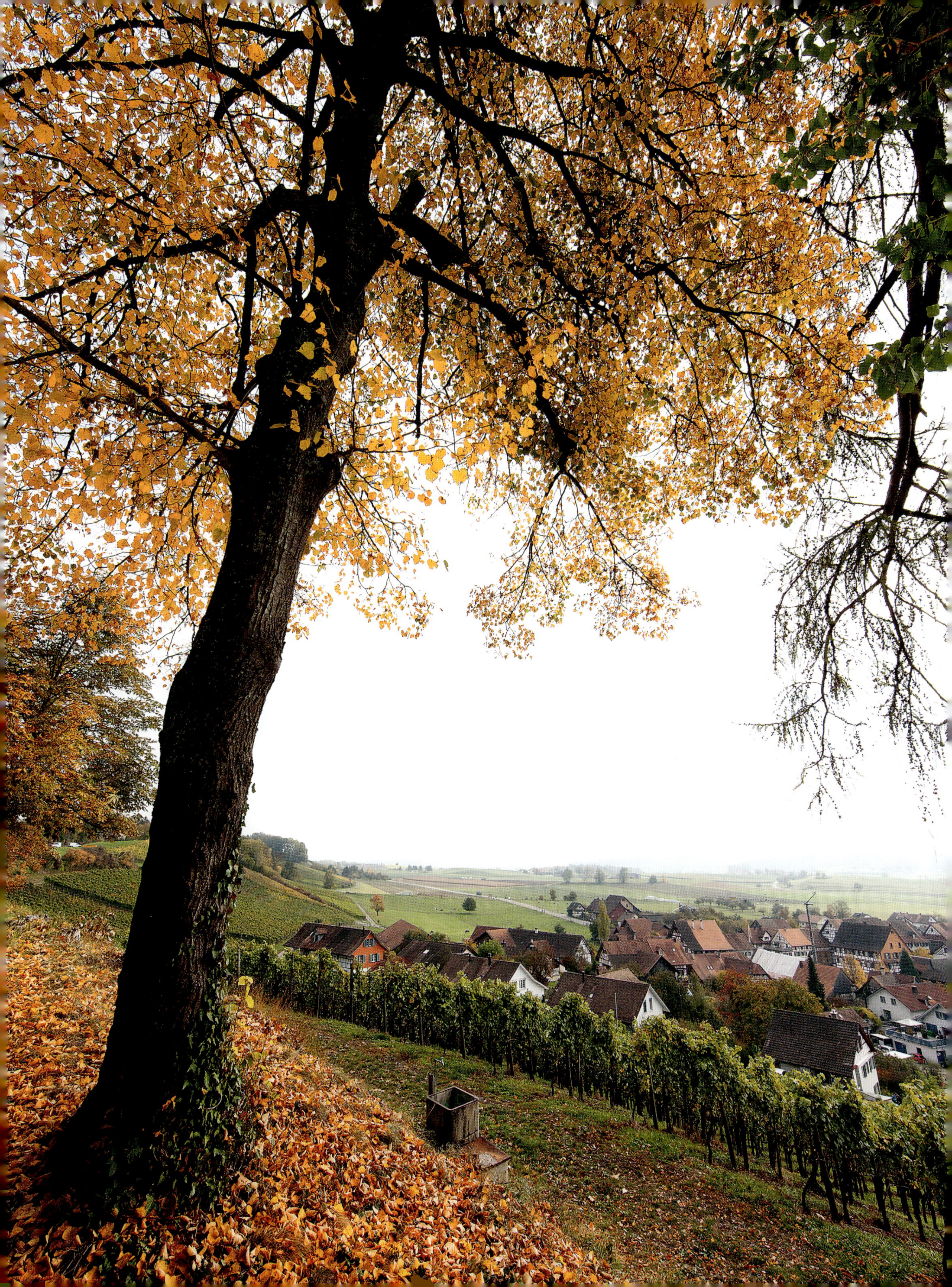

Die einmaligen Rheinschlaufen mit der Klosterinsel Rheinau und dem Rheinfall sind in der Natur- und Heimatschutzbewegung verbunden mit dem denkwürdigen und erfolglosen Kampf gegen den Bau des Kraftwerks Rheinau und für den Landschaftsschutz. Seit der Inbetriebnahme des Kraftwerks 1957 wird der Rhein 10 Kilometer bis zum Rheinfallbecken eingestaut, die Stromschnellen sind verschwunden. Der Rhein ist ein langsam fliessendes Gewässer geworden. Die Fallhöhe des Rheinfalles reduziert sich im Winter um 1,83 Meter und im Sommer um 0,59 Meter. Dennoch markiert der Kampf gegen das Kraftwerk Rheinau einen wichtigen Wendepunkt zu neuem Respekt vor der Landschaft. Renaturierungen wie an der Thur bezeugen eine neue Grundhaltung im Gewässerschutz.

The meanderings of the Rhine have created this unique shallower area with its monastery island Rheinau and the Rhine Falls. These are a historic part of the Nature and Heritage Protection movement through the memorable, but unsuccessful fight against the construction of the Rheinau Power Plant. Since the commissioning of the power plant in 1957, the Rhine has been backed up 10 kilometres – all the way to the Rhine Falls Basin, and all the rapids have disappeared. The Rhine has become a slow-flowing stretch of water. The drop height of the Rhine Falls is reduced in winter by 1.83 metres and by 0.59 metres in the summer. Nevertheless, the fight against the Rheinau Power Plant marks an important turning point in achieving a new respect for landscapes. Renaturations, such as on the Thur River, bear witness to a new attitude towards water protection.

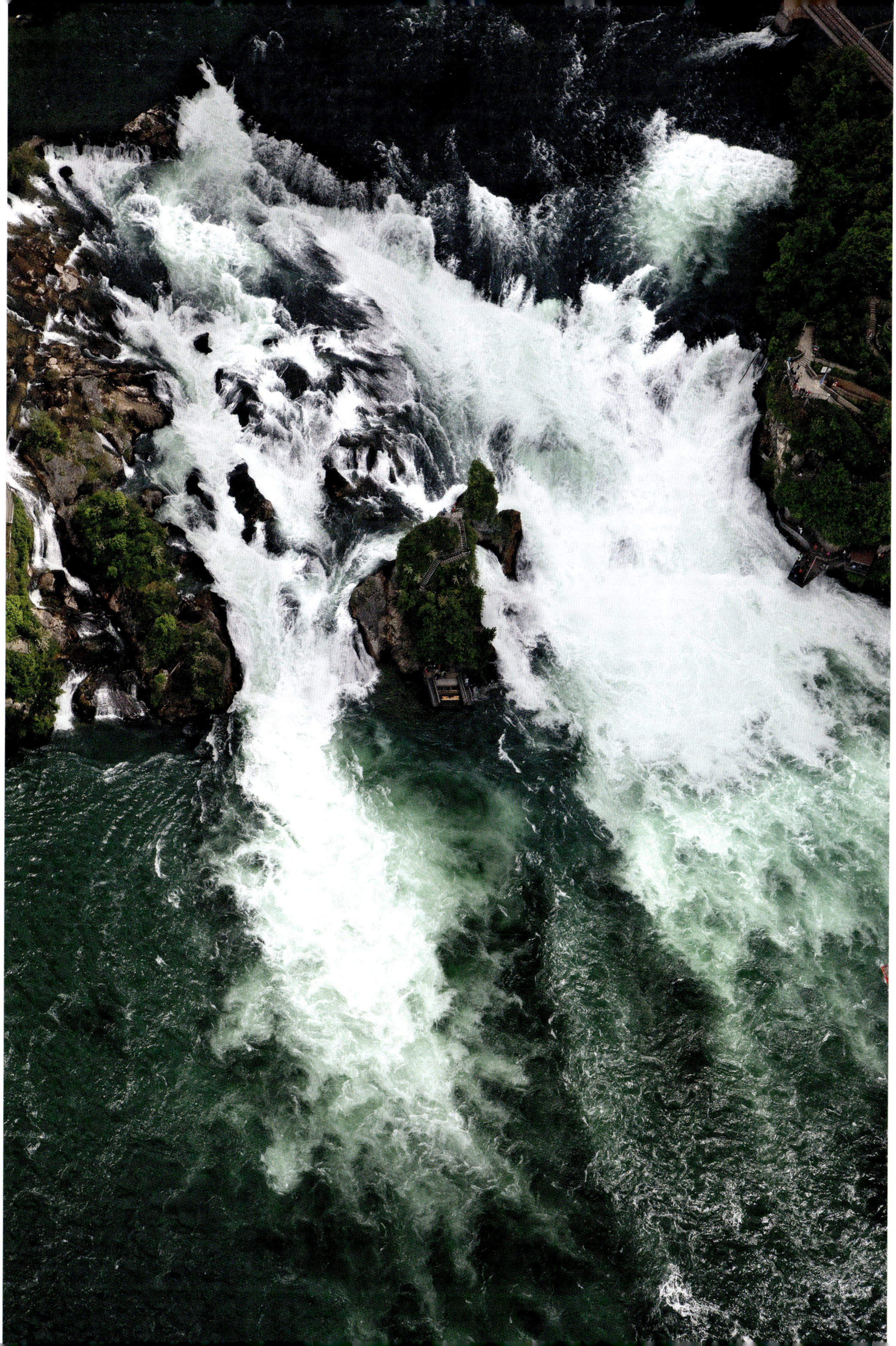

Das Bachsertal hat seinen praktisch unversehrten ländlichen Charakter bewahren können, obwohl die benachbarten Dörfer im unteren Glatttal und im Wehntal in den letzten Jahrzehnten städtisch überprägt worden sind. Das Relief der Landschaft mit abschirmenden bewaldeten Hügelzügen und die Endmoräne Heitlig dürften die bemerkenswerte Resistenz gegen urbane Tendenzen und die positive Haltung zu einer nachhaltigen, naturorientierten Landwirtschaft gefördert haben.

The Bachsertal has preserved its virtually intact rural character, even though the neighboring villages of the Lower Glatttal and Wehntal have experienced some urban transformation in recent decades. The contour of the landscape with its protected, rolling wooded hills and the end moraine Heitlig were allowed a remarkable level of resistance against urban tendencies and have promoted a positive attitude for a sustainable, nature-oriented agriculture.

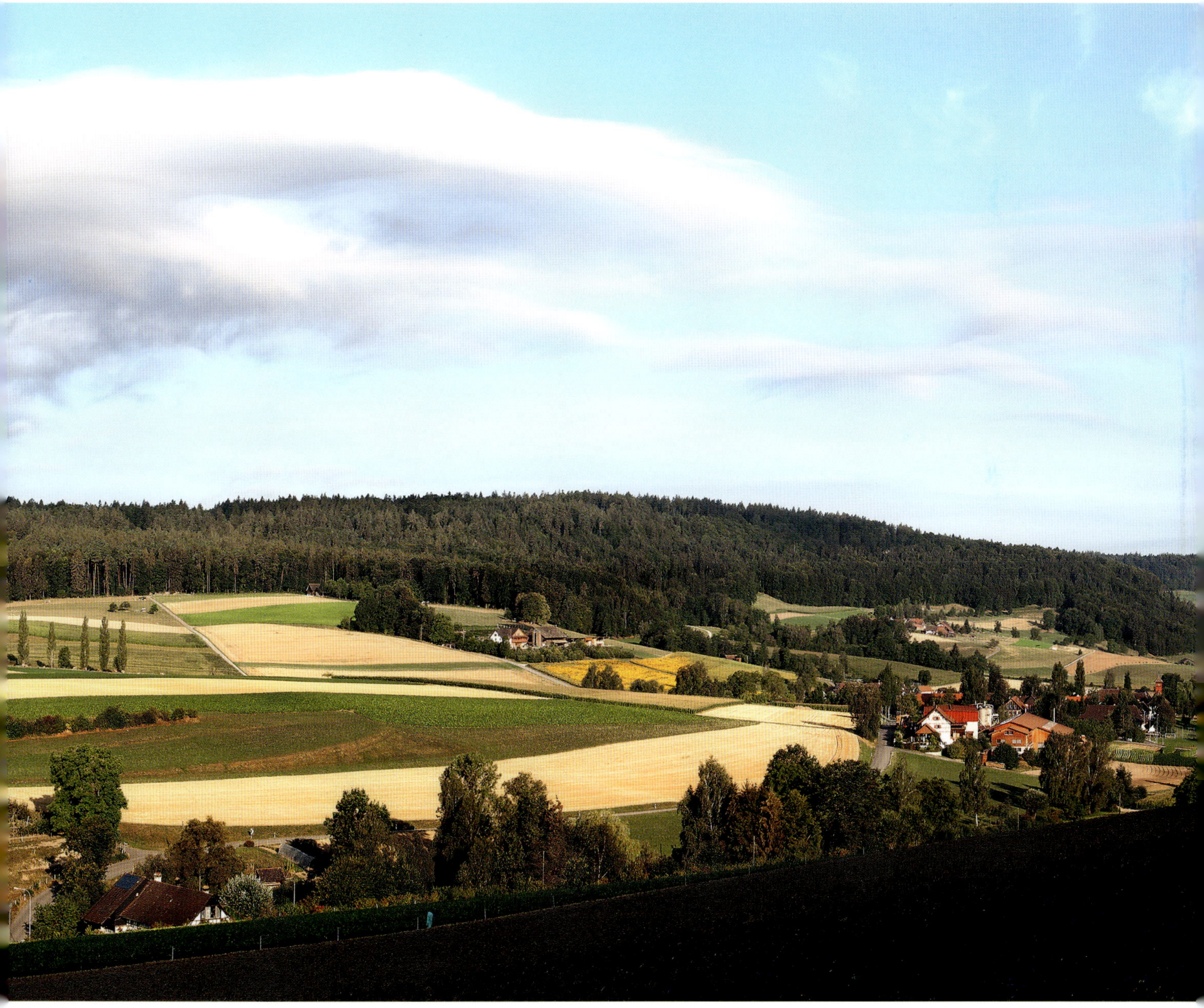

Voralpin geprägte Landschaften
Characteristic Prealpine Landscapes

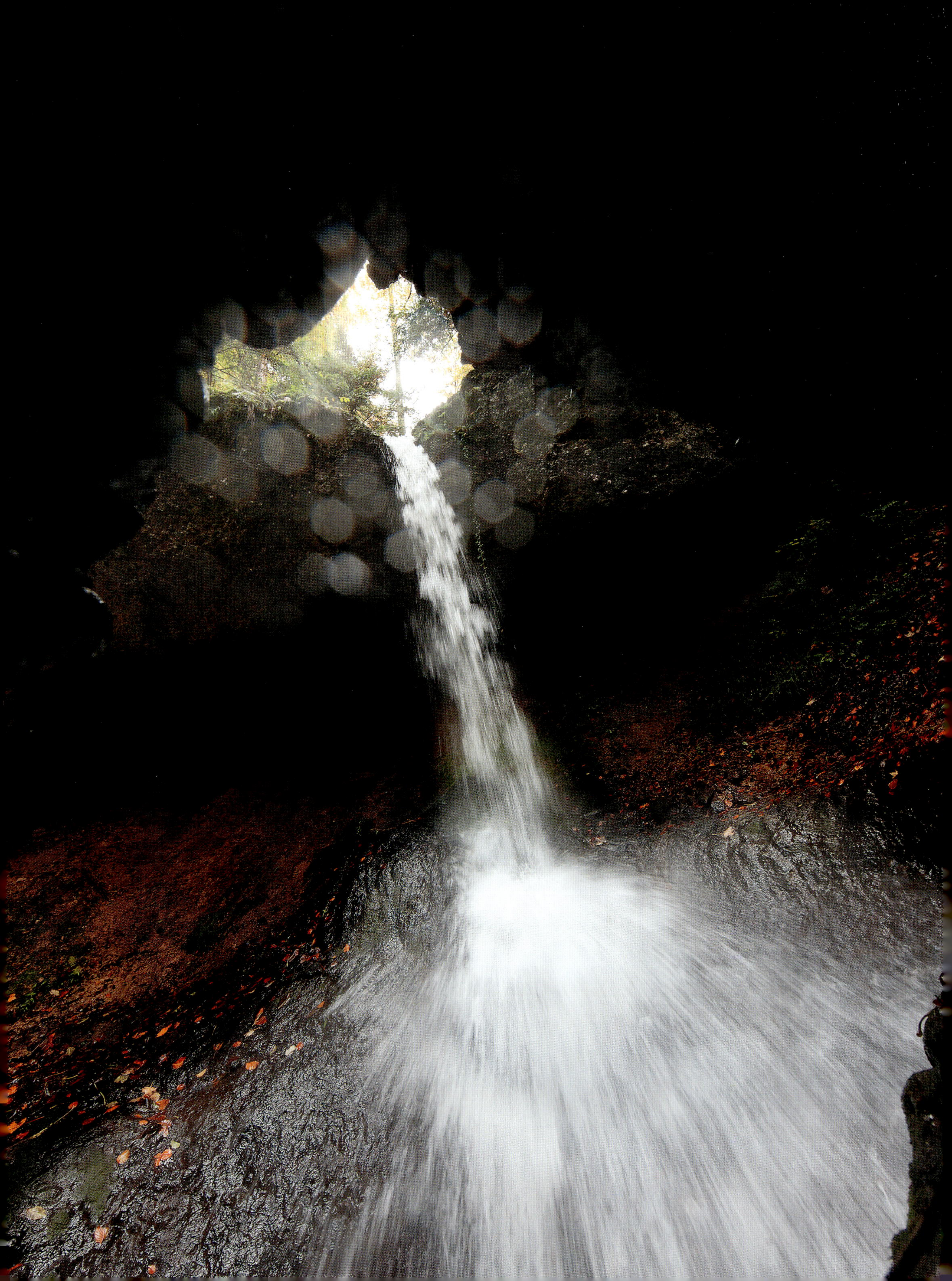

> *«Die Erholungslandschaft ist nicht museal, nicht als Park zu denken, sondern als bewirtschaftet-naturnahe Landschaft.»*
>
> Emil Egli (Kulturgeograph, 1905–1993)

> *'A recreational landscape is not like a museum, is not to be thought of as a park, but as a farmed natural landscape.'*
>
> Emil Egli (Cultural Geographer 1905–1993)

Was für eine stiebende Dusche! Das breite Umfeld der scharf bespritzten Fläche und die Weite der im weniger widerstandsfähigen Fels ausgewaschenen Höhle sind ein Abbild der erosiven Kraft des Baches.

What an amazing shower! The broad surroundings of the sharp splattered surface and the expanse of the eroded cave carved out of less resistant rock is an image of the erosive power of a stream.

Zürich trägt das Etikett eines Mittellandkantons, doch im Charakter der Landschaft liegt eine Fülle topographischer Varianten. Zunehmend voralpin geprägt sind im Osten die Hörnli- und Bachtelkette mit Nagelfluhwänden und Wasserfällen und im Süden der Albisrücken, der den Zürichsee begleitet. Als Ausläufer des Juras bietet die Lägern topographisches Bergland auch im Westen.

Der auf die Voralpen orientierte Blick richtet sich in erster Linie auf das Zürcher Oberland mit seinem in der letzten Kaltzeit, der sogenannten «Würm-Eiszeit» entstandenen zweiteiligen Grundcharakter. Eher sanft moduliert gibt sich das durch den Linth/Rhein-Gletscher überformte obere Glatttal mit verlandenden Seen, Mooren und der einmaligen Drumlin-Landschaft zwischen Rüti, Pfäffikon und Uster. Der Begriff Drumlin ist verwandt mit dem gälisch und irischen «druman», das heisst Rücken: Drumlins sind unter Eis geformte und in die Länge gezogene elliptische Hügel aus Lockermaterial wie Grundmoränenschutt oder Schotter. Die Längsachse liegt in der Richtung der einstigen Gletscherbewegung. Dank dem sanften Abschmelzen des nördlichen Seitenarms des Linth-Gletschers bis zurück über die Hombrechtikoner Felsschwelle und dem Wegfall grösserer Zuflüsse wurde das einmalige und national bedeutende Drumlinfeld nicht durch Erosion abgetragen.[1]

In kleinräumiger Vielfalt präsentiert sich dagegen das Tössbergland mit der durch Fliessgewässer scharf zerfurchten Molasse, den stufigen Wasserfällen und der hügeligen Wiesen- und Waldlandschaft als immer wieder überraschende Natur-, Kultur- und Wanderlandschaft. Das Tössbergland mit der Bachtel- und Hörnlikette verdankt seine besondere und markante voralpine Prägung im Wesentlichen der Tatsache, dass es auch zur Zeit der maximalen Vergletscherung während der letzten Eiszeit, vor rund 24 000 Jahren, wie eine zerklüftete Insel aus dem Eismeer ragte, knapp verbunden mit dem Irchel, der im Endstadium der Vergletscherung wie auch die Lägern

The Canton of Zurich is certainly located in Central Switzerland, but the character of its landscapes offers a much wider range of topographical variations. For example, in the east, the Hörnli and Bachtel ranges are increasingly pre-alpine in character with sharp ridges, waterfalls and very steep slopes. The Albis range accompanies Lake Zurich along its south side and the Lägern Mountains, an extension of the Jura Mountains, offers mountainous terrain in the west.

Looking at it from a pre-alpine perspective, one turns first of all to the Zurich Oberland that owes its fundamental bipartite character to its origins in the last Ice Age, the so-called Würm glaciation. The rather gently rolling profile of the Upper Glatttal (tal = valley) was modelled by the Linth-Rhine Glacier which left behind lake-filled silt basins, moors and the unique Drumlin landscape between Rüti, Pfäffikon and Uster at the end of Lake Zurich. The term Drumlin is related to the Gaelic and Irish *druman*, which means 'back'. The Drumlins were formed under moving ice leaving long, drawn-out elliptical hills made of loose material, such as ground-down moraine rubble and rocks broken into gravel. The long axis indicates the direction of the glacier's movement. Thanks to the gentle retreat of the northwest arm of the Linth Glacier back to the Hombrechtikon bedrock and the disappearance of larger tributaries, the unique landscape of the nationally important Drumlin Field was not carried away by erosion.[1]

In contrast, the Tössbergland (bergland = highlands) present great diversity in a small space with sharp-furrowed molasse shaped by fast flowing water, stepped waterfalls, hilly meadows and forest landscapes. This element of an always surprising nature has created a natural and cultural landscape for walking and hiking. The Tössbergland, along with the Bachtel and Hörnli ranges, owe their special and distinctive pre-alpine character essentially to the fact that at the time of maximum glaciation during the last Ice Age, about 24,000 years ago, they loomed like

weitgehend eisfrei blieb (siehe Abbildung Seite 13). Der im Vergleich zum Tössbergland niedrigere Albisgrat vermochte vom Uetliberg aus einen schmalen Kamm ins Eismeer zu zeichnen, überliess aber den Bereich Hirzel und Schönenberg dem Schliff des Gletschers bis zur erneut eisfreien Höhronen in den Schwyzer Voralpen. Der Molasserücken des Pfannenstiels war im Kaltzeitmaximum indessen vom Eis überflossen und tauchte erst in den spätwürmzeitlichen Abschmelzphasen wieder auf.

Der zweiteilige Grundcharakter des Zürcher Oberlandes widerspiegelt sich auch in der Art der Besiedelung. Vor allem in den weiten und offenen Lagen des Glatttals ist eine anhaltende Verstädterung im letzten halben Jahrhundert unübersehbar. Im wenig zuwanderungsfreundlichen engen Tössbergland verlief die Besiedelungsgeschichte fordernder und härter. Neben Dörfern in den Talsohlen entstanden weit und locker gestreute Weiler und abgelegene Einzelhöfe. Die auf 800 bis 900 Meter ü. M. liegende Gemeinde Sternenberg umfasst über 50 zum Teil schwer zugängliche kleine Hofgruppen und Einzelhöfe. Es war ein Siedeln im Kampf gegen die Natur und, infolge der Staulagen, verbunden mit oft mehr Schnee als in den inneren Alpen. Das Tössbergland war als Hirtenland und Ort der Köhlerei ein Gebiet des kargsten Bauerntums. Erst mit der Heimindustrie, dem Spinnen von Baumwolle, Korben oder Schnitzen von Kellen (daher «Chelleland»), war eine knappe wirtschaftliche Basis erreichbar.[2] Noch im 19. Jahrhundert bestimmten Existenzprobleme den Alltag. Demut, Gottergebenheit und eine religiöse Naturbe-

jagged islands out of the ice ocean, barely connected with the Irchel, an elevation in the north of the canton, and the Lägern Mts in the west, all of which remained extensively free of ice during the end phase of the glaciers (see Illustration, page 13). Although the Albis Ridge is much lower in comparison to the Tössbergland, it was still able to push a small crest up through the ice ocean: Zurich's Uetliberg. However, the glacier left its mark on the towns of Hirzel and Schönenberg and all the way to the ice-free Höhronen in the pre-Alps of the Canton of Schwyz. On the east side of Lake Zurich, the molasse ridge of the Pfannenstiel was also covered with ice during the maximum cold period and only reappeared in the retreat phase of the late Würm Period.

The bipartite character of the Zurich Oberland is also reflected in the kind of settlements that have taken hold. In particular, the Glatttal's wide, open areas have experienced a prolonged – and conspicuous – urbanisation over the last half-century. In the less migration-friendly Tössbergland corridors, the settlement history indicates that it has been harder and more demanding to maintain. In addition to the villages in the valley, distant and loosely strewn hamlets and remote farms are a characteristic of Tössbergland. At 800 to 900 meters above sea level, the community of Sternenberg comprises over 50, in part hard to access, small and isolated farms. It was always a settlement in a battle with nature and, as a result of the topography, often collected more snow than the inner Alps. With its pastureland and collieries Tössbergland lay along the edges of the poorest

Zwischen Hinwil, Wetzikon und Uster liegt eines der landesweit schönsten Drumlinfelder. Drumlins entstehen unter dem Gletschereis im Kontakt mit lockerem Grundmoränenschutt; Rundhöcker sind vom Gletschereis abgeschliffene Felsbuckel. Die Stromlinienform und die einheitliche Ausrichtung sind das Resultat der dominierenden Eisbewegung – sie erinnern an eine ziehende Schafherde. Drumlins sind häufig bewaldet, dazwischen liegen feuchte Mulden, Streuwiesen oder frühere Torfstichparzellen.

Between Hinwil, Wetzikon and Uster lies one of the nation's most beautiful Drumlin fields. Drumlins are formed underneath glacial ice in contact with loose ground moraine rubble; rock hummocks or sheep-back rocks are formed by glacier ice abrading the rocks. The streamlined shape and the uniform alignment are the result of a dominant ice movement – they resemble a flock of passing sheep. Drumlins are often wooded, interjacent with damp depressions, wet meadows or former peat-ditch parcels.

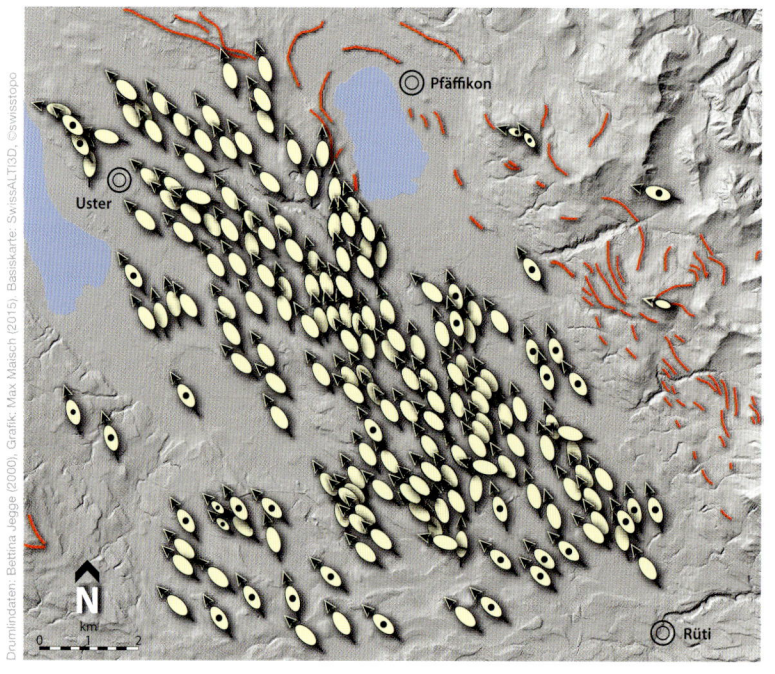

Drumlinfeld oberes Glatttal

— Moränenwall
⬬ Drumlin
👁 Rundhöcker

Drumlin field in Upper Glatttal

— Moraine Wall
⬬ Drumlin
👁 Rounded Hump

ziehung waren im einsam erlebten Voralpenklima mit langen Wintern eine segensreiche Stütze. Die Suche nach Gold in den Bächen hingegen war eher Ausdruck von Wunschdenken. Man traf sich und befreite die Seele durch gemeinsames Arbeiten, Erzählen, Singen. Das Zürcher Oberland ist auch heute noch eine Landschaft der Sekten und Freikirchen. Damit und mit dem landschaftlichen Grundcharakter zeigt es eine bemerkenswerte Wesensverwandtschaft mit dem Napfgebiet und mit Appenzell Ausserrhoden.

Mit der wirtschaftlichen Entwicklung der Agglomeration Zürichs und dem ausufernden Wachstum der städtischen Zentren im letzten halben Jahrhundert gerieten die nebelarmen Voralpenlagen immer mehr in die Sonntagsklasse der vielbesuchten Naherholungsgebiete. Der stadtnächste und ganzjährig besuchte Aussichtsgipfel ist zweifellos der mit guten Fusswegen und einem Fahrsträsschen erschlossene Bachtel mitsamt Turm, geräumiger Wirtschaft und einer Schwingarena für den Bachtel-Schwinget. Das als Aussichtsberg ebenso bekannte Hörnli ist rundum eingebettet in die Wanderlandschaft der Tössbergregion. Mit der geförderten Erschliessung auch durch den öffentlichen Verkehr rückte die Stadt dem Oberland noch näher, wurden die Pendlerdistanzen kürzer und die geschätzte Landschaft gewann unvermittelt an Ansehen als schöne und gesunde Wohnlage – die Existenz des Sanatoriums Wald auf dem Faltigberg bezeugt es. Diese Wertschätzung und die wieder wachsende Geborgenheit in der Landschaft äusserten sich auch in einer Welle der Sanierung und oft beeindruckend sorgfältigen Pflege älterer Gebäude. Selbst früher eher als schäbig eingestufte bäuerliche Bauten, wie die unter dem Druck der zürcherischen Obrigkeit entstandenen Flarzhäuser, wurden teilweise zu eigentlichen Perlen. Mit gutem Erfolg hatte man sich auch um die ganzheitliche Erhaltung wichtiger Bauten wie jene des eindrücklichen Industrie-Ensembles Neuthal bemüht. Man ist immer wieder überrascht, wie harmonisch mächtige alte Textil-Industriegebäude in die Landschaft gesetzt wurden: Harmonie trotz kraftvollem Auftritt, bedingt durch den zwingenden Standort in der Talsohle und die vielen Fenster für ausreichendes Licht. Unterhalt erfordern auch die verschiedenen, ab 1890 von Adolf Guyer-Zeller für seine Arbeiterinnen und Arbeiter in der Baumwollspinnerei mit Brücken und Treppen über waldige Gipfel und durch tiefe Tobel angelegten Wanderwege. Mit Leidenschaft der Mitglieder verbunden ist der Betrieb von Fahrten auf der stillgelegten Strecke Bauma – Hinwil durch den Dampfbahnverein Zürcher Oberland.[3]

Die heutige Bedeutung der voralpinen Lagen als Erholungslandschaft widerspiegelt sich auch im dichten Wanderwegnetz – das Angebot reicht von kinder-

peasant farms. With the start of cottage industries in the 18th century, such as spinning cotton, weaving baskets and ladle making, a marginal economic basis came within reach.[2] However, well into the 19th century, the problems of basic existence determined everyday life. In the solitary pre-alpine climate with long winters, humility, resignation to God's will and a religious relationship to nature were a beneficial support. The search for gold, found in several areas, was more like an expression of wishful thinking. People would meet up and free their souls through community work, exchanging stories, and singing. Even today, the Zurich Oberland is such a landscape of religious sects and free churches. This aspect and the landscape's basic character show a remarkable affinity with the Napf highlands area on the cantonal border between Luzerne and Bern and with the Canton of Appenzell Ausserrhoden in northeast Switzerland.

With the economic development of Zurich's agglomeration and the sprawling growth of other urban centres in the last 50 years, the less foggy, pre-alpine areas have become popular recreational areas. Closest to Zurich and open year-round, the Bachtel Mountain outlook point is without a doubt the most visited site. With good footpaths and connected by a road, Bachtel includes a tower, a spacious restaurant and an arena for the Bachtel Schwingfest (Schwingen is a traditional Swiss wrestling sport). Also well known as a beautiful lookout mountain, the Hörnli is embedded in the hiking landscape of the Tössberg region. With increased connections, including public transport, Zurich got closer to the Oberland, the commuter distance got shorter, and this treasured landscape suddenly gained a reputation as a beautiful and healthy place to live – the existence of the Wald Sanatorium on the Faltigberg testifies to that. This new appreciation of the landscape and the growing feeling of comfort in using it are also being expressed in a wave of renovations and often impressive, very meticulous care of older buildings. Even structures that were earlier classified as shabby farm buildings, such as the Flarzhäuser, composite buildings created under pressure from the Zurich authorities, are sometimes considered architectural 'pearls'. Those responsible took pains to ensure that the comprehensive preservation of important buildings was as successful as those of the impressive Industrial Ensemble of Neuthal. One is always surprised by how harmoniously even large, old textile industrial buildings were set into the landscape: harmony in spite of a powerful appearance, required through the compelling location in the valley and the many windows for sufficient light. The various *Wanderwege* (hiking or walking paths), established by Adolf Guyer-Zeller from 1890 onwards require maintenance. Built for his

wagenfesten Routen bis zu Wegen, die alpinen Charakter haben und sicheren Halt bietende Bergschuhe erfordern. Auf Routen wie im oberen Früetobel oder auf diversen Gratwegen im Raum Stralegg-Schnebelhorn ist streckenweise Trittsicherheit geboten. Das gilt auch für den Gratweg über die Lägern in der Westecke des Kantons und für den Albisgrat. Bei der Fallätschen in ihrer Funktion als Erosionstrichter des Rütschlibaches wird der Albisgrat erniedrigt und nach Westen verschoben. Der Geologe Heinrich Jäckli rechnet in einem Gedankenspiel damit, dass der Rütschlibach bis in einer Million Jahren den Albisgrat völlig durchschnitten haben wird, die Reppisch unterhalb Stallikon auf 550 Meter ü. M. anzapft und sich auf 430 Meter als linksseitiger Zufluss der Sihl neu erfindet.[4] Der Bergweg von Unter-Leimbach zum Albisgrat ist zwar immer wieder etwas rutschig, in unserer zeitlichen Perspektive allerdings nicht gefährdet. Bei der grossen postglazialen Sackung von Mittelleimbach, bei der die Sihl an den Entlisberg gedrängt wurde, liegt die Abbruchkante oben am Albisgrat zwischen Mädikon und der Balderen. Entlang der ganzen Albiskette, bis in den Wildnispark Zürich, kann geologische Dynamik nach wie vor erlebt werden. Rutschungen schaffen dabei immer wieder Lebensraum für Pionierarten, für die stets bereiten Erstbesiedler unter den Pflanzen und Tieren.

workers in the cotton spinning mills, the paths have bridges and stairs and lead over forested summits and through deep ravines. The Steam Engine Railway Association of the Zurich Oberland operates journeys to the abandoned railway stretch from Bauma to Hinwil, supported mainly by the passion of its members.[3]

The importance of the pre-alpine areas as recreational landscapes today is reflected in the extensive network of hiking and walking trails – ranging from paved paths for prams and pushchairs up to routes that have an alpine character and require mountain boots with appropriate soles. Some routes, like those in the upper Früetobel or diverse narrow ridge trails in the area of Stralegg-Schnebelhorn, offer firm footing, but only on certain stretches. That is also true for the Gratweg trail over the Lägern in the southwest corner of the canton as well as for the Albis Ridge. In its function as an erosion slope, the Fallätschen area of the Uetliberg has reduced the Albis Ridge and pushed it in a westerly direction, and continues to do so. The Fallätschen is also the source of the Rütschlibach, a stream that flows into the Sihl River at Leimbach. The geologist Heinrich Jäckli calculated in a personal 'mind game' that the Rütschlibach will have completely cut through the Albis Ridge in about one million years, and will tap into the Reppisch River below Stallikon, which will then be at 550 metres above sea level. At 430 metres, the Reppisch will re-invent itself as a left-side feeder to the Sihl River.[4] Although the mountain path from Unterleimbach to the Albis Ridge is certainly always somewhat slippery, within our time perspective, it is certainly not an endangered feature. The great post-glaciation settling of Mittelleimbach, which pushed the Sihl River onto the Entlisberg, also placed the brim above on the Albis Ridge between Mädikon and the Balderen. Along the entire Albis Range, right up to Zurich's Wilderness Park in Langnau am Albis, the geological dynamics can still be felt. Landslides create new living spaces for pioneers, those ever-ready first settlers among the plants and animals.

In der Pionierzeit der Segelfliegerei war die Scheidegg ein viel benutzter Startplatz – bis Ende der 1940er-Jahre Bergstarts zu aufwändig wurden. Die Rampe wird heute mit leichten Hängegleitern genutzt.

In the pioneering days of gliders, the Scheidegg was a much-used starting platform – until the end of the 1940s when mountain starts got too expensive. The ramp is now used by light hang-gliders.

Panorama von der Scheidegg an einem typischen winterlichen Hochnebeltag. Der Blick reicht von den Glarner über die Zentralschweizer bis zu den Berner Alpen.

The panorama seen from the Scheidegg on a typical wintery day with high fog. The view extends from the Glarner Alps across the Central Swiss Alps to the Bernese Alps.

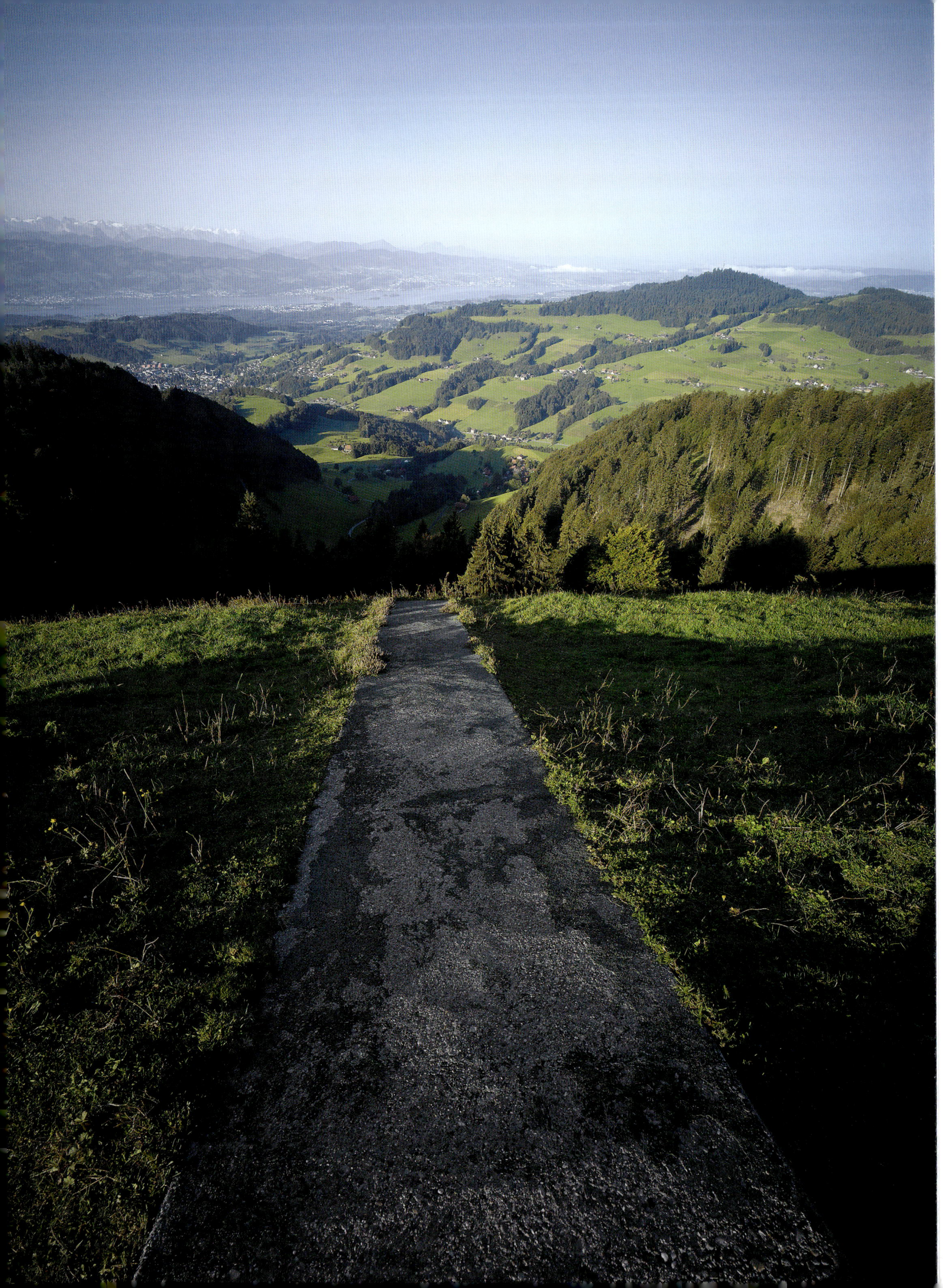

73

Flug über die bewaldete Kuppe des Roten mit Blick in Richtung Bachtel, Rigi und Pilatus. Die schlichten Farben und der zarte Nebelschleier werden zu vereinheitlichenden Elementen der Landschaft (folgende Doppelseite).

Flying over the wooded crest of the Roten with a view of the Bachtel, Rigi and Pilatus mountains. The sober colours and the delicate mist become unified elements of the landscape (following double-page).

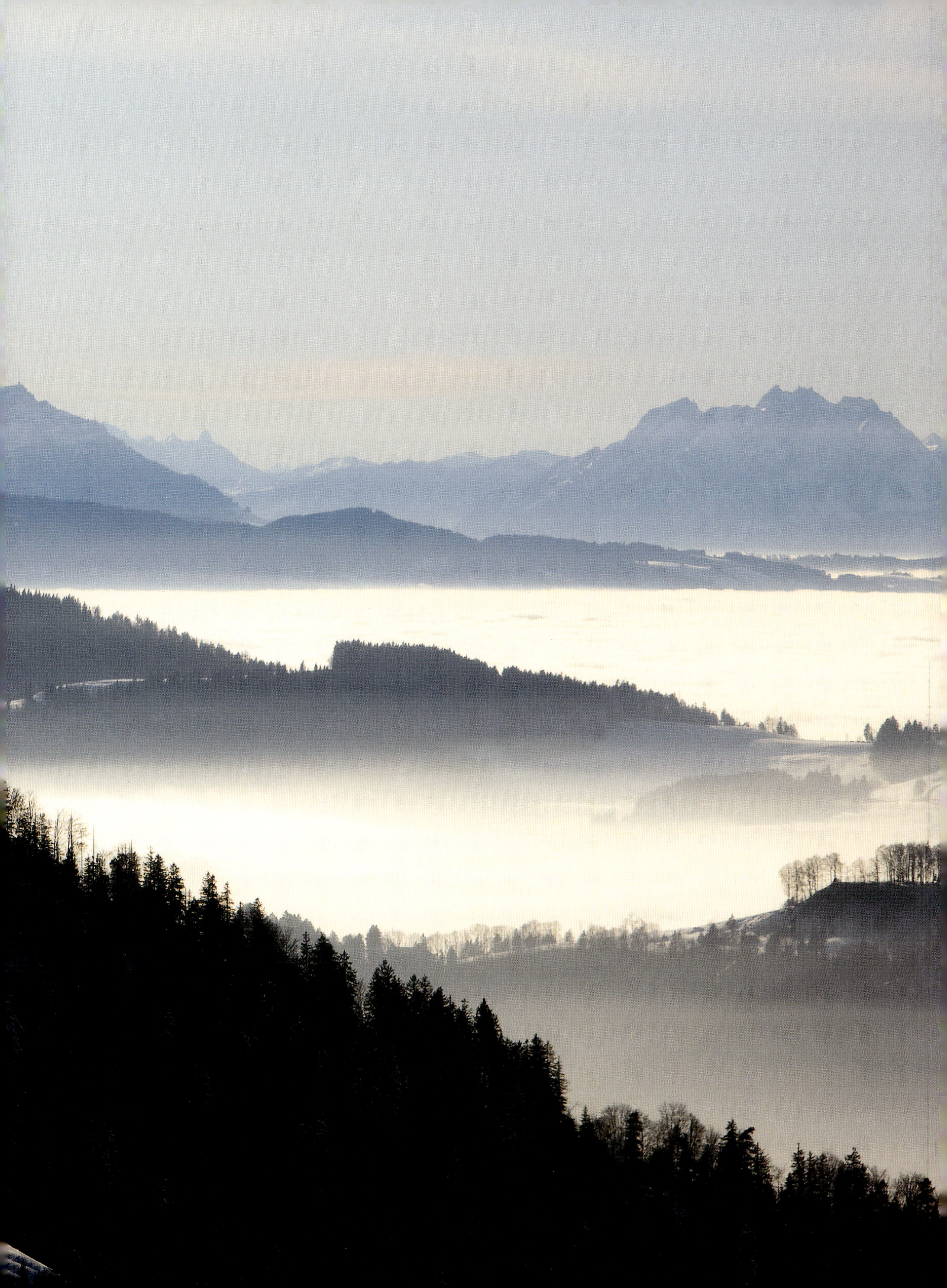

Der Gipfelgrat auf dem Schnebelhorn wäre schöner und ökologisch reicher, wenn Wald und Weide nicht scharf voneinander getrennt wären, sondern in einer offenen Landschaft ineinander übergingen. Die mächtigen Fichten im dunklen Bildteil links würden dazu passen, und auch Arten wie Vogelbeere, Mehlbeere, Waldföhre, Buche oder Bergahorn sind in einem stufigen Waldrand wirkungsvoller. Auch Stechpalmen oder Wildrosen dürften dabei sein.

The summit ridge on the Schnebelhorn would be more beautiful and ecologically richer, if the forest and meadows were not so sharply separated, but instead would merge into one another in an open landscape. The mighty spruce trees in the dark part of the image on the left would fit in well and species, such as the rowan berry, whitebeam berry, Scots pine, beeches or sycamores, are more striking and effective with a stepped edge of a forest. Even holly or wild roses would be suitable.

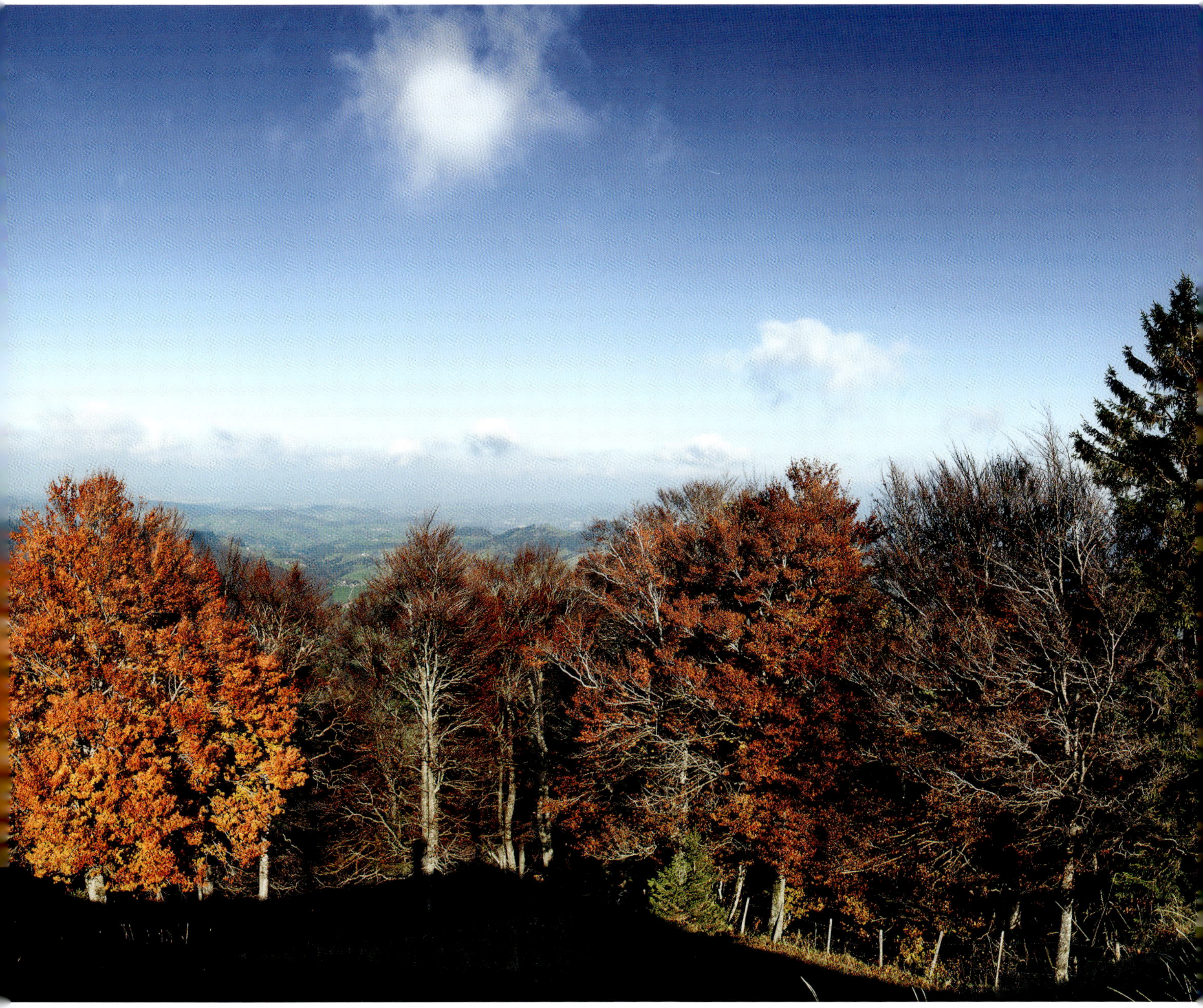

Kleinere Häusergruppen und zahlreiche Einzelhöfe mit Kreuzgiebeln sind charakteristisch für das obere Tössbergland. Gfell, Sternenberg (links).
Tierhag mit Blick auf die Sömmerungsweide der Alp Schnebelhorn (rechts).

Smaller groups of houses and numerous single farms with cross gables are characteristic of the upper Tössbergerland, Gfell, Sternenberg (left).
Tierhag with a view of the Schnebelhorn Alp and its summer pasture (right).

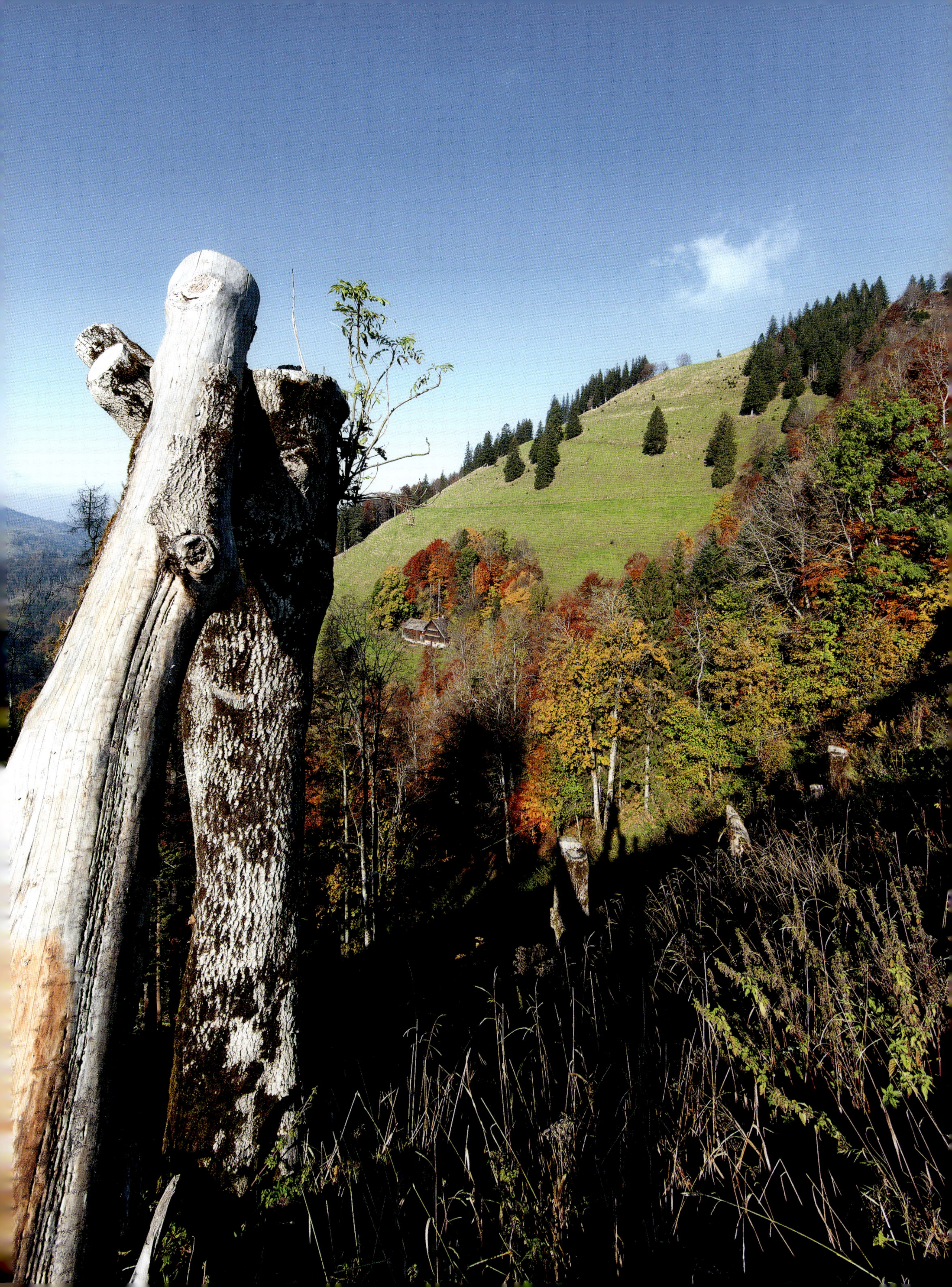

Auf dem Hörnli: Die offene Weite überrascht nach dem Aufstieg durch eine vielfältige, attraktive Waldlandschaft mit Einblicken in das forstwirtschaftlich nicht mehr genutzte, fast unbegehbare wilde Bärtobel (siehe auch Seiten 220–223).

On top of the Hörnli: the open expanse is a surprise after climbing through a diverse, attractive forest landscape with a glimpse of the areas that are no longer under forestry care and are therefore the unused and nearly impassable parts of the wild Bärtobel (see also pages 220–223).

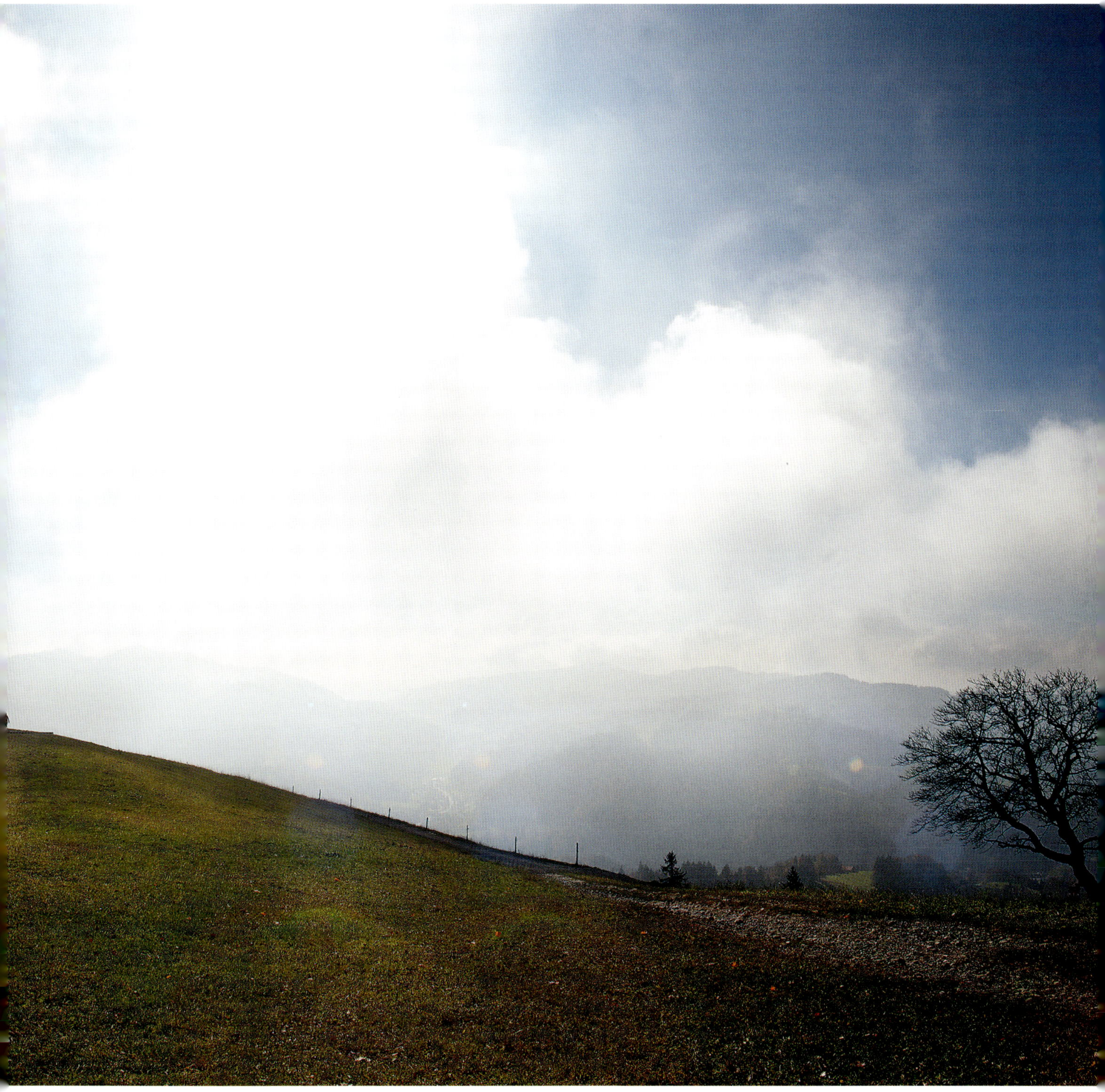

In der Tössscheidi: Steile Nagelfluh-Felswände sind Standorte von Vertretern einer alpinen Kalkflora – an trocken-warmen Wänden zum Beispiel Felsenmispel, Blaugras und Horstsegge, in eher feuchten oder wechselfeuchten Zonen Safrangelber Steinbrech und Fettkraut (links).
Mit dem zunehmenden Holzbedarf im 18. Jahrhundert und nach dem Bau einer Zufahrtsstrasse wurde der Wald am Tössstock nahezu vollständig abgeholzt. In der Folge kaufte der Kanton zahlreiche Parzellen – zur grössten Zürcher Staatswaldung (rechts).

In the Tössscheidi: Steep cliffs of molasse conglomerate are locations with representative alpine limestone flora: on dry, warm walls, for example, one finds rock medlar, bluegrass and horst sedge; in rather humid or changing wet-dry zones, saffron-yellow saxifrage and butterwort (left).
With the increasing demand for wood in the 18th century and after the construction of an access road, the forest on the Tössstock was almost completely cleared. As a result, the Canton of Zurich bought numerous parcels – and it became the largest state-owned forest (right).

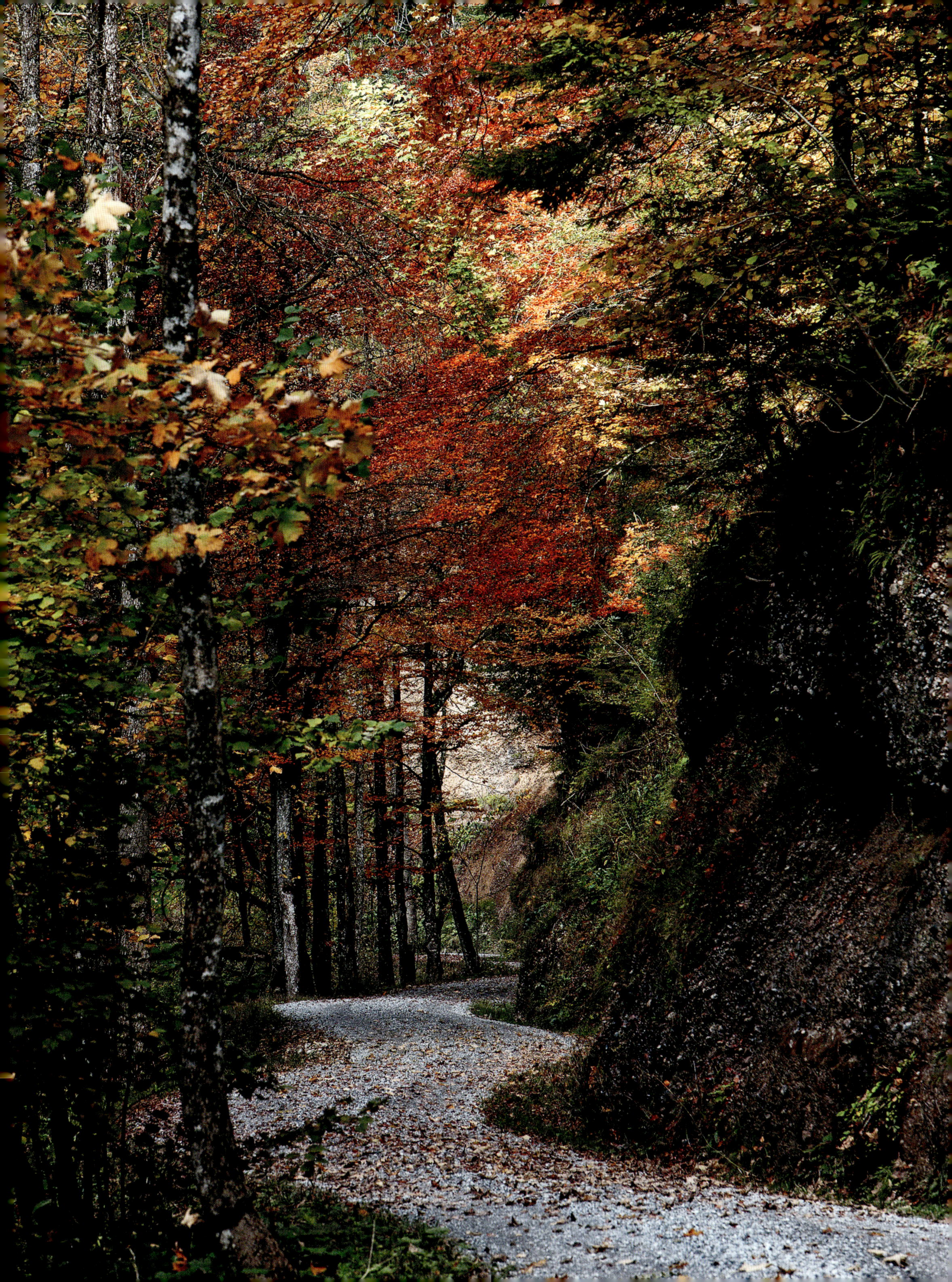

Tief eingeschnittene Bachläufe und steile Felswände gehören zum Relief der Oberländer Landschaft. Das treppenartige Profil vieler Bäche beruht auf der Schichtung von erosionsfesten Nagelfluhbänken über weichem Mergel- und Sandstein. Dieser wird ausgeschwemmt und im Hangschutt der nächsten Treppenstufe weitergegeben. Eingefügte Holz- oder Steinstufen verstärken den Treppencharakter. Im Sagenraintobel ob Wald schimmern die so entstehenden Wasserfälle in geheimnisvollem Zauberglanz.

So wie im Sagenraintobel haben die Wälder in den Tobeln in vielen Fällen einen urwaldnahen Charakter. Sie werden forstlich kaum genutzt, da ihre Bewirtschaftung an den steilen, oft erosionsgefährdeten und schwer zugänglichen Standorten aufwändig und oft auch gefährlich ist. Partien mit flachen Flusssohlen sind rar (folgende Doppelseite).

Deeply incised streams and steep cliff walls are part of the contours of the Zurich Oberländ landscape. The step-like profile of many streams is based on the stratification of erosion-resistant banks of molasse conglomerate over soft marlite and sandstone. This one has been washed out and passed the colluvial deposits onto the next step. Inserted wood or stone steps reinforce the stairs' character. In the Sagenrain ravine above Wald, these waterfalls shimmer in a mysterious brilliance.

In many cases, as in the Sagenrain ravine, the forests in these ravines have a jungle-like character. They are hardly ever used in forestry, as their control on steep, often eroded and inaccessible locations, is expensive and often dangerous. Sections with shallow riverbeds are rare (following double-page).

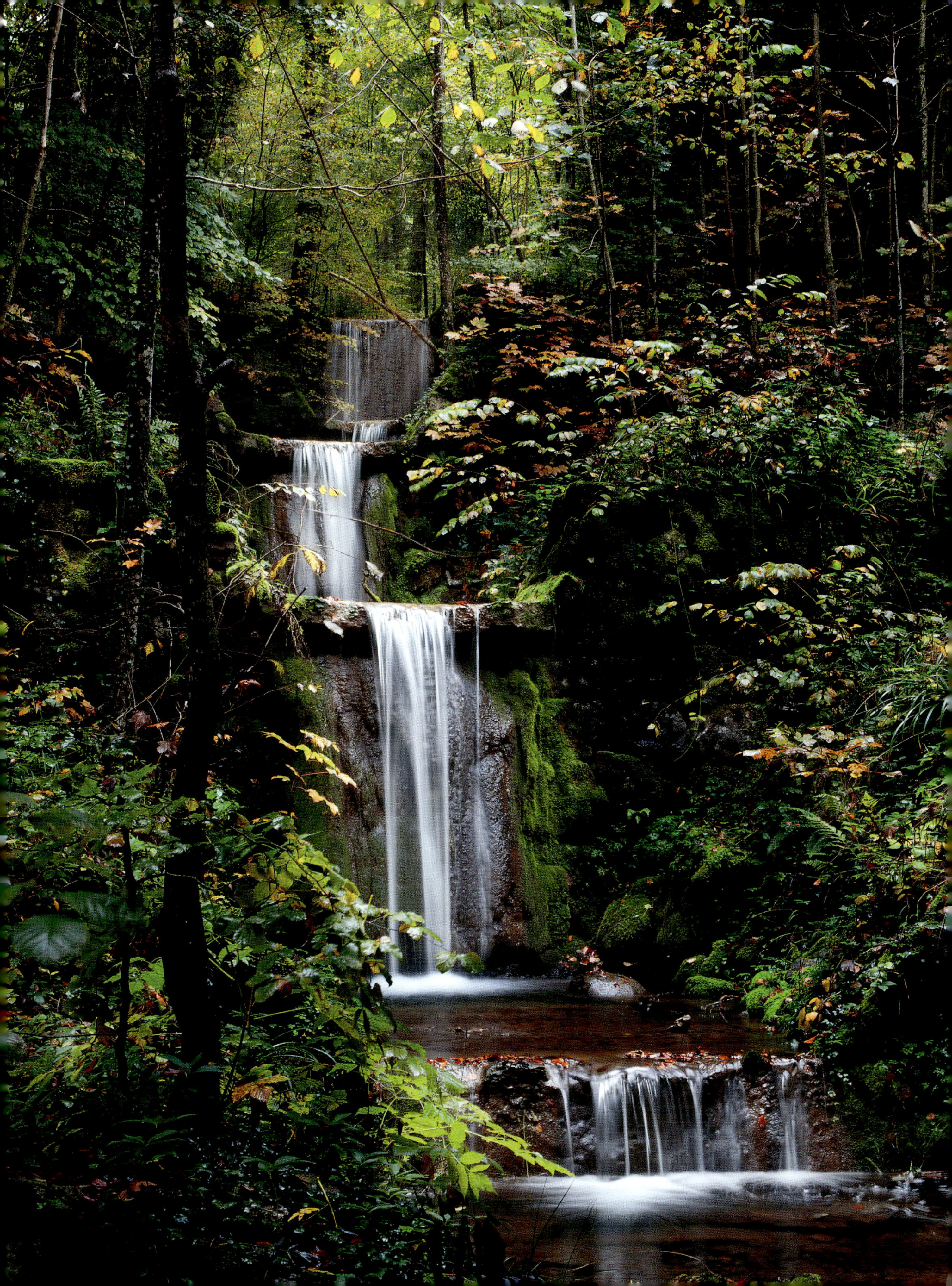

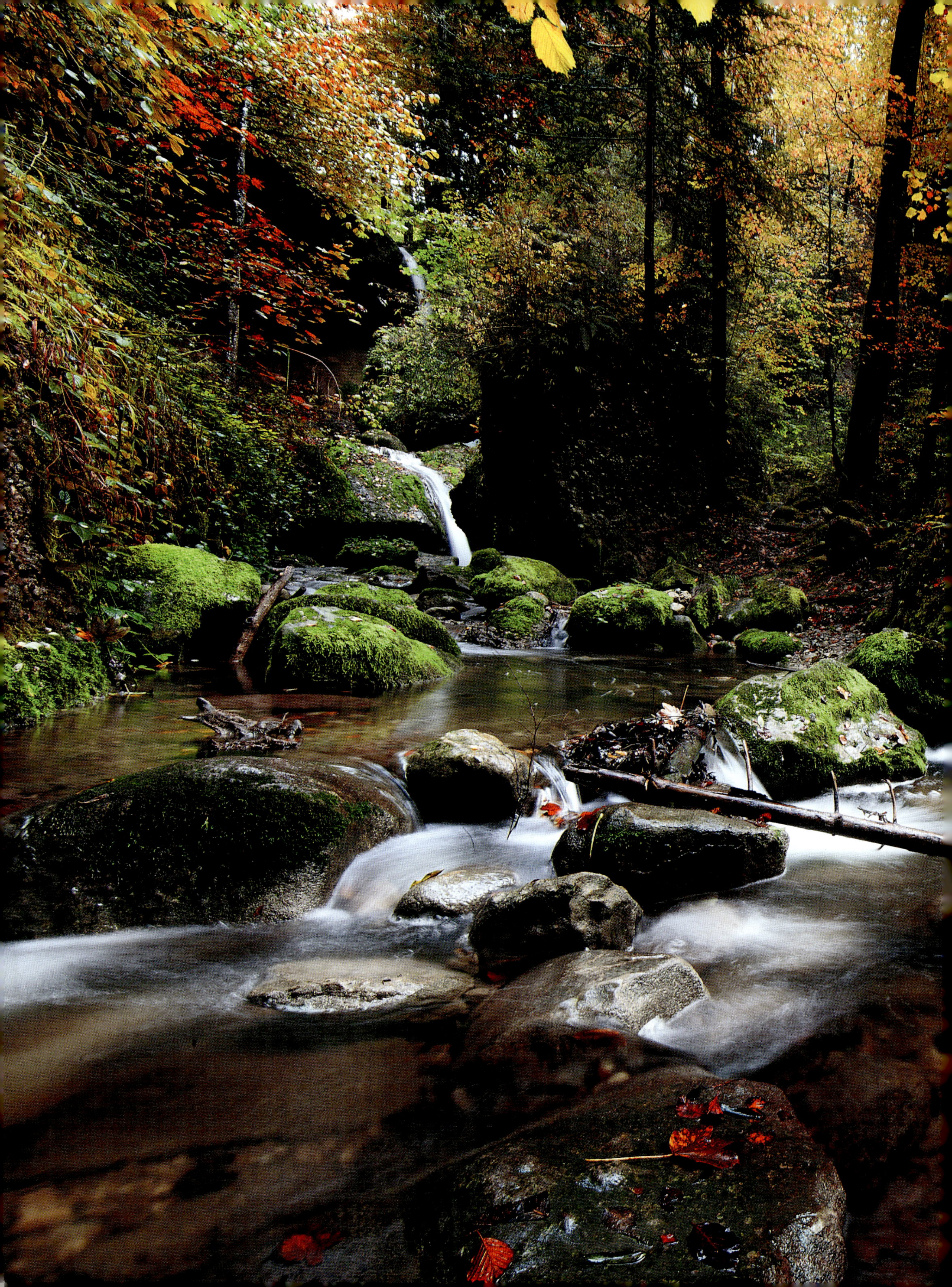

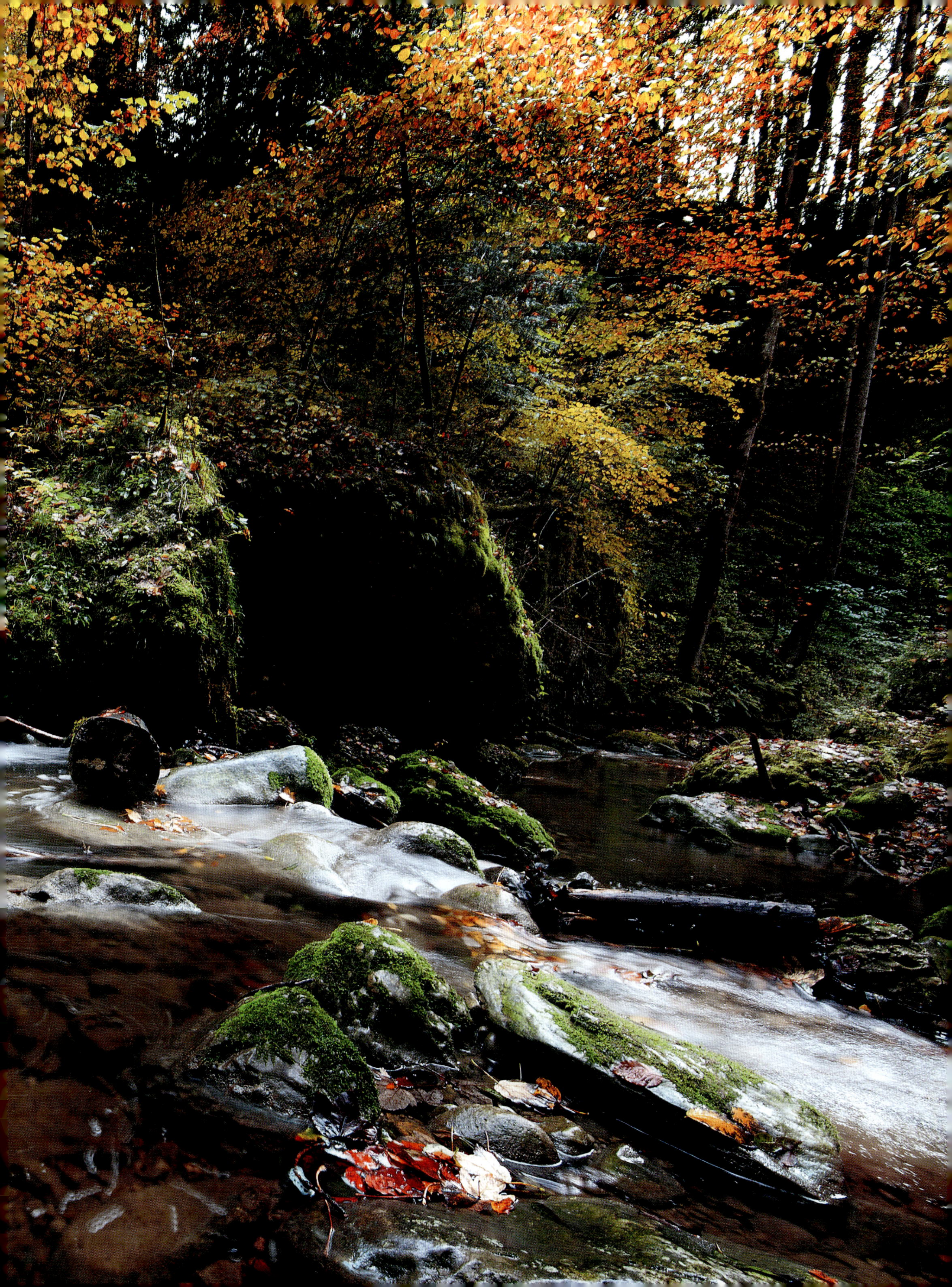

Im Spinnerei-Ensemble Neuthal bei Bauma kann der Betrieb der Anlage dank den intakten räumlichen Strukturen und den funktionsfähigen Maschinen auch in Details nachvollzogen werden. Die Fabrik wurde ohne Elektrizität durch Wasserkraft aus gestauten Weihern betrieben. Die Kraftübertragung vom Turbinenhaus zur Spinnerei erfolgte mit einer Seiltransmission mit Zwischenstütze (links).
Ein römischer Brunnen schmückt den kleinen Park vor den Stallungen im Neuthal, rechts daneben steht das Ökonomiegebäude (rechts).

Der Wissengubel bei Gibswil. Dem herabfallenden Rieselwasser würde man bei Niederwasser kaum zutrauen, dass es in dieser mächtigen Arena imstande war, die Nagelfluhplatten zu polieren und die dazwischen gelagerten weicheren Mergel- und Sandsteinschichten herauszuwaschen. Hinter dem Wasserfall entstanden Hohlräume, darunter Erosionstrichter. Dafür brauchte es aber geologischen Zeitspannen, die unser Vorstellungsvermögen übersteigen (folgende Doppelseite).

In the Spinning Mill Museum of Neuthal, close to Bauma, the operation of the plant can be reconstructed in detail thanks to the intact premises, and the still-functioning machines. The factory was operated without electricity, using only hydroelectric power from dammed ponds.
The power transmission from the turbine house to the spinning mill was carried out by cable transmission with an intermediate support (left).
A Roman fountain adorns the small park in front of the stables at Neuthal. Next to it on the right are the barns (right).

The Wissengubel by Gibswil. It is hard to believe that water trickling down during the low-water season would be able to polish the molasse conglomerate plates and wash out the deposited soft marl and sandstone layers. Behind the waterfall, cavities and hollows are created, including erosion funnels. This takes place in geological time periods, which usually exceeds our imagination (following double-page).

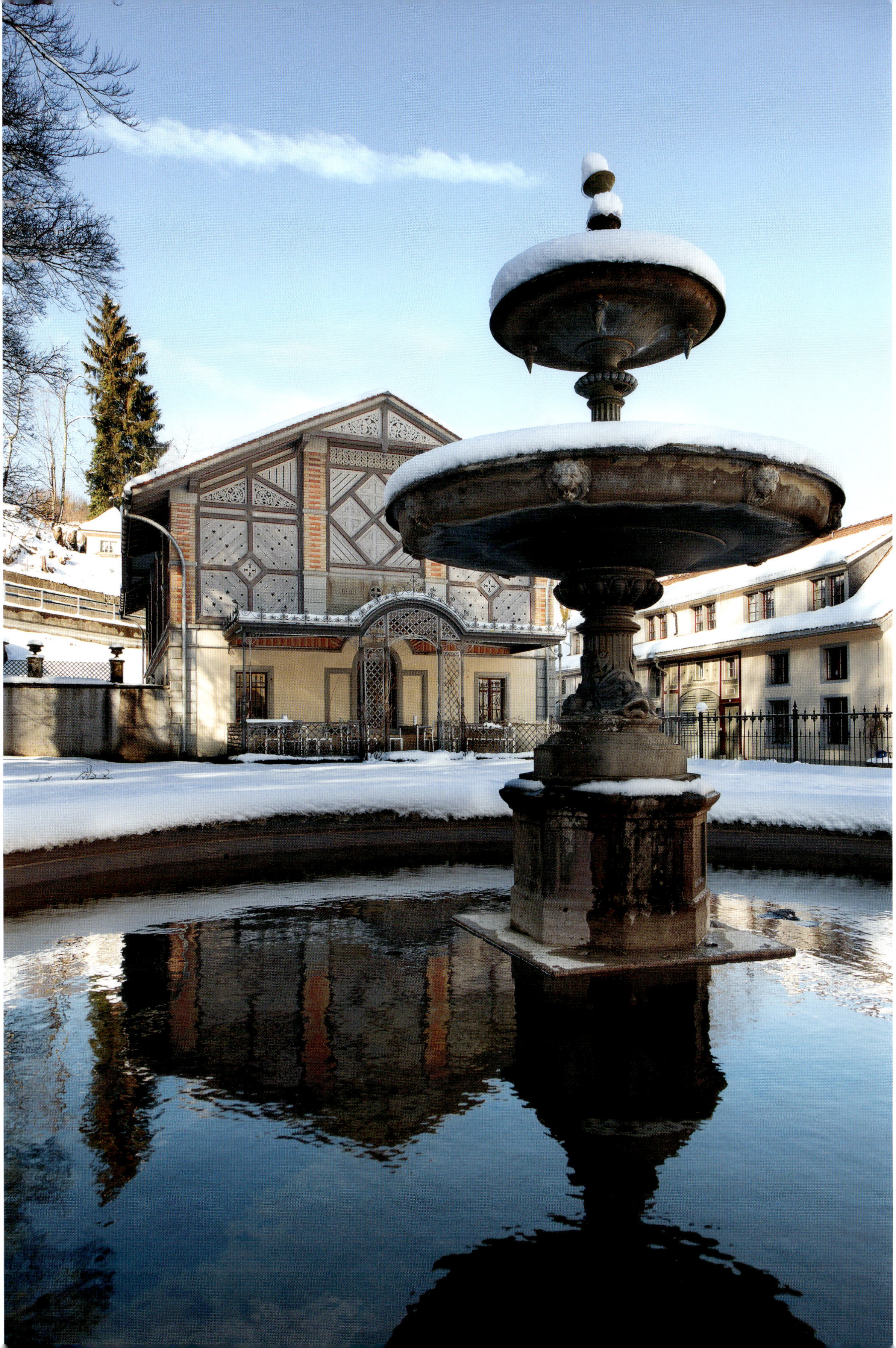

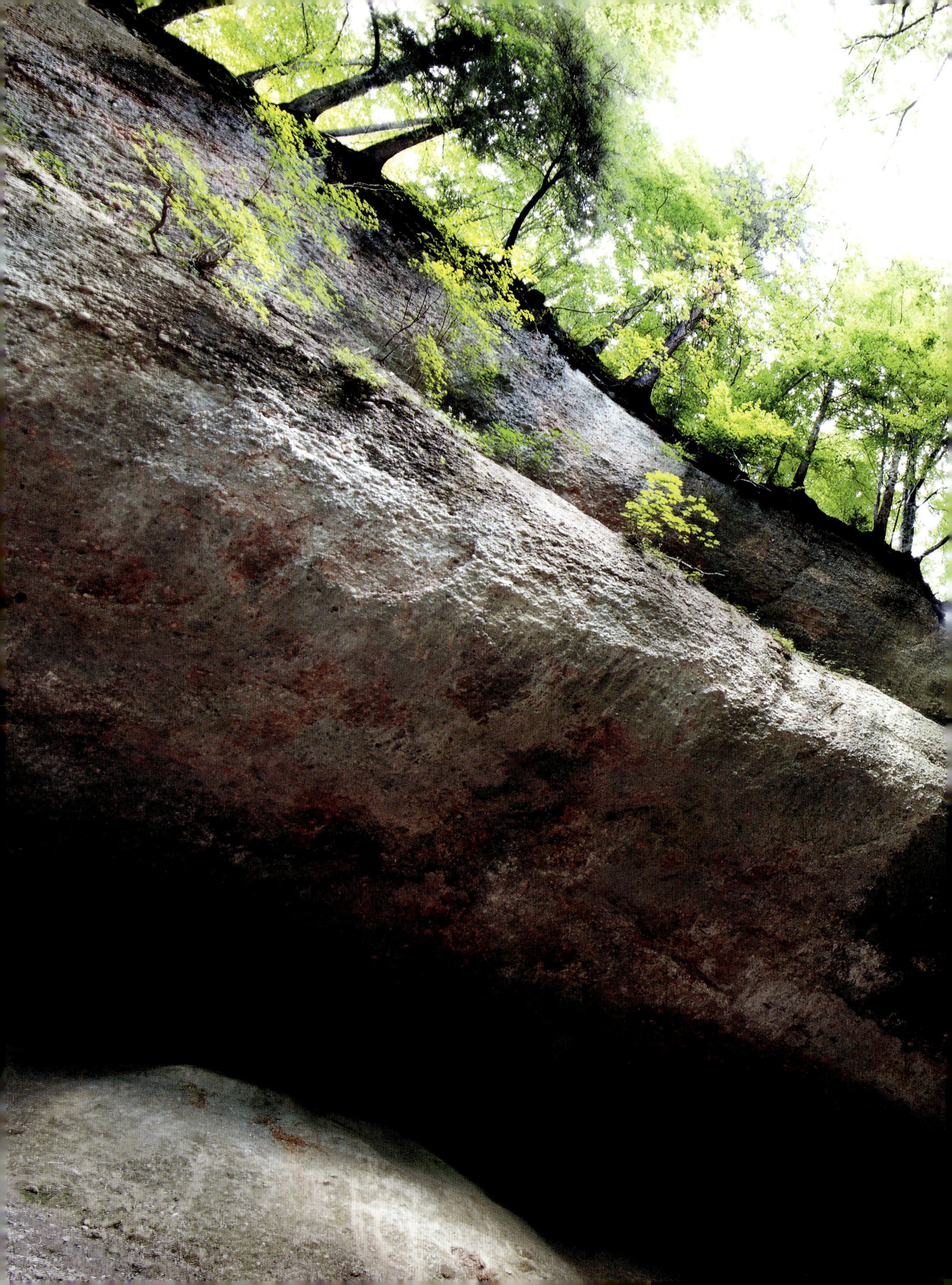

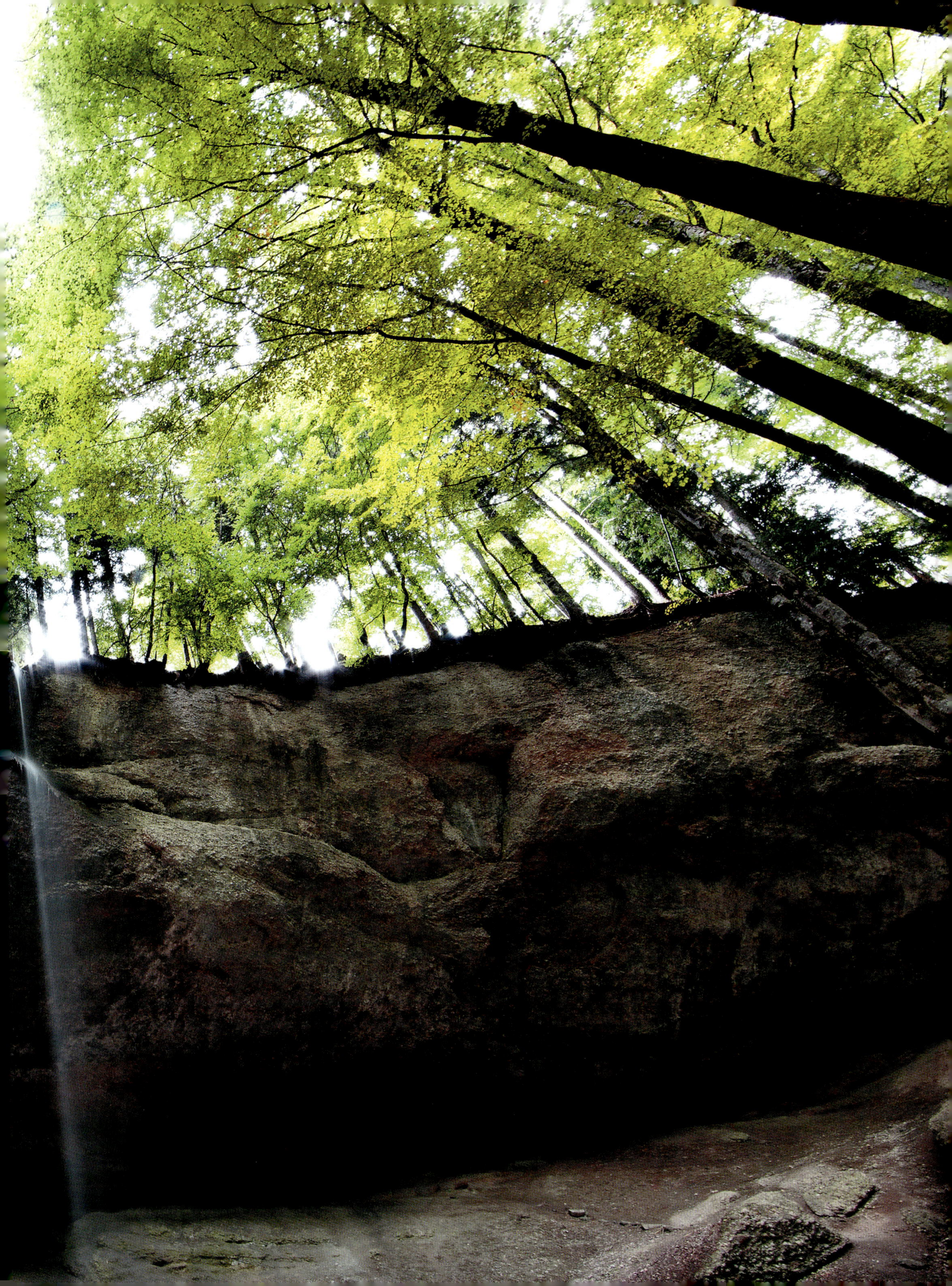

Im Bäntal bei Kollbrunn schuf die Natur in jahrzehntelanger Arbeit die Tüfelschilen, ein eigentliches Tuffsteinwunder – und sie arbeitet noch immer daran. Im 19. Jahrhundert, bis 1873, baute man an dieser von vier Quellen bewässerten Stelle mit einer Steinsäge Tuffstein als Baumaterial ab. Im Tobel- und Waldschattenklima und unter der Dauerbewässerung durch kalkhaltiges Quellwasser verfeinerte die Natur die treppenförmige Basisstruktur. Die im feuchten Milieu präsente reiche Moosflora baut seither an diesem Natur-Kunstwerk immer weiter.

In the Bäntal by Kollbrunn, nature has created the Tüfelschilen over decades of work: a real Tuffstein miracle – and, it is still working on it. In the 19th century, up until 1873, Tuffstein was mined for building material using a rock saw that was built on an irrigated point with four springs. In the ravine with a shade forest climate and continuous irrigation from hard spring water, nature refined the basic structure of the steps. The rich moss flora prominent in wet environments continues to build upon this natural work of art.

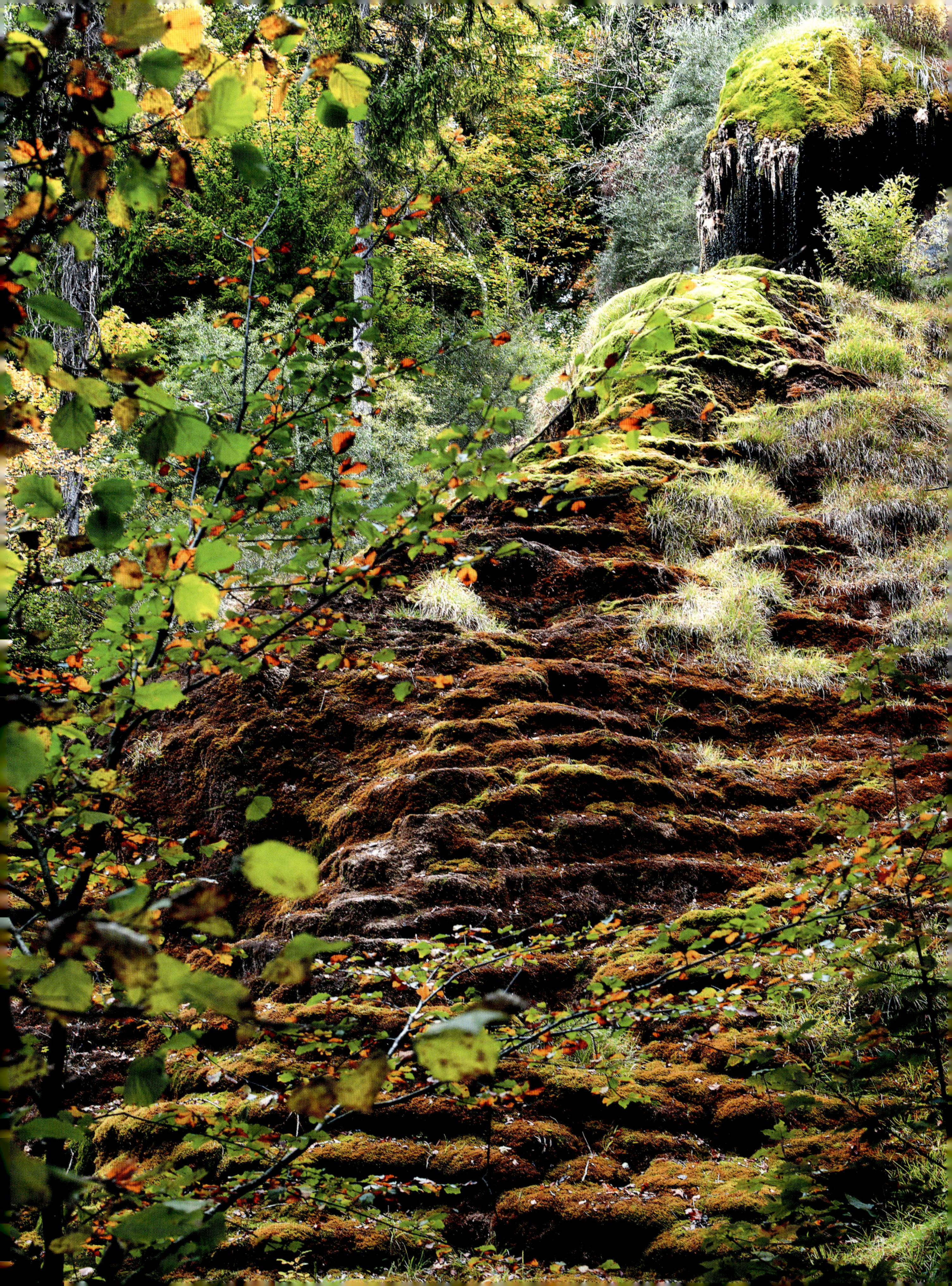

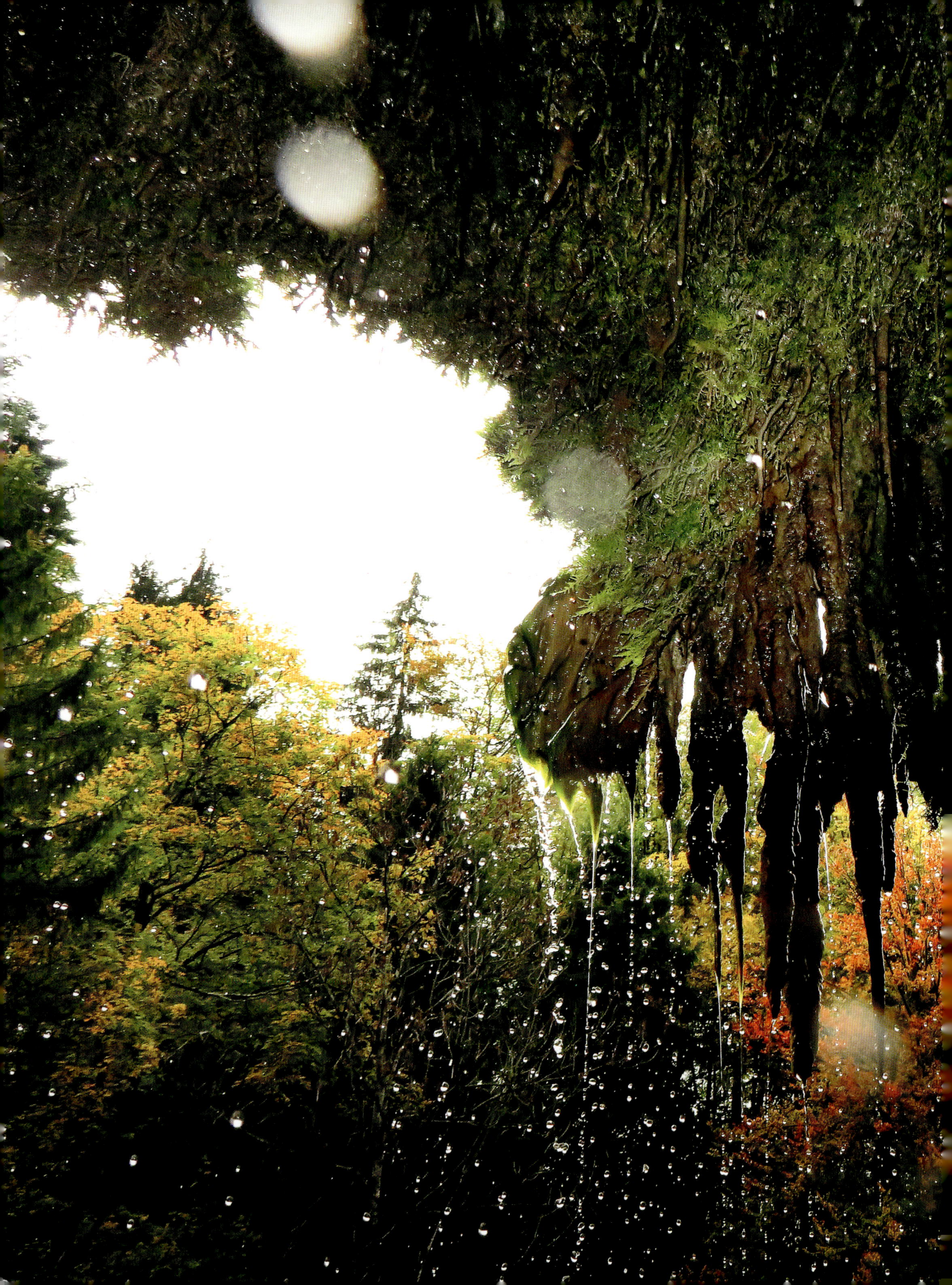

Die Morgensonne hat den Fotografen auf dem Bachtelturm erreicht und überstrahlt den Speer und fast auch den Säntis, während die Tössberge mit ihren bewaldeten Bachtobeln noch beschattet sind. Über der Linthebene und dem Zürichsee zeichnen sich die Spitzen der Glarner, Zentralschweizer und Berner Alpen ab, ganz rechts, bereits hell besonnt, Rigi und Pilatus. Herrlich besonnt ist auch der Allmen, der nördliche Nachbar in der Bachtelkette.

Die Tüfelschilen bei Kollbrunn – ob der Teufel bei seinem Kirchgang hier Kühlung sucht? (vorhergehende Doppelseite)

The Tüfelschilen near Kollbrunn: Does the devil look for something cooling when he goes to church? (previous double-page)

The morning sun has reached the photographer on the Bachtel Tower and outshines Speer Mt. and almost the Säntis as well, while the Töss Mountains with their wooded mountain-stream ravines are still in the shade. Above the Linth Plateau and Lake Zurich, the tips of the Glarus Alps, Central Swiss Alps and Bernese Alps are emerging, while far on the right, are the already brightly sunlit Rigi Mt. and the Pilatus. Magnificently illuminated is also the Allmen, the northern neighbor within the Bachtel mountain range.

Die Täuferhöhle am Westhang des Allmen erinnert an die Täuferbewegung im 16. Jahrhundert in Zürich. Als die Vereinigung verboten und die Täufer mit aller Härte verfolgt wurden, versammelten sich die Gläubigen in Privathäusern und in Wäldern. Ein Fluchtort war die Täuferhöhle. Unter einer mächtigen Nagelfluhdecke führt die geräumige Höhle 30 Meter ins Berginnere. Herabrieselndes Wasser hat den Mergel herausgespült (links).
Der 70 Meter lange, abenteuerliche Bachtelspalt am Osthang des Unterbachtels ist das Resultat einer wohl vergleichsweise jungen Sackung (rechts).

The Täuferhöhle (Baptist Cave) on the western slope of the Allmen, is reminiscent of the Baptist/Anabaptist movement of the 16th century in Zurich. When the association was banned and the Baptists/Anabaptists persecuted with the utmost severity, the believers gathered in private homes and in the forests. One of the refuges was the Täuferhöhle. Underneath a massive ceiling of molasse conglomerate, the spacious cave reaches 30 metres into the mountain. Trickling water has flushed out the marl (left).
The 70 m adventurous Bachtel Gap on the eastern slope of the Unterbachtel is probably the result of a comparatively young ground settling (right).

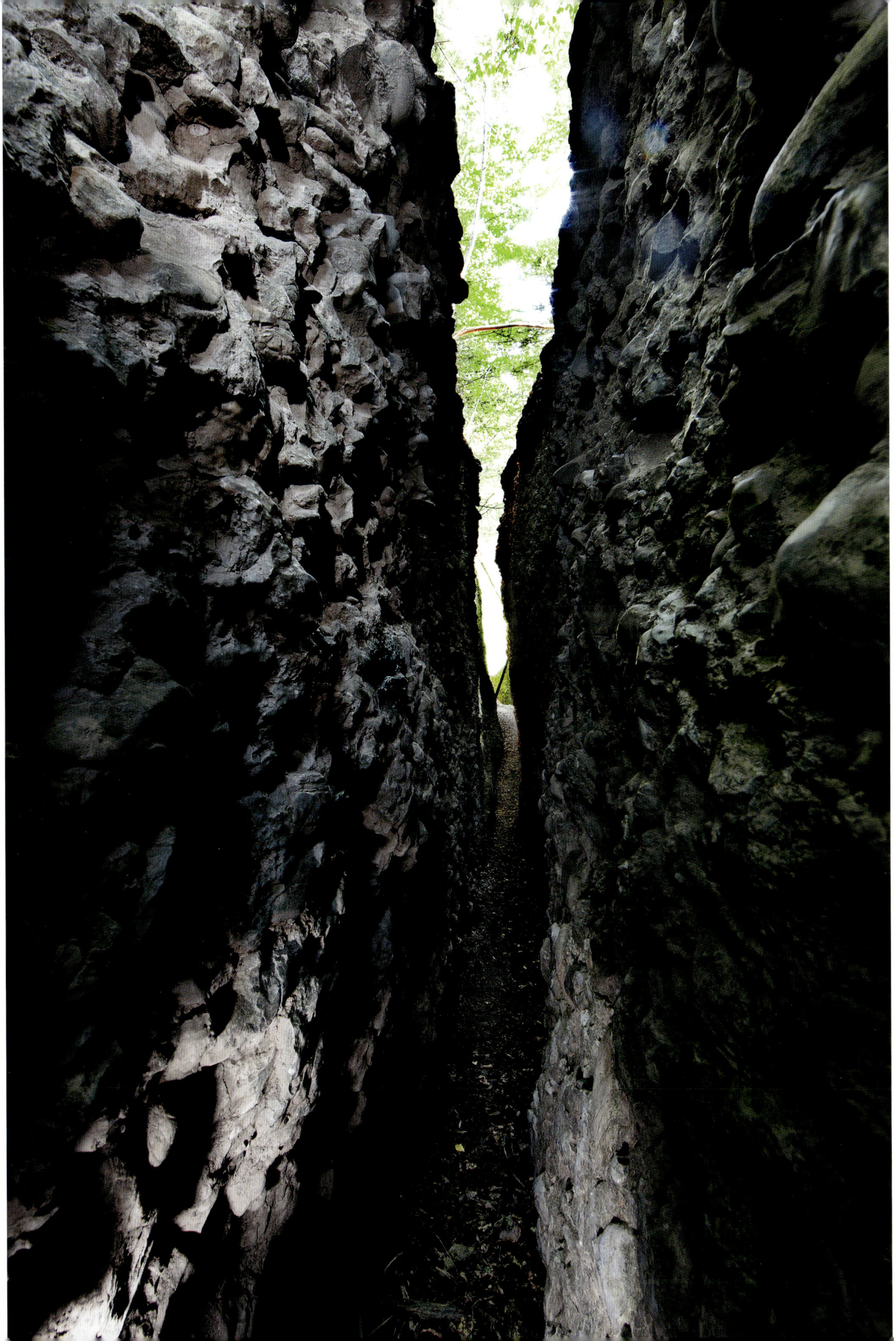

Der Hasenstrick bietet als Terrasse am Bachtel am Rande der eiszeitlichen Gletscherlandschaft nicht nur Platz für eine Flugpiste und für grössere Anlässe, sondern auch eine offene Aussicht Richtung Zürichsee. Der mit den grösseren Dörfern Hinwil, Dürnten und Wald dichter überbaute eigentliche Hangfuss liegt unterhalb der Sichtlinie zum See.

On the Bachtel, there is a terrace called the Hasenstrick at the edge of an Ice Age glacier landscape, which is not only spacious enough for an airstrip and big events, it also has an open view towards Lake Zurich. The large villages of Hinwil, Dürnten and Wald lie below the line of sight of toward the lake at the base of a densely built up slope.

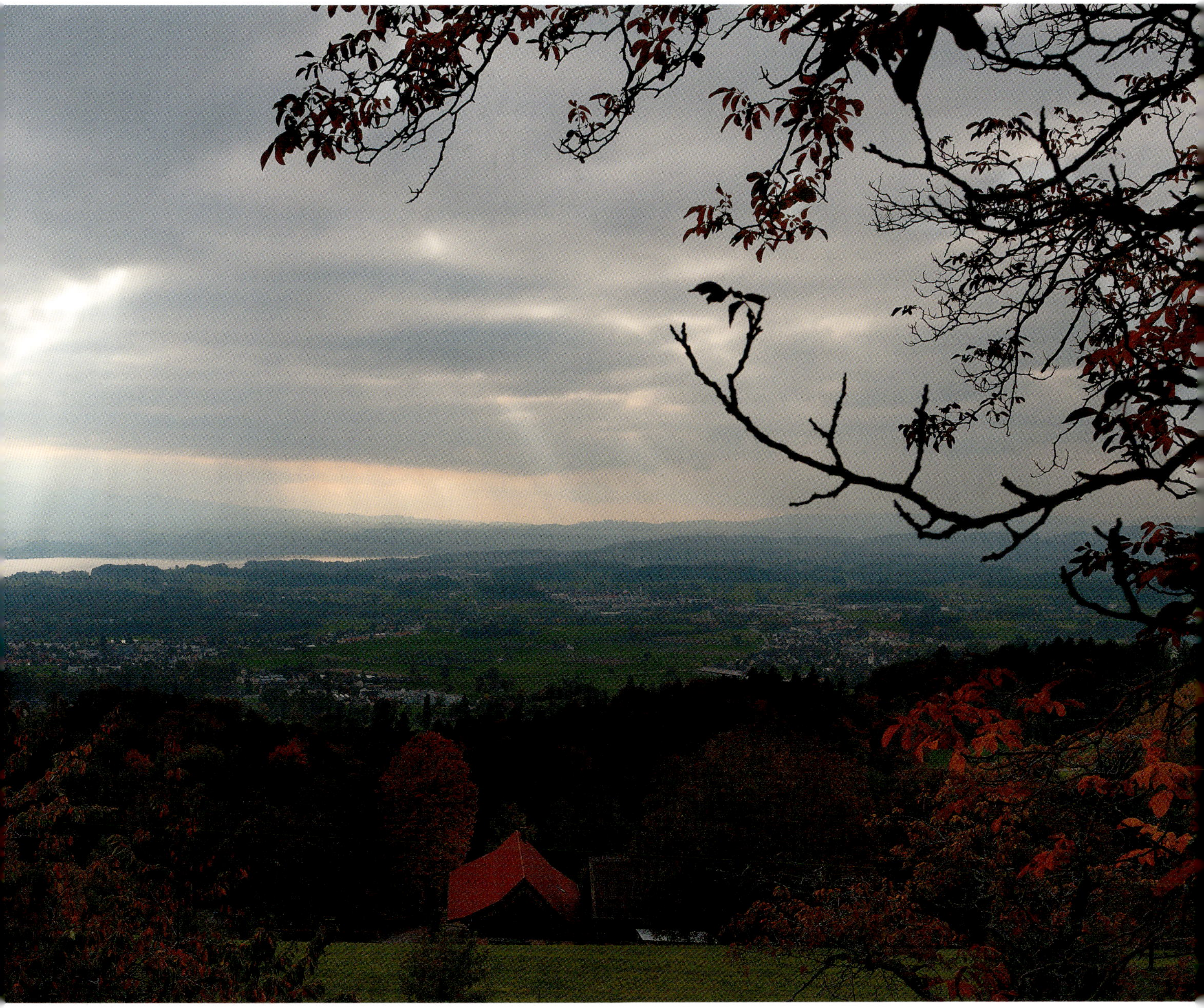

Linden sind eigentliche Landmarken auf den Kuppen der eiszeitlichen Gletscherlandschaft Hirzel. Einer dieser markanten Hügel bietet als sozialer Treffpunkt von Herdentieren auch Übersicht während dem Wiederkäuen.

Linden trees are actually landmarks along the summits of the Ice Age glacier landscape of the Hirzel. One of the prominent hills serves as a social meeting place for herd animals as well as a good view while chewing the cud.

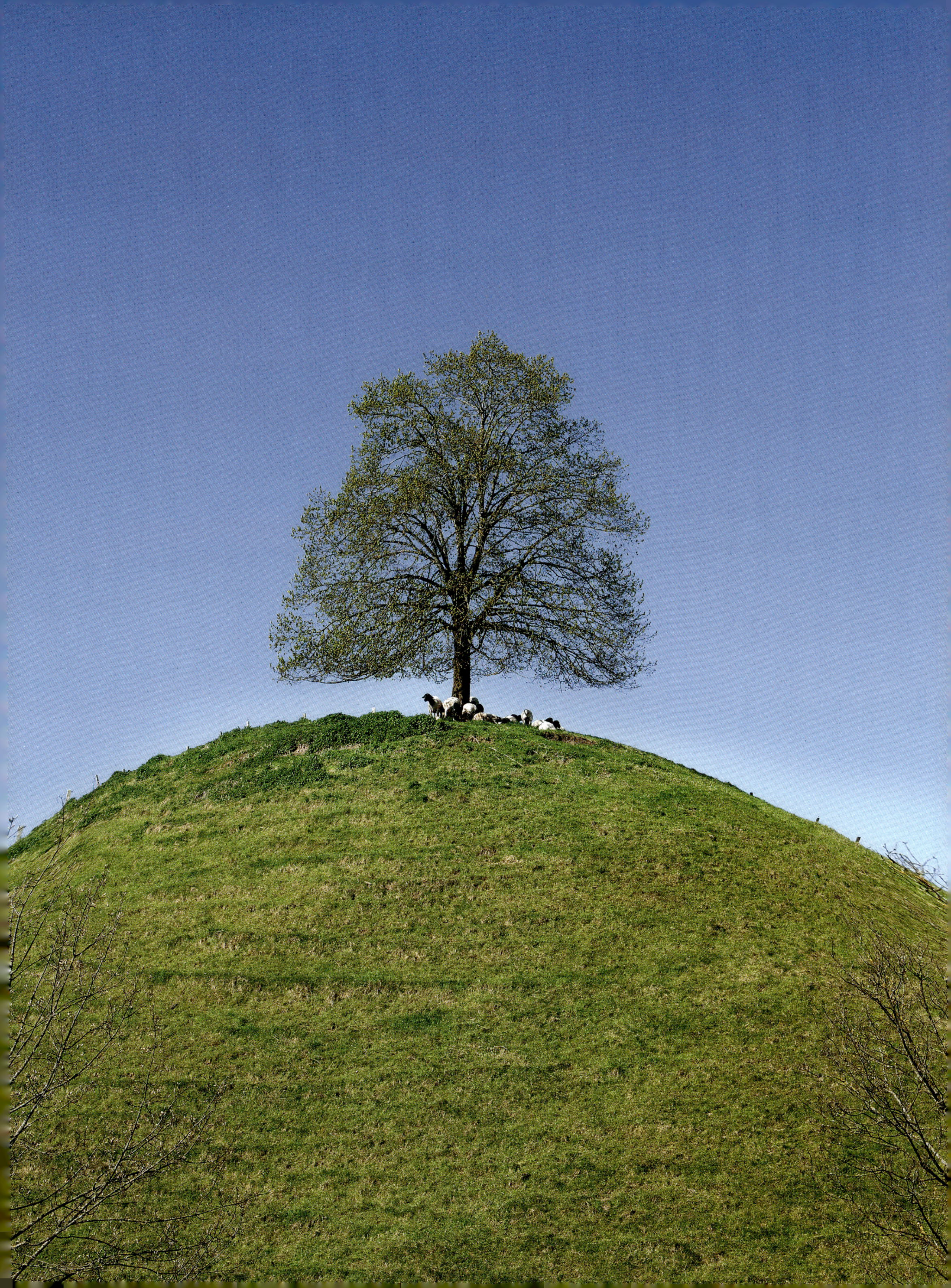

Die vom Gletscher geschliffene, sanft modellierte Landschaft im Raum Bubikon-Grüningen liegt südlich des bedeutenden Drumlinfeldes (siehe auch Seite 66).

Ground down by the glacier, a gently contoured landscape in the Bubikon-Grüningen area is located south of the most significant Drumlin field (see also page 66).

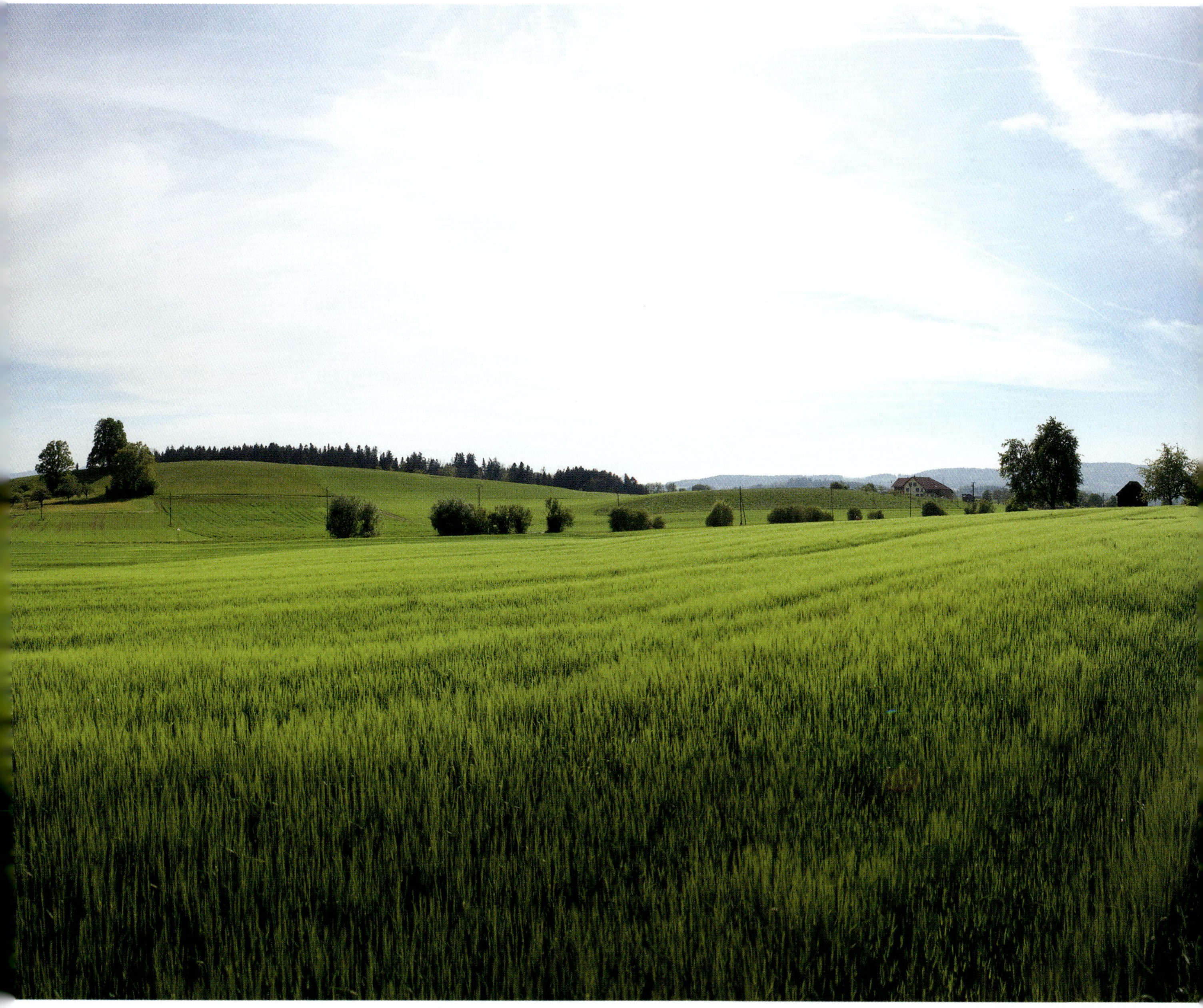

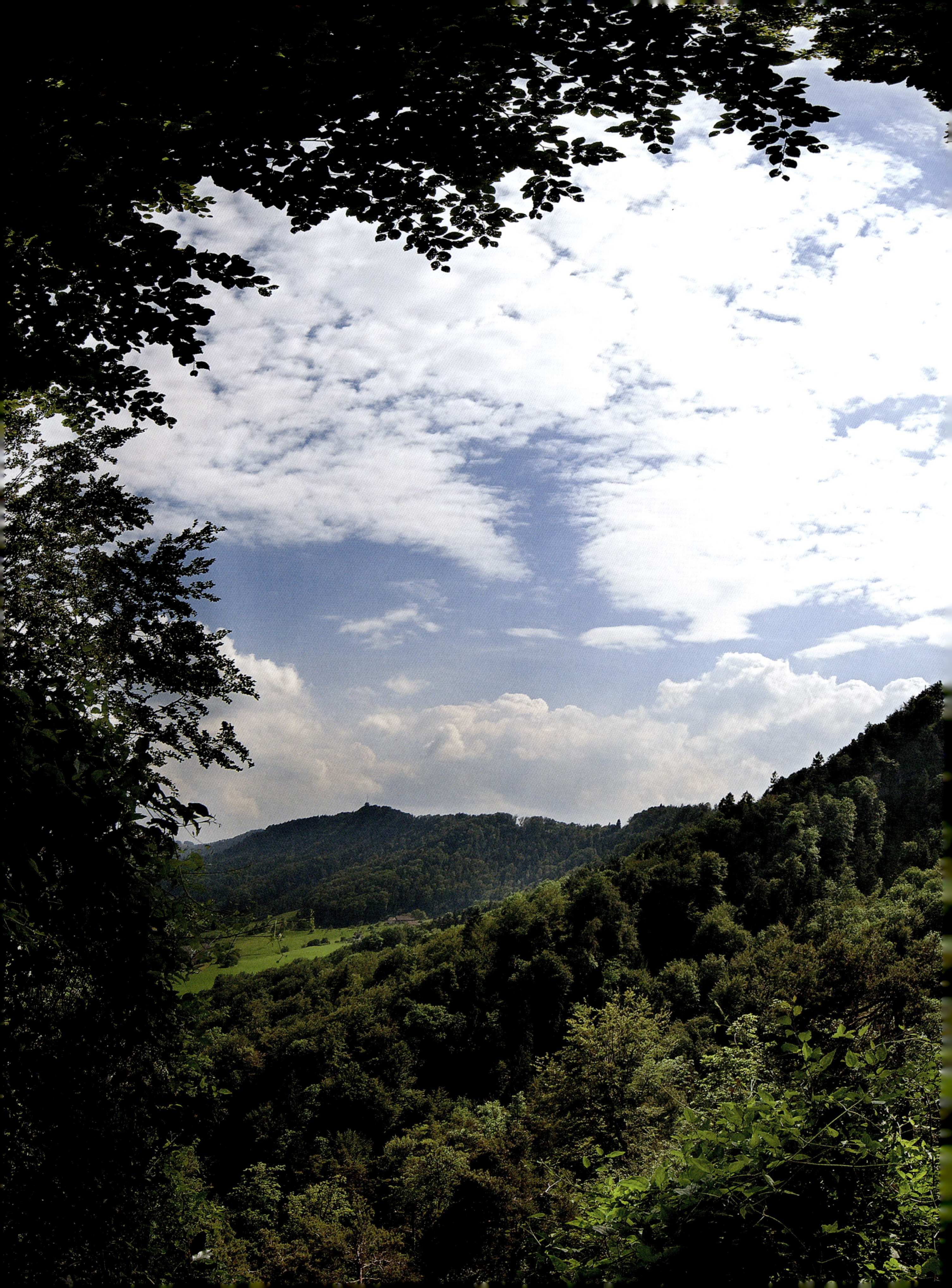

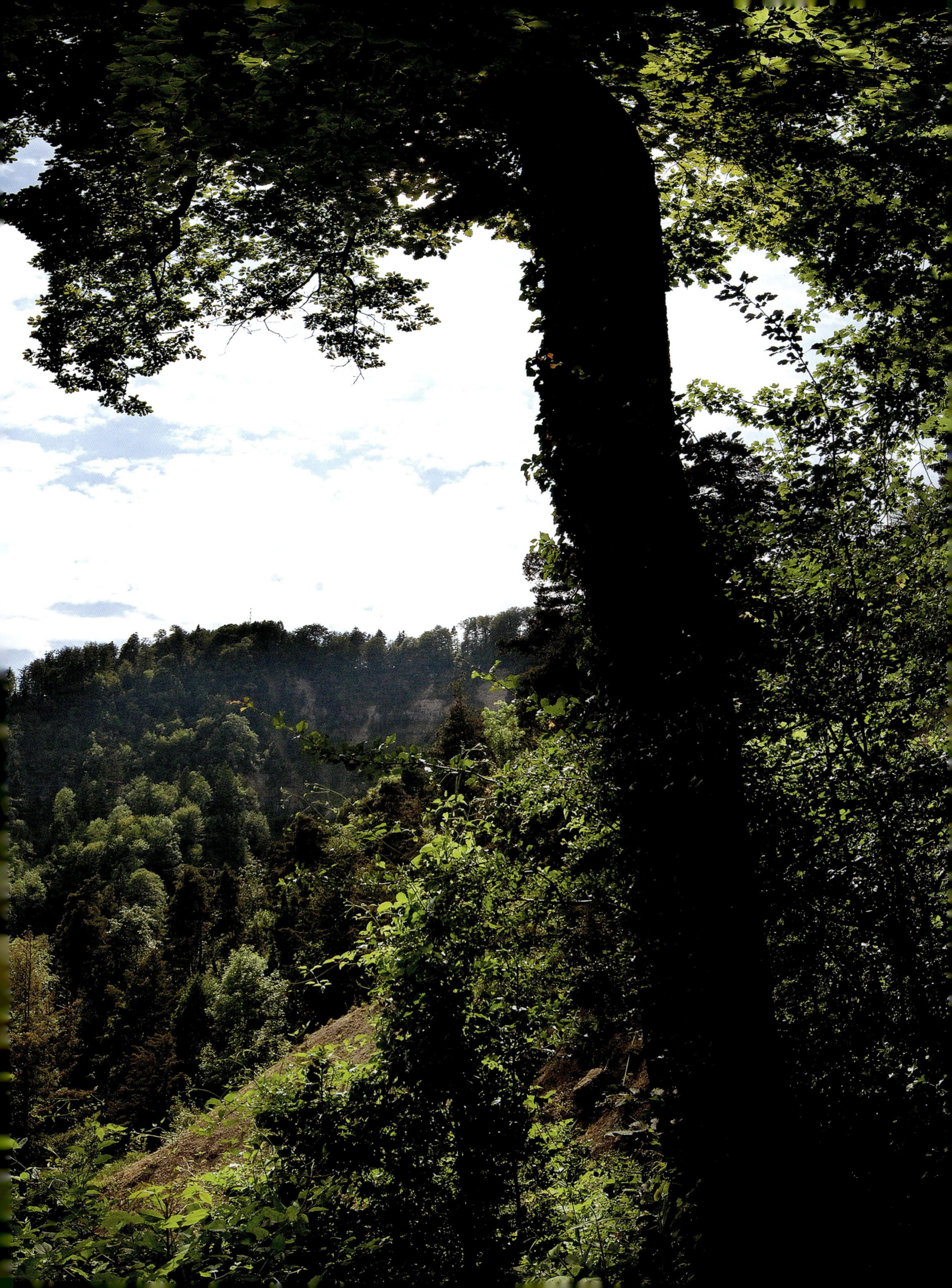

Unerwartet in unmittelbarer Stadtnähe: Die Fallätschen zeigt sich in Ansätzen zuweilen grün überwachsen und gefestigt, unvermittelt auch wieder im traditionellen Graubraun (vorhergehende Doppelseite).

Am Rande der Fallätschen, dem Erosionstrichter des Rütschlibaches, ist in wildem, steilem und rutschigem Gelände Trittsicherheit gefragt.

Die Lägern, ein langgezogener, abschnittweise scharfkantiger Ausläufer des Juras, tritt als Nebelspalter auf (folgende Doppelseite).

Unexpected so close to the city: The Fallätschen, an eroded slope above Wollishofen, changes its face during the climb: sometimes green with overgrowth and steady, then abruptly back to its traditional gray-brown (previous double-page).

On the fringes of the Fallätschen, the erosion chutes of the Rütschlibach. Surefootedness is required in the wild, steep and slippery terrain.

The Lägern mountains, a long-drawn out, sometimes sharp-edged extension of the Jura Mountains, appears here as a fog-splitter (following double-page).

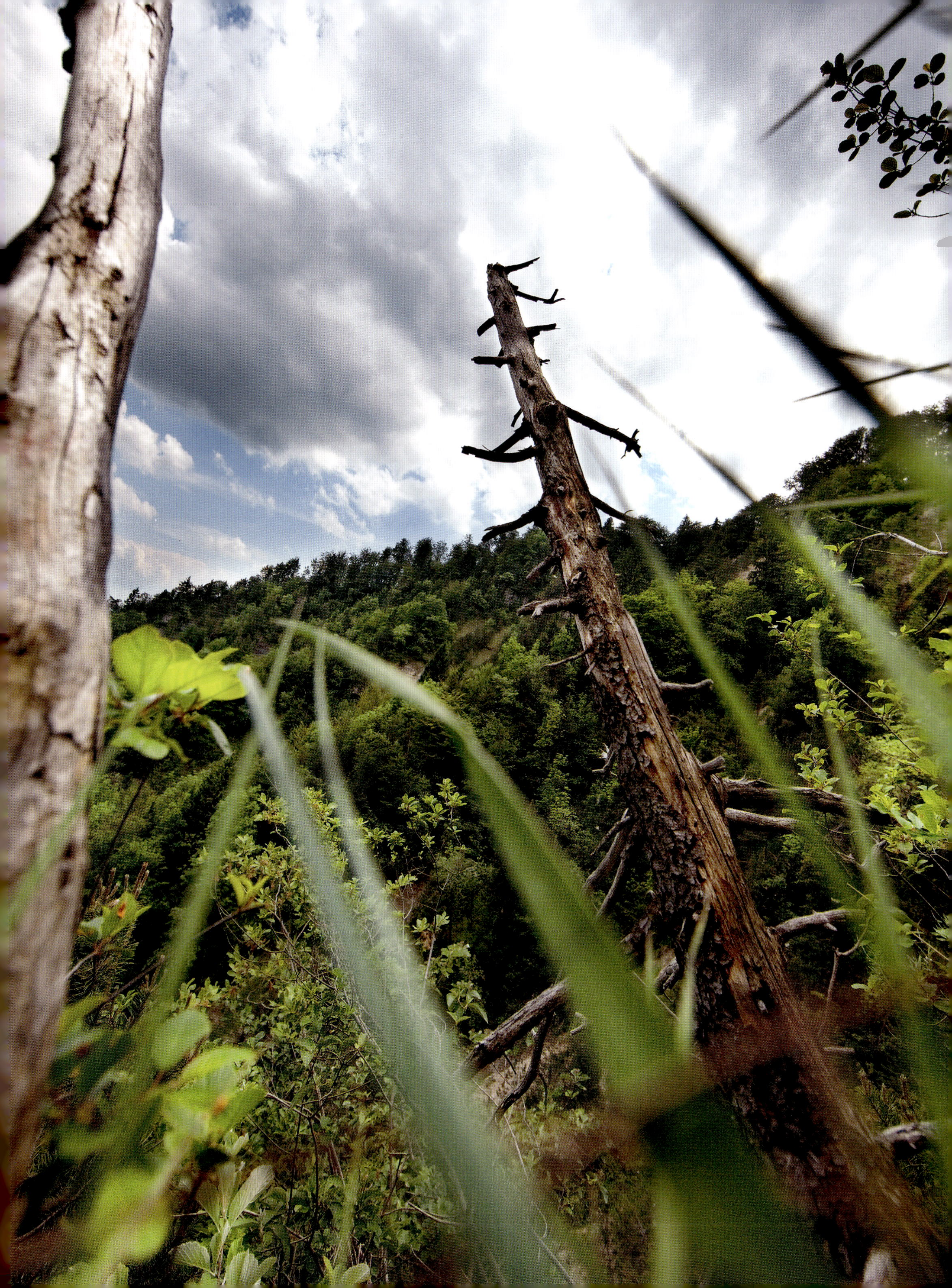

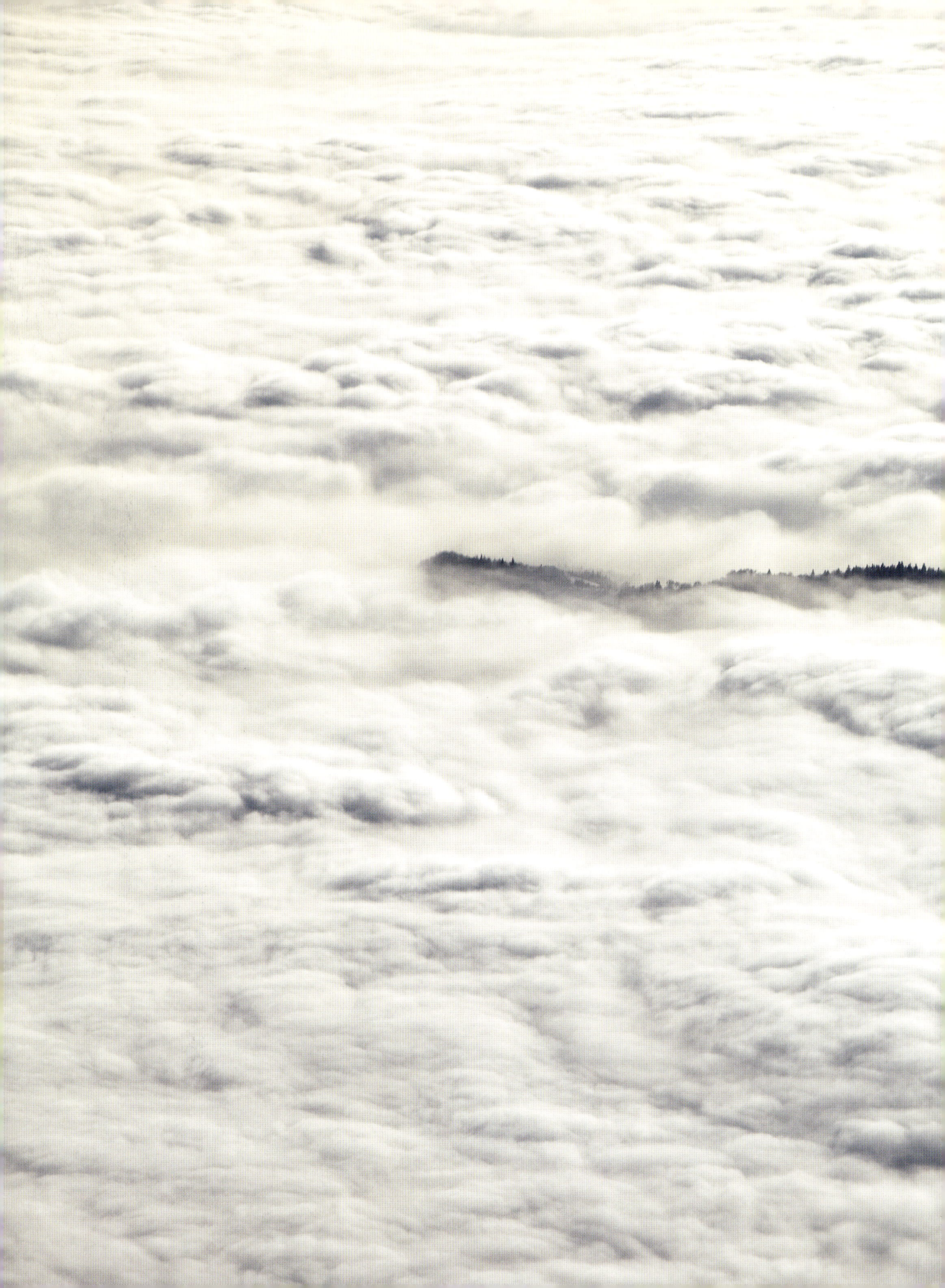

Seen- und Flusslandschaften

Lake and River Landscapes

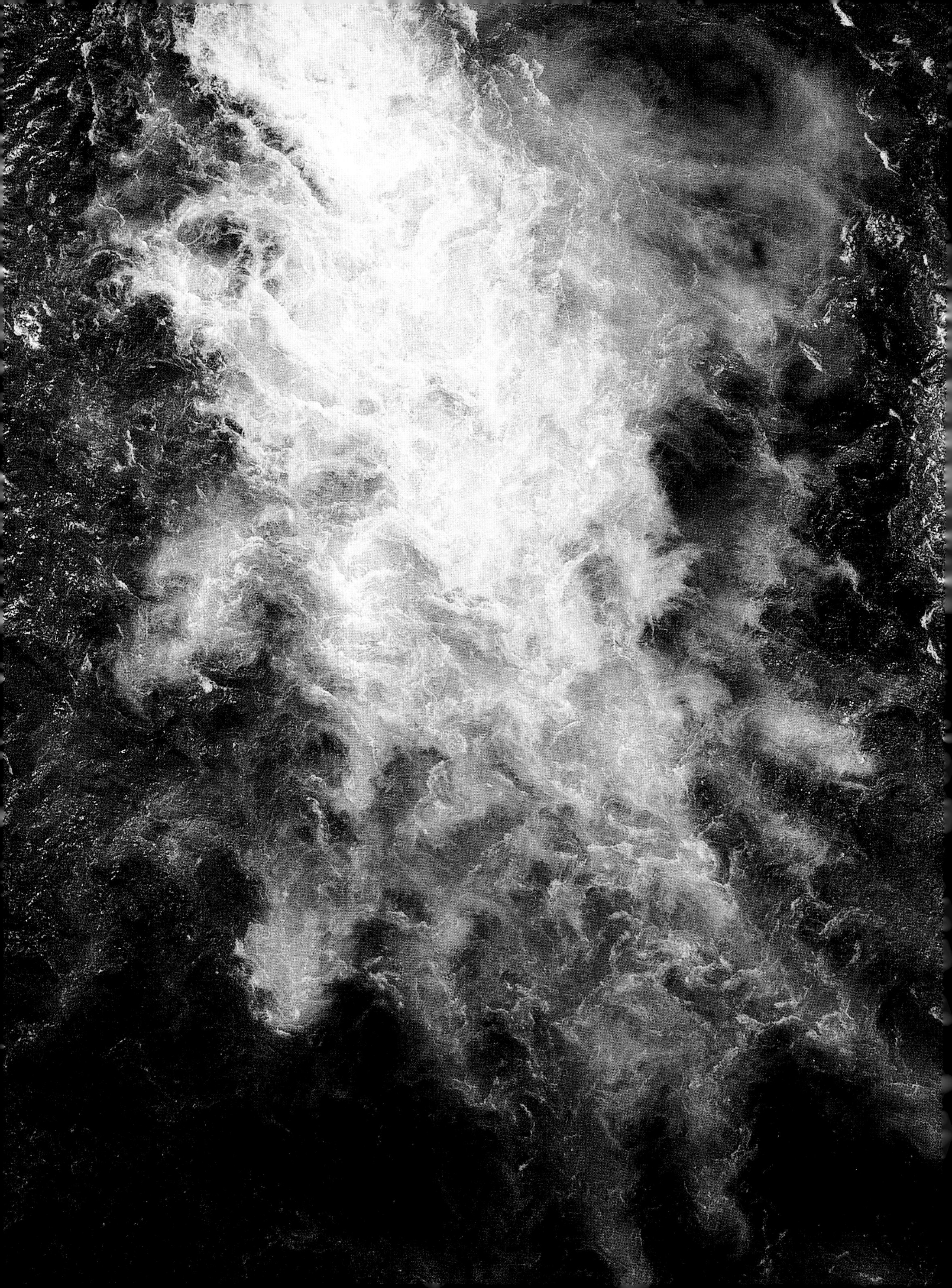

«Da die Gebirgsflüsse schnell und reissend sind, scheinen die Seen von der Natur geschaffen, um deren Ungestüm zu mässigen.»

Josias Simmler (Humanist, 1530–1576)

'Because mountain rivers are fast and torrential, lakes seem created by nature to moderate their turbulence.'

Josias Simmler (Humanist, 1530–1576)

Der Rheinfall ist mit seiner Form und Mächtigkeit ein Sonder-Fall unter den helvetischen Wasserfällen. Auch ausschnittweise bietet er ein Schauspiel wilder Schönheit, und das Dauerrauschen ist eine akustische Demonstration geballter Kraft.

The Rhine Falls with its dramatic form and power is a special case amongst Helvetic waterfalls. Even in a partial view, it offers a spectacle of wild beauty and the continuous noise is an acoustic demonstration of concentrated power.

Zürichs Gewässernetz lässt eine nach Nordwesten gerichtete topographische Grundstruktur des Kantons erkennen, wie sie durch würmeiszeitliche Gletscherarme vorgespurt wurde und vereinfacht sogar im Zürcher Wappen angedeutet ist. In der Tat entspricht die schräge Trennlinie zwischen den Standesfarben Blau und Weiss dem Verlauf von Still- und Fliessgewässern: ganz im Westen ein Abschnitt der Reuss als Grenzfluss, wenig östlich davon Türlersee mit Reppisch, dann folgen Sihl, Zürichsee mit Limmat, Greifensee mit Glatt, Pfäffikersee und Kempt und schliesslich, in zunehmend wilderem Gelände, die Töss, die, ebenfalls nordwestlich orientiert, bei der Tössegg in den Rhein fliesst.

Gewässer sind landschaftsprägend. Ruhende wie Seen und Weiher laden ein zum Verweilen; Fliessgewässer, Flüsse und Bäche, setzen mit ihrer Dynamik ein forderndes Zeichen. Eine festliche Grundstimmung dürfte die Ortsentscheide für Landesausstellungen an Seen begünstigt haben: Die Landi 1939 am Zürichsee als Ort der Weitsicht, die Expo 1964 am Genfersee und die Expo.02 am Neuenburger-, Bieler- und Murtensee vielleicht als Orte der Umsicht und wohl auch Einsicht. Seen laden zu ruhigem Sehen ein. Der grosse Geologe und Gletscherforscher Albert Heim schrieb 1891 in einem Beitrag zur Geschichte des Zürichsees:[1]

«Für das Naturbild von Zürich ist der Gegensatz von Zürichberg, Limmat und See einerseits, von Albis und Sihl andererseits sehr bezeichnend. Hier in der Limmat ein Fluss frei von Geschieben, leicht lenksam und friedlich; er kommt aus dem See, einem alten, schon vor der Eiszeit rückgebildeten, vollständig schlummernden Talstück, das der Gletscher der Diluvialzeit gütig vor vollständiger Schuttausfüllung bewahrt hat – er ist ein Bild der Ruhe; beschaulich sinnend klärt sich hier das Wasser und spiegelt den Himmel in seiner Flut.

Dort in der Sihl ein Wildwasser, unvermittelt aus den Alpen durch ein junges, noch ganz unfertiges

Taking an aerial view of the Canton of Zurich's network of lakes and rivers reveals a topographical structure oriented towards the northwest that was pre-determined by the arms of the Linth-Rhine Glacier during the Würm Ice Age. This is actually suggested in the Zurich coat of arms in simplified form. In fact, on Zurich's standard, the diagonal line that divides the colours of blue and white, corresponds to the paths of both still and flowing water: At the most western point of the canton, a section of the River Reuss forms a border with the Canton of Aargau, and a little east of that is the Türlersee (see = lake), which gives rise to the Reppisch River. East again is the Sihl River, which flows parallel to Lake Zurich for a bit and joins the Limmat River, which flows out of Lake Zurich. The Greifensee gives rise to the Glatt River, and the eye moves on to the Pfäffikersee and the Kempt River. The Töss River, which is also oriented northwest amid increasingly wild terrain, finally flows into the River Rhine at Tössegg.

Water is a strong element in the landscape. Restful lakes and ponds invite people to linger; while the dynamic movement of flowing water, rivers and streams has a more challenging character. A festive atmosphere may have worked in favour of the decision to allow national exhibitions to take place on lakes: The 1939 Landi (Swiss National Exhibition) on Lake Zurich as a place of far-sightedness, the Expo 1964 on Lake Geneva and for the Expo.02 on the Lakes of Neuenburg, Biel and Murten perhaps as places of circumspection and possibly also insight. Lakes invite one to peaceful thoughts. The great geologist and glacier researcher and explorer, Albert Heim, wrote in a contribution to the history of Lake Zurich in 1891:[1]

'The contrast between the Zurichberg, the Limmat River and Lake Zurich on one side of the valley, and the Albis and the Sihl River on the other, is very characteristic of the natural image of Zurich's landscape. Here, the Limmat, a river free from rubble and

121

Tal uns zuströmend, Ausgangslinie zahlreicher Abrutschungen und Wildbachschluchten, reich an bedeutenden, oft plötzlichen Anschwellungen, gewaltig und wechselvoll im Geschiebetransport und schwierig in gleichmässige Bahnen zu zwingen; da beobachten wir einen Talbildner in voller Arbeit, der feilt und schleift, um ein enges Tal zu vertiefen und zu erweitern, […].

See und Sihl aber, beide, sind in altem alpinen Schutt eingebettet durch die Arbeit der Wasser. Dort ist die Arbeit vollendet, der See liegt in der Sonntagsruhe, hier ist strenger Werktag.»

Seen sind Kernelemente der Landschaft. Wer im Zug von Zürich nach Chur reist, überlegt sich bei der Wahl des Sitzplatzes, auf welcher Seite man den Zürich- oder Walensee sieht. Der offene Blick auf das Landschaften und Wetter spiegelnde Wasser, die visualisierte Horizontale und Weite, ist eine von der Natur geschenkte Qualität. Zu einem kultivierten Umgang mit Seelandschaften gehört es, unverbaute Seeufer und eine möglichst freie Sicht auf den See zu erhalten und zu fördern. Die Zürcher Regierung hat während 90 Jahren nach 1850 aus heutiger Sicht allzu grosszügig Aufschüttungen in den biologisch wichtigen Flachwasserzonen offiziell zugelassen.[2] Ob die dadurch entstandene, wie ein Pfeil auf die Stadt weisende Uferlinie des Zürichsees als Anklage an die Behörden interpretiert werden kann? Immerhin ist dem See im Zusammenhang mit den Uferschüttungen auch ein Dauerkorsett in der Form von harten Mauern verpasst worden. Eine sichere Abwehrlinie unterbindet Rückeroberungsversuche. Trotz der nicht nur in der Stadt breit geschätzten Qualität der gepflegten See-Anlagen ging die Nähe zum Wasser verloren – mit punktuellen Ausnahmen vor allem beim Zürichhorn. Mit der Höhe der Mauer wird auch die Beziehung der Bewohner zum See distanzierter. Deshalb sind dem See weitere mutige Revitalisierungsschritte zu wünschen. Jeder Abschnitt mit wasser- und landseitigen Flachufern bereichert das Leben und das Erlebnis des Zürichsees. Im Schwyzer Teil des Sees mit der Ufenau, dem Frauenwinkel und weiteren Teilen jener Naturlandschaft stützte das Kloster Einsiedeln Bemühungen im Sinne des Naturschutzes. Kantonsübergreifender Widerstand war gefordert bei einem geplanten Bauprojekt im Frauenwinkel. Dieser Kampf hatte 1927 zur Gründung des Verbandes zum Schutz des Landschaftsbildes am Zürichsee VSLZ geführt, seit 1998 Zürichsee Landschaftsschutz ZSL.[3] Der Zürichsee ist ein Geschenk, die Wasserqualität konnte markant verbessert werden, und das Landschaftsbild vom Bürkliplatz über den zwischen Albis und Pfannenstiel eingebetteten See ist in der Netzhaut jedes

detritus, easily managed and peaceful, flows out of the lake – an old dormant part of the valley carved out well before the Ice Age started, and which a Pleistocene glacier benignly protected from being filled with debris. It is an image of quiet; a contemplative reflection clears the water and reflects the sky in its flush.'

'While over in the Sihl, a torrent erupts from the Alps through a young, still unfinished valley, streaming towards us; the starting lines of numerous landslides and torrent ravines, rich in powerful, often sudden high waves, violent and erratic in transporting rubble and difficult to force into smooth channels; there we observe a valley's creation in full force, filing and grinding in order to hollow out and widen a narrow valley […].'

'However, Lake Zurich and the Sihl River are both embedded in old alpine debris left by the effects of water. There, the work is complete, the Lake lies in a Sunday quiet, while here, it is a strenuous workday.'

Lakes are core elements of the landscape. Anyone travelling by train from Zurich to Chur thinks about the choice of seats, or what side of the train to sit so one can see Lake Zurich or the Walensee. The open view of the landscape and weather-reflecting water, the visualised horizon and distance is one of nature's eminent gifts. It appears to me that to sustain and promote undisturbed lake banks and the best possible open view of a lake is part of a cultivated approach to lake landscapes. From 1850 to about 1940, the cantonal government had officially allowed, from today's perspective, an all too generous volume of earth fill in the biologically important shallow water zones.[2] Can the thus created shoreline of Lake Zurich, pointed at the city like an arrow, be interpreted as an accusation of the authorities? In any case, in connection with the shore embankment, the lake was also given a continuous corset in the form of solid walls. A secure defence line prohibited any recapture attempts. In spite of the, not only in the city, widely treasured quality of the well-kept parks along the lake, proximity to the water was lost: with selected exceptions, mainly at the Zürichhorn. The height of the walls also makes contact with the lake more difficult for the residents. Therefore, additional courageous revitalisation steps are much to be desired. Every section with water and low banks enriches the life and the experience of Lake Zurich. In the part of the lake located in the Canton of Schwyz, with the island of Ufenau, the Frauenwinkel and other parts of this natural landscape, the Monastery of Einsiedeln supported efforts for nature protection. Resistance arose across cantonal borders in 1927 when a construction project was planned for the Frauenwinkel. This conflict led to the founding of the 'Verbande zum Schutz des Landschaftsbildes am Zürichsee'

Zürchers eingebrannt, mitsamt den Voralpen und der Wucht der alles überragenden Alpen.

Im Umfeld des städtisch umbauten Zürichsees ist auf weitere ebenfalls nacheiszeitlich entstandene kleinere, reizvolle Seen zu verweisen wie etwa den Greifensee, Pfäffikersee, Chatzensee und den Türlersee, der als einziger nicht eine nach dem Rückzug des Linth/Rhein-Gletschers gehobelte, kleinere oder grössere Wanne übernahm. Vielmehr entstand dieses landschaftlich reizvolle Juwel durch eine mächtige nacheiszeitliche Sackung am Nordosthang des Aeugsterberges, welche die Reppisch zum heutigen See staute. Alle diese kleineren Seen kamen bereits in der ersten Hälfte des letzten Jahrhunderts unter zunehmenden Druck durch Wochenendaktivitäten – sei es durch den Bau von Hütten, das Ausreissen oder Zertrampeln von Pflanzen oder das Zurücklassen der Abfälle. Die ausufernde Situation rief nach ordnenden Händen und Aufsicht. Diese wurde zunächst vor allem auf privater Basis und gestützt durch Naturschutzorganisationen wahrgenommen, dann jedoch trug sie die Öffentliche Hand politisch mit. Mit differenzierten, mehrfach aktualisierten Schutzverordnungen gelang es am Greifensee, Türlersee und Chatzensee – alle drei waren und sind besonders stark besucht – in vorbildlicher Weise, die Erholungsnutzung von den vorrangigen Naturschutzflächen räumlich zu trennen und diese damit zu schützen.

Im Unterschied zu den stehenden Gewässern sind Fliessgewässer Lebensadern mit der Schlüsselfunktion, das Quell- oder Einzugsgebiet von Flüssen mit ihrem Mündungsgebiet zu verbinden. Mit seiner naturgegebenen Gestaltungskraft korrigiert und erneuert das Wasser das Flussbett immer wieder. «Werktägliches Wirken» nannte es Albert Heim mit Bezug auf die Sihl. Der besondere Reiz noch weitgehend naturbelassener wie auch wiederbelebter Bäche und Flüsse liegt im räumlich und zeitlich variantenreichen Landschaftsbild und oft auch in der raumfüllenden akustischen Präsenz. Ein Erlebnis der Sonderklasse für alle Sinne ist der grossartige Rheinfall. Für seinen Schutz sind neben dem Bund die Kantone Schaffhausen und Zürich gemeinsam verantwortlich.

Die optisch und auch akustisch bedingte Anziehungskraft der Fliessgewässer ist mit dem Erlebnis von Dynamik verbunden, das bei den wilderen und unberechenbaren Gewässern auch Respekt gebietet. Die bei naturbelassenen Bächen spielerische Vitalität und die damit verbundene akustische Vielfalt ist vom böhmischen Komponisten Smetana für die gurgelnde «junge» Moldau feinfühlig musikalisch eingefangen. Die im Schlussabschnitt des Werkes umgesetzte Würde der «reifen» Moldau als meerwärts ziehender Strom, die dabei als Stillwasser wahrgenommene Weite und Ruhe ist bei uns indessen nur

(VSLZ; Association for the Protection of Lake Zurich Landscapes), which was changed to the 'Zürichsee Landschaftsschutz' (ZSL) in 1998.[3] Lake Zurich is a gift: The water quality was markedly improved and the view from Bürkliplatz of the landscape between the Albis and Pfannenstiel peaks with the lake embedded in between, including the alpine foothills and the impact of the Alps towering over everything else, is burned into the retina of every Zürich inhabitant.

In the surroundings of the urban modifications to Lake Zurich, additional post-ice age processes caused small, appealing lakes to appear, e.g. the Greifensee, Pfäffikersee, Katzensee and Türlersee. The latter is the only lake that did not fill one of the small or large planed-out troughs caused by the retreat of the Linth-Rhine Glacier. This delightful scenic jewel came into being because of a powerful post-Ice Age settling of the north face of the Aeugsterberg, which dammed the Reppisch River forming today's lake. In the first half of the last century, all of these smaller lakes were already under increasing pressure from weekend activities, whether it was building huts, rooting up plants, trampling down vegetation or leaving waste behind. The escalating situation called for order and supervision. These were first carried out mainly on a private basis and supported by nature protection organisations; later, the public authorities put it on a legal basis. As a kind of test case, the Greifensee, Türlersee and Katzensee – all three were and are especially heavily visited – received differentiated, consistently updated protection regulations and have managed to spatially separate recreational use from the priority nature protection areas and to protect these areas.

In contrast to still water, flowing waters have a key function as life arteries: to connect the source or catchment areas of rivers to their estuaries. With its naturally given creative power, water corrects and renews the riverbed again and again. 'A strenuous workday' is what Albert Heim called it in regard to the Sihl River. The special attraction of streams and rivers left in their natural state or revitalised to a great extent, lies in the spatial and temporal variety-rich landscape and often in the surrounding acoustic presence as well. A very special experience for all the senses is the magnificent Rhine Falls. The governments of the Cantons of Schaffhausen and Zurich are both responsible for its protection.

The optical and acoustic powers of flowing water are connected with the experience of dynamics – and with wild and unpredictable waters, it also demands respect. The playful vitality of streams left to their natural course and their acoustic diversity has been sensitively captured by the Bohemian composer Smetana in the young gurgling headwaters of his

in gestauten Abschnitten wie bei Eglisau am Grenzfluss Rhein zu erleben.

Sichtbarer als bei den Stillgewässern begann sich in den letzten Jahrzehnten im Umgang mit Fliessgewässern eine neue Kultur des offenen Denkens durchzusetzen. Statt in geometrischen Kanälen Wasser möglichst ohne Schäden abzuleiten begann man, Flüsse und Bäche als dynamische und biologisch vielfältige Systeme zu verstehen, die sich im grösseren Raum des Flussbettes immer wieder neu hydrologisch und biologisch anpassen. Bei diesem Lernprozess spielte die im Säntisgebiet entspringende Thur eine Schlüsselrolle. Ohne Passage durch einen ausgleichenden See neigt sie zu Hochwasser und bewahrt auf den 125 Kilometern bis zum Rhein ihren Charakter als Wildbach. Mit Begradigungen und Dammbauten wurde in der Thurebene die landwirtschaftliche Nutzfläche vergrössert, die Thur indessen nicht gezähmt. Beim Hochwasser vom 7./8. August 1978 schuf sie sich nach einem Dammbruch bei Ellikon das fehlende Hochwasserrückhaltebecken selbst und überschwemmte fünf Quadratkilometer Kulturland.[4] Auch wenn die Planungen zuweilen harzig verliefen, so wurden doch die Aspekte der Natur und Landschaft immer mehr beachtet, und der naturnahe Wasserbau wurde im ganzen Kanton zur leitenden Devise. Mit dem Projekt «Hochwasserschutz und Auenlandschaft Thurmündung» entstand unter Mitarbeit der Thur eine dynamische, sich weitgehend selbst überlassene «Naturlandschaft», und im Raum Altikon bis Gütighausen gelang es mit dem Einbau von Buhnen dem Hochwasserschutz, dem Landschaftsbild und der biologischen Vielfalt Rechnung zu tragen. In der Thur wurde in einem durch den Kanton geförderten Programm wie auch in weiteren Flüssen – unter anderen der Töss, der Reppisch, der Sihl und der Limmat – mit gezielten baulichen Eingriffen der natürliche Wiederbelebungsprozess erfolgreich angestossen.

Mit Blick auf den naturnahen Wasserbau wurden auch die zahlreichen in früheren Jahrzehnten eingedolten Bäche nach Möglichkeit geöffnet. Gleichsam vor der Haustüre entstanden aus eingedolten Wiesen- und Dorfbächen sowie aus Bächen in urbanen Räumen oft breit gesäumte, erlebbare Bach-Lebensgemeinschaften. Mit der von der Natur inspirierten Wasserführung wird der ganze Uferbereich reich strukturiert und bietet damit eine Standortvielfalt, die sich auch in einer variantenreichen, hohen Biodiversität widerspiegelt. Der breite Übergang vom Wasser zum Land und umgekehrt wird zum bereichernden Element im Landschaftsbild: Das sind die Auen. In diesem vielfältigen, aber im Falle von etwas grösseren Fliessgewässern von Natur aus unberechenbaren Lebensraum leben zahlreiche Pflanzen

work, *The Moldau*. In the closing sequence, the full dignity of the mature river flowing north to meet the Elbe, carries the perceived breadth and calm of still water, which we can only experience in dammed sections of the River Rhine, for instance at Eglisau.

More visible than the handling of still waters, in recent decades, a new culture of open thinking began to be accepted and implemented in the approach to flowing water. Instead of diverting water into geometric canals thought to cause the least possible damage, rivers and streams began to be understood as diverse dynamic and biological systems that would continue to adapt hydrologically and biologically in the larger space of a riverbed. The Thur River, which has its source in the Säntis area, played a key role in this learning process. Because the river does not pass through a counterbalancing lake, it tended toward high-water and in its 125 kilometres to the Rhine had proved its character as a torrential river. The useful agricultural area was enlarged in the Thur Plain by straightening sections and building dams. The Thur River, however, refused to be tamed. On 7 and 8 August 1978, a dam broke near Ellikon and, because there was no floodwater control basin, the floodwaters poured out over five square kilometres of cultivated land.[4] Although planning does not always live up to the expectations, the process itself led to more observation and better solutions. Indeed, after this event, this aspect of nature and landscape was carefully observed and using the closest-to-nature hydraulic constructions became the leading solution throughout the entire canton. With the project, Floodwater Protection and Water Meadow Landscapes of the Thur River Estuary, developed 'in cooperation with the Thur River', a dynamic, largely left to itself natural landscape emerged. In the area from Altikon to Gütighausen, the installation of jetties not only provided floodwater protection; it also managed to accommodate the needs of the landscape's image and biological diversity. In addition to the Thur River, the canton also funded programmes with specific structural interventions for other rivers, such as the Töss, Reppisch, Sihl and Limmat Rivers, thus successfully initiating the natural revitalisation process.

With a view to promoting close-to-nature hydraulic engineering, countless streams forced into channels in earlier decades were also opened when possible. As if originating right before your door, previously covered meadow and village streams as well as streams in urban spaces offer broadly lined perceptible symbiotic stream communities. With its nature-inspired flow, the entire bank is luxuriously structured and presents a local diversity that also reflects a variant-rich, high level of bio-diversity. The broad passage from water to land and the reverse becomes

und Tiere. Bei Hochwasser werden im oft natürlicherweise nährstoffreichen Lebensraum ganze Lebensgemeinschaften immer wieder überspült, Pflanzen und Tiere weggeschwemmt, verletzt und durch Sedimente zugeschüttet. Die unter diesen Verhältnissen immer wieder selektiv getesteten Arten regenerieren jedoch schnell und sind Meister darin, die durch den Fluss freigeräumten Flächen oder neuen Aufschüttungen zu erobern. Die im Forstwesen als Pionierart bekannte schnellwüchsige Weiss- oder Grauerle kommt mit Phasen der Überschwemmung wie auch der Trockenheit zurecht. Spezialisiert hat sich die Gelbe Schwertlilie. Sie versteht es, den für Schönheiten eingerichteten Logen-Standort am Gewässerrand mit ihren schwimmenden Samen zu sichern.

Ein besonderer Spezialist in diesem Lebensraum ist der durch Revitalisierungsmassnahmen von Flüssen wie der Thur geförderte Flussregenpfeifer, der zum Brüten die vom Hochwasser freigeputzten Kiesflächen nutzt. Sein Gelege ist durch das Farbmuster wunderbar getarnt. Aus diesem Grund werden die raren Nistplätze während der Brutzeit durch Informationstafeln und Absperrungen vor Störungen geschützt. Es ist jedoch ein wichtiges Anliegen, dass Menschen jeden Alters die herrlichen Natur-Räume erleben können: das vielfältige Leben entlang der Wasserkannte, Graureiher, Fische, Wasserinsekten, oder Nagespuren der scheuen Biber.

an enriching element in the scenic landscape. A multitude of plants and animals thrive in exactly this diverse habitat, but in cases of somewhat larger flowing waters, these wet meadows are by nature demanding and unpredictable living spaces. In these often naturally nutrient-rich living spaces, entire symbiotic communities can be washed over by floodwaters, plants and animals swept away, injured or scoured through the sediment. Under these conditions, however, certain selectively tested types regenerate very quickly and are masters in conquering areas cleared by floods or new embankments. Those known in forestry as pioneer types are fast-growing white or grey alders that manage quite well with phases of flooding or drought. The yellow water iris is a specialist in this; its swimming seeds need moving water to ensure a place at the water's edge to display its beauty.

An outstanding specialist in living in such a space is the little ringed plover, which benefits from the revitalisation measures of rivers like the Thur. The plover uses the gravel washed clean by floodwaters for nesting because its clutch of eggs is wonderfully camouflaged by their colour patterns. These rare nesting places are protected from people during the breeding season by information boards and barriers. However, it is an important concern that people of every age group are able to experience wonderful natural spaces: the diverse life forms along the water's edge, grey herons, fish, water insects or the clear evidence of shy beavers at work.

Andere Stadtbäche haben es schon erlebt, der Hornbach wartet noch darauf: im engen Bereich eine fischfreundliche naturnahe Form und im untersten Abschnitt mehr Platz zu erhalten. Beim Zürichhorn wäre der Platz vorhanden (links).
Jean Tinguelys Anti-Maschine «Heureka» war ein Spektakel an der Landesausstellung 1964 in Lausanne. Mit ihrer ausgeklügelten Leerlauf-Botschaft ist sie auch am Zürichhorn eine Attraktion. Der Ort passt zum tiefen Ernst, Humor und spontanen Witz, den der ungebundene Künstler ausgestrahlt hat. Keine Mauer und kein Geländer behindern den direkten Zugang zum Wasser (rechts).

Other city streams have had the experience, but the Hornbach is still waiting to have a more fish-friendly, natural form in the narrow portion and more space at the lowermost section. At the Zurich Horn, there would be space available (left).
Jean Tinguely's anti-machine 'Eureka' was a spectacle in 1964 at the National Exhibition in Lausanne. With its ingenious 'idle cycle' message, today it is still an attraction at the Zurichhorn. The site matches the deep earnestness, humour and spontaneous wit that the untethered artist radiated. No walls or railings obstruct direct access to the water (right).

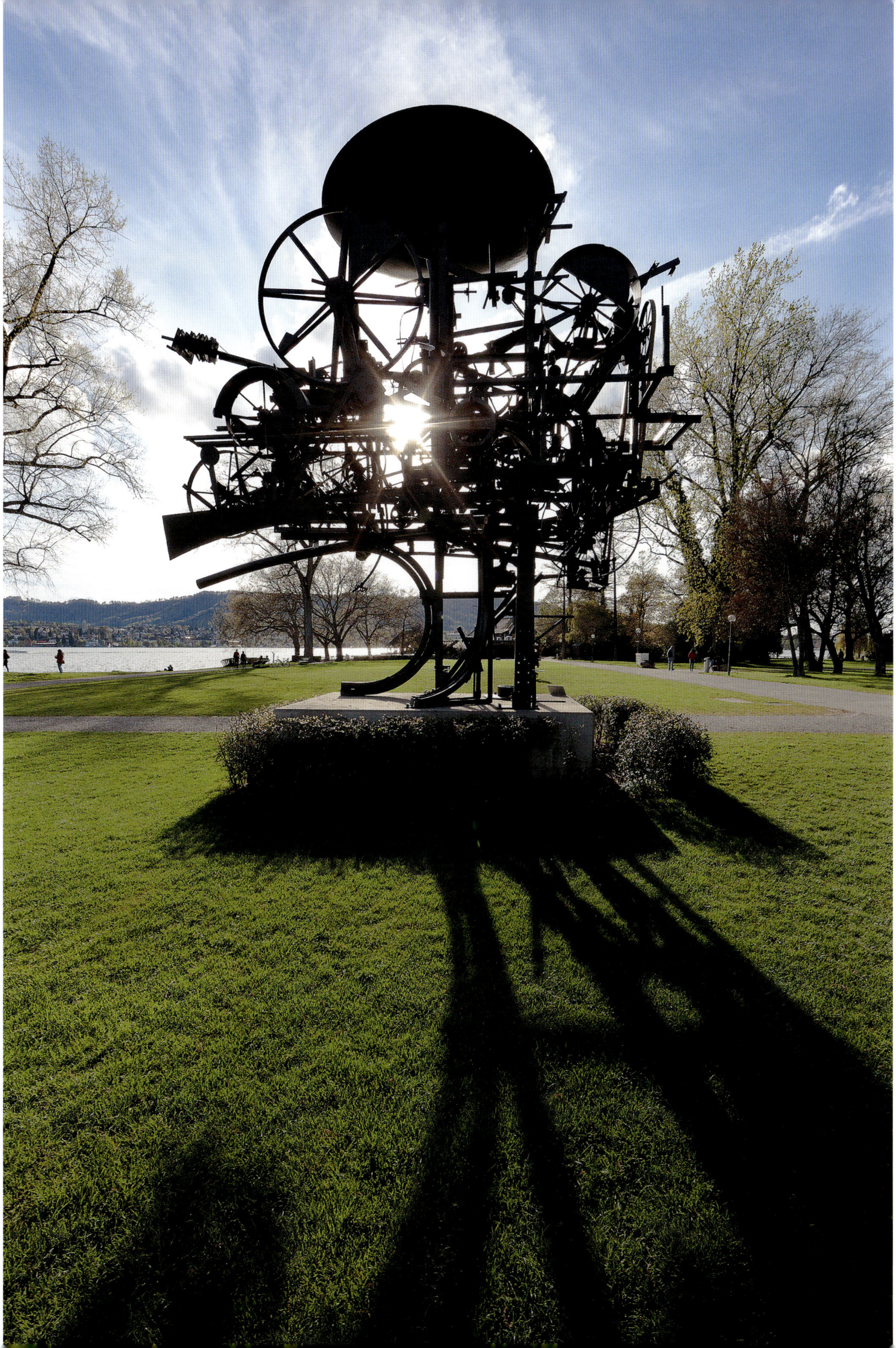

Dorfbäche wie jener durch das Küsnachtertobel beleben die Dorfstruktur und das Uferdelta. Solche einfachen Uferzonen laden zum Bade – so wie auch das gepflegte Strandbad Tiefenbrunnen (links).
Die vielleicht einzige erfreuliche stehende Autokolonne im Raum Zürich ist jene in der Fähre während der unbesorgten Überfahrt zwischen Meilen und Horgen (rechts).

Village streams, such as the one flowing through the Küsnachtertobel, animate the village structures and the shoreline. Such simple shore areas are an invitation to swim – just like the well-kept public beach of Tiefenbrunnen in Zurich (left).
Perhaps the only enjoyable traffic holdup in the Zurich area is the one on the ferry during the carefree crossing between Meilen and Horgen (right).

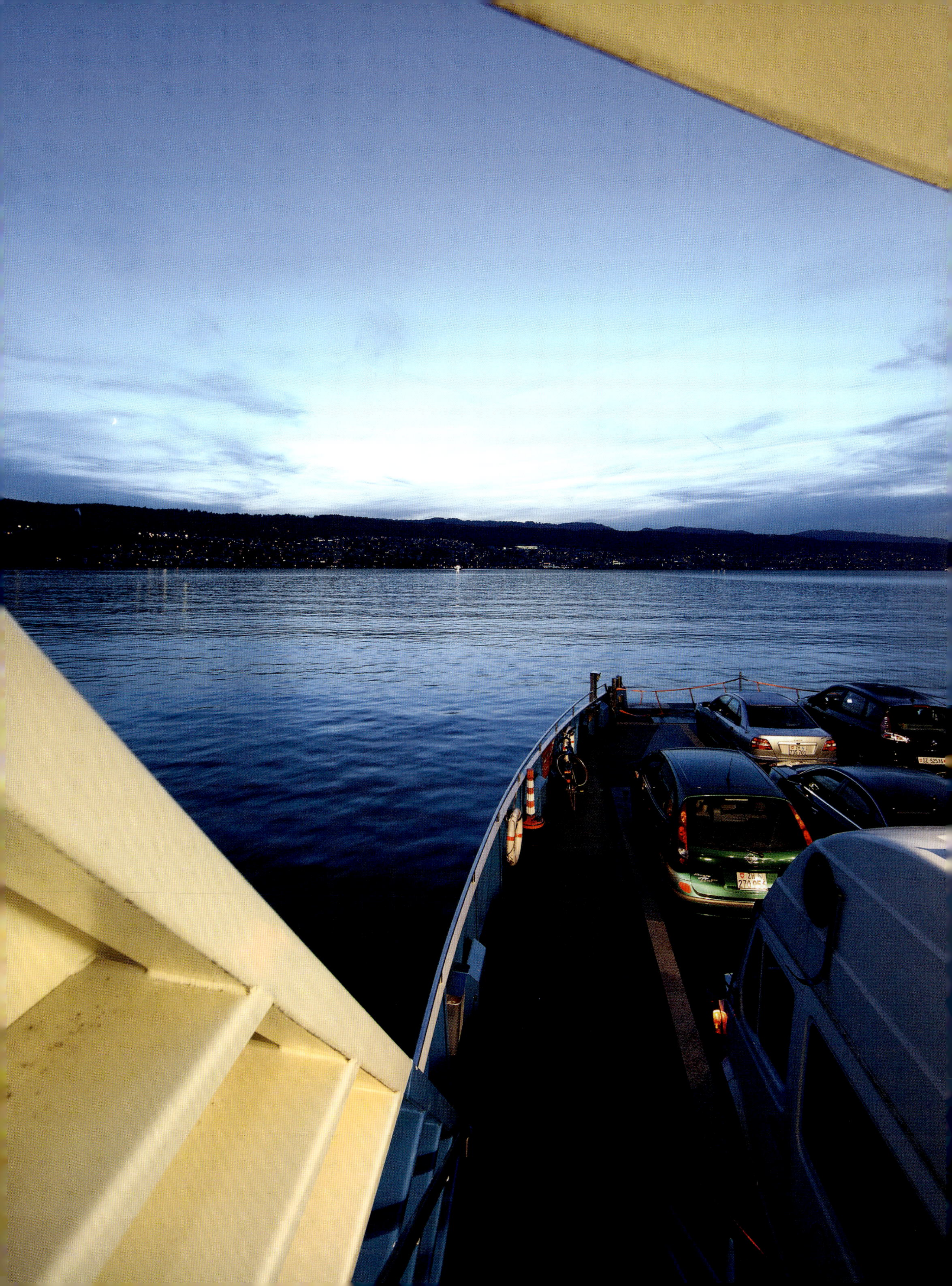

Gemeinsam verfolgen Kanton und Stadt Zürich das Ziel, die Limmat erlebbar zu machen und mehr Nähe zum Wasser zu schaffen. Der Wipkingerpark (links) mit einem breiten Zugang zum Wasser passt in dieses Konzept, ebenso die Badi Unterer Letten und die renaturierten Ufer der Werdinsel.
Mit der Erneuerung der Konzession des Kraftwerks Wettingen konnte der Flussraum des Limmatkanals erweitert werden. Zu diesem Zweck baute man den rechtsseitigen Damm zurück. Das Bild, vom flacheren Damm der Limmat aus in Richtung Oetwil aufgenommen, zeigt: Die Limmat nutzt den bei erhöhtem Wasserstand wieder erreichbaren Raum (rechts).

The Canton and City of Zurich both pursue the goal of giving their residents an experience of the Limmat and creating more access to the river. The Wipkingerpark (left) with its open access to the water fits into this concept, as well as the public swimming baths Unterer Letten and the renatured banks of the Werdinsel.
With the renewal of the Wettingen Power Station's licence, the river basin of the Limmat canal could be enlarged, leading to lowering the dam on the right side. The image, taken from the lower dam of the Limmat towards Oetwil, shows that the Limmat can once again use this extra area when water levels are elevated (right).

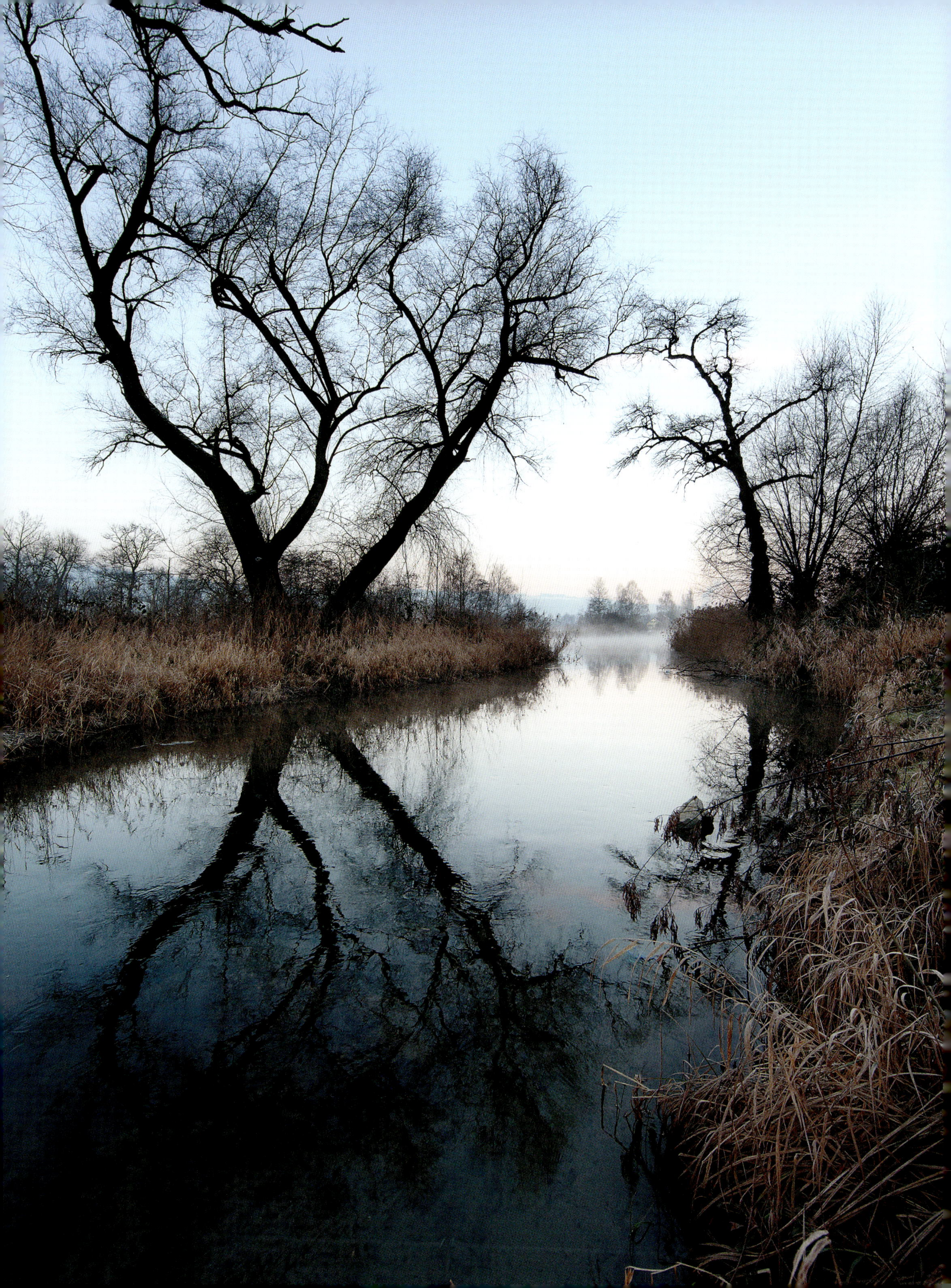

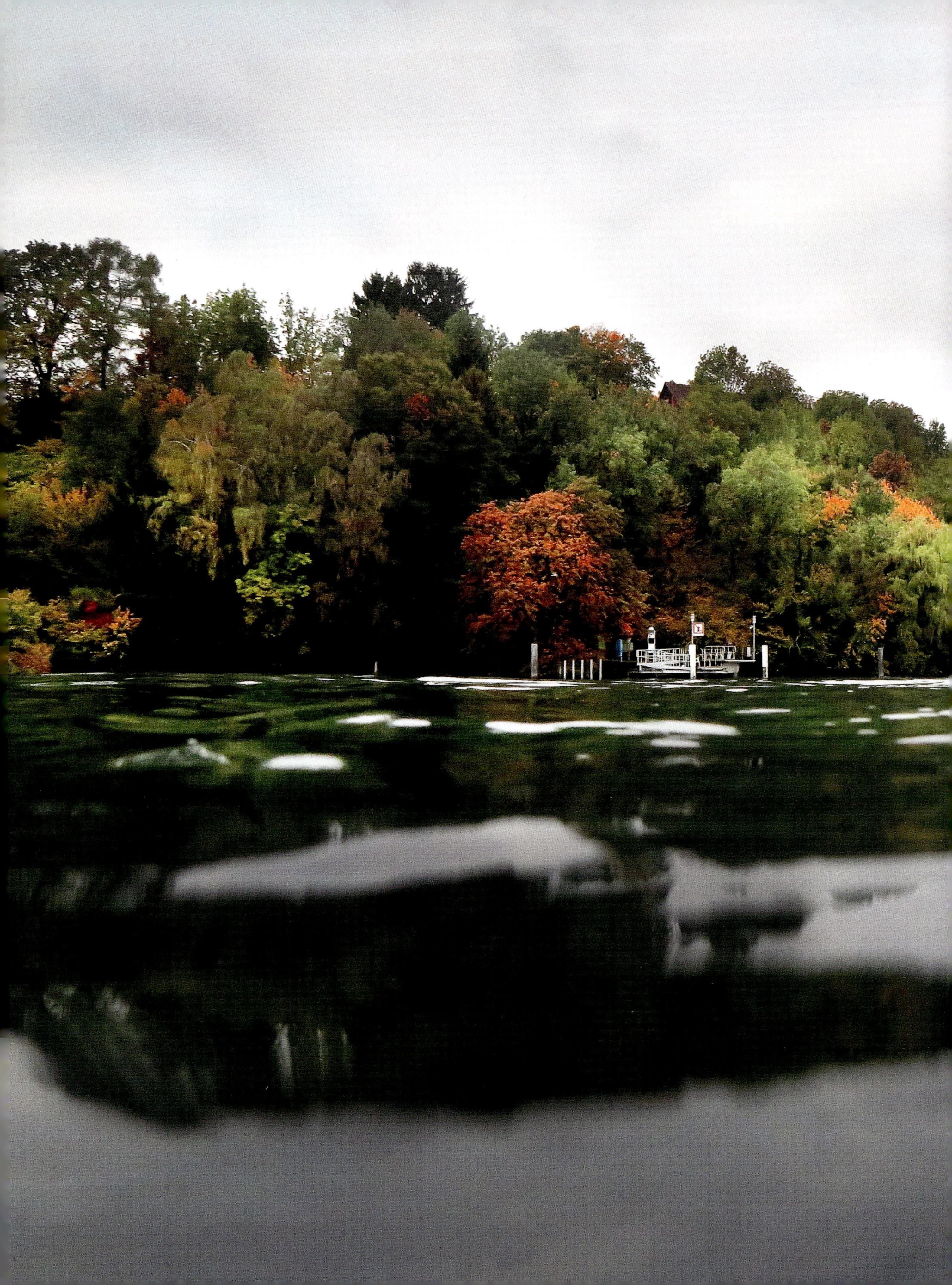

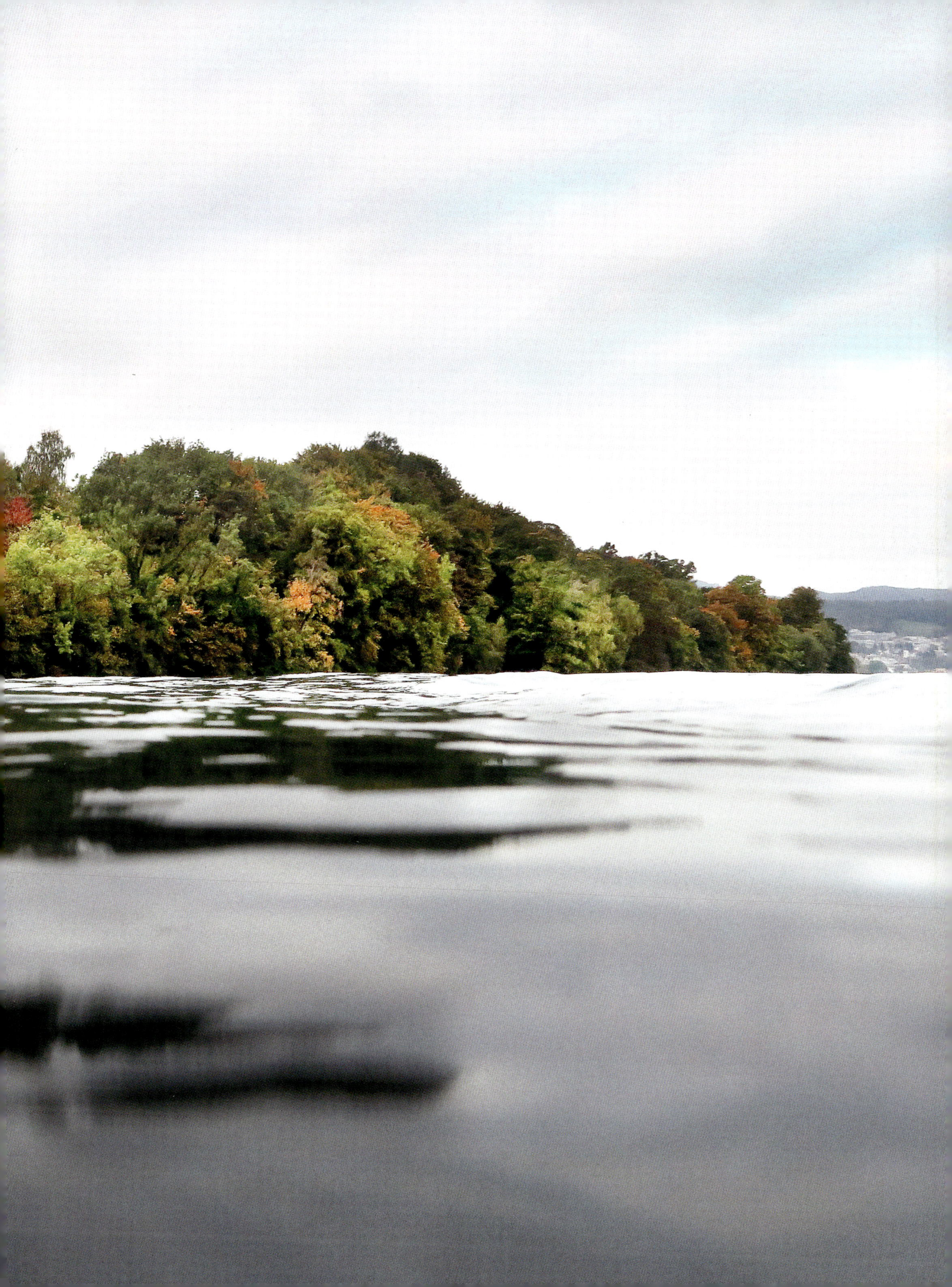

Die Halbinsel Au ist rundum ein Gesamtkunstwerk. Der Wald auf der Seeseite mit dem schlichten Schiffssteg ist nur eines von zahlreichen stimmigen Landschaftselementen (vorhergehende Doppelseite).

Schirmensee und Feldbach, das Gebiet der Gemeinde Hombrechtikon südlich der Seestrasse, ist Teil der zürcherischen Seeuferschutzzone und einer der letzten Flecken im Kanton mit natürlichem Ufer am Zürichsee (links).
Die Ufenau (Kanton Schwyz) ist mit der Kirche Peter und Paul und der Kapelle St. Martin eine Klosterinsel und mit ihren Flachufern und dem weiteren Umfeld Teil eines national bedeutenden Naturschutzgebietes (rechts).

The Au peninsula is altogether a total work of art. The forest on the lakeside with the simple dock for the boats is just one of its many harmonious landscape features (previous double-page).

Schirmensee and Feldbach, the area of Hombrechtikon south of Seestrasse, is part of the Zurich Lakeshore Protection Zone and one of the last spots in the Canton that still has natural shores on Lake Zurich (left).
The Ufenau (Canton of Schwyz) with its Church of Peter and Paul and the Chapel of St. Martin is a monastery island, and its flat banks and broader surroundings are part of a nationally important nature reserve (right).

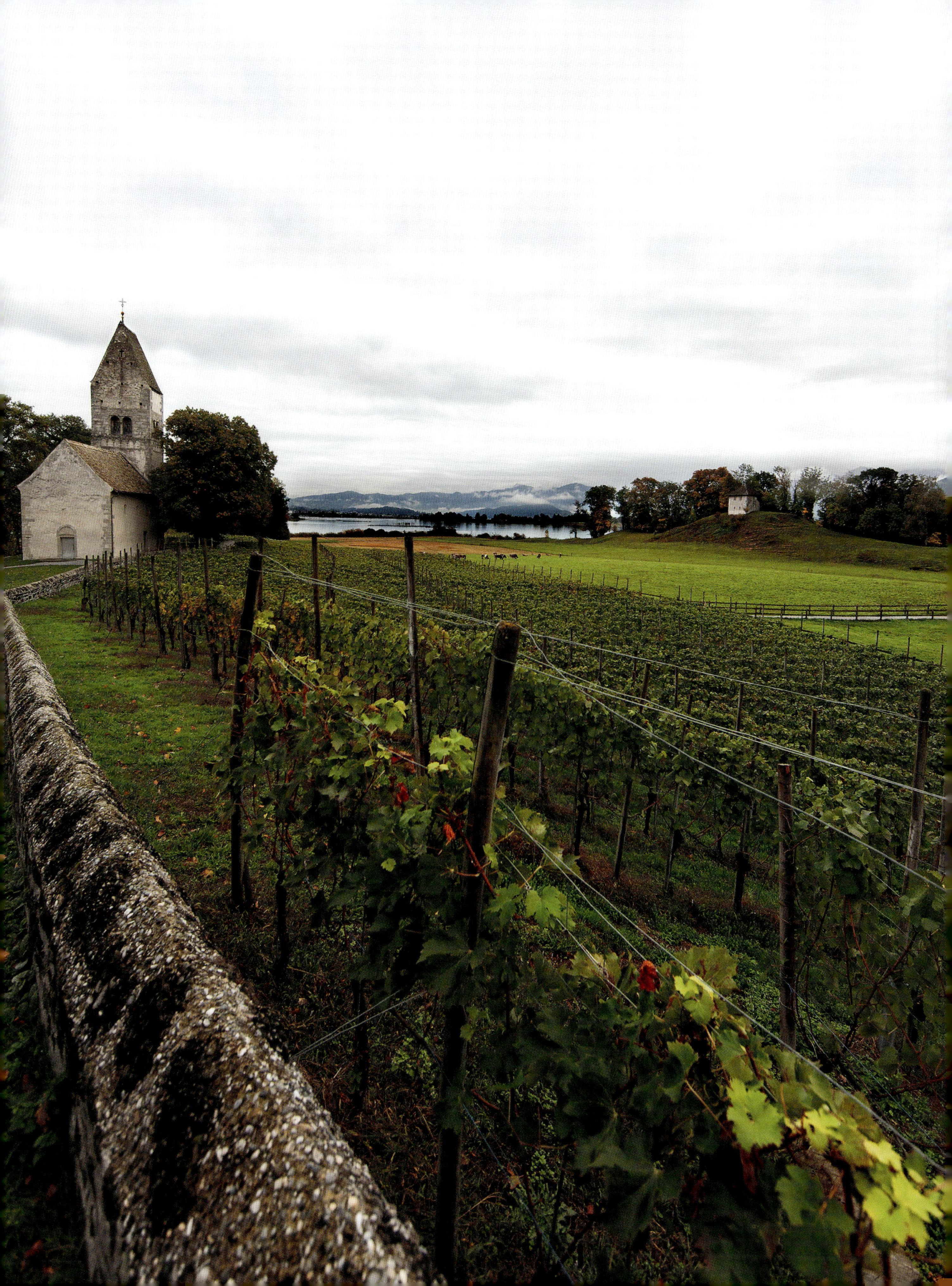

Nicht immer ist die Sihl beim Sihlsprung ein harmloses Gerinne, in dem sich das Ufer spiegelt. Der breite, durch Erosion geweitete Raum des Flussbettes lässt Dynamik ahnen: Bei Hochwasser dominiert hier der reissende Fluss das Bild bis an den unteren Rand.

At the Sihlsprung, the Sihl River isn't always just a harmless channel that reflects the banks. The area of the riverbed widened by erosion hints at the dynamics: At high water, the torrential river dominates the image all the way to the lower edge.

Die biologische Bedeutung der Reusstal-Landschaft ist aussergewöhnlich. Der zürcherische Beitrag hat seinen Schwerpunkt im Reussspitz und der Maschwander Allmend. Sie liegen in dieser Luftaufnahme im Dreieck zwischen der Reuss und der im Auenwald (nahe dem Kieswerk) in die Reuss einmündenden Lorze. Die Aufnahme zeigt, wie geometrische Landwirtschaftsflächen und die ursprünglichen Flachmoore und Nasswiesen in Gewässernähe beieinanderliegen. Der Zugersee ist nebelbedeckt, darüber erheben sich links der Zugerberg und der Rossberg und in der Mitte die Rigi (folgende Doppelseite).

The biological significance of the Reuss Valley landscape is extraordinary. The focal point of Zurich's contribution is the Reussspitz and the Maschwander Allmend (Commons). In this aerial view, they can be located in the triangle between the Reuss River and the alluvial forest (near the gravel plant) where the River Lorze flows in. The photo shows how geometric agricultural land and the original low moors and wet meadows lay side-by-side close to the water. Lake Zug is covered by fog, while the Zugerberg and Rossberg mountains soar to the left and the Rigi stands in the middle (following double-page).

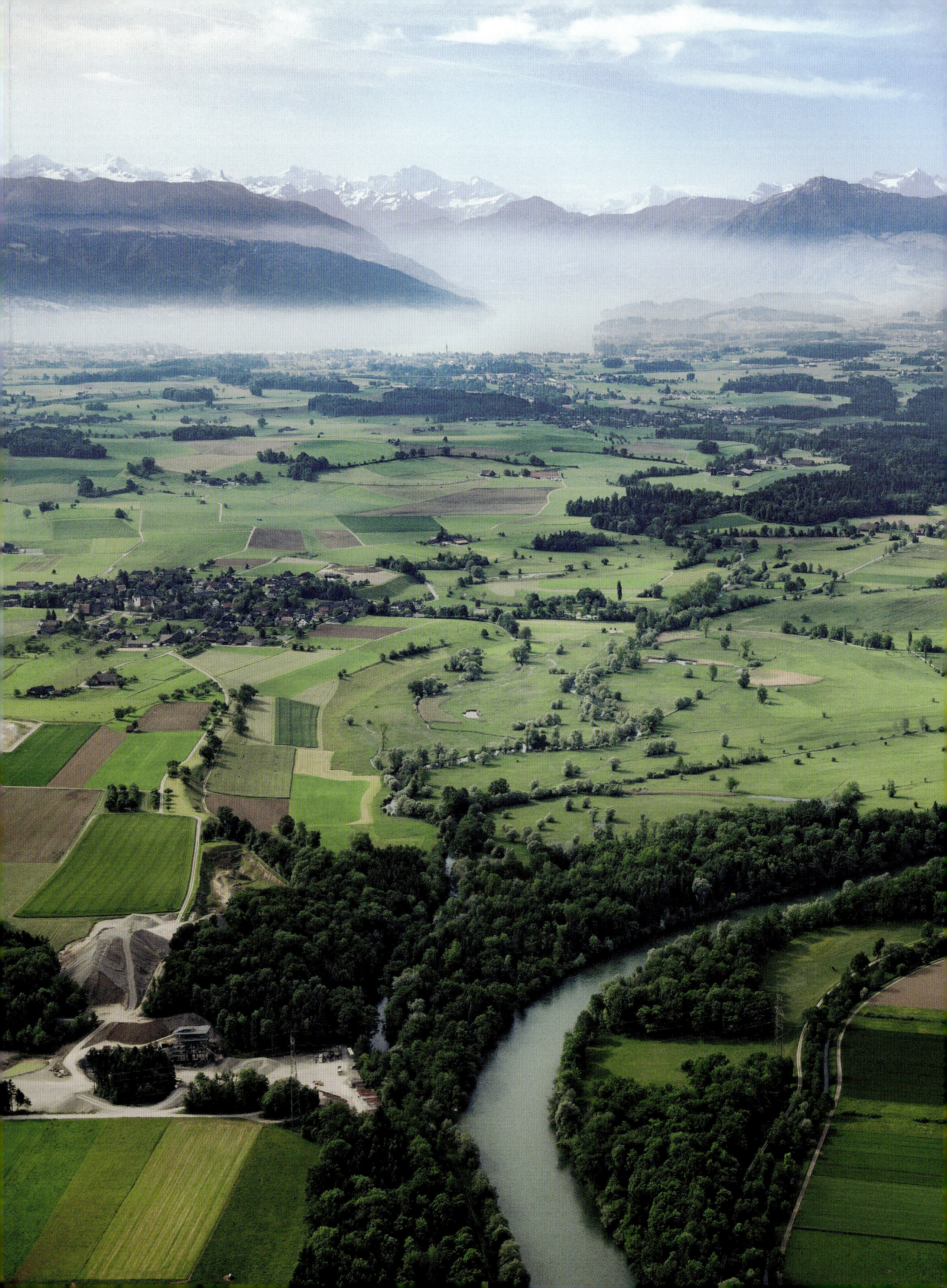

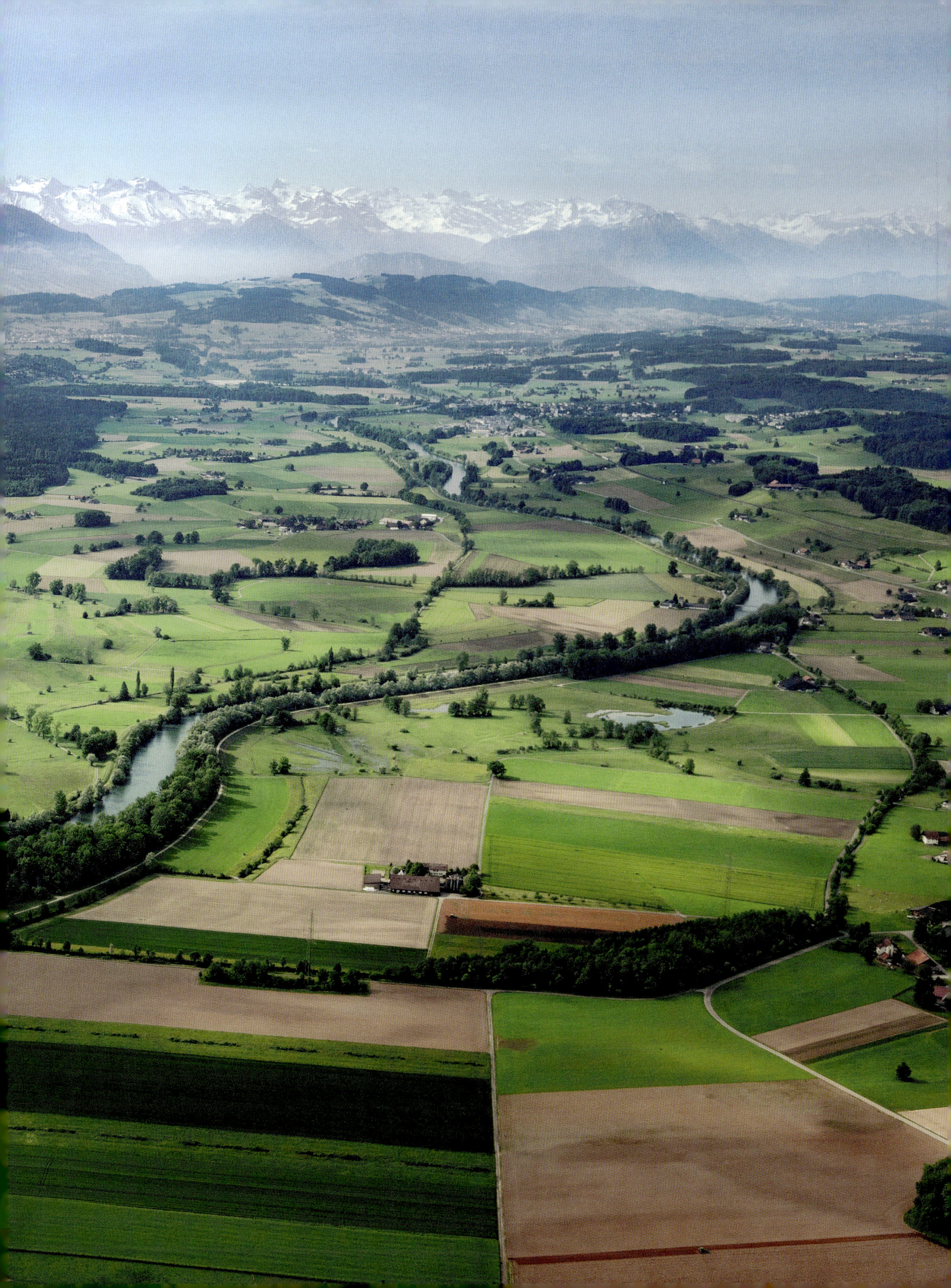

Ein wenig unterhalb des Türlersees eingerichtetes Speicherbecken dient dazu, den Wasserstand des Türlersees und die Wasserführung der Reppisch naturgerecht zu regulieren (links).
Der Türlersee zieht Erholung suchende Menschen an, die Kapazität ist aber begrenzt. Sehr früh konnten hier wichtige Erfahrungen gewonnen werden, wie sich Naturschutz und Erholungsnutzung nebeneinander vertragen (rechts).

A storage basin a little below the Türlersee serves as a nature-oriented regulator for the water levels of the Türlersee and the channel flow conditions of the Reppisch River (left). The Türlersee attracts recreation seekers, however, the capacity is limited. Important experience was gained early on how nature conservation and recreational use could get along side by side (right).

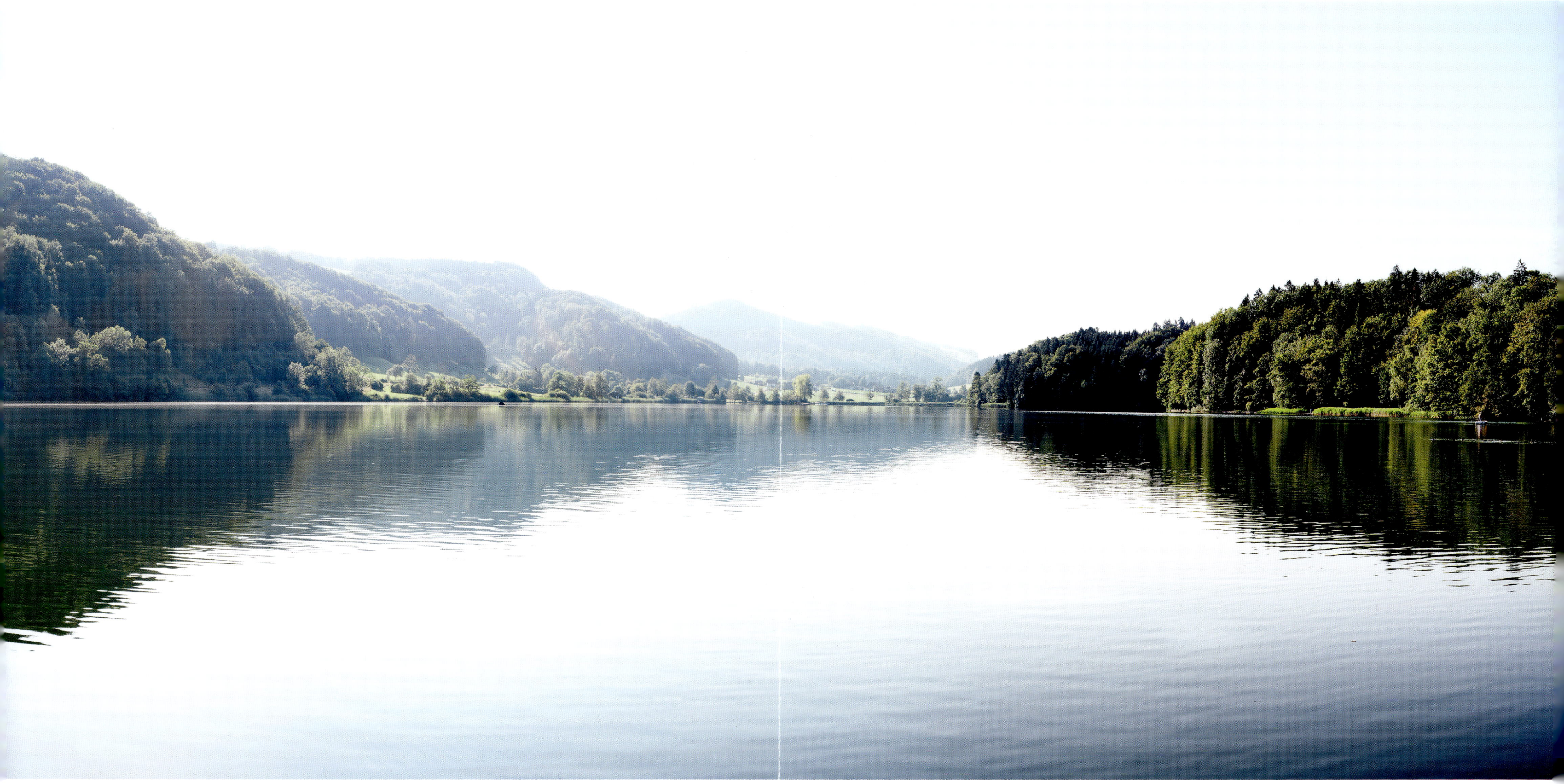

Der Pfäffiker- und der Greifensee haben dank rechtzeitig eingeführten Schutzbestimmungen fast durchwegs unverbaute Ufer bewahren können. Wohl fehlen die Unterwasserwiesen, und das Schilf wächst nicht nur im Wasser, sondern auch als Landschilf, das von Vögeln kaum genutzt wird. Aber im Vergleich zum Zürichsee hat der Ufersaum einen natürlichen Grundcharakter. Ein Abschnitt am Pfäffikersee (links) und ein überlanger Steg am Greifensee, der verhindert, dass beim Ein- und Auswassern von Booten das geschützte Röhricht beschädigt wird (rechts).

Thanks to a timely introduction of protection measures, the Pfäffikersee and the Greifensee could maintain almost entirely unobstructed shores. However, they lack underwater meadows and the reeds grow, not only in the water, but also on land as Chinese giant miscanthus, where birds hardly ever live. But, compared to Lake Zurich, the shoreline has a basic natural character. One section of the Pfäffikersee (left) and an overly long jetty at the Greifensee prevents damage to the reeds from boats entering and exiting the water (right).

Der Türlersee mit seiner landschaftlichen Idylle ist erst nach der Eiszeit entstanden: Der Aeugsterberg war nach Abschmelzen der Gletscher, aus denen er herausragte, nicht mehr stabil, so dass von seinem Nordosthang (in der Bildmitte) in einem einmaligen Abbruch 60 Millionen Kubikmeter Gestein ins Tal stürzten und die Reppisch zum Türlersee aufstauten.

The Türlersee with its scenic idyll arose only after the end of the Ice Age. After the glaciers melted, the Aeugsterberg, which stood out above the glacier, became unstable and 60 million cubic metres of rock from its northeastern slopes (centre) fell into the valley and dammed up the Reppisch River to create the Türlersee.

141

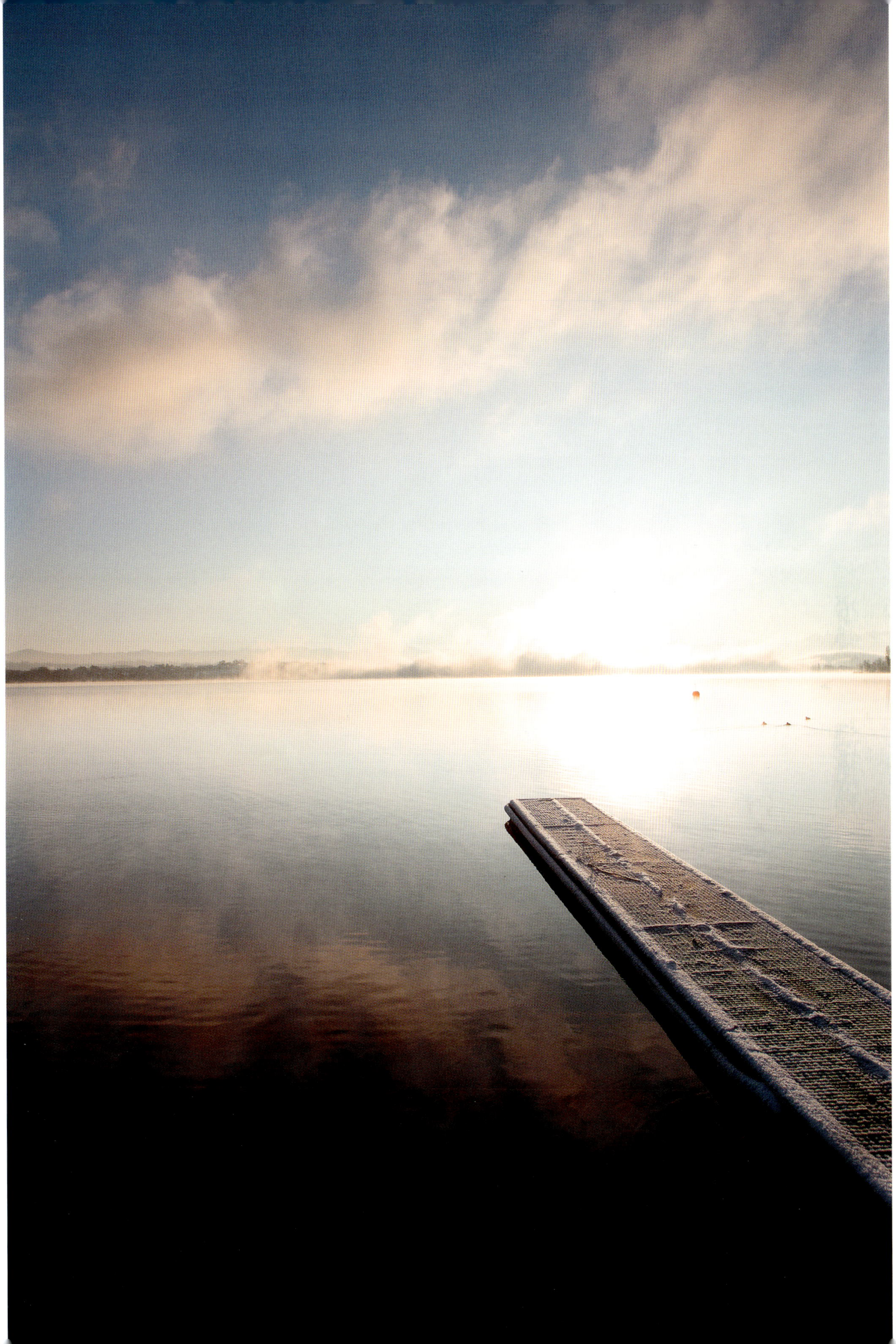

Die Tössscheidi am Fuss des Tössstocks ist der Ort, wo die Vordere und die Hintere Töss zusammenfinden. Bei Niederwasser ist wenig von der geballten Kraft der beiden Bäche zu erkennen, dafür erhalten sie Zuschuss aus einem Brunnen (links).
Entlang der Töss im bewaldeten Leisental konnte abschnittsweise der Längsverbau entfernt und der Töss damit mehr Spielraum zugestanden werden – dies auch zugunsten einer grösseren Vielfalt an Wasserlebewesen (rechts).

The Tössscheidi at the foot of the Tössstock is where the two sources of the Töss River come together (right). During low water, the combined power of the two streams is not obvious, however, here they have the extra benefit of a well (left).
Along the Töss River, in the wooded Leisental, sections of the strong barriers alongside the stream could be removed in order to grant more latitude to the river, which also favours a greater variety of aquatic life (right).

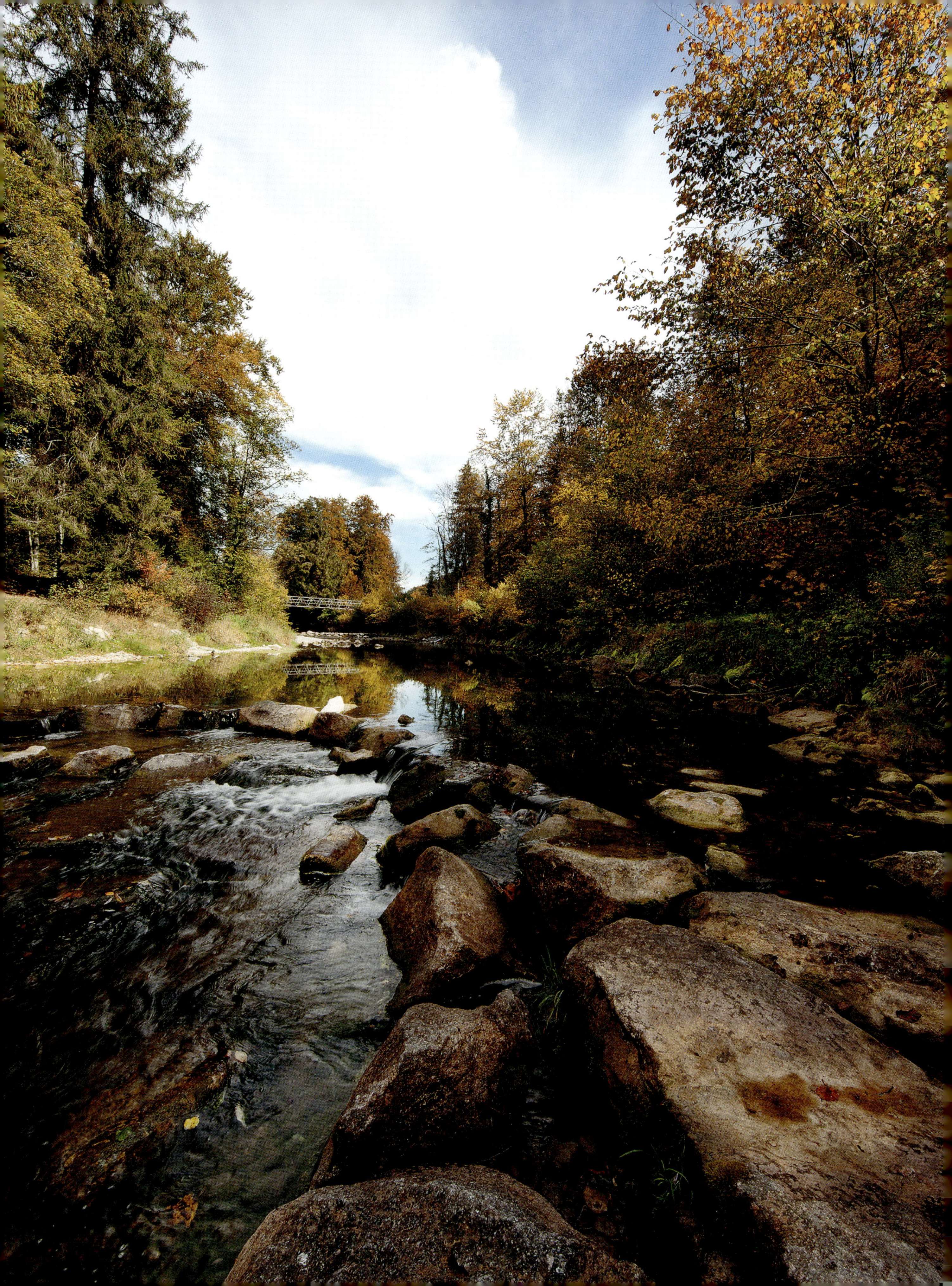

Zwischen dem Raum Frauenfeld-Uesslingen und Gütighausen (rechts, im Vordergrund) verläuft die Thur in einer langen S-Schlaufe. Nach der nahezu geraden Strecke des Thurkanals bricht der Fluss bei einer sachten Linkskurve durch das rechtsseitige Ufer (links, vom Thurgauer Ufer aus gesehen). Bis um die Jahrtausendwende war die Thur auf beiden Seiten mit Blocksteinen hart verbaut. Aus der Einsicht heraus, dass eine möglichst freie Dynamik auch den Hochwasserschutz verbessert, entfernte man die Blocksteine zugunsten von weiträumig gesicherten Leitlinien. Die Thur hat in harter Arbeit diese Chance genutzt und eine vielfältige, strukturreiche neue Flusslandschaft geschaffen. Der Flussregenpfeifer hat seit über 100 Jahren wieder auf den Kiesbänken gebrütet und seine Jungen aufgezogen.

In the area between Frauenfeld-Uesslingen and Gütighausen (right, in the foreground), the Thur River runs in a long S-curve. After the almost straight stretch of the Thur Canal, along a gentle left curve, the river breaks through the right side of the bank (left, as seen from the Thurgau shore). Until the turn of the millennium, the Thur was lined on both sides with massive stone blocks. With the insight that the best possible dynamic also improved flood control, the stone blocks were removed in favour of broad, secured guard lines. The river seized this opportunity and created, with much hard work, a diverse, structurally rich, new river landscape. For more than 100 years now, the river plover (little ringed plover) has bred and reared their young on the gravel banks.

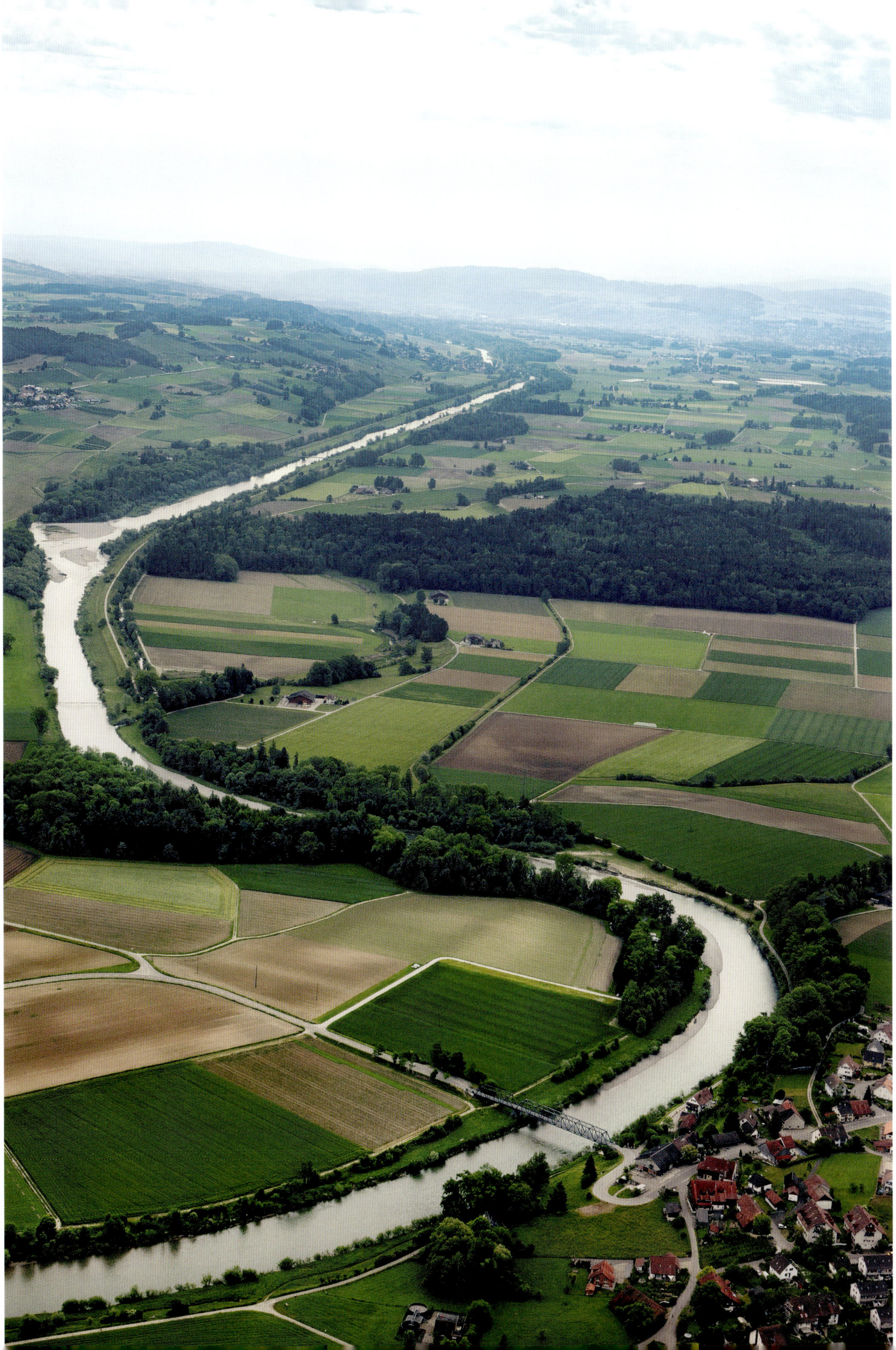

In der Mäanderlandschaft bei Gütighausen wurden in einzelnen Aussenkurven der Thur massive, mit Weiden verankerte Querriegel – sogenannte Buhnen – eingebaut. Ihr Effekt ist ein doppelter: Die Hauptströmung wurde in die Flussmitte gedrängt, und zwischen den Buhnen entstand neues Wasserleben (links).

Eine Schwarzpappel und eine Birke markieren den Thurspitz, die Mündung der Thur in den Rhein. Die Renaturierungen an beiden Flüssen und in den sie begleitenden Auenlandschaften haben die Bedeutung der dynamischen Auenwälder als natürlicher Hochwasserschutz erkennen lassen (rechts).

Der Rhein bei Eglisau, drei Kilometer unterhalb der markanten Eisenbahnbrücke gestaut, zeigt sich als ruhiger Fluss mit Würde und Gelassenheit (folgende Doppelseite).

In the meandering landscape of Gütighausen, some massive jetties were built, using crossbars anchored with willows, into some individual outer curves of the Thur. Their effect is twofold: The mainstream was pushed into the middle of the river and new aquatic life was created between the jetties (left).

A black poplar and a birch tree mark the Thurspitz, where the Thur flows into the Rhine. The renaturation projects on both rivers and their accompanying wet meadow landscapes have revealed the importance of dynamic wet forests as natural flood protection (right).

The Rhine near Eglisau, dammed three kilometres below the distinctive railway bridge, appears as a calm river with dignity and serenity (following double-page).

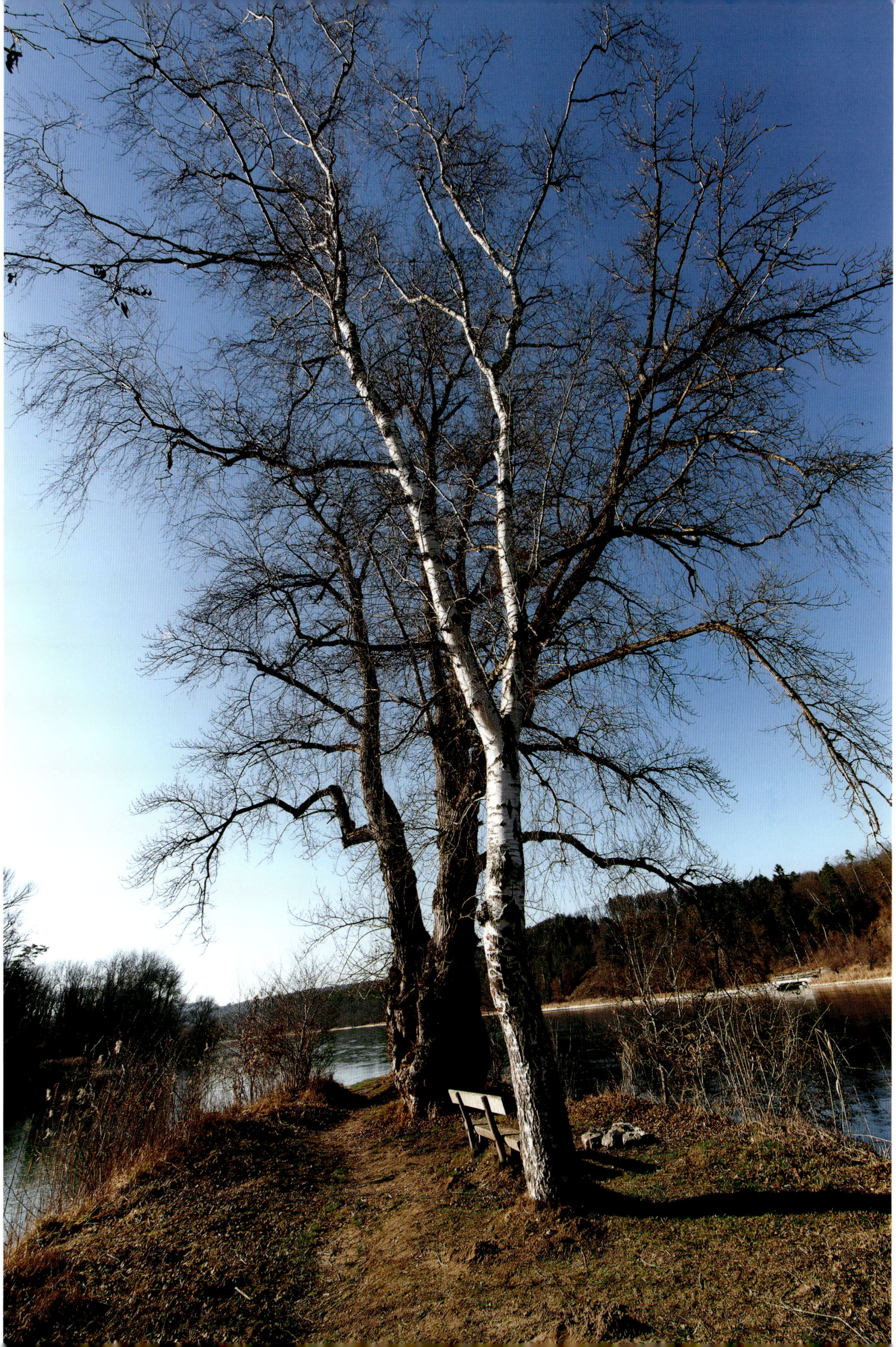

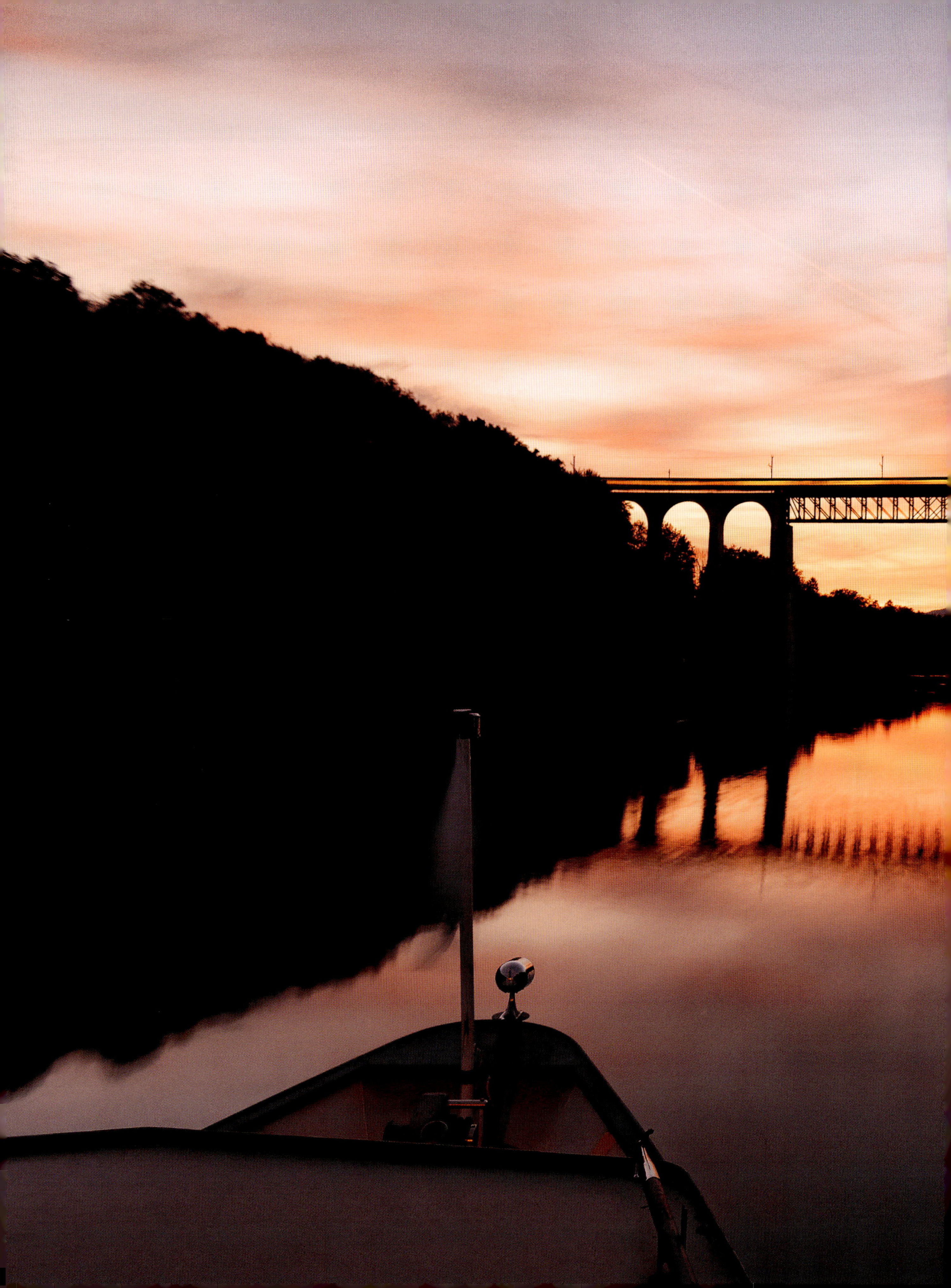

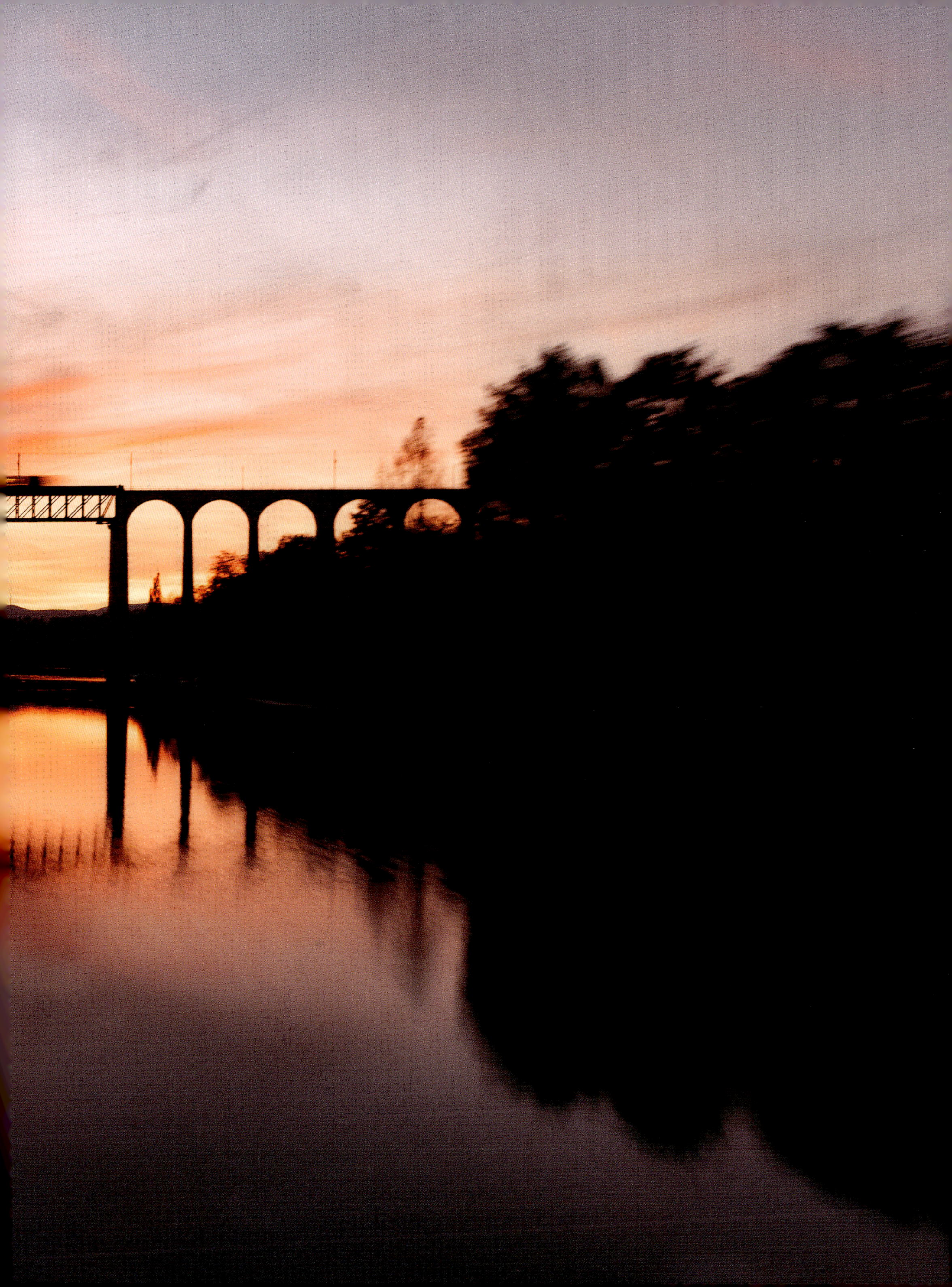

Die Seilfähre über den Rhein bei Ellikon wurde 1905 eingerichtet, nachdem man das Übersetzen von Personen mit Weidlingen wegen der wechselnden Strömungsverhältnisse als zu gefährlich erachtet hatte. Die Fähre rund zwei Kilometer oberhalb der Thurmündung bietet ein besonderes Flusserlebnis. Führt die Thur unvermittelt Hochwasser, staut dies den Rhein sehr rasch auf und erfordert vom Fährmann angepasstes Steuern oder auch Rudern (links).
Blick vom landschaftlich vielfältigen Irchel Richtung Rüdlingen. Der auf beiden Flussseiten von natürlichen Ufern gesäumte Abschnitt des Rheins ist eine Rarität unter den grösseren Flüssen der Schweiz. Für schwimmend querende Wildtiere sind Abschnitte dieser Art Schlüsselstellen (rechts).

The cable ferry across the Rhine at Ellikon was set up in 1905 after it was considered to be too dangerous to ferry people using a Weidling (punt) because of the changeable current conditions. The ferry, approximately two kilometres upstream of the confluence with the Thur, offers a special river experience. During a sudden flood of the Thur, the Rhine dams up very quickly and requires the ferryman to adjust his piloting or even switch to rowing (left).
View from the diverse landscapes of the Irchel in the direction of Rüdlingen. The sections of natural banks lined up on both sides of the Rhine are a rarity amongst the major rivers of Switzerland. For wildlife floating across, sections of this kind are key points (right).

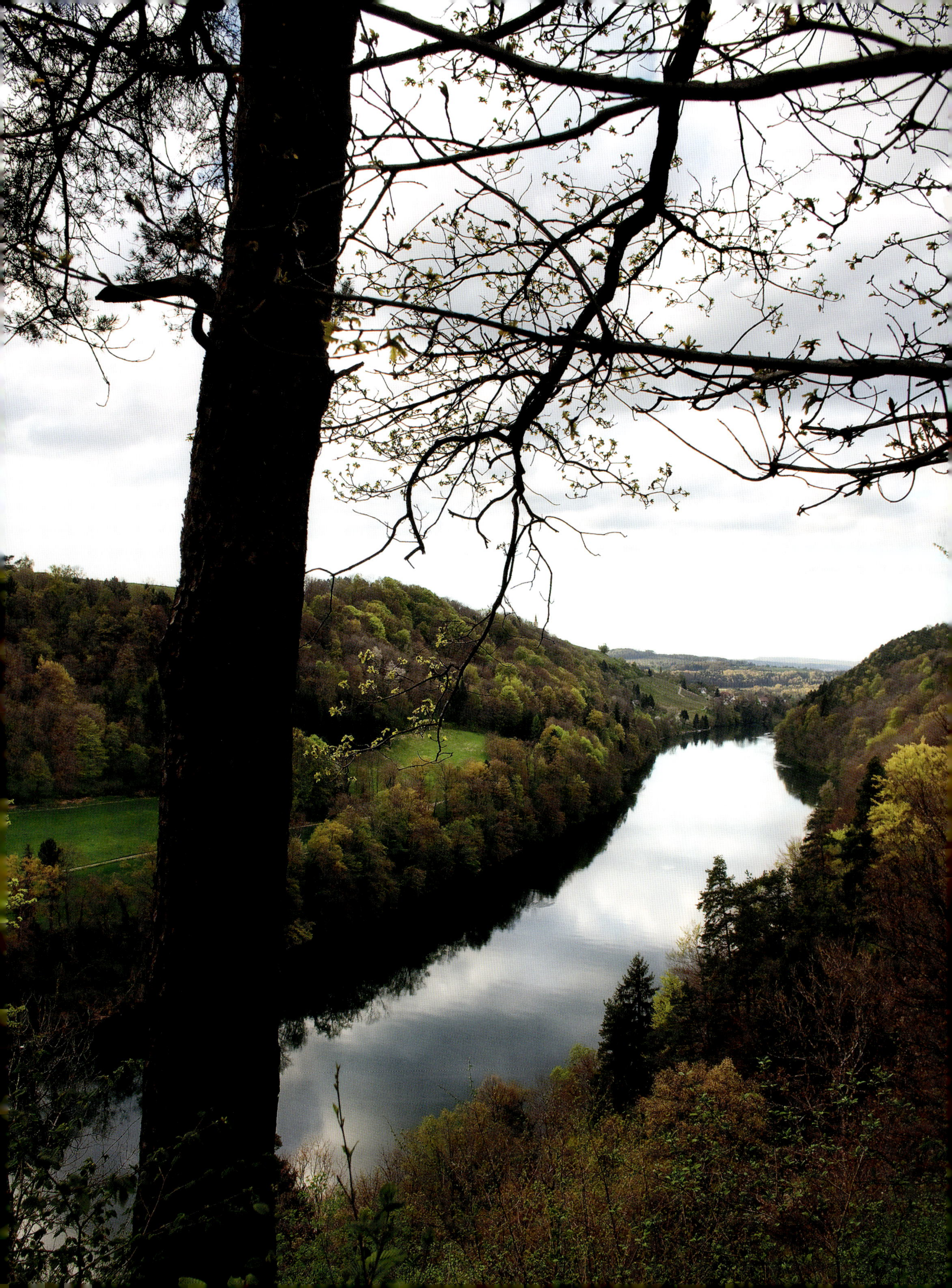

Im Abschnitt zwischen Rüdlingen und dem Thurspitz liegen der Alte Rhein und der kanalisierte Rhein nebeneinander. Lücken im trennenden Damm bereichern die Dynamik und das Bild der Landschaft. Das Potenzial für Renaturierungen am hier noch kaum angetasteten Rheinkanal ist aber noch nicht ausgeschöpft.

In the section between Rüdlingen and Thurspitz, the Old Rhine and the channeled Rhine are parallel to each other. Gaps in the separating dam enrich the dynamics and the image of the landscape. The potential for renaturation projects here on the almost untouched Rhine Canal has not yet been exhausted.

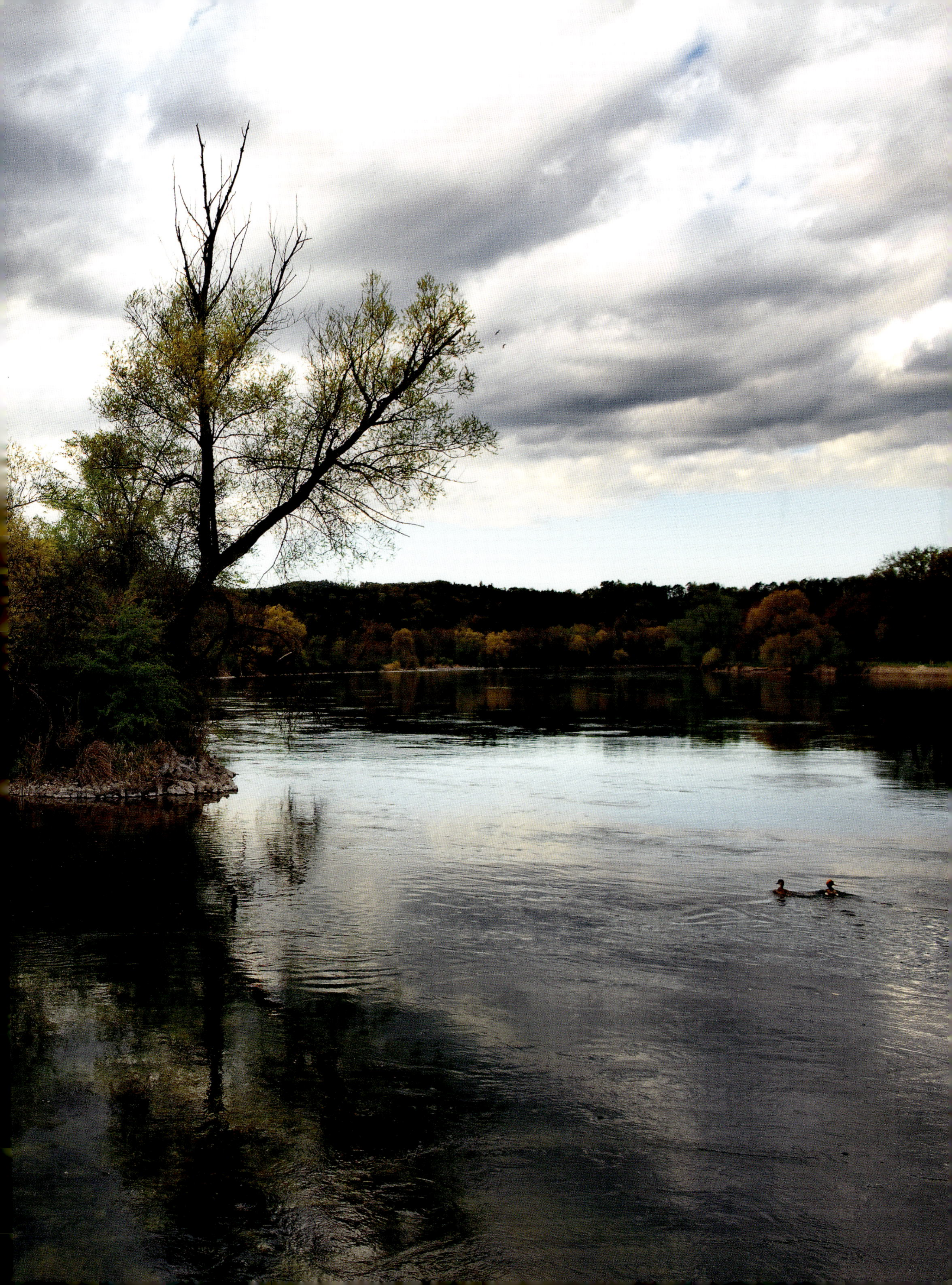

Landschaften der Auen und Moore

Water Meadows and Moor Landscapes

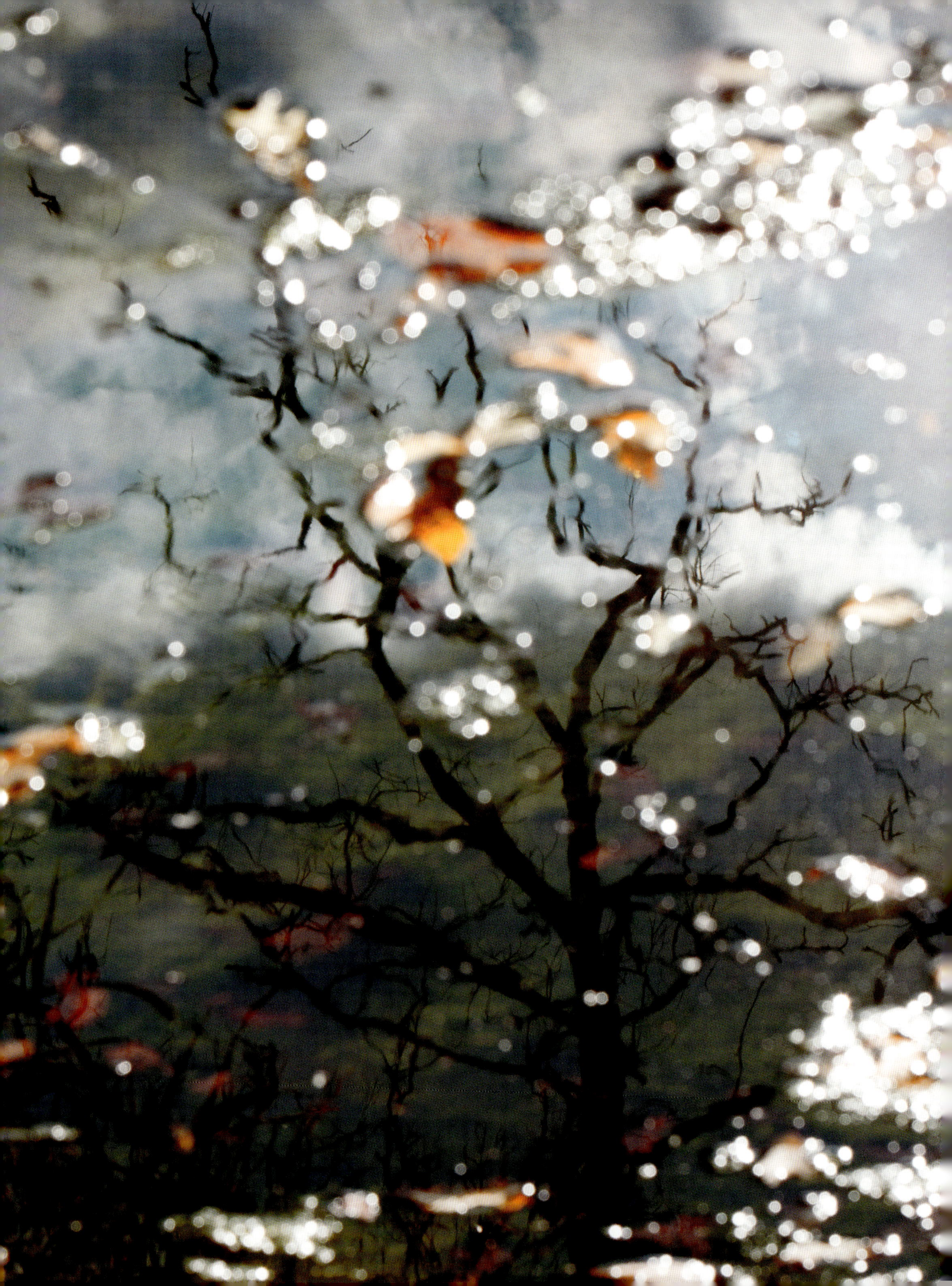

«Nach dem Rückzug der Gletscher und Verlanden der Gletscherrandseen folgten Moore.»

'After the retreat of the glaciers and the silting up of the lakes at the edge of the glaciers, moors followed.'

Ein Uferbaum? Wasser? Blätter? Mystisch verzauberte Vielfalt?

A tree on a river bank? Water? Leaves? Mysterious enchanted diversity?

Auenwälder, Auen und Flussauen sind faszinierende Uferlandschaften, die sich in ihrem Erscheinungsbild im Wechsel des Wasserstandes verändern. Im 19. Jahrhundert hatten die Überschwemmungen von Flüssen und Bächen dazu geführt, dass man die grösseren Flüsse zwischen massiven Hochwasserdämmen in ein sicheres Flussbett zwang. Bis anhin wechselfeuchte Auenwälder, die unter der natürlichen Flussdynamik durch Hochwasser kurzzeitig überflutet und dabei auch gedüngt wurden, verloren in der Folge den Charakter von Auenwäldern.[1]

Mit den aktuellen Revitalisierungen wie dem Thurauen-Projekt wurde der Hochwasserschutz auf die ufernahen Siedlungen konzentriert und der zum Schutz der Wälder eingerichtete harte Längsverbau entfernt. Künftige Hochwasser dürften den früheren Auencharakter des Waldes und seine Funktion als Rückhaltebecken wieder fördern. Das begünstigt raschwüchsige Weichhölzer wie Weiden, Pappeln und Grauerlen, die in ihrer Stammesgeschichte darauf selektiert wurden, mit Überflutungen zurechtzukommen. In der Forstwirtschaft sind diese Arten von geringem Wert. Vorzugsweise Weiden, Espen und Pappeln werden indessen durch den Biber genutzt. Besonders in der kalten Jahreszeit hat er es auf die nährstoffreiche Rinde der obersten Zweige dieser Bäume und Sträucher abgesehen. Als Nicht-Kletterer hat er mit seinen meisselartigen und lebenslang nachwachsenden Nagezähnen das «Mundwerk» zum Fällen von Bäumen mitbekommen. Mit seinem rundlichen Körper mitsamt Pelz und Fett hätte der Schwerarbeiter allerdings ein Überhitzungsproblem, wenn nicht das Leben im Wasser, der flache, unbehaarte Schwanz und das nächtliche Arbeiten die nötige Kühlung brächten. Im weiteren Raum der Thurlandschaft haben sich Biber vor allem in ruhigen Gewässern mit weichen Ufern, kleineren Nebenflüssen, Binnenkanälen, Waldweihern und stillen Buchten angesiedelt. Der Biber war im 19. Jahrhundert in der Schweiz ausgerottet worden – mitbedingt durch die eingangs

Alluvial forests, water meadows and river floodplains are fascinating riverside landscapes that change their appearance in accordance with the fluctuations in water levels. In the 19th century, the solution to floods caused by overflowing rivers and streams was to force the larger rivers between massive high-water dams with a secure riverbed as a solution. As a result of this intervention, the wet-dry forests, which are flooded short-term by the natural river dynamics and thus fertilised, have lost their character as alluvial forests.[1]

With the current revitalisations, such as the Thurauen Project, to reinstall the floodplains of the Thur River in the Canton of Zurich, flood protection using dams is being concentrated on settlements near riverbanks and the strong barriers protecting forests alongside the stream are being removed. Thus, future floods may once again promote the earlier meadow character of the forest and its function as a storage basin. This favours fast-growing soft woods, such as willow, poplar and grey alder, which were selected to help manage flooding because of their biological evolution. In forestry, these types are considered to have little economic value. Beavers primarily use willow, aspen and poplar trees for building homes and dams. Especially in the cold seasons, beavers zero in on the nutritionally rich rind of the uppermost branches of these trees and shrubs. As a non-climber, the beaver evolved chisel-like teeth to fell trees and a mouth full of gnawing teeth that continue to grow throughout his lifetime. However, his round body, including the pelt and fat, causes an overheating problem for this hard worker if he is out of the water too long, luckily, the flat, hairless tail and night-time work provide the required cooling. In the broader space of the Thur River landscape, beavers have mainly settled in quiet waters with soft banks, smaller tributaries, inland canals, forest ponds and quiet coves. The beaver became extinct in the 19th century in Switzerland – caused by the activi-

erwähnten Korrekturen von Fliessgewässern. Verfolgt wurde er wegen seines dichten Fells und als geschätzte Fastenspeise – denn aufgrund des Lebens im Wasser und des schuppigen Schwanzes hatten ihn katholische Würdenträger den Fischen zugeordnet. Seit 1962 sind Biber bundesrechtlich geschützt, gestützt auf das Bundesgesetz über die Jagd und den Schutz wildlebender Säugetiere und Vögel.[2] Sie wurden erfolgreich wiederangesiedelt und tragen mit den erreichten Beständen dazu bei, die landschaftliche Strukturvielfalt und Biodiversität zu fördern.

Von Auen sind kleinere nasse Wälder mit vergleichsweise stabilem hohem Grundwasserstand zu unterscheiden, wie zum Beispiel stockende Schwarzerlen oder Birken in einem verlandenden Flussaltlauf oder im Bereich von Mooren, wie im Umfeld des Chatzensees. Sie haben nicht den unberechenbaren Charakter der Auen und gehören in den Kreis der oft sehr sauren Bruchwälder. Der durch eine von Bibern verursachte Stauung entstandene «Biberwald» bei Marthalen zeigt sich in diesem Sinne eher als angehender Bruchwald und weniger als Aue, die nach kurzen Nassphasen wieder trocknet.

In den Moorlandschaften ist die Dynamik der Natur berechenbar. Mit ihrer über mehrere Jahrhunderte dauernden Entwicklungsgeschichte lassen sie sich auch nicht annähernd so leicht wiederherstellen wie Auen.[3] Ausserdem sind Moore mit dem Handicap belastet, dass die wirtschaftliche Nutzung mit ihrer Zerstörung verbunden ist. Das Seleger Moor im Knonauer Amt, in dem mit moortauglichen Pflanzen, vor allem Rhododendren und Azaleen, eine gärtnerische Parklandschaft gestaltet wurde, ist diesbezüglich eine Ausnahme, weil der gewachsene Torfboden am Ort verbleibt. Moore wurden landesweit entwässert, um Weideland zu gewinnen und um den trocknenden Torf als Brennmaterial oder im Gartenbau verwenden zu können. Vor allem während der beiden Weltkriege im letzten Jahrhundert, als Brennholz rar wurde, stach man auch in bis dahin weitgehend intakten Hochmooren Torf, zum Teil auf Anweisung der Behörden. Der wichtige strenge gesetzliche Schutz der Moore ist in der Schweiz verbunden mit der eidgenössischen «Rothenthurm-Initiative», die am 6. Dezember 1987 vom Stimmvolk überraschend angenommen wurde. Auslöser war ein von der Armee geplanter Waffenplatz, den die lokale Bevölkerung intensiv bekämpfte. Seitens des Naturschutzes wies man auf den weich federnden und extrem trittempfindlichen Hochmoorboden hin und auf die prächtige noch erhaltene offene Hochebene, die nach dem Stau des Sihlsees und damit dem Verlust jenes noch grösseren nahen Moores nicht auch noch geopfert werden darf. Vielleicht wäre bei einem fachübergreifenden Beginn der aufwendigen Planung des Waffenplatzes die mi-

ties of the above-mentioned 'corrections' to flowing water. The beaver was also hunted for his thick fur and as a treasured fasting food; based on their life in the water and scaly tails, Roman Catholic authorities had them classified as fish. Since 1962, beavers are federally protected, supported by the federal law on hunting and the protection of wild living mammals and birds.[2] They were successfully reintroduced to Switzerland in 1956 by Maurice Blanchet and with their newly achieved protected status, they now contribute to structural diversity in the landscape and promote bio-diversity.

Small alluvial forests with comparatively stable high groundwater levels should be differentiated from meadows, for example, standing black alder or birch in a silted-up old river course or in the area of moors, as in the surroundings of the Katzenseen in Zurich. These alluvial forests do not have the unpredictable character of meadows and belong instead to the category of carrs, which are often very acidic. In this sense, the forest in Marthalen, brought into being by beaver dams, is more of a prospective carr and less a meadow, as meadows soon dry out again after a short wet phase.

The dynamics of nature are more predictable in a moor landscape. With its development history lasting over several centuries, it does not allow reestablishment as easily as meadows.[3] More important, moors are burdened with the handicap that their economic benefit is connected with their destruction. The Seleger Moor in the District of Knonau, in which a garden-like park landscape has been created with suitable plants for moors, mainly rhododendron and azaleas, is an exception in this regard, because the existing peat floor remains in place. Nationwide, moors are being drained in order to gain pastureland, to use dried peat as fuel or for use in gardening. Some severe destruction took place during the two World Wars in the last century; as firewood became rare, people dug up the high moor peat, in part, on the recommendation of the authorities. Otherwise, the moors were extensively intact up to that point. In Switzerland, the strict legal protection of moors is connected with the Federal Rothenthurm Initiative that was surprisingly accepted by the voting public on 6 December 1987. The trigger was a military training area planned by the army, which the local population was fighting intensively. The nature protection supporters pointed out that the soft springy high moor ground was extremely sensitive to being stepped on and that the grand open high plateau, still preserved, should not be allowed to be sacrificed – as had a still larger nearby moor after the dam was built on Sihl Lake. Perhaps an interdisciplinary start to the complex planning needed for a military training

litärische Untauglichkeit eines Hochmoores frühzeitig erkannt worden.

Moore gehören zu den Feuchtgebieten und entstanden beispielsweise im Uferbereich verlandender Seen oder Weiher oder über dem wasserundurchlässigen Grundmoränen-Lehm. Erforderlich ist auch ein feucht-kühles Klima, bei dem mehr Wasser zurückgehalten wird, als durch Verdunstung und Abfluss verloren geht. Im anhaltend wassergesättigten Milieu und dem damit verbundenen Luftabschluss werden abgestorbene Pflanzen nicht vollständig zu Humus, sondern nur teilweise zu Torf abgebaut (wie in einem Bruchwald). Die so entstandenen Flachmoore sind artenreich und vielfältig je nach dem Nährstoffgehalt des die Pflanzen speisenden Grundwassers. Ein Hochmoor ist eine völlig neue Lebensgemeinschaft. Es entsteht, wenn unter dem Wirken von Torfmoosen (Sphagnum-Arten) die Torfschicht in die Höhe und über den Einflussbereich des Grundwassers hinauswächst. Die sich nach oben streckenden Torfmoose können in ihrem Zellsystem das 10- bis 20-fache ihres Volumens an Regenwasser aufnehmen. Der jährliche Zuwachs von zunächst wenigen Zentimetern wird in der Folge durch die Wasserlast auf höchstens wenige Millimeter gepresst. Die wenigen bis um drei Meter hohen, noch erhaltenen Hochmoorparzellen sind neben der naturkundlichen auch von kultureller Bedeutung. Mit den in verschiedenen Schichten eingelagerten Blütenpollen sind sie wertvolle Archive für die Erforschung der nacheiszeitlichen Landschaftsgeschichte.[4] Blütenpflanzen, die sich auf dem Moos-Polster des Hochmoors ansiedeln, müssen an die extrem nährstoffarmen Verhältnisse angepasst sein. Der Sonnentau kann kleine Insekten, die sich von klebrigen Blättern nicht mehr lösen können, ohne den Chitin-Panzer verdauen. Hochmoore sind nach wie vor bedroht durch (illegale) Entwässerung wie auch wegen ihrer hohen Sensibilität gegenüber Luftschadstoffen.

area would have recognised earlier that a high moor was unsuitable for military use.

Moors belong to the category of wetlands and originate, for example, in the banks of silted lakes or ponds or in the silt above a water impermeable ground moraine. A cool damp climate is also required, in which more water will be retained than is lost through evaporation and drainage. In the continuously water-saturated environment and the resulting absence of air, the dead plants will not turn completely into humus, rather it will only be partially broken down into peat (as in a carr). A fenland generated from this will have a rich diversity of species, depending on the nutritional content of the plant feeding ground water. A raised bog emerges with a completely new symbiotic community when the peat layer grows taller and above the influence zone of the ground water due to the effects of peat moss (sphagnum types). As the peat moss stretches upwards, their cell system can take up to 10 to 20 times its volume of rainwater. The annual growth from an initial few centimetres will be pressed down a few millimetres, at most, as a result of the weight of the water. The few still preserved high moor parcels of up to about three metres high, are in addition to their natural history, also of cultural importance. The various layers of embedded flower pollen are a valuable archive for research into post-Ice Age landscape history.[4] Flowering plants that settle on the moss cushion of a high moor must adjust to extreme nutrient-poor conditions. The sundew plant (Drosera) has evolved to be able to digest small insects without a chitin shell, which cannot detach themselves from the sticky leaves. Today, high moors are still threatened by illegal drainage and now, in addition, by their high sensitivity to air pollution.

Im Torfriet nordwestlich des Pfäffikersees haben sich auf früher abgetorften Moorflächen nach Aufgabe der Nutzung vor allem Waldföhren breitgemacht, die stellenweise aufgelichtet wurden. In weniger trockenen Teilen wie am Rande des alten Torfstichweihers fördern Seggen den Verlandungsprozess. Birken markieren den Standort eines ehemaligen Bruchwaldes (siehe auch folgende Seite).

In Torfriet, a high moor northwest of the Pfäffikersee, where peat cutting was abandoned after peat went out of use as fuel, mainly Scots pines have spread out, which were thinned out here and there. In less dry parts, such as the edge of a previously dug peat pond, sedges are promoting the silting process. Birch trees mark the location of a former forest mire (see also the following page).

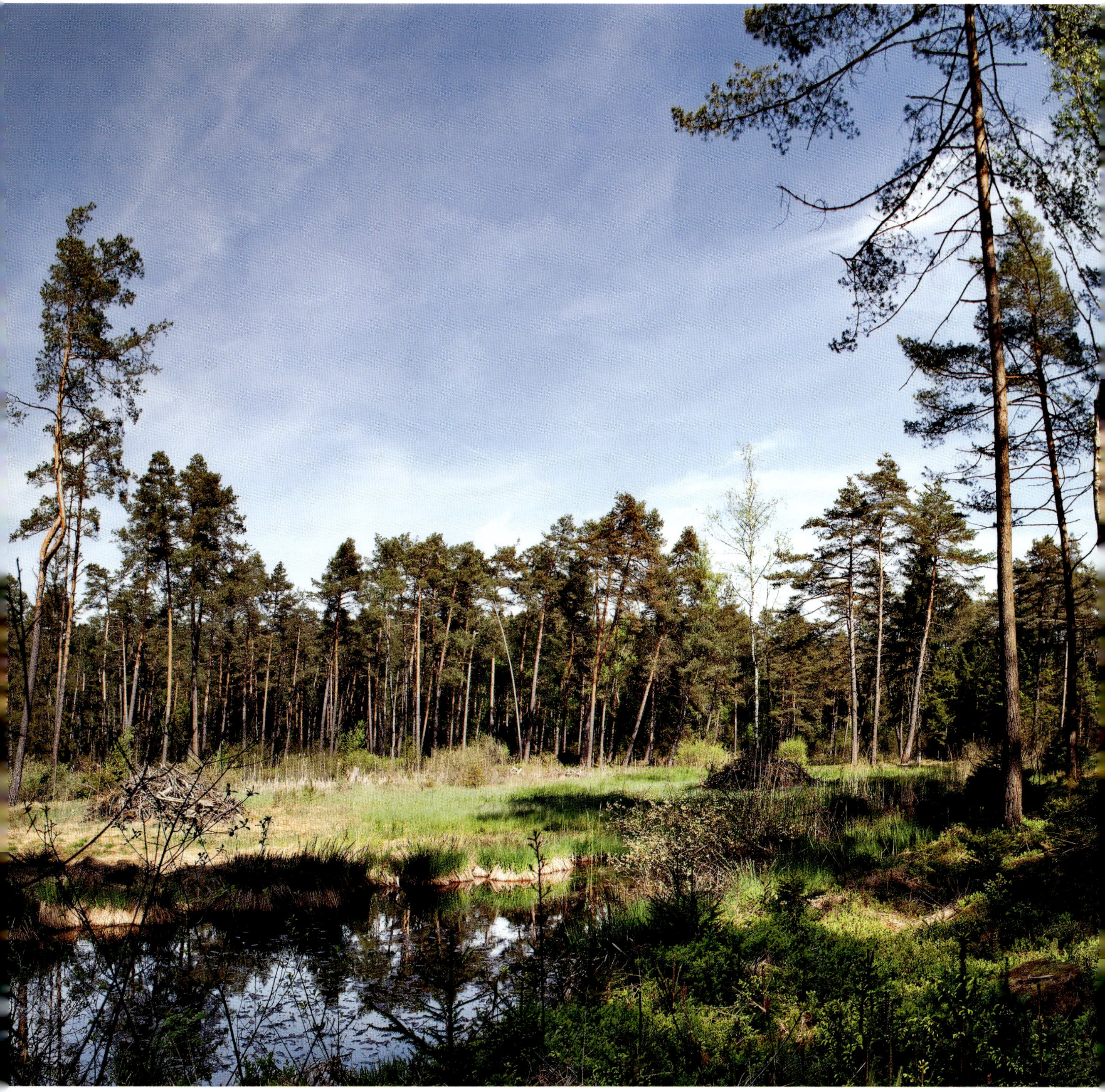

Moorwildnis prägt die Vielfalt in diesem Teil des Torfriets am Pfäffikersee. Im wenig Halt bietenden, weichen Moorboden hat wohl der Wind zwei Fichten samt ihrem flachen Wurzelteller umgeworfen. In den entstandenen dauernassen Löchern wird Holz unvollständig abgebaut und vertorft – die Basis für Bruchwald (links; siehe auch die Doppelseite am Schluss des Buches).
Die beiden Wäldchen mit Birken und Föhren wie auch der alte Torfstich bereichern das Grossseggenried im Robenhauserriet. Das Zusammenspiel von nährstoffarmen und -reichen, eher trockenen und nassen Mooren, Rieden und Wiesen führt am Pfäffikersee zu einer grossen Vielfalt von naturnahen Lebensgemeinschaften (rechts).

Moor wilderness characterises the diversity in this part of the Torfriet near the Pfäffikersee. The soft peaty ground offered little support to the two spruce trees that the wind turned over, along with their shallow root mat. In the permanently wet holes, wood degrades incompletely and peat forms – the foundation for a carr forest, an area of bog with scrub willows (left; see also the double-page spread at the end of the book).
The two copses with birches and pines, as well as old peat, enrich the sedges of Robenhauserriet. The interaction of nutrient-poor and nutrient-rich, rather dry and wet marshes and meadows, leads to a wide variety of natural symbiotic communities at the Pfäffikersee (right).

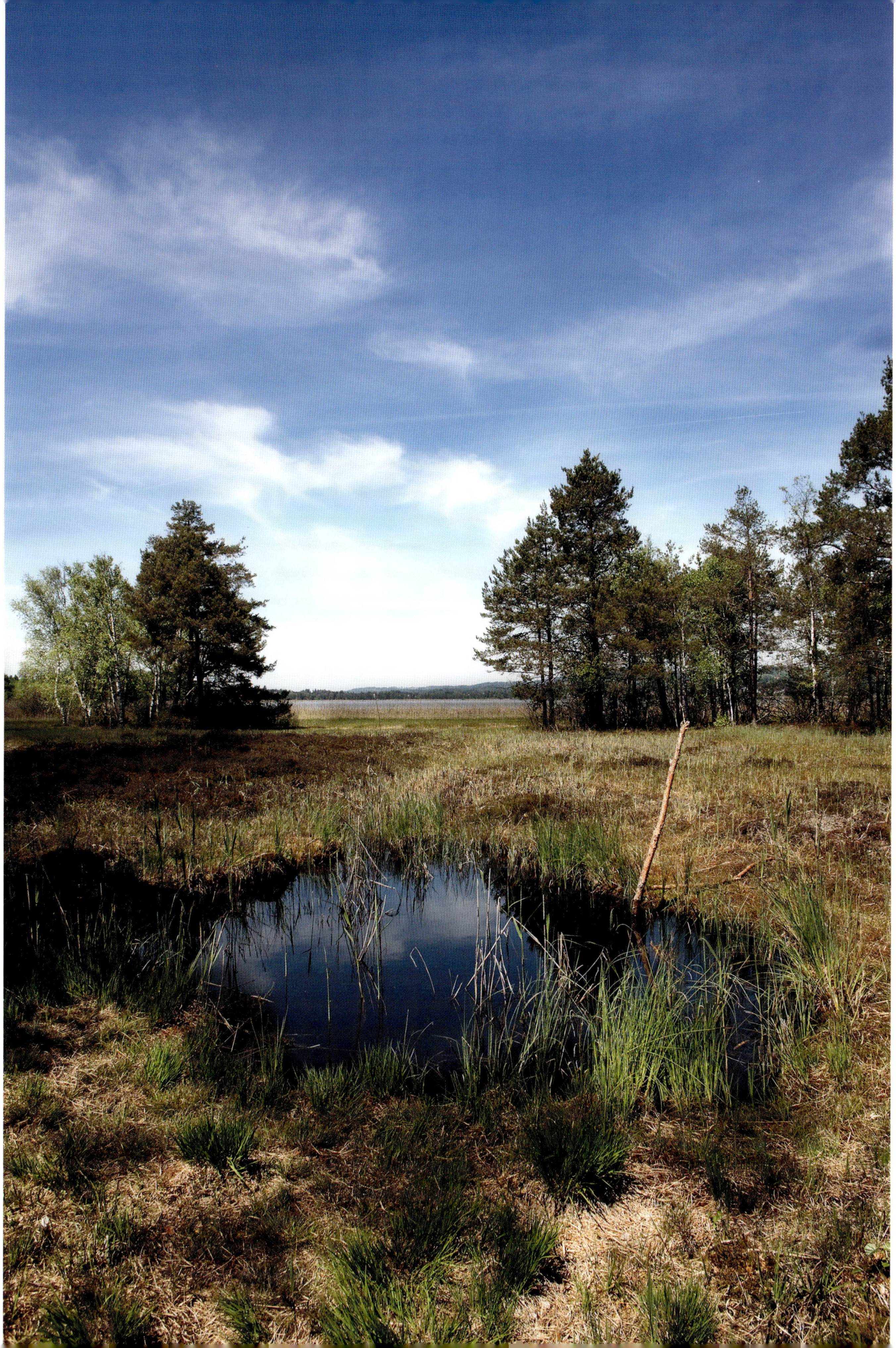

Ried und Streuwiese mit grosser Vielfalt am oberen Ende des Greifensees mit einladenden Wegen – zumeist angelegt neben Wiesenbächen oder sonst nasser Vegetation. Der Greifensee ist an seinen beiden geschützten Schmalseiten gesäumt von im Wasser stehendem echtem Schilfröhricht. Entlang der Längsseiten sind die Ufer an mehreren Orten leicht zugänglich. Für die meisten Besucher ist der See in erster Linie ein selbstverständliches und wichtiges Nächsterholungsgebiet (links). Landschaft beim Ausfluss der Glatt (rechts).

Marshes and wet meadows with a large plant diversity at the upper end of the Greifensee has some inviting trails – mostly laid out next to meadow streams or otherwise wet vegetation. On its two protected narrow sides, the Greifensee is lined with standing real reed beds. Along the length of the lake, the banks are easily accessible in several locations. For most visitors, the lake is primarily a self-evident and important local recreation area (left). Landscape at the outlet of the Glatt River (right).

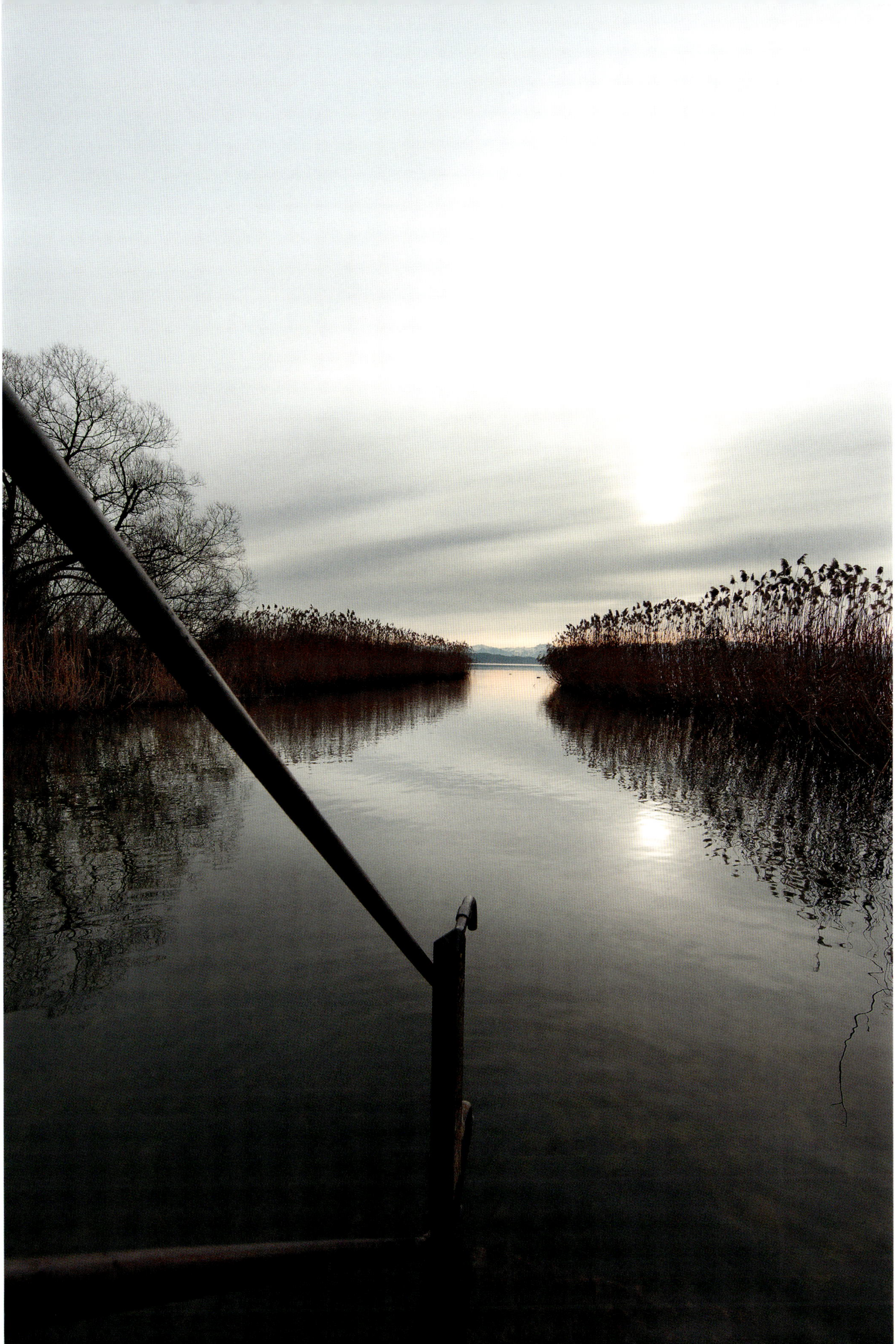

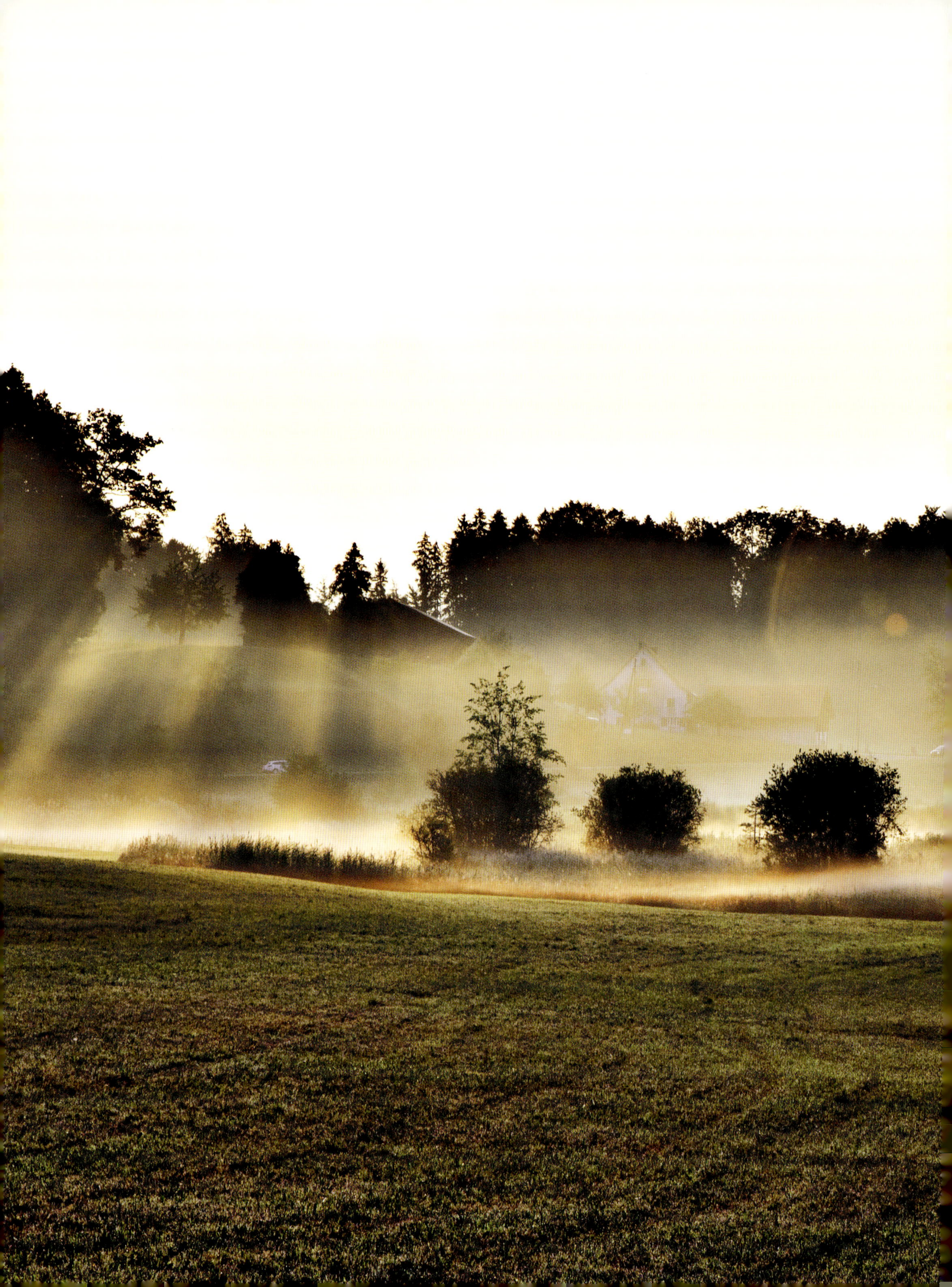

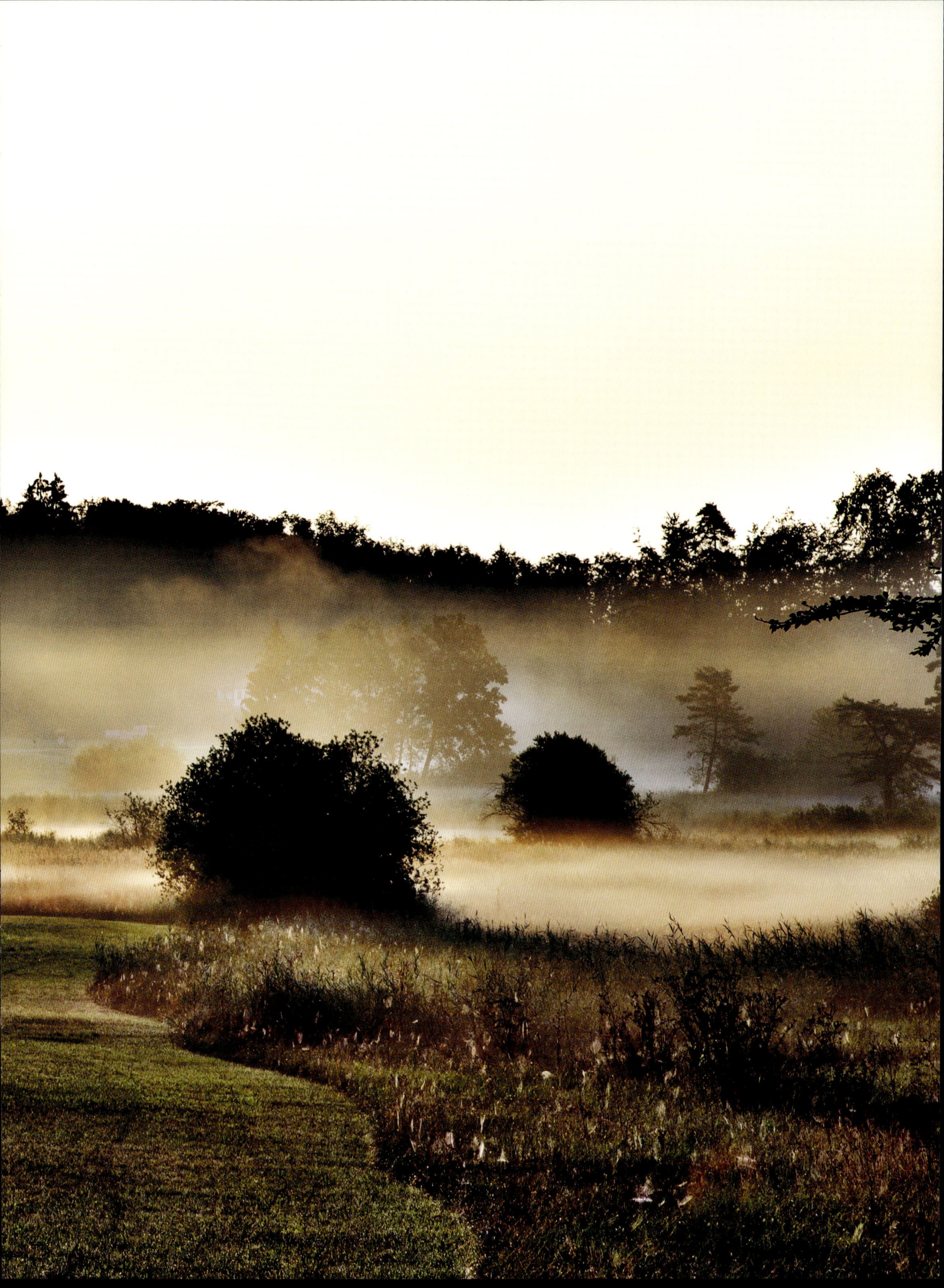

Das biologisch reiche Torfmoor Ützikerriet liegt zusammen mit dem Seeweidsee, dem Lützelsee und dem Lutikerriet in einer gemeinsamen kantonalen Schutzzone. Sie gehört zur landschaftlich reizvollen Hombrechtiker Passlandschaft, die vom Nordast des Linth-Rhein-Gletschers geformt wurde (vorhergehende Doppelseite).

Zwei beliebte Badeseen, beide in unmittelbarer Nachbarschaft zu einem bedeutenden Torfried: Der Untere Chatzensee nördlich vom Hänsiried zwischen Zürich-Affoltern und Regensdorf (links) und der Egelsee, ein biologisch reiches Waldried in der Gemeinde Bubikon (rechts).

The biologically rich Ützikerriet, a peat bog, lies in a joint cantonal protection zone, together with the Seeweidsee, the Lützelsee and the Lutikerriet. It is part of the attractive landscape of the pass above Hombrechtikon that was formed by the northern branch of the Linth-Rhine Glacier (previous double-page).

Two popular swimming lakes, both in the immediate vicinity of a major peat bog: The lower Chatzensee north of Hänsiried between Zurich-Affoltern and Regensdorf (left) and the Egelsee, a biologically rich wet forest in the community of Bubikon (right).

Der Lützelsee mit Blick gegen den Bachtel. Der See hat weitgehend natürliche Ufer und ist dank seinem Umland, vor allem dem Lutikerriet im Nordwesten, als Kleinsee nicht nur eine isolierte Insel in der Kulturlandschaft, sondern auch in seinem Naturhaushalt mit der Landschaft verbunden (folgende Doppelseite).

The Lützelsee with a view of the Bachtel. The lake has largely natural banks and thanks to its surroundings, especially the Lutikerriet in the northwest, the small lake is not just an isolated island in the cultural landscape; it is also connected to the landscape by its own natural environment (following double-page).

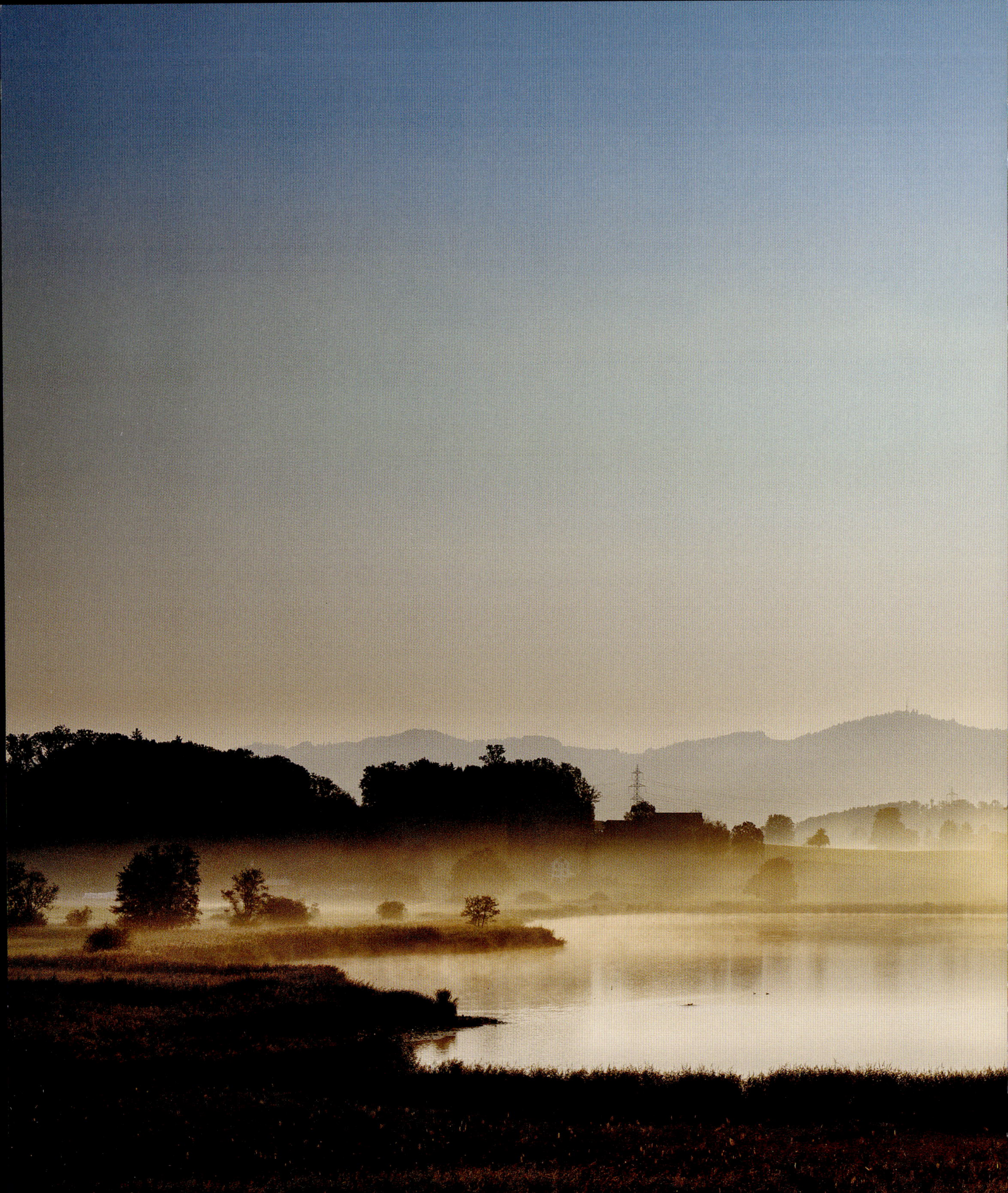

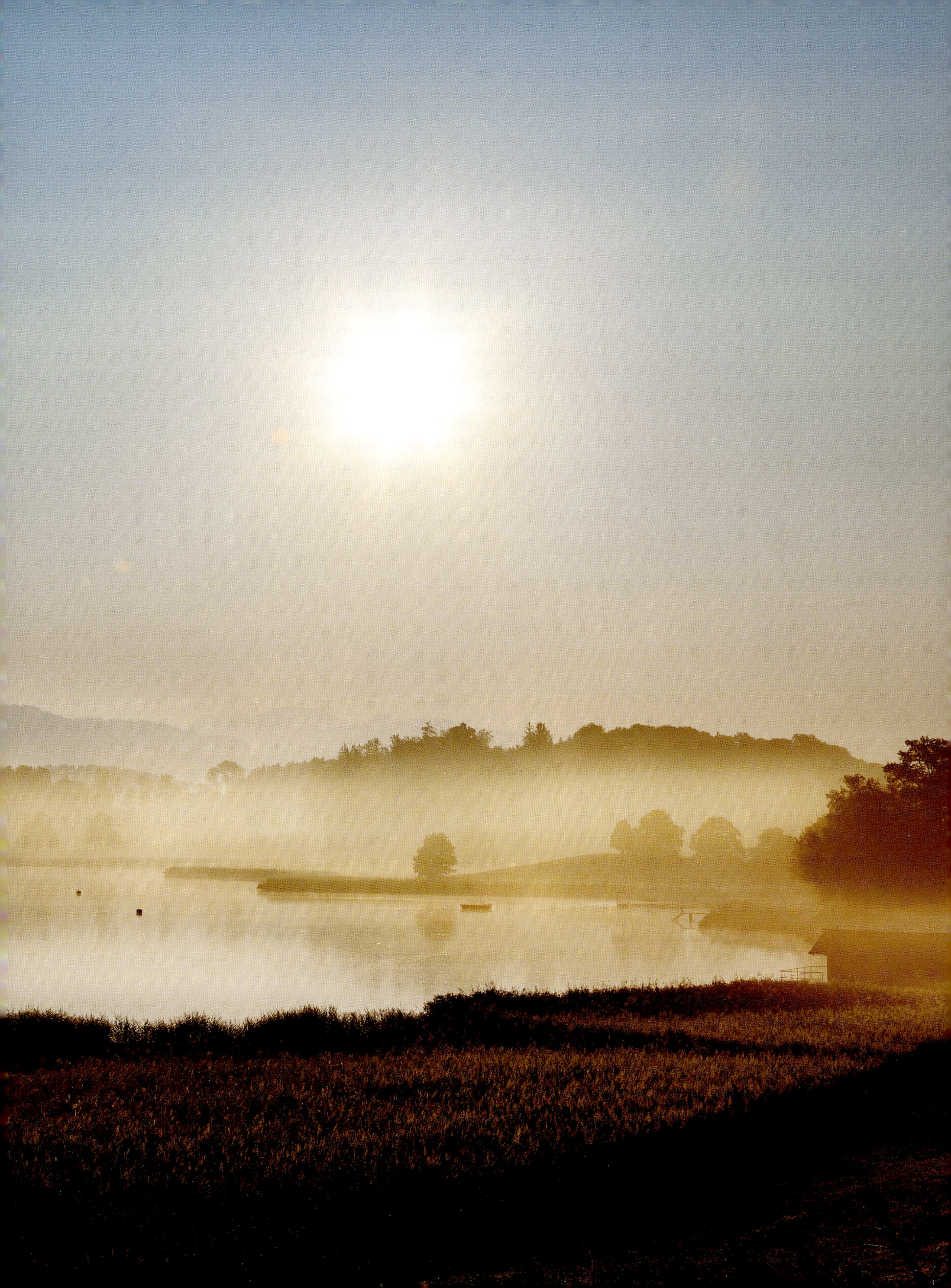

Der Rumensee in Itschnach wurde als Fabrikweiher künstlich angelegt. Sein Wasser trieb eine Mühle und eine Sägerei an. Für den Naturschutz waren solche Fabrikweiher vor allem aufgrund des unnatürlich wechselnden Wasserstandes praktisch wertlos. Das änderte sich mit der Stilllegung und der bewussten Umnutzung und Pflege als reizvolles und viel besuchtes Naturschutz- und Erholungsgebiet.

The Rumensee in Itschnach was artificially created as factory pond. Its water powered a mill and a sawmill. As far as nature protection goes, such factory ponds were virtually worthless, especially because of the unnaturally changing water levels. This changed with the closedown of the factory and a conscious rehabilitation effort and is now an attractive and well-visited nature sanctuary and recreational area.

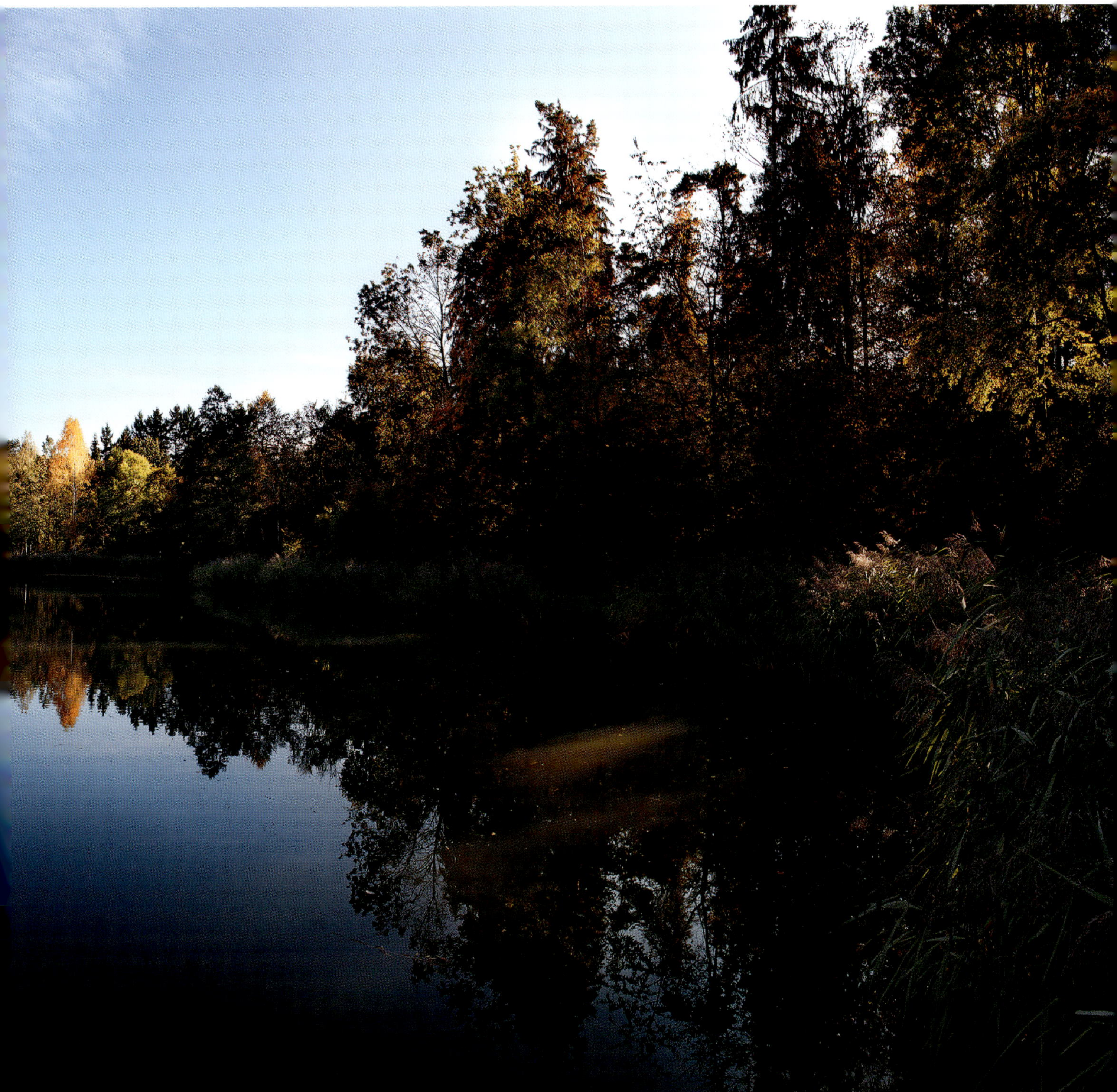

Das knapp ausserhalb des Flughafengeländes liegende «Goldene Tor» ist ein Grundwasseraufstoss in einem flachgründigen Quellweiher. Durch Öffnungen in der Moränendecke wird unter Druck stehendes Grundwasser «brodelnd» aus dem älteren Schotter nach oben gepresst (links).

Der Flughafen Zürich liegt mit seinen über 70 Hektaren Streuwiesen und Flachmooren in der grössten Ebene des Kantons. Zum Schutz vor Vogelschlag, also vor Zusammenstössen grösserer Einzelvögel oder Vogelschwärmen mit Flugzeugen, hat sich eine extensive Langgrasbewirtschaftung bewährt. Der weniger häufige Grasschnitt verringert für Greifvögel das erreichbare Angebot an Kleintieren (rechts).

Just outside the Zurich airport grounds lies the 'Golden Gate', a groundwater output in a shallow source pond. Through openings in the moraine ceiling, pressurized groundwater 'bubbles' are pressed upward through the older gravel (left).

The Zurich Airport, with its more than 70 hectares of wet meadows and low moors lies in the largest plain in the Canton of Zurich. To protect against bird strikes – collisions with large individual birds or flocks of birds with airplanes – an extensive long-grass cultivation has proven useful. Cutting the grass less frequently also limits the opportunities for birds of prey to find small animals (right).

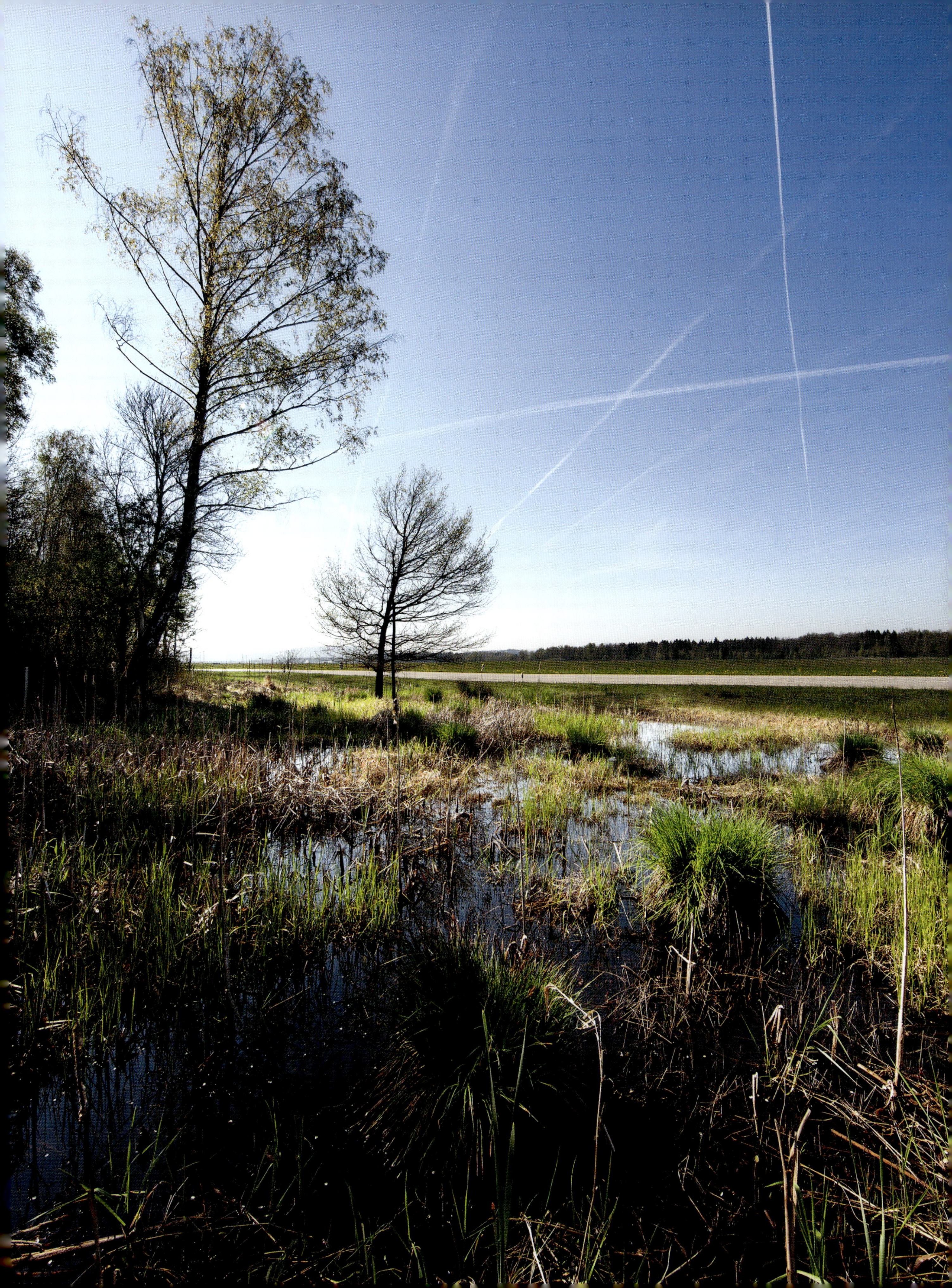

Als eines der letzten grossen Flachmoore der Schweiz ist das Neeracherried vor allem für seine Vorkommen von Brut- und Zugvögeln bekannt. Im Naturzentrum von BirdLife Schweiz gelangt man auf einem kurzen, attraktiven Pfad durch Hecken, Flachmoor und Röhricht zu zwei Beobachtungshütten und kann von diesen aus mit Feldstecher und Fernrohr den Watvögeln, Reihern und Enten oder Raritäten wie dem Eisvogel zuschauen (rechts).
Die Weissstörche lassen sich vom Verkehr zum Glück nicht stören: Sie haben sich nach jahrzehntelanger Abwesenheit im Jahr 2008 wieder im Gebiet angesiedelt (links).

As one of the last remaining fenlands in Switzerland, the Neeracherried is primarily known for its numbers of breeding and migratory birds. In the nature centre run by BirdLife Switzerland, a short, attractive path through hedges, fens and reed beds leads to two observation cabins. With binoculars or a telescope, one can observe waders, shore birds, herons and ducks or rarities like the kingfisher (right).
Luckily, white storks are not disturbed by traffic; they settled back in the region in 2008 after decades of absence (left).

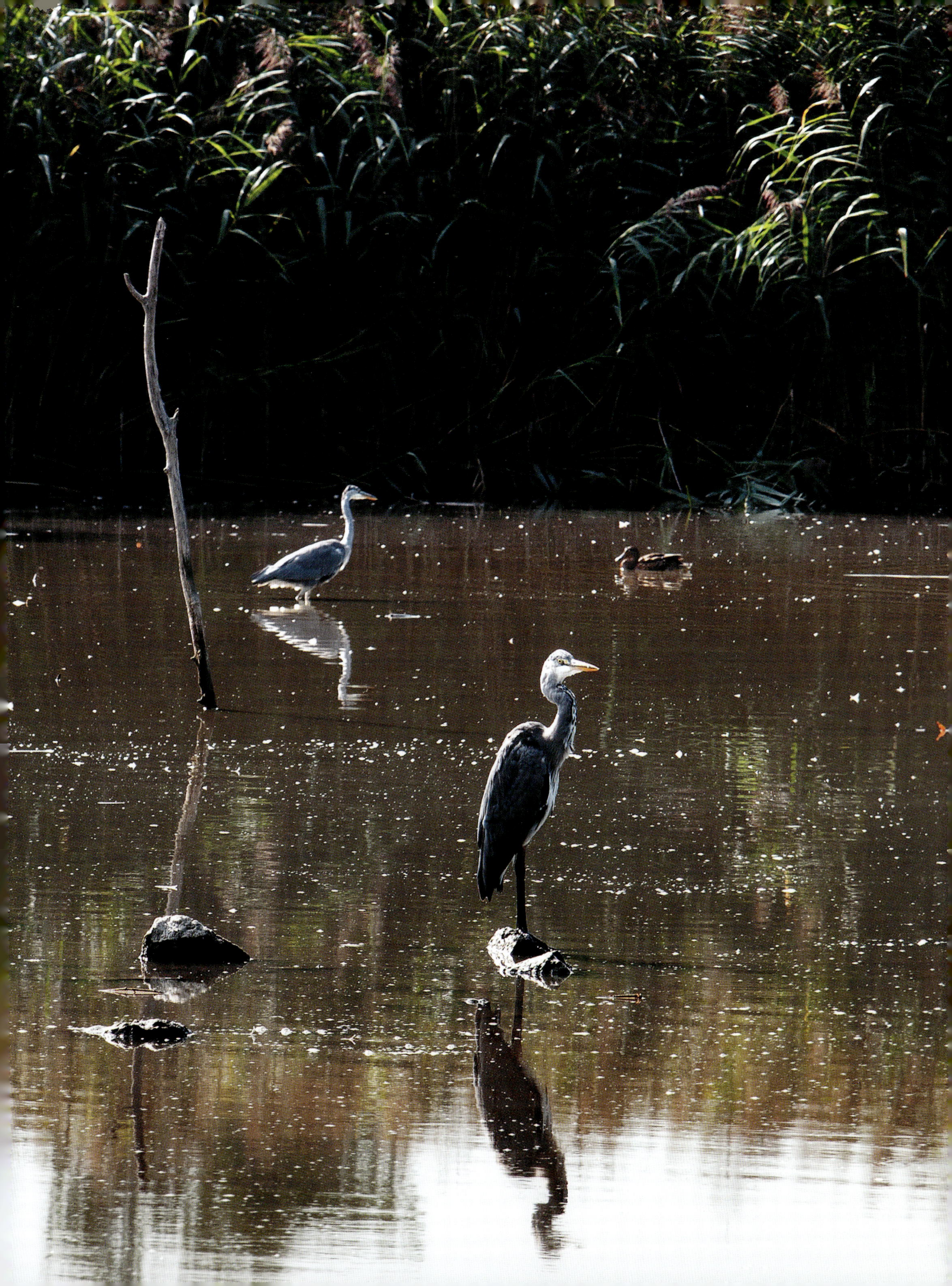

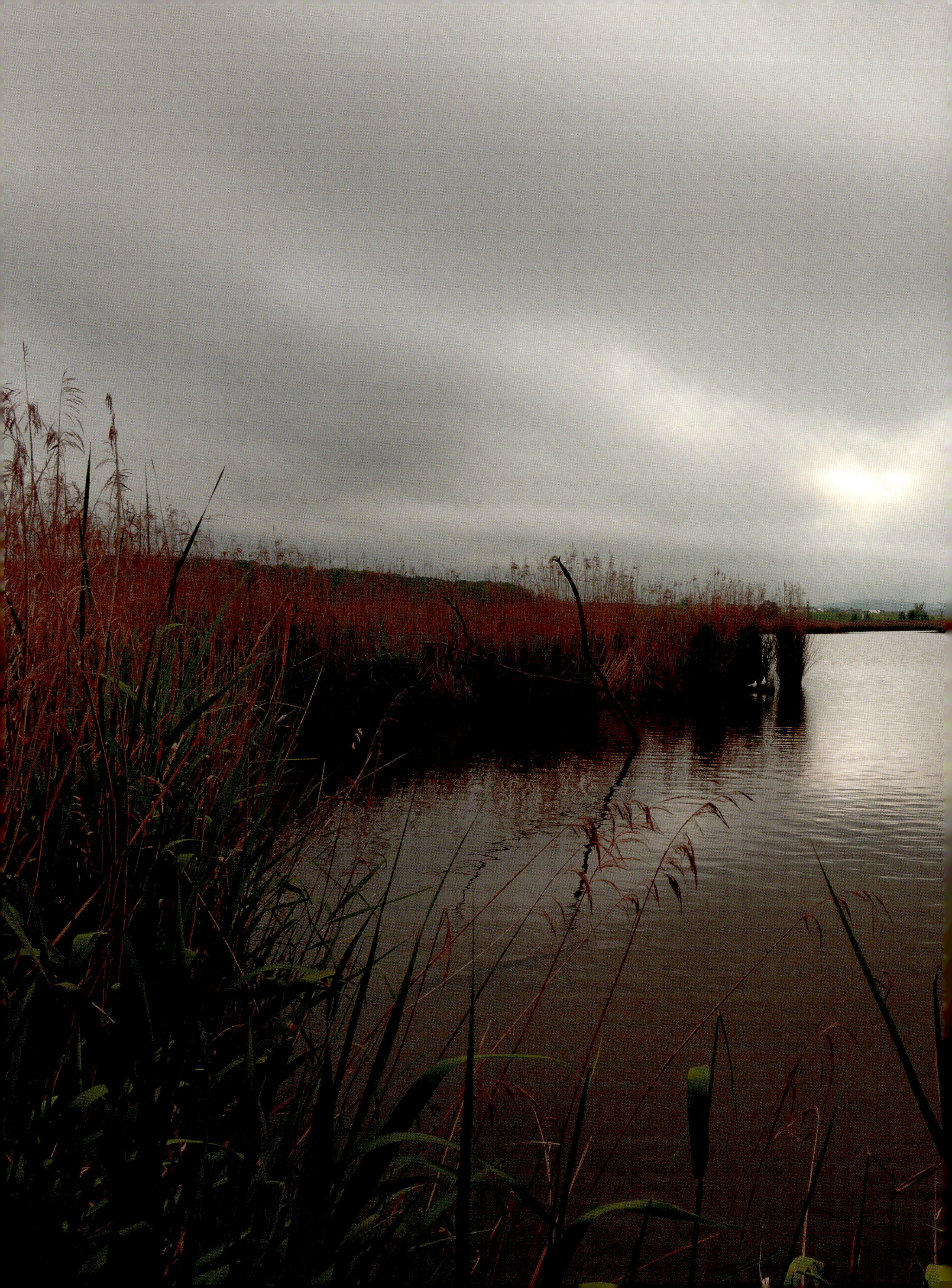

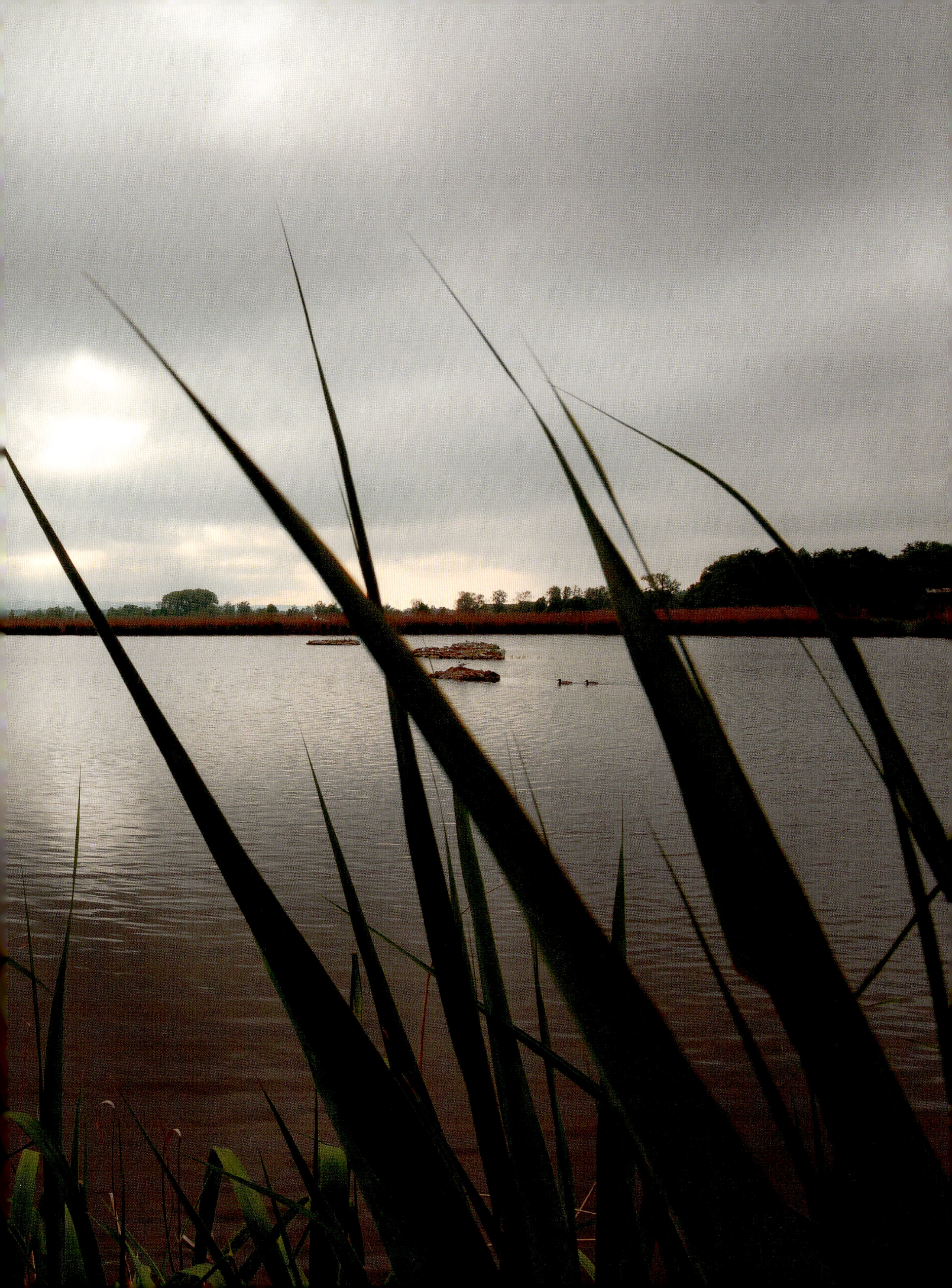

Das Neeracherried ist eine Insel der Natur in einer intensiv genutzten Landschaft – und wird durch zwei Strassen in drei Teile zerschnitten. Exemplarisch zeigt sich hier der Konflikt zwischen dem Erhalt der biologischen Vielfalt in einer einmaligen Landschaft und der ungehinderten Mobilität. Schon seit Jahren plant der Kanton Zürich eine Umfahrungsstrasse um das Ried. Blick aus der Beobachtungshütte auf das weite Flachmoor (vorhergehende Doppelseite).

Der Husemersee (links) und der Nussbaumersee – im Uferbereich mit Teichrosen (rechts) – liegen im Thurgauer Seebachtal, nahe an der Grenze zu Zürich. Sie sind Teil der biologisch reichen Glaziallandschaft zwischen Thur und Rhein mit den Seen südlich von Nussbaumen und der Andelfinger Seenplatte. Die zahlreichen, oft kleinen Flachmoore, Weiher und Tümpel waren nach der Eiszeit Teil eines grossen, zusammenhängenden Feuchtgebietes. Beim Rückzug des Gletschers blieben einzelne mächtige Eisbrocken zurück, wurden vom Moränenschutt überdeckt und später, nachdem sie allmählich aufgetaut waren, zu Toteisseen (Söllen).

The Neeracherried is an island of nature in an intensively used landscape – and it is cut into three parts by two roads. Taken as an example, it shows the conflict between the conservation of biological diversity in a unique landscape and unhindered mobility for humans.
For years, the Canton of Zurich has been planning a ring road around the marsh. The view over the vast moor from the observation cabin (previous double-page).

The Husemersee (left) and the Nussbaumersee with water lilies along the banks of water (right), lie in the Seebach Valley in the Canton of Thurgau, close to the border with Zurich. These two lakes are part of the biologically rich glacial landscape between the Thur and Rhine Rivers, together with the lakes south of Nussbaumen and the lake area of Andelfingen. After the Ice Age, the numerous, often small fenlands, ponds and pools were part of a large, contiguous wetland. When the glaciers were retreating, single huge chunks of ice were left behind. These were covered by moraine rubble and later, after they had gradually thawed, turned into dead ice (now drainage basins or kettle lakes).

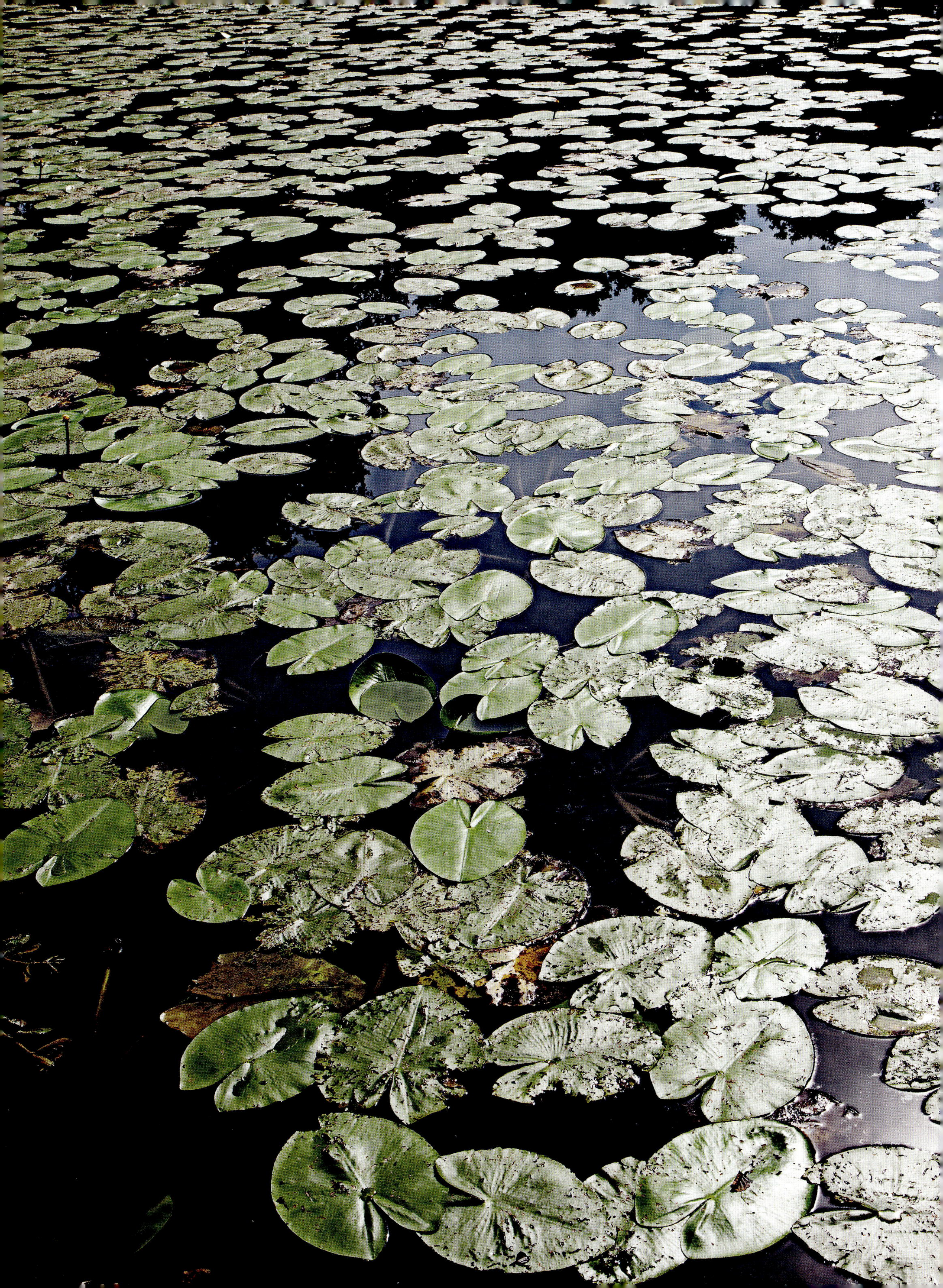

Im Raum Marthalen entstand ein eigentlicher kleiner See, nachdem Biber einen Waldbach gestaut hatten. Wasserlinsen bildeten rasch einen grünen Teppich. Etliche der «Stangenhölzer» des betroffenen Jungwaldes starben. Für Biber sind sie bedeutungslos. Im Winter, wenn Krautnahrung fehlt, fällen Biber voll im Saft stehende und häufig am Gewässerrand wachsende Bäume, um an die besten Zweige zu gelangen.

In the area of Marthalen, a proper small lake was formed after beavers had dammed a forest stream. Duckweed quickly formed a green carpet. Several of the 'pole wood trees' of the young forest died – for beavers, these are irrelevant. During winter, when herbage is missing, beavers fell young trees that often stand along the shorelines in order to reach the best branches.

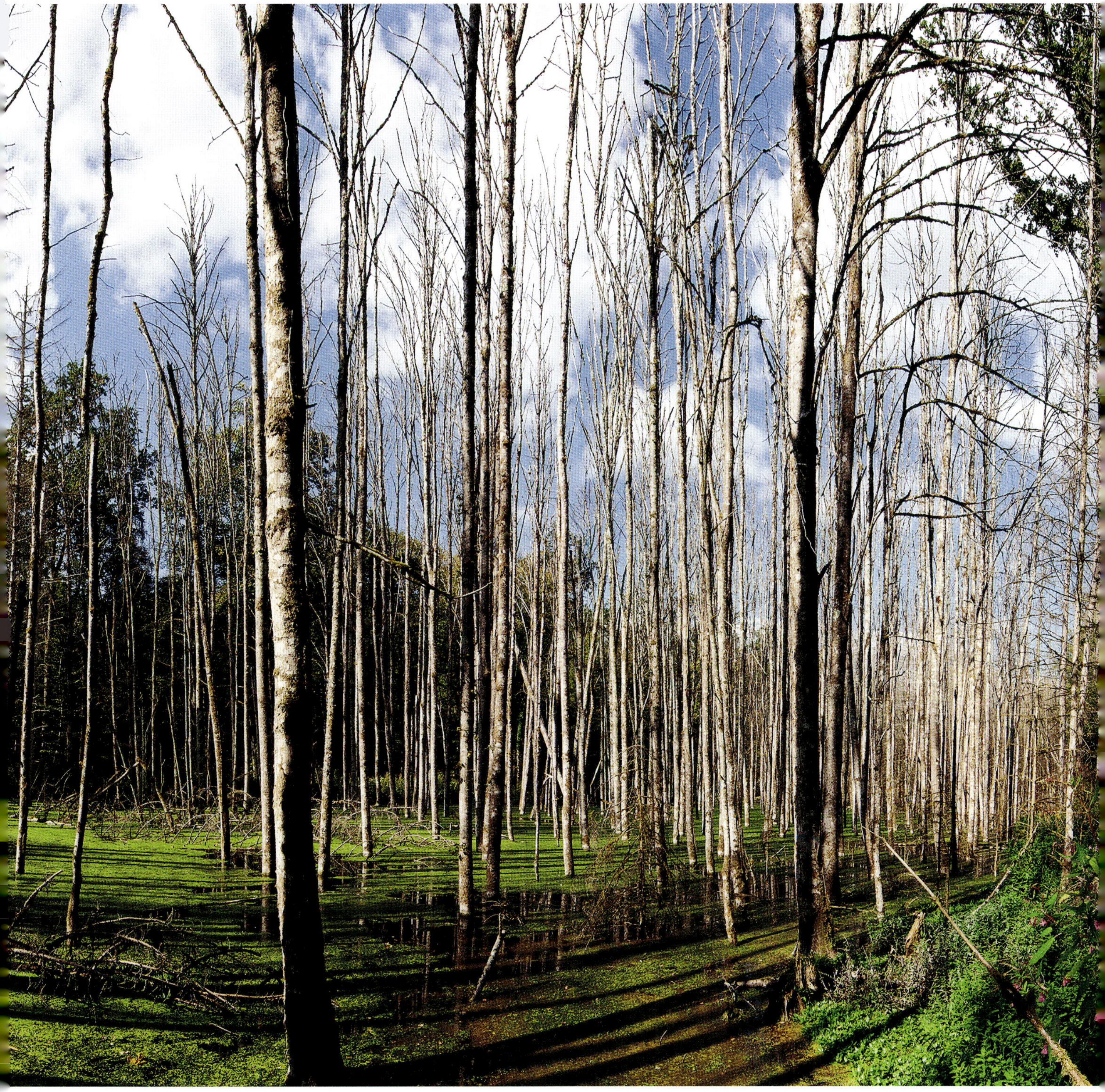

Der kaum metertiefe See böte Platz für eine Biberburg mit Zugang durchs Wasser und einem trockenen Raum über dem Seespiegel (links). Ansätze zu Bautätigkeit wurden beobachtet. Ob der Platz ausreichend störungsarm ist? Ob die Nahrungsressourcen genügen? Eine Kraftprobe seines Mundwerkzeuges bietet das in einen Baumstumpf am Seeufer gemeisselte Zahnmuster (rechts).

The barely one-metre-deep lake offers enough space for a beaver lodge with underwater access and a dry room above the water level (left). Approaches to construction activities were observed: Does the location have a sufficiently low interference level? Are the food resources sufficient? A demonstration of his powerful mouth and teeth can be seen in the tooth patterns carved into the tree stump on the lakeshore (right).

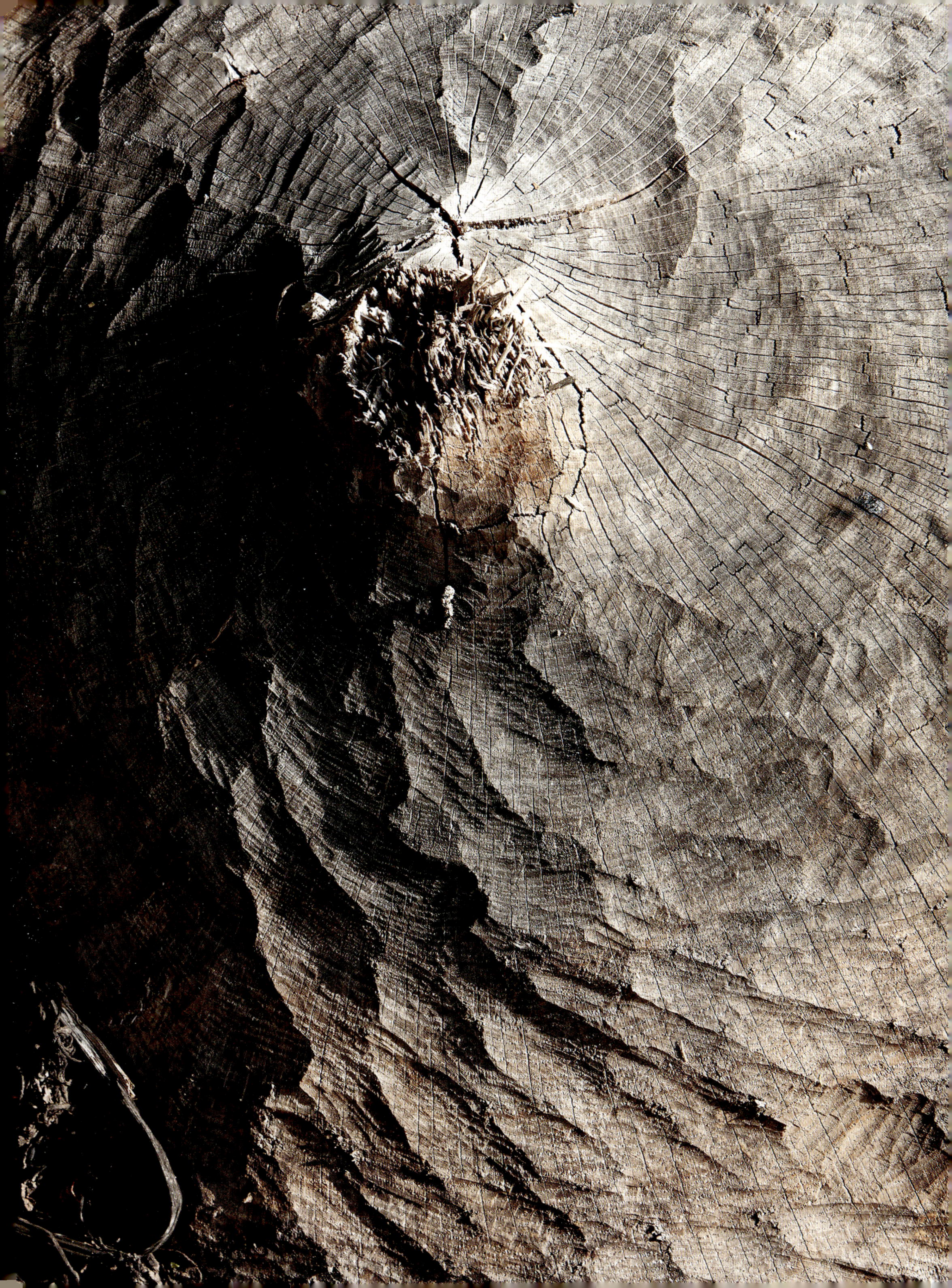

Die Lebensbedingungen der Auenwälder sind abhängig vom Wasserregime der Flüsse: Auf Überschwemmungen folgen trockene Phasen, Uferbänke und kleine Inseln können weggerissen und an anderen Stellen wieder deponiert werden, offene und dichte Waldpartien wechseln sich ab. Wenn in Mulden Wasser nicht abfliessen kann und Totholz unter Luftabschluss nur teilweise abgebaut zu Torf wird, kann Bruchwald entstehen. Wo die oft wilde Thur in den Rhein mündet, liegen die Thurauen – eine Erlebnislandschaft im Bereich des Naturzentrums bei Flaach.

Der markante Eggrank der Thur unterhalb Andelfingen ist im Rahmen des Auenprojektes zu einem wunderbaren Badeplatz geworden. Eine nach Osten bis Süden gerichtete, breite Kiesbank, lockerer Mischwald im Hintergrund und eine Feuerstelle: ein Ort für sommerliche Temperaturen und Badewetter (folgende Doppelseite).

The living conditions of wet forests are dependent on the water regime of the rivers: Floods are followed by dry phases, riverbanks and small islands can be torn away and deposited somewhere else, open and densely wooded areas alternate. If water cannot drain from the hollows and deadwood is hermetically sealed in, it can only become partially degraded to peat, then carr forests may arise. Where the, often wild, Thur flows into the Rhine, that is where the Thur wet meadows lie – an experience landscape in the area of the Nature Centre in Flaach.

The distinctive region of Eggrank at the Thurspitz just below Andelfingen, has become a wonderful swimming spot as part of the wet meadow project. A broad gravel bank facing east to south, light mixed forest in the background and a fireplace: a place for summery temperatures and bathing weather (following double-page).

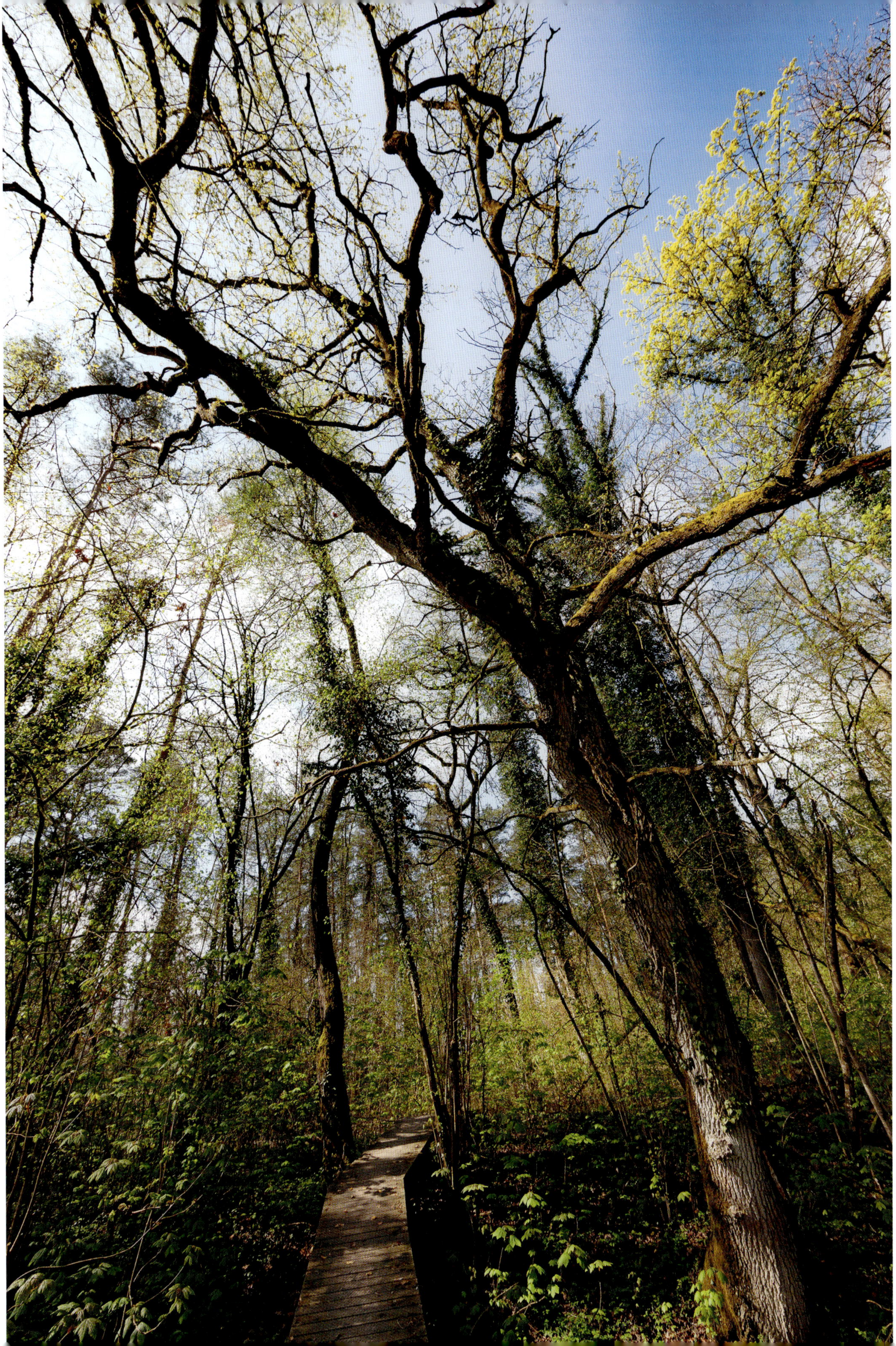

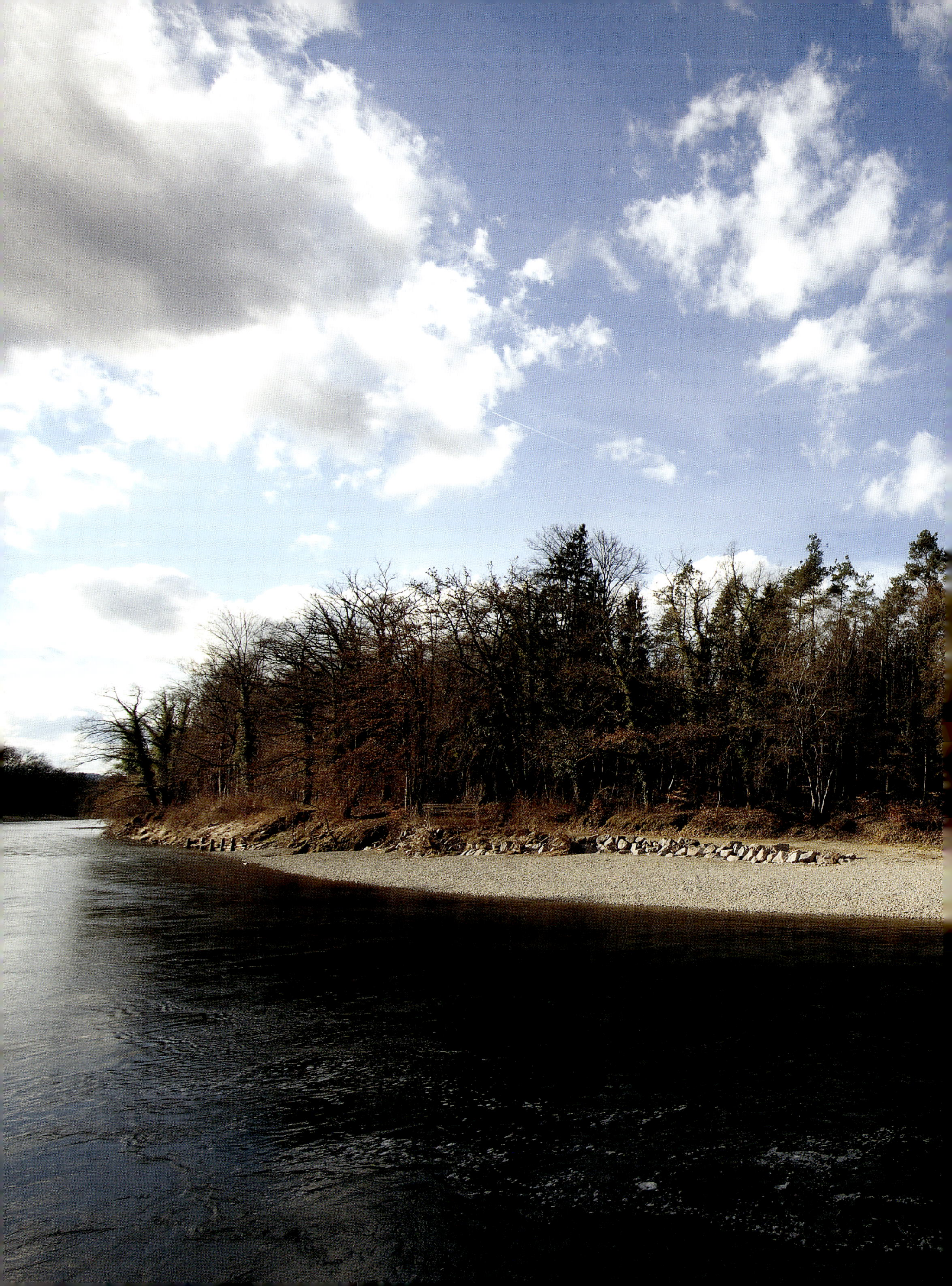

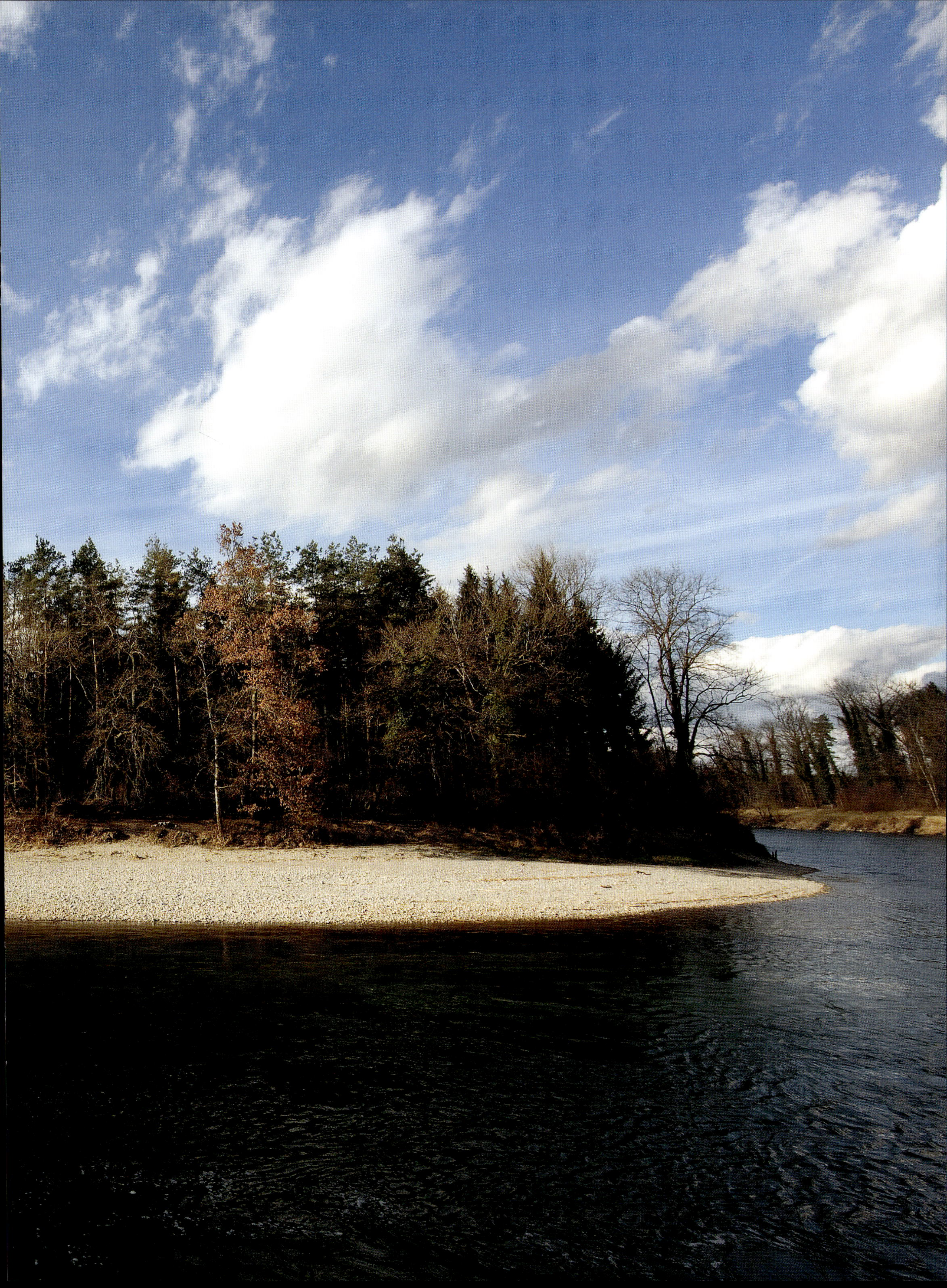

Für den Überwinternden Schachtelhalm ist charakteristisch, dass er meist herdenweise vorkommt – so wie in diesem nassen und lichten Waldabschnitt in der Maschwander Allmend (links).

Das Hochmoorgebiet Hagenholz in Kappel am Albis entstand zwischen zwei Moränenwällen und war Teil eines grösseren Feuchtgebietes. Schon am Ende des 19. Jahrhunderts wurden Teile der einmaligen Bergföhren-Hochmoorfläche geschützt; seit 1988 sind Regenerationsversuche im Gang. Der Hochmoorrand ist überwachsen mit Moor- und Heidelbeeren (rechts).

For the rough horsetail, it is characteristic that it usually appears in a great mass – as in this wet and light forest section by the Maschwander Allmend (left).

The raised bog area of Hagenholz in Kappel am Albis arose between two moraine ridges and was part of a larger wetland. By the end of the 19th century, parts of the unique Scots pine-bog area were already protected and regeneration attempts have been in progress since 1988. The edge of the high moor is overgrown with moorberries and blueberries (right).

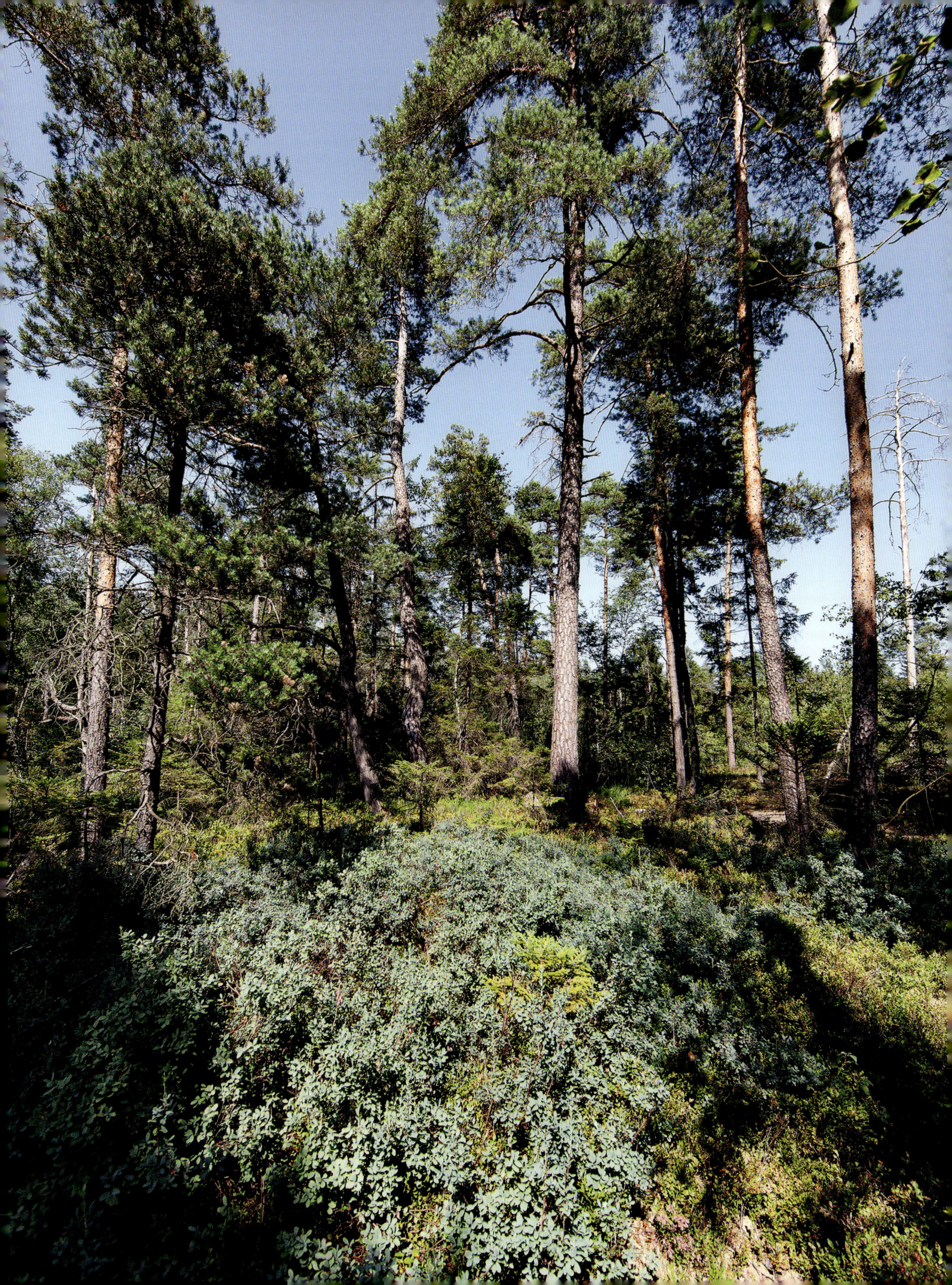

Azaleen und Rhododendren in der Blüte sind das Vorzeigeprogramm im Seleger Moor. Wie alle Heidekrautgewächse (Ericaceen) sind es Holzpflanzen; viele unter ihnen sind angepasst an Moorböden oder saure Rohhumusböden. Einheimische Arten dieser Pflanzenfamilie sind Zwergsträucher wie die Alpenrose, die Alpenazalee oder die Heidelbeere. Heute gehört es zum Allgemeinwissen, dass die letzten Reste noch bestehender Moore in unserem Land geschützt sind und die Verwendung von Hochmoortorf im Gartenbau nicht mehr gesellschaftsfähig ist. Die Bretterwege im Seleger Moor sind eine Schutzmassnahme, weil Moorböden trittempfindlich sind. Passend hinter dem Streifen mit bunten Azaleen und Rhododendren sind die Birken, die auch im sauren Moorboden gut gedeihen.

Azaleas and rhododendrons in bloom are the flagship programme in Seleger Moor. Like all of the heather family (Ericaceae), they are woody plants and many of them have adapted to boggy soils or acidic raw humus soils. Native species of this plant family are dwarf shrubs like the Alpenrose, the Alpenazalee (alpine trailing azalea) or the blueberry. Today, it is common knowledge that the last remnants of the remaining moors are protected in Switzerland and the use of peat in horticulture is no longer socially acceptable. The wooden walkways at Seleger Moor are a protection measure because boggy soils are sensitive to tramping. Behind the strip of colourful azaleas and rhododendrons are birches, which grow well in acidic peaty soil.

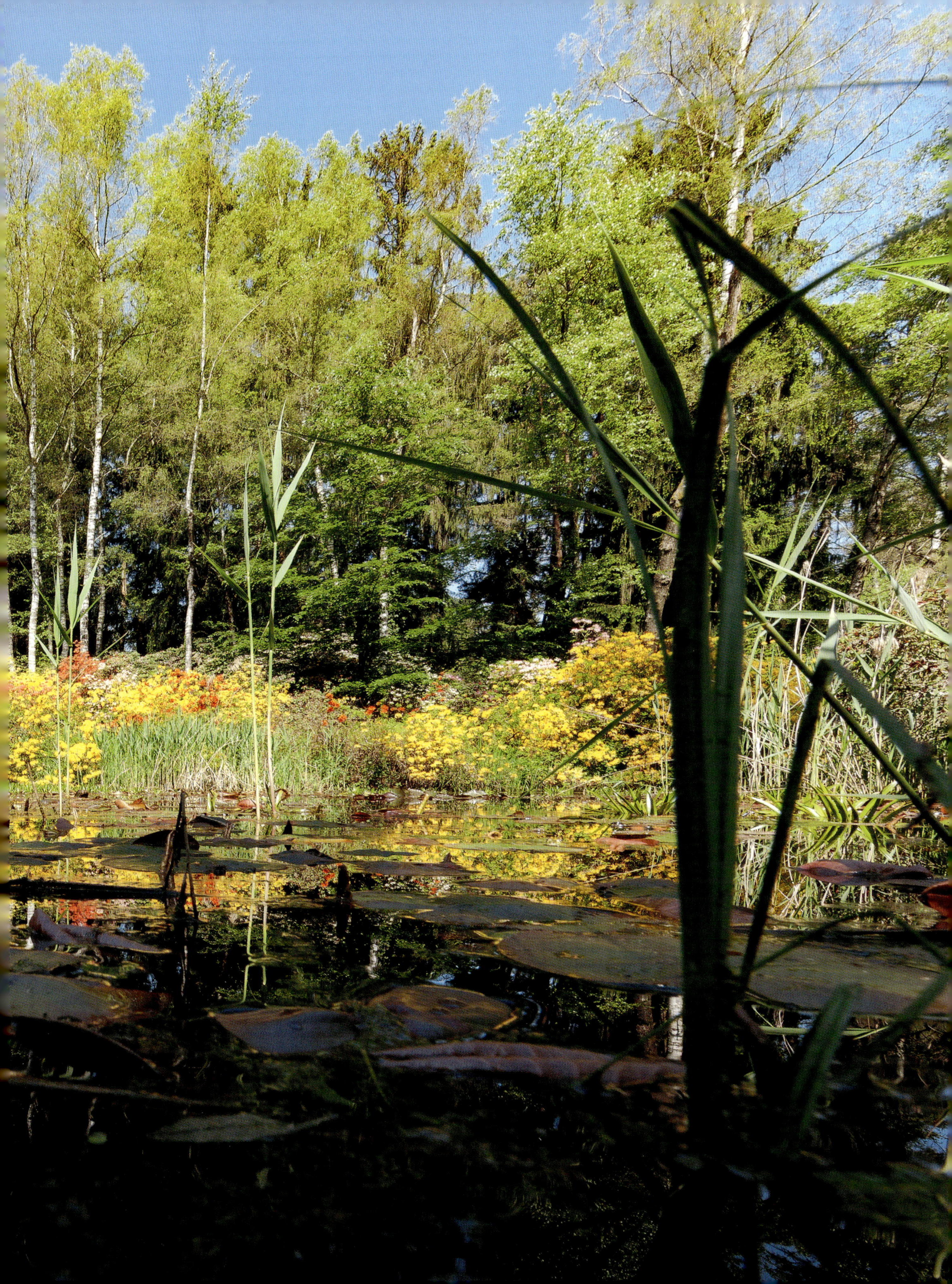

Die einheimische Weisse Seerose hat grosse rundliche Schwimmblätter und, anders als die zahlreichen grossen Hybrid-Seerosen, Blüten mit einem Durchmesser bis zu neun Zentimeter, die etwas aus dem Wasser ragen.

The native white water lily has large round floating leaves and, unlike many large hybrid water lilies, have flowers with a diameter of up to nine centimetres that protrude slightly from the water.

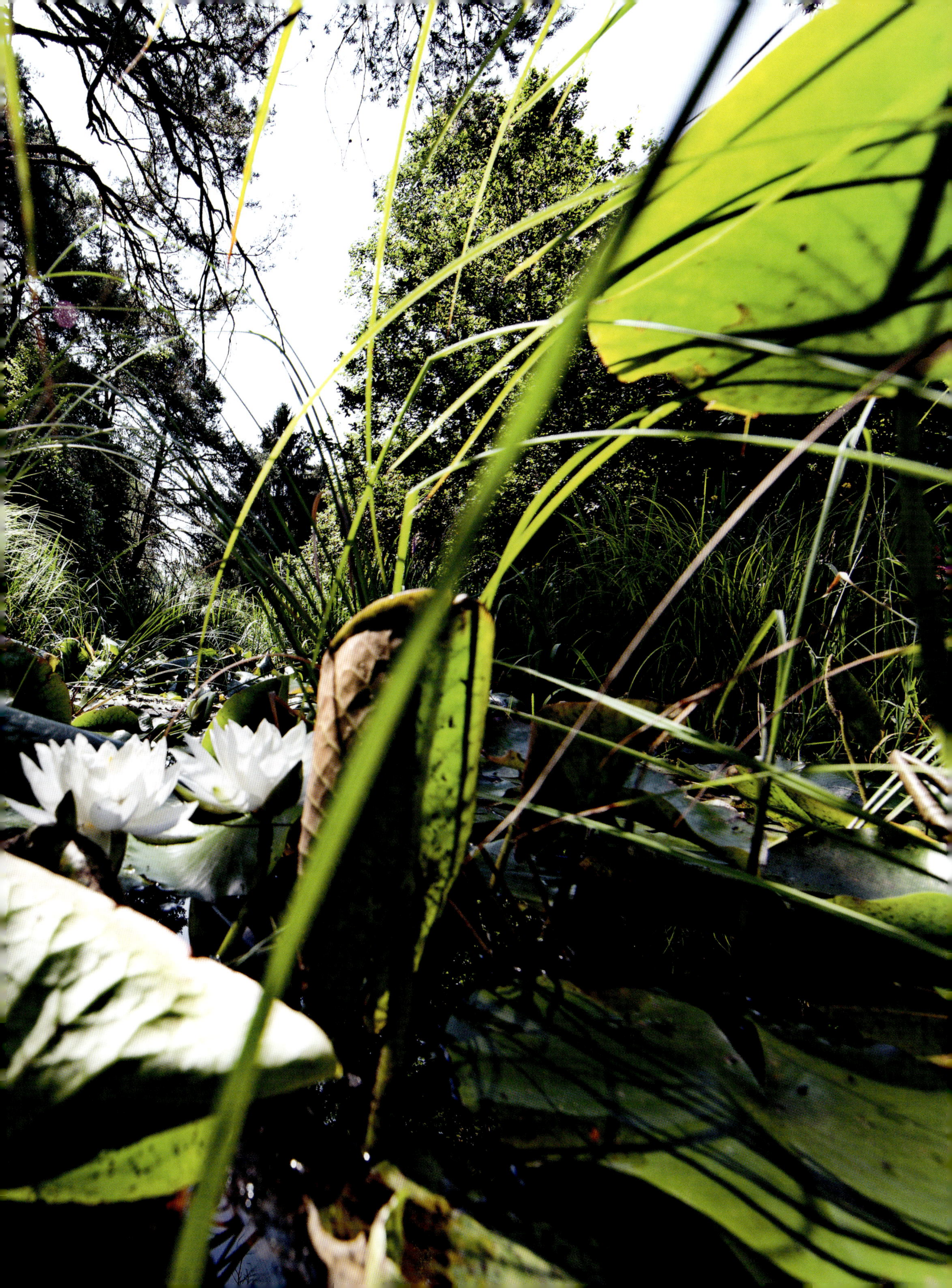

Waldlandschaften

Forest Landscapes

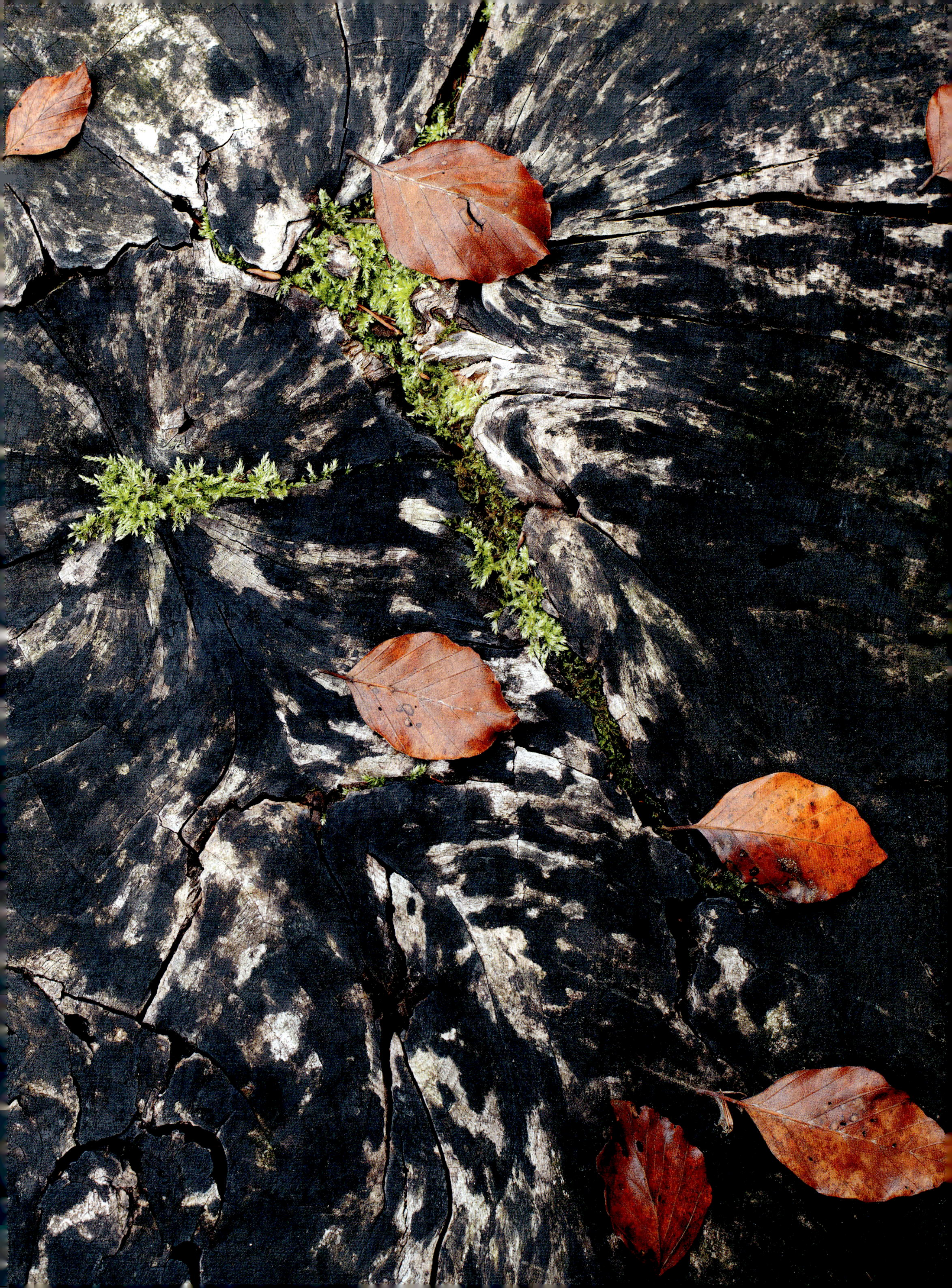

«Der Forstwirth dieses Landes wird seine Wälder nicht retten, wenn er seine Augen nur auf Holz zu richten versteht.»
Albrecht Karl Ludwig Kasthofer (Forstmeister, 1777–1853)

'The forester of this country will not save its forests, if he is only able to focus his eyes on wood.'
Albrecht Karl Ludwig Kasthofer (Forester, 1777–1853)

Buchenblätter im Altersglanz, zerfallendes Holz und einwachsendes Moos in einem künstlerischen Zusammenspiel von Waldelementen.

Beech-tree leaves shining from old age, decaying wood and ingrown moss in an artistic interplay of forest elements.

Wälder sind in unseren Breitengraden die komplexesten Lebensgemeinschaften. Wenige Baumarten wie Buchen, Eichen, Eschen, Fichten, Tannen, Föhren und Eiben gestalten die räumliche Struktur des Waldes. Sie bestimmen massgeblich die Lebensbedingungen für das Heer der weiteren im Wald wohnenden Arten von Pflanzen, Tieren und Pilzen. Als langlebigste, mächtigste und beständigste Lebewesen sind Bäume Individuen. Jeder hat seine eigene Geschichte, die aus seiner «Black-Box» im Stamm abzulesen ist. Die Härte oder Gunst der einzelnen Lebens- und auch bestimmter Kalenderjahre und früherer Nutzungen lassen sich dank dem zyklischen Wachstum der Bäume erkennen und mit dendrochronologischen Methoden beurteilen. So führen die Bäume gleichsam ein «Grundbuch der Landschaft», das menschliche Generationen weit überspannt. Und nicht zufällig spielen Bäume in der Kulturgeschichte eine wichtige Rolle – als Marchlinden, Freiheitsbäume, Hausbäume oder Alleen. Bäume von symbolischem Charakter sind etwa die Linden auf den Moränenhügeln im Raum Hirzel, die zweizeilige Rosskastanien-Allee beim Bahnhof Eglisau, die mächtige Brockmann-Eiche am Adlisberg, die Tiefenhoflinde am Fröschengraben in Zürich oder die tausendjährige Wolfhartsgeereneiche in Gottfried Kellers Novelle «Das verlorene Lachen».

Wälder und Landwirtschaftsflächen liegen in getrennten Zonen. Das war nicht immer so. Das durch Wälder zum einen und Wiesen und Äcker zum anderen gezeichnete Raummuster ist – neben geländebedingten Vorgaben – eine Folge des eidgenössischen Forstpolizeigesetzes, das seit 1876 für die Gebirgswälder und seit 1902 für das Territorium der ganzen Schweiz in Kraft steht. Es schützt das Waldareal und verbietet Kahlschläge wie auch landwirtschaftliche Nutzungsformen im Wald.

In früheren Zeiten war die Nutzung des Waldes bäuerlich geprägt: In etlichen Gebieten weideten Kühe, Ziegen und Schweine im Wald, und die Bauern

In our latitude, forests are the most complex biological communities. A few tree species, such as beech, oak, ash, spruce, fir, pine, and yew, shape the spatial structures of the forest. They significantly determine the living conditions for the host of additional kinds of plants, animals and fungi living in the forest. As the longest living, most abundant and enduring life form, trees are individuals. Each has its own story that can be read from the 'black box' in its trunk. The severity or favourability of the weather, along with the full details of life for a specific calendar year and early uses can be identified thanks to the cyclical growth of the tree, which can be evaluated with dendrochronological methods. Trees allow us to read their 'Journal of the Landscape', thus giving us information that far exceeds the span of human generations. It is not by chance that trees also play an important role in our cultural history: The Marchlinde that identifies boundaries, the Liberty Tree; trees that emphasise the location of a house, or impressive avenues of trees. Trees of symbolic character are, for example, the lindens on the rolling morainic hills in the Hirzel area, the double aisle on Horse Chestnut Avenue near the Eglisau railway station, the mighty Brockmann Oak on the Adlisberg, the Tiefenhof Linden on the Fröschengraben in Zurich or the thousand-year-old oak, *Wolfhartsgeereneiche*, in Gottfried Keller's novel, *Das verlorene Lachen* (The Lost Laugh).

Forests and agricultural landscapes lie in separate zones. This was not always the case. In addition to the terrain conditions, the spatial patterns defined by forests and those defined by meadows and agricultural land are the result of the federal Forest Law, that began in 1876 for mountain forests, and since 1902 is in force for all territories in the entire country. It protects the forest areas and bans clear-cutting, as well as the agricultural use of forests.

In earlier times, the use of forests was shaped by farming: In certain areas, cows, goats and pigs pastured in the forests and the farmers trimmed branch-

schnaitelten Äste von Laubbäumen für Streue und Winterfutter. Eine andere häufige Nutzungsform war der Mittelwaldbetrieb. Dabei erntete man etwa alle 20 Jahre auf einer Fläche die so genannte Hauschicht als Brennholz, vor allem Hagebuchen, Hasel und Birken. Nur wenige Einzelbäume mit wertvollem Stammholz wie Eichen, Buchen oder Kirschen blieben auf der Fläche stehen. Diese intensiven Nutzungsformen brachten es mit sich, dass die Wälder im Vergleich zu heute hell und vor allem im breiten Waldrandbereich mit dazwischen angelegten Äckern und Fruchtbäumen oft lichtdurchflutet waren.

Das Forstwesen und die mit der ETH aufgebaute junge Waldforschung förderten im 19. Jahrhundert die Trennung der Land- von der Waldwirtschaft, die mit dem Forstpolizeigesetz besiegelt wurde. Ihr Ziel war die Abkehr von den bis dahin verbreiteten Mittelwäldern hin zu naturgerechten Dauerwäldern und einer naturnahen Waldwirtschaft, die ein hohes Erntealter der Waldbäume ermöglichte. Bei der Wahl der Baumarten wurden in diesem Sinne vegetationskundliche Standortkarten zur Leitlinie. In der Vorstellung des späten 19. Jahrhunderts sollte der Wald auf diese Weise drei Hauptfunktionen dauernd und uneingeschränkt erfüllen können: Schutz, Nutzen und Wohlfahrt. Postuliert wurde, dass der Wald als Folge der primären Holznutzung automatisch auch die weiteren geforderten Funktionen erfüllen würde. Heute ist in Forstkreisen allgemein anerkannt, dass ein solcher Anspruch nicht umsetzbar ist. So fehlte dem Wald etwa die natürliche Altersphase, wenn die Bäume bei der damals üblichen Bewirtschaftung schon im mittleren Alter gefällt wurden. Als neue Philosophie etablierte sich der «Plenterwald». Dieser orientierte sich an der natürlichen Entwicklung der Bäume und förderte über die gezielte Nutzung von Einzelstämmen stufige Bestände von ungleichem Alter. Im Laufe des zwanzigsten Jahrhunderts wuchs schliesslich die Einsicht, dass im Wirtschaftswald neben der nachhaltigen Produktion von Wert- und Energieholz auch dem Naturschutz und der Erholungsnutzung Rechnung getragen werden muss.

Zu einer neuen Herausforderung für die Anliegen des Naturschutzes wurde indessen die landesweit festgestellte Entwicklung zu dunkleren, artenärmeren Wäldern und der extrem reduzierte landschaftliche Zusammenhalt zwischen Wald und Feld durch schmale Waldgrenzen ohne biologisch wertvolle Übergangsgebiete. Sie sind eine negative Folge der konsequenten Trennung von Forst- und Landwirtschaft. Um diese für die Naturwerte gravierende Entwicklung zu korrigieren, legte der Regierungsrat 1995 im kantonalen Naturschutz-Gesamtkonzept fest, dass neben naturgerecht genutzten Wirtschaftswäldern auch naturkundlich bedeutende Wälder be-

es from broad-leafed trees for spreading and winter fodder. Another common form of woodland management was coppicing. In this form, trees were harvested every 20 years or so with a cut of the understorey for firewood, mainly hornbeam, hazel and birch. Only a few single trees with valuable trunk wood, such as oak, beech or cherry remained standing in the space. This intensive form of management brought about the condition that forests, in comparison to today, were often flooded with light, especially in the broad forest edge area, with cultivated areas and fruit trees in-between.

Forestry and the ETH's new field of forest research promoted the separation of the land from forest management, which was sealed by the Forest Police Law in the 19th century. The goal was to move away from coppicing, until then the most widely practiced form of forest management, to more natural timber forests and a close-to-nature forest management that would make it possible to raise the harvesting age of forest trees. To accomplish this, the selection of tree species used vegetation survey site maps as guidelines. In the late 19th century concept, the forest should thus be able to fulfil three main functions continuously and indefinitely: protection, use and welfare. It was postulated that the forest, as a result of the primary wood use, would also automatically fulfil the additional required functions. Today, it is generally recognised in forestry circles that such an approach is not implementable. Because, the forest is missing, for example, the natural aged phase, because under the old method, trees would already be felled in middle age. A new philosophy established itself, selection forestry, in which single trees are selected for cutting. This is oriented to the natural development of the trees and promotes stepped inventories of different ages through the targeted use of individual trunks. In the course of the 20th century, the insight finally grew into the awareness that, in an industrial forest, in addition to the sustainable production of valuable wood and energy wood, the protection of nature and recreational use must also be taken into account.

A new challenge in the matter of nature protection was, however, the realisation that nationwide forests had developed into dark landscapes with few species and offered an extremely reduced scenic cohesion between forest and field because the narrower forest boundaries did not have biologically important transition areas. This was the negative result of the consistent separation of forest and agriculture. In order to correct this and move toward the serious development of natural values, in 1995 the cantonal government specified in the Nature Protection Master Plan that, in addition to nature-compatible industrial forests in use, historically important forests should

stimmt werden können.¹ So sollen vor allem lichte Wälder geschaffen und genutzt werden, wie sie früher die bäuerliche Form der Nutzung hervorgebracht hatte.² Zahlreiche Vergleichsstudien haben ergeben, dass sich mit dem Weidebetrieb in Wäldern eine höhere und besondere Artenvielfalt einstellt. Mit diesen Massnahmen sind in erster Linie lokale Naturschutzziele im Visier; keineswegs sollen die landwirtschaftlichen Nutzungsformen aus dem frühen 19. Jahrhundert grossflächig reaktiviert werden. Deshalb dürfte eine weiche Grenze zur stillen Duldung von Einzelfällen mit dem weniger strengen Waldgesetz von 1991 wohl erreicht sein.³

In diesem Zusammenhang ist auch die Frage nach dem ursprünglichen Naturwald von Bedeutung. Welches waren in Mitteleuropa die natürlichen Verhältnisse, die natürlichen Waldbilder und Lebensgemeinschaften gewesen, bevor der Mensch die Flora und Fauna massgeblich mitbestimmte? Noch vor wenigen Jahrzehnten widersprach niemand der Aussage, dass der Wald von Natur aus die gesamte Landschaft bedeckt hatte. Heute ist man sich ziemlich einig, dass der Wald nicht geschlossen gewesen sein konnte, wenn die grossen Pflanzenfresser wie Wald- und Steppenwisent, Auerochse, Wildpferd und Riesenhirsch darin lebten – nicht zu reden von den Elefanten und Nashörnern, die vor 30 000 Jahren auch in Zürich wirkten. Alle diese Arten förderten ähnlich wie bei einer Waldweide eine offene, lichtreiche, teilweise vielleicht savannenartige Waldlandschaft. Was waren die Ursachen für das Aussterben der grossen Pflanzenfresser? Nur den erdgeschichtlichen Wandel mit den Eiszeiten für verantwortlich zu erklären, wäre zu einfach. Menschen konnten beim Niedergang mehrerer Arten sehr wohl mitgewirkt haben (siehe Seite 16).⁴ So gesehen lässt sich der lichte Wald durchaus als natürliche Waldform einstufen, und wenn wir Hausrinder als ökologische Ersatztierart für den ausgerotteten Urochsen akzeptieren, erhält auch die halboffene bäuerliche Wald-Weide-Landschaft eine zusätzliche Akzeptanz als naturgerechte Form der Nutzung. Und es sind auch schöne Waldbilder. Ob uns Menschen der offene, lichte Wald vielleicht deshalb besonders gut gefällt und wir in Stadtpärken eine Savanne gestalten, weil der Mensch ursprünglich ein Savannenbewohner war? Dies vermutet jedenfalls der Ökologe Gordon Orians.

Der naturgerechte Umgang mit dem Wald ist in den letzten Jahren komplizierter geworden und kann nicht allein dem Forstwesen übertragen werden. Die Herausforderungen sind zahlreich: die zunehmende Rolle des Waldes für den Klimaschutz, die Frage seiner optimalen Nutzung angesichts des Klimawandels, die wechselnde Bedeutung der Holznutzung, die Rolle als Erlebnisraum, für Erholungsaktivitäten,

also be identified.¹ Most important, therefore, was that light forests should be created and used in the same way they were produced in the previous form of forest management.² Numerous comparison studies have shown that meadow management in forests brings a higher number of species and with it, a special species diversity. These measures are intended to fulfil the local nature protection goals. And, in no way should the agricultural forms of use from the early 19th century be reactivated on a large scale. However, tolerance of single cases may well be achieved with the less strict forest law of 1991.³

In this connection, the question about the original natural forest is also important. What were the natural relationships, the natural forest landscape and the biological communities like in Central Europe before mankind started significantly co-determining the flora and fauna? Even a few decades ago, no one contradicted the statement that the forest had covered the entire landscape – determined by its own nature. Today, we pretty much all agree that the forest could not have had a closed canopy when the large herbivores, such as forest and steppe bison, aurochs, wild horses and giant deer lived in them – not to mention the elephants and rhinoceroses that 30,000 years ago would also have had an effect on Zurich. All of these species preferred surroundings similar to a forest meadow: an open light-filled forest, or perhaps a partially savannah-like forest landscape. What was the reason for the decline of the large herbivores? To declare that the Ice Ages are solely responsible for the Earth's historical changes would be too simple. Humans could very well have played a part in the decline of several species (see page 16).⁴ Seen this way, the light forest can be classified as a natural forest form and, when we accepted domesticated cattle as an ecological replacement for the extinct aurochs, the half-open peasant forest-meadow landscape also received an additional acceptance as a 'natural' form of use. And, these are also beautiful forest landscapes. Perhaps we humans find open, light forests especially pleasing or plan a savannah design for our city parks because humans were originally savannah dwellers? In any case, the ecologist Gordon Orians suspects this is true.

Following a natural approach to forests has become more complicated in recent years and cannot be attributed to forestry alone. The challenges are many: the increasing role of forests as climate protection, the question of its optimal use in regard to climate change, the pursuit of various kinds of nature protection goals and the changing importance of using wood. In addition, there is the role of the forest as an experiential space, a place for recreational activities, and, especially in forests close to urban areas,

für verschiedenartige Naturschutzziele und, vor allem in stadtnahen Wäldern, als Raum für neue Trendsportarten, die nur sehr begrenzt auf derselben Fläche wahrgenommen werden können. Ein weiteres Thema ist der Artenschutz. Es ist ein wichtiges Ziel, dass sich Arten möglichst unter Bedingungen der natürlichen Selektion entwickeln können. Der gemeinsame Lebensraum von Raubtieren, Beutetieren und Konkurrenten prägte die Stammesgeschichte, und so trägt die Präsenz von Wolf und Luchs bei Rehen und Wildschweinen dazu bei, dass ihre hoch entwickelten Sinnesleistungen weiter geschärft werden und ihr wachsames Verhalten erhalten bleibt.

Jeder Wald muss also in seiner Individualität begriffen werden und darf nicht nur als anonymer Vertreter einer «Kategorie» verstanden werden: Es gibt auch Wälder mit einem dynamischen Auencharakter wie jene im Bereich der Thurauen und des «Biberwalds» bei Marthalen. Die durch Hausschweine beweideten Eichenwälder im Norden des Kantons regten den jungen Gottfried Keller zu seinem herrlichen «Waldlied» an.[5] Lichte Wälder wurden vor allem in kargen und steilen Südlagen eingerichtet wie am Irchel, an der Hohflue im Bachsertal, an der Lägern oder am Uetliberg und im Oberland.

Der Sihlwald und das Bärtobel beim Hörnli im Oberland sind zu Naturwäldern bestimmt worden. In ihnen wird bewusst nicht lenkend eingegriffen – die Natur kann mit sich selbst experimentieren. Dies gilt auch nach Windwürfen; der natürliche Abbau von stehendem Totholz wird Mikroorganismen, Pilzen, Bock- und Borkenkäfern und Spechten überlassen. Der gut zugängliche Wildnispark Zürich Sihlwald trägt das Label «Naturerlebnispark – Park von nationaler Bedeutung» und stellt so die vielleicht anspruchsvollste Herausforderung an die Verantwortlichen für den Zürcher Wald dar. Wildnis spricht uns in unserer Grundhaltung zur Natur und Kultur an – es ist wunderbar, wenn ansatzweise Naturwald-Erlebnisse vermittelt werden können, wie sie Hermann Hesse nach Tagen in Sumatra in seinem Gedicht «Abschied vom Urwald» beschrieben hat:[5]

Hier in dieser unendlichen leuchtenden Wildnis
War ich weiter als je entrückt von der Menschenwelt –
O und niemals sah ich so nah und unverstellt
Meiner eigenen Seele gespiegeltes Bildnis.

a space for new sport trends that can only be experienced in a very limited way on similar spaces. Another theme is the protection of forest species. It is an important goal that species should be able to develop under the best possible conditions of natural selection. The common living spaces of hunters, prey and rivals affect the evolution of the species involved. Thus, the presence of wolves and lynx near deer and boar contributes to a further sharpening of a prey animal's highly developed sensory performance and preserves their alert behaviour.

Each forest must also be recognised in its individuality, and, may not be understood only as an anonymous representative of a 'category'. There are also forests with a dynamic wet forest character, such as those in the area of Thurauen and the 'beaver forests' near Marthalen. Domestic pigs helped create the meadows in the oak forests in the northern area of the Canton of Zurich that stirred the young Gottfried Keller to his wonderful *Waldlied* (Forest Song).[5] Light forests were mainly established in sparse, steep southern areas, such as the Irchel, the Hohflue in Bachsertal, the Lägern Mountains, the Uetliberg and in Zurich's Oberland.

The Sihl Forest and the Bärtobel near Hörnli in the Oberland were designated as natural forests. The intention is conscious non-intervention: Let Nature do the experiments herself. This is true as well for windfalls: the natural decomposition of standing dead wood will be taken over by microorganisms, fungi, longhorn and bark beetles and woodpeckers. The easily accessible Wilderness Park Zurich in the Sihl Forest carries the label 'Nature Adventure Park – A Park of National Importance' and thus represents perhaps the most demanding challenge for forest managers. Wilderness speaks to our most basic attitudes towards nature and culture. It is wonderful when rudimentary natural forest experiences can be communicated, as Hermann Hesse did in his poem *Abschied vom Urwald* (Farewell to the Forest Primeval) where he described his days in Sumatra:[5]

Here in this endless luminous wilderness
I was further than ever removed from the human world –
O and never did I see so close and undisguised
My own soul's reflected image.

«Kernzone» bedeutet im Wildnispark Sihlwald, dass die Natur Vorrang hat und die Besucher die Wege nicht verlassen dürfen. Die mächtigen Buchen profitieren vom hellen Licht in den Baumkronen, der trockene Standort am Abbruchrand ist aber nachteilig. Mit weiten Wurzeln zum sicheren Waldboden finden sie Wasser und erreichen damit auch Standfestigkeit.

The Core Zone in the Wilderness Park Sihlwald means that in this area nature takes precedence and visitors may not leave the paths. The strong beech trees profit from the bright light in the treetops, however, the dry location at the edge is disadvantageous. With wide roots in the safe forest floor, it finds water and achieves stability.

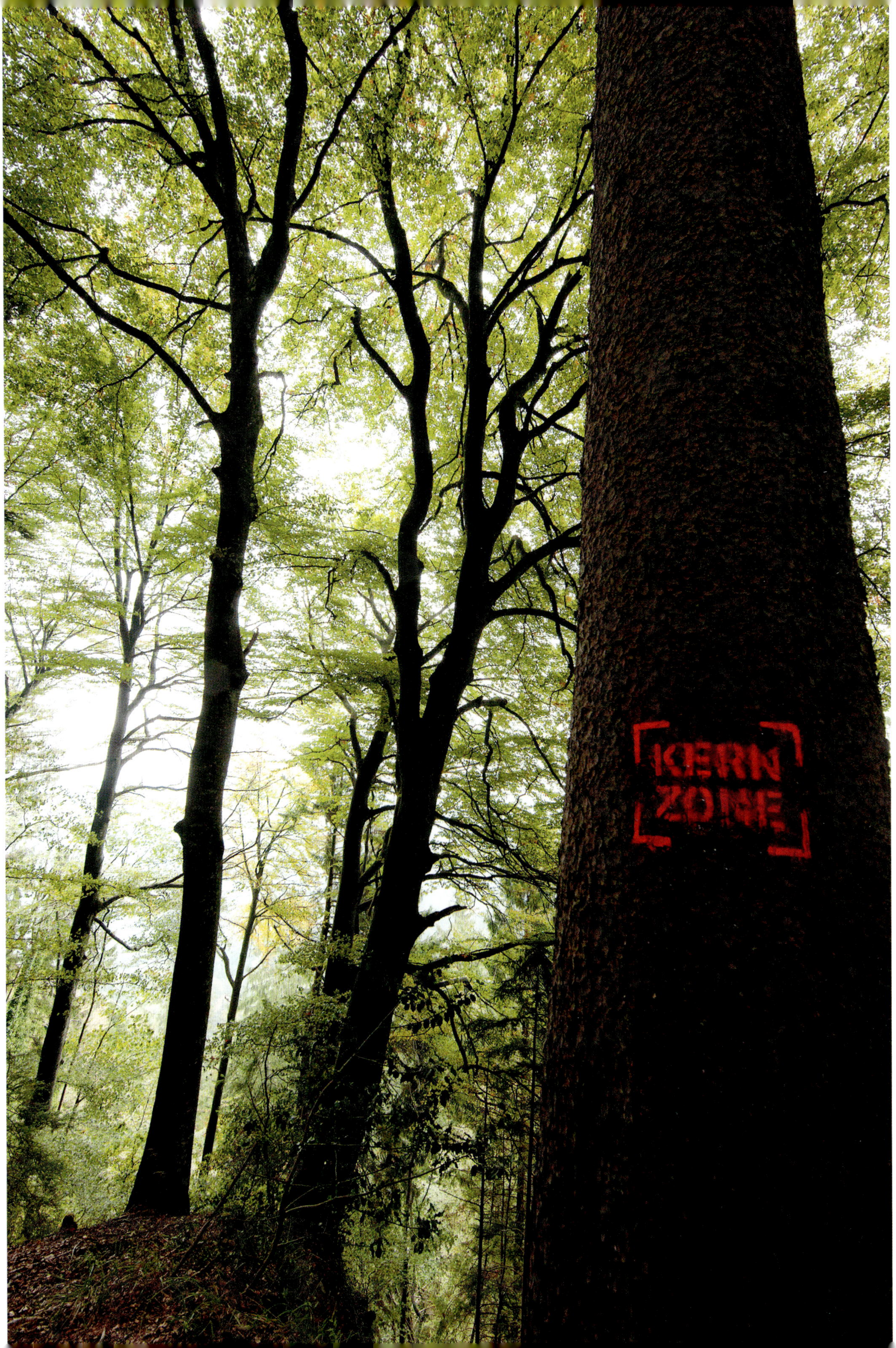
KERN
ZONE

Eindrücke von der Vielfalt des Laubmischwaldes im Sihlwald, in dem Buchen zwischen Nadelbäumen wie Fichten, Föhren und vor allem der rotstämmigen Eibe vorherrschen. Ihr üblicher Platz ist in der zweiten Etage des Waldes (links). Eiben sind harzfrei, schattenertragend und langsamwüchsig, ihr Holz ist hart und dauerhaft. Ausser der roten Beerenhülle sind Eiben von den Wurzeln bis in die Nadeln giftig – vor allem für Pferde und auch für Menschen, aber kaum für Rehe. Im Uetliberg-Albis-Gebiet stehen die europaweit reichsten Eibenbestände.

Impressions from the variety in the mixed deciduous forest in the Sihlwald, where beech trees are in between conifers, where spruce and Scots pine and especially the red-stemmed yew prevail. Their usual place is on the second floor of the forest (left). Yews are resin-free, shade tolerant and slow-growing, their wood is hard and durable. Apart from the red berry shell, yews are poisonous from the roots to the needles – especially for horses and people, but rarely for deer. The Uetliberg-Albis region has Europe's richest yew stock.

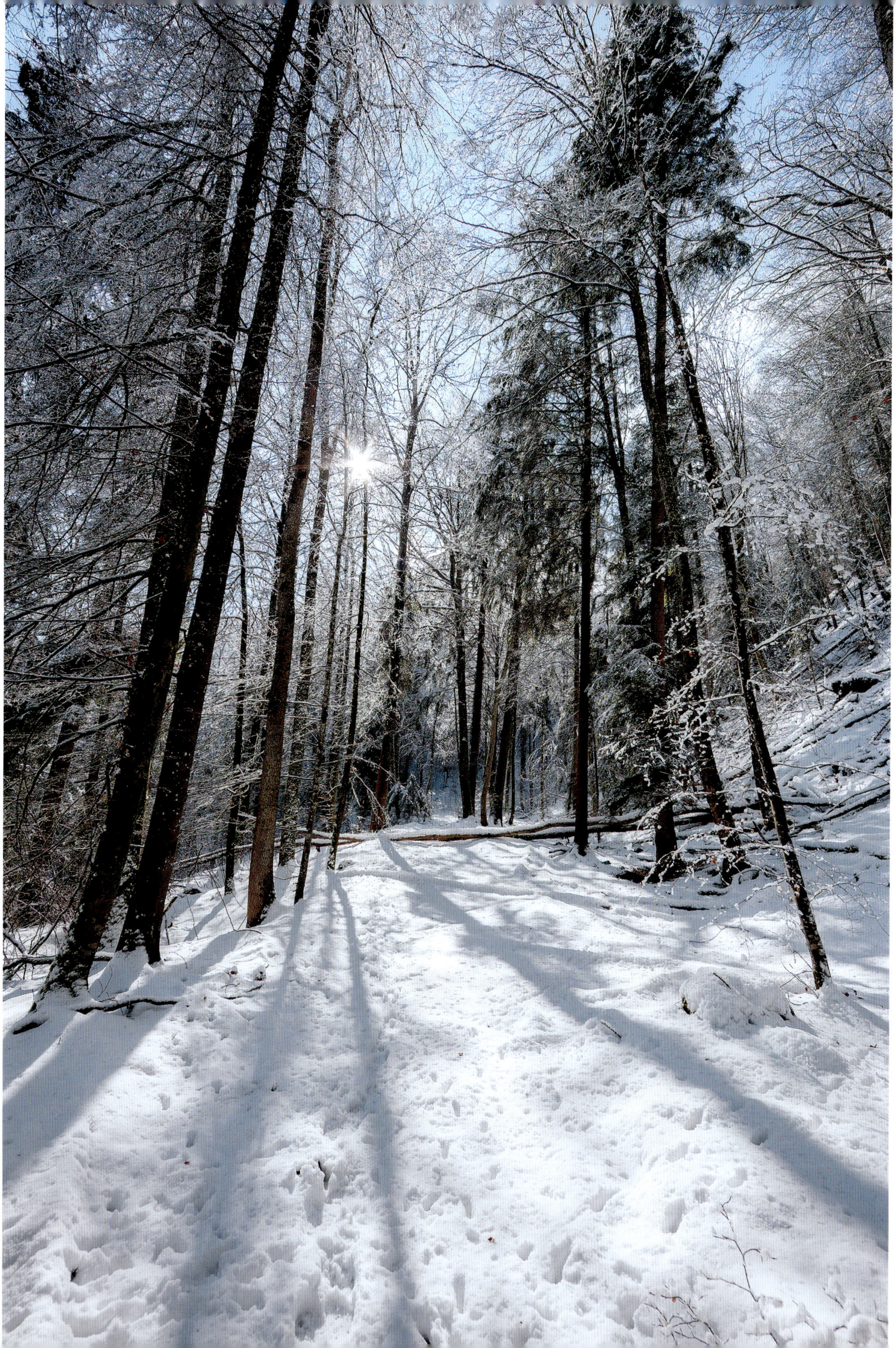

Vielfältige Formen der Pilze: Trametes, ein Baumpilz mit mehrjährigem konsolenartigem Fruchtkörper, bei dem an der Vorderkante und Unterseite jedes Jahr eine neue Zuwachszone gebildet wird. Darunter der Buchen-Schleimrübling, ein baumbewohnender Ständerpilz (links).
Neben Totholz wächst das Kleine (einheimische) Immergrün: Die Pflanze treibt unterirdisch weit kriechende Rhizome, so dass offen ist, ob in einem ausgedehnten Bestand einzelne Büschel, Sprosse oder das ganze Feld als eine Pflanze, ein Individuum gelten sollen (rechts).

The many forms of fungi: Trametes, a tree fungus with a perennial, console-like fruiting body, on which a new growth ring is formed every year at the front edge and the bottom. Underneath is the porcelain fungus (Oudemansiella mucida), an arboreal column mushroom (left).
Myrtle, a small native evergreen, has extensive creeping rhizomes underground, therefore, in an extended population, it is unclear whether the plant should be considered as one plant, as a single clump, as a sprout, or as the entire field (right).

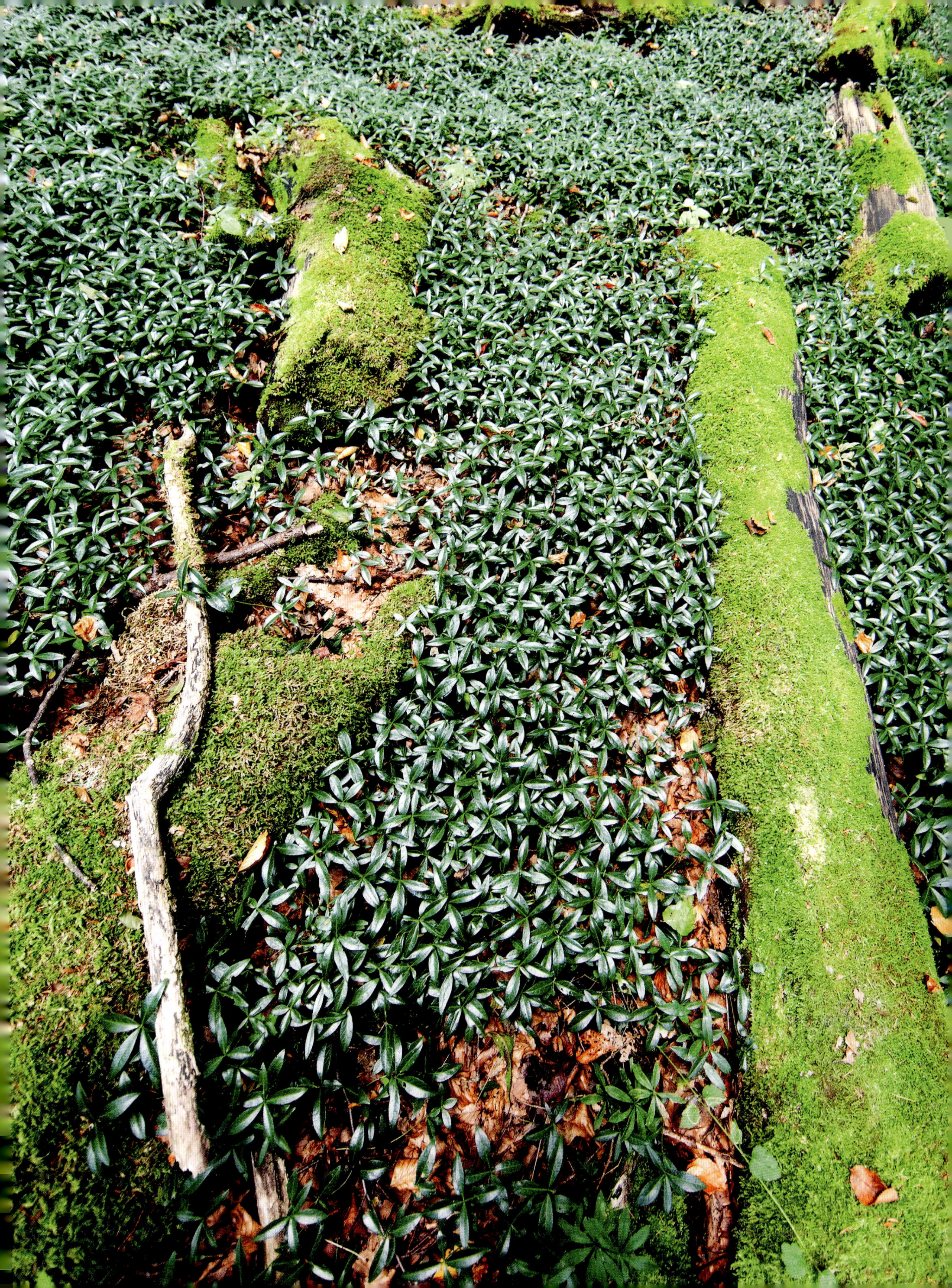

Die Würm-Eiszeit war für den Wildnispark Sihlwald ein Glücksfall: nicht nur weil die Gletscher den Albiskamm bewahrten, sondern auch weil die Böden der Hangterrasse Waldmatt/ Weienbrunnen durch die Grundmoräne abgedichtet wurden und immer wieder – teilweise auf Zeit – spiegelnde Kleinstgewässer entstehen (links).
Die Wintersonne lässt Buchenzweige und -knospen glitzern und gibt dem offenen Raum eine feingliedrige Struktur. Im Sommer bilden die Äste und Zweige ein breites, beschattendes Blätterdach. Pflanzen, die auch im Schatten leben können, sind damit den lichthungrigen Arten gegenüber begünstigt (rechts).

The Würm Ice Age was a stroke of luck for the Wilderness Park Sihlwald: not only because the glaciers preserved the Albis Ridge, but also because the bottom of the hillside terrace of Waldmatt/Weienbrunnen was sealed off by a ground moraine, leading to the creation of small reflecting bodies of water, again and again over time (left).
The winter sun makes the beech twigs and buds sparkle and gives the open space a delicate structure. In summer, the limbs and branches form a broad, shady canopy. Here, plants that can live in the shade have an advantage over 'light-hungry' species (right).

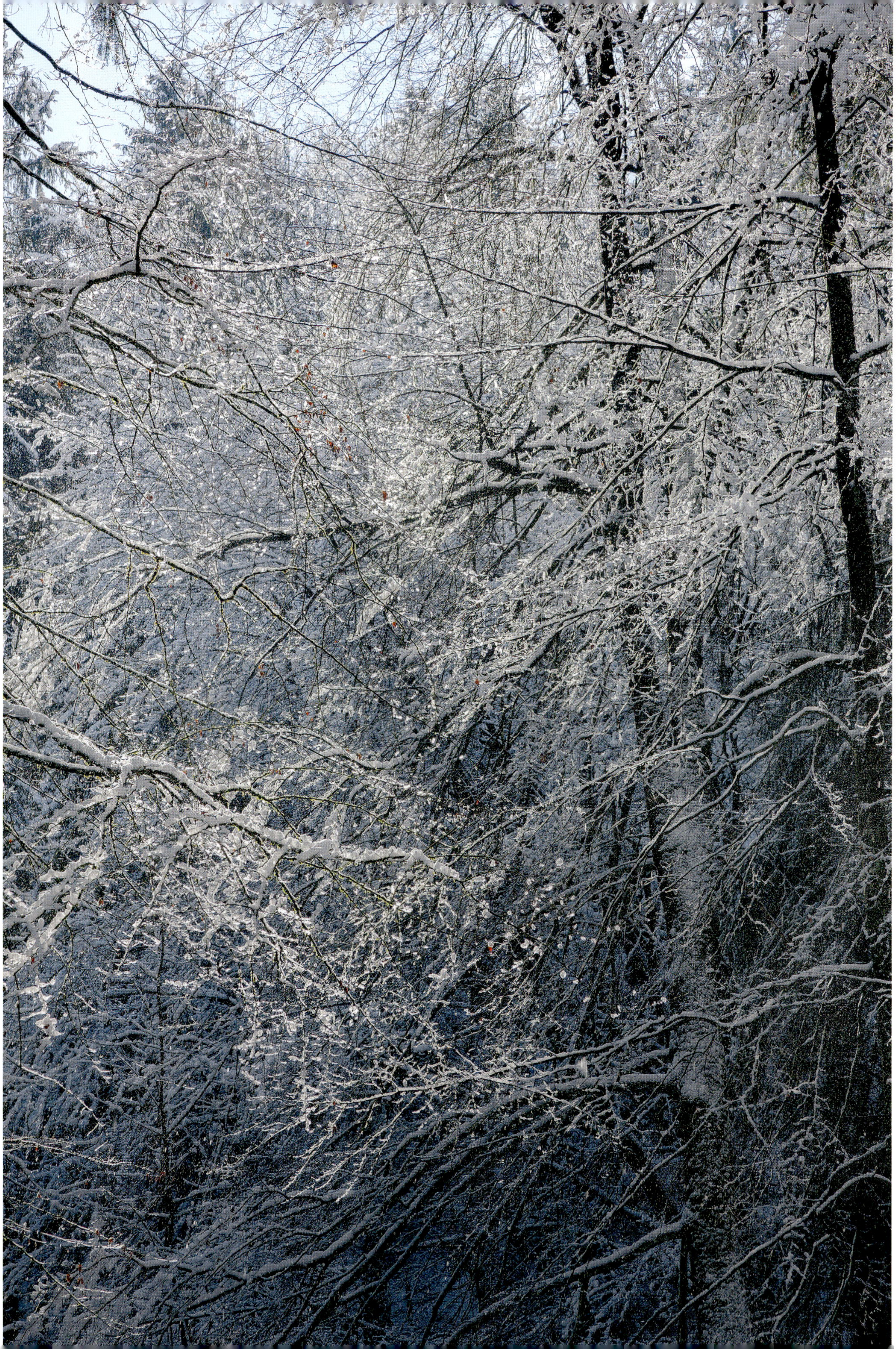

Mit dem herbstlich rotbraunen Buchenlaub, das den Boden teppichartig bedeckt, wird der Wald fast zum wohnlichen Innenraum. Unter Förstern wird die Buche zuweilen «Mutter des Waldes» genannt. Dies nicht nur, weil Falllaub vielen Kleinlebewesen einen wärmenden Winterschutz bietet, sondern auch, weil das ohne hemmende Gerbstoffe langsam verrottende Buchenlaub als ideales Keimbett gilt – nicht nur für Buchen (links).

Über den mit Moosen und Sauerklee überwachsenen Resten einer Buche hat sich ein Rotrandiger Baumschwamm für den Abbau des Holzes eingenistet. Mit den attraktiven Zuwachsringen ist er ein kleines Kunstwerk geworden (rechts).

When autumn's russet beech leaves cover the ground like a carpet, the forest almost becomes a homely interior space. Amongst foresters, the beech is sometimes called the 'mother of the forest'. This is not only because the falling leaves provide warming winter protection to many small beings, but also because the slowly decomposing beech leaves, without inhibiting tannins, are considered the ideal seeding bed – and not only for beeches (left).

On top of the remains of a beech tree overgrown with moss and sorrel, a Red-Belt Conk (Fomitopsis Pinicola) has taken root to degrade the wood. With the attractive growth rings, it has become a work of art (right).

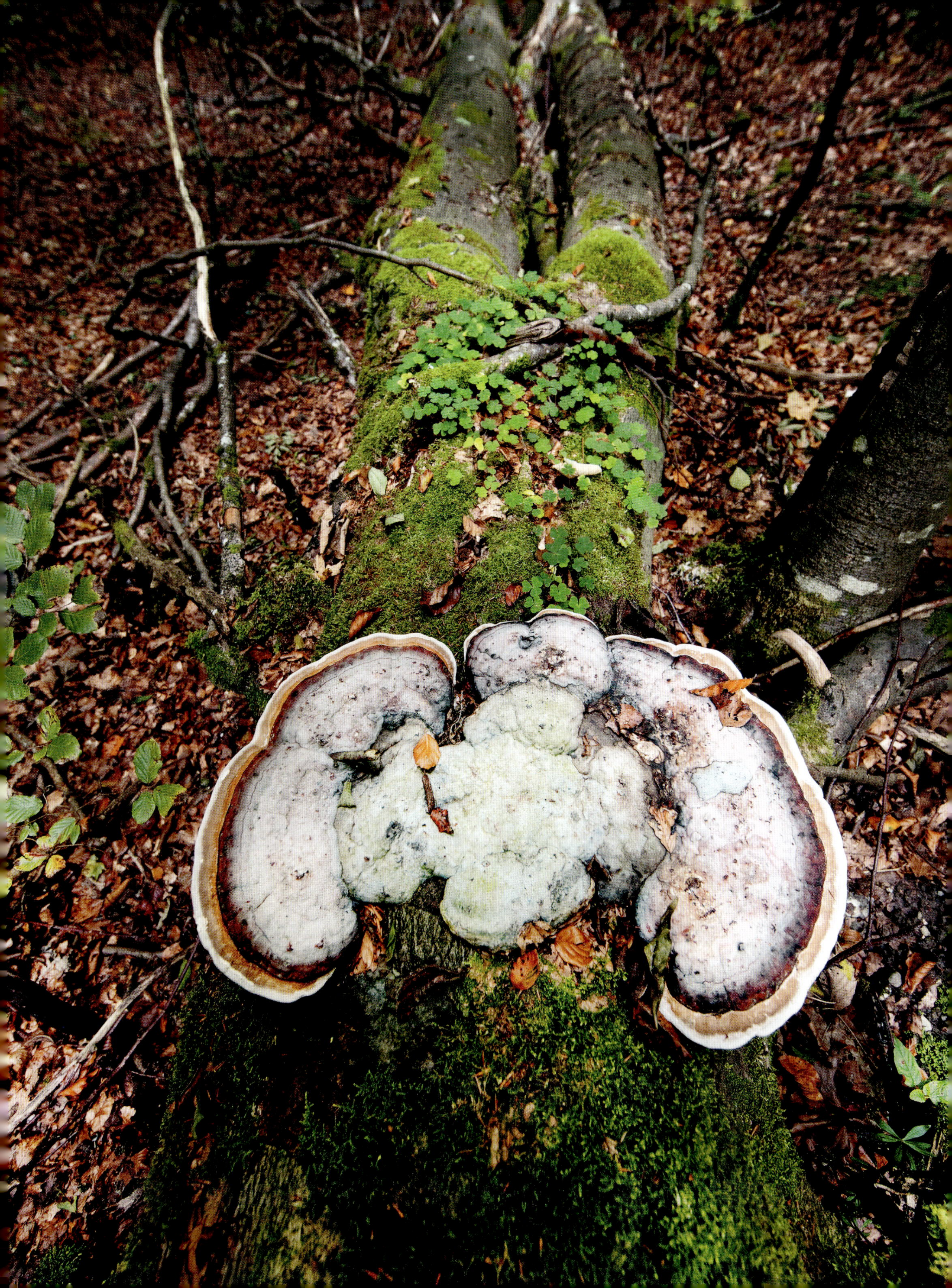

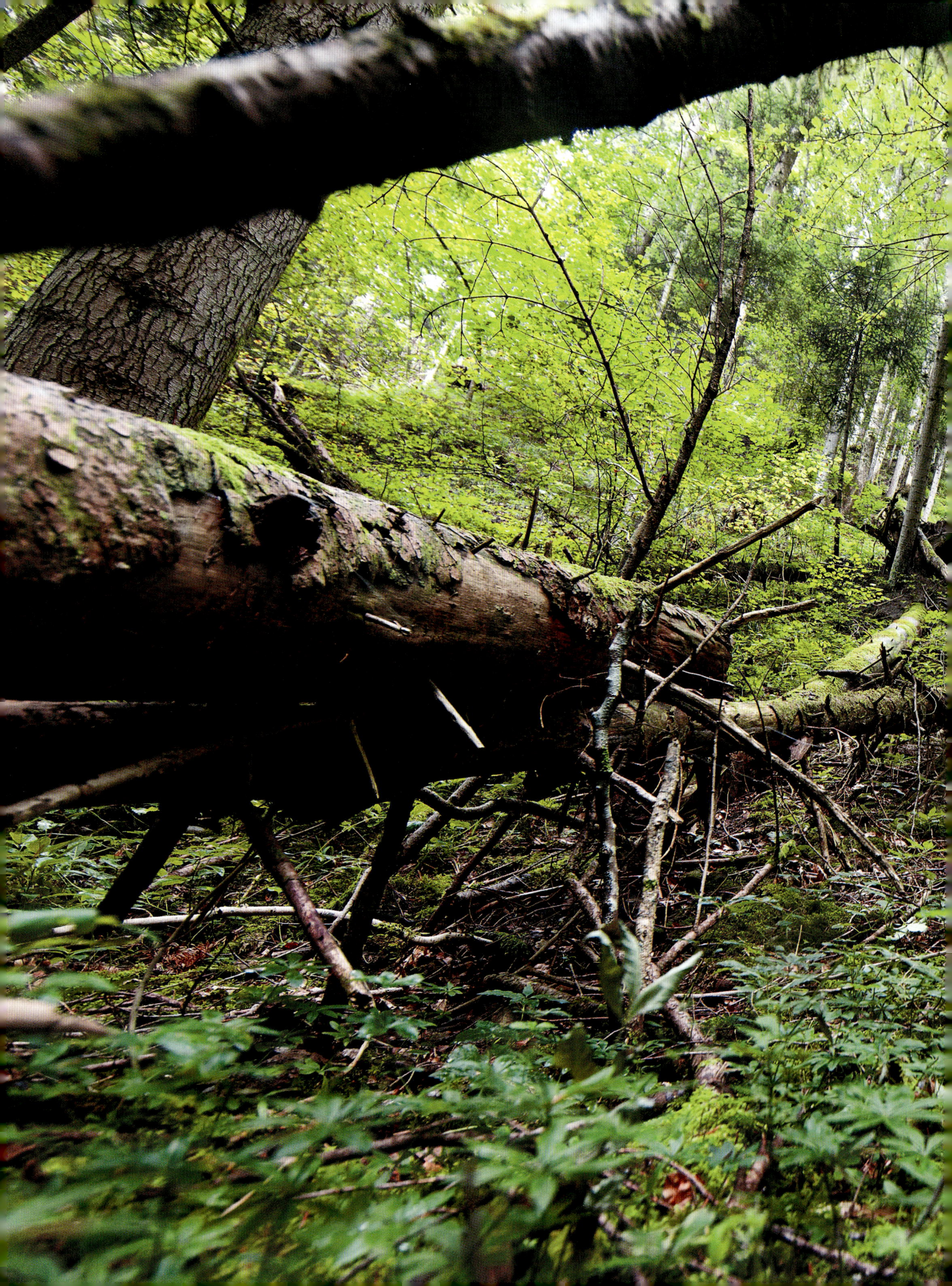

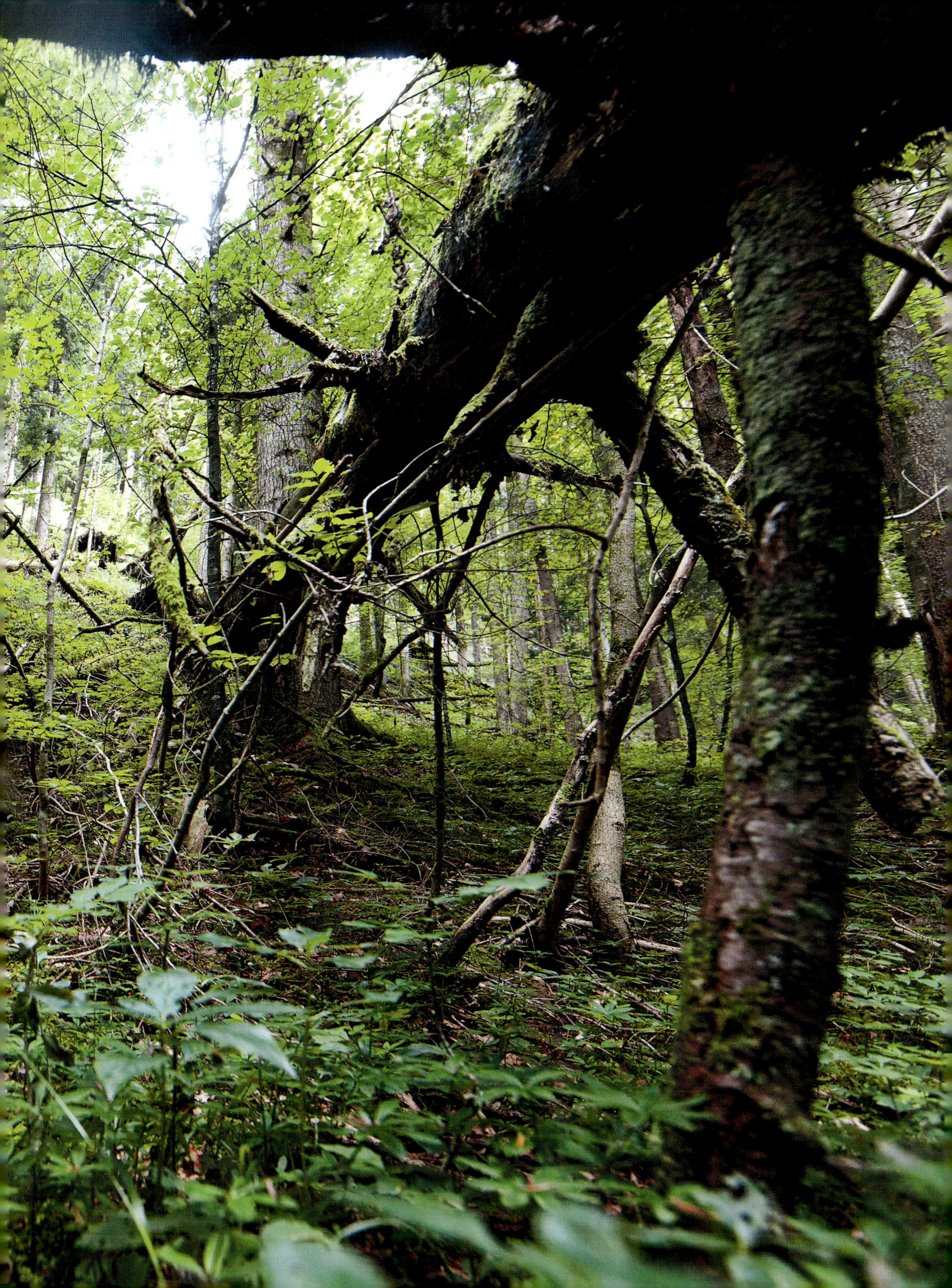

Im schwer zugänglichen Bärtobel-Wald, seit 1981 Schutzgebiet von Pro Natura, wird mit dem Schutzziel «Naturwald» die weitere Entwicklung dem Wald selbst überlassen. Das Waldbild, das sich so entwickelt, steht im Kontrast zu einem forstlich gepflegten, stabilen Wald. Die Natur bietet auch Labilität und Dynamik: links hinten die frühe Dickungsphase, rechts hinten die Optimalphase, vorne die Zerfallsphase. Das räumliche Nebeneinander des zeitlichen Nacheinanders ist im Naturwald charakteristisch (vorhergehende Doppelseite).

Brennholz, das im wilden Bärtobel wohl schon vor Jahrzehnten gesägt und nicht abgeholt wurde, fördert im Verrottungsprozess neues Leben (links).
Der vielbegangene Wanderweg von Gfell zum Hörnli führt der Geländekante über dem Bärtobel entlang. Die alte Buche wäre längst talwärts gestürzt, gäben ihr die Wasser suchenden kräftigen Wurzeln nicht sicheren Halt. Gelitten hat der Baum dennoch – wohl mehr noch durch die Bodenverdichtung am Wanderweg als durch die in die Rinde eingeschnittenen Zeichen (rechts).

The hard to reach Bärtobel forest has been a protected reserve of Pro Natura since 1981. In order to achieve their protection goal of becoming a 'natural forest', the further development of the forest is being left to nature itself. The image of a forest left to its own development is a contrast to a neat, forestry groomed, stable forest. Nature also provides instability and dynamics: behind on the left is the early Thickening Phase, behind on the right is the Optimal Phase and in the front, the Decaying Phase. The spatial juxtaposition of a chronological sequence is characteristic of a natural forest (previous double-page).

Firewood that was probably cut in the wild Bärtobel decades ago and was never collected facilitates new life in the rotting process (left).
The much-frequented hiking trail from Gfell to the Hörnli leads along the edge of the terrain above the Bärtobel. The old beech would have long ago plunged downhill if the strong water seeking roots didn't give it a strong firm hold. Despite that, the tree has suffered – even more from the soil compaction along the hiking trail, than by the marks cut into the bark (right).

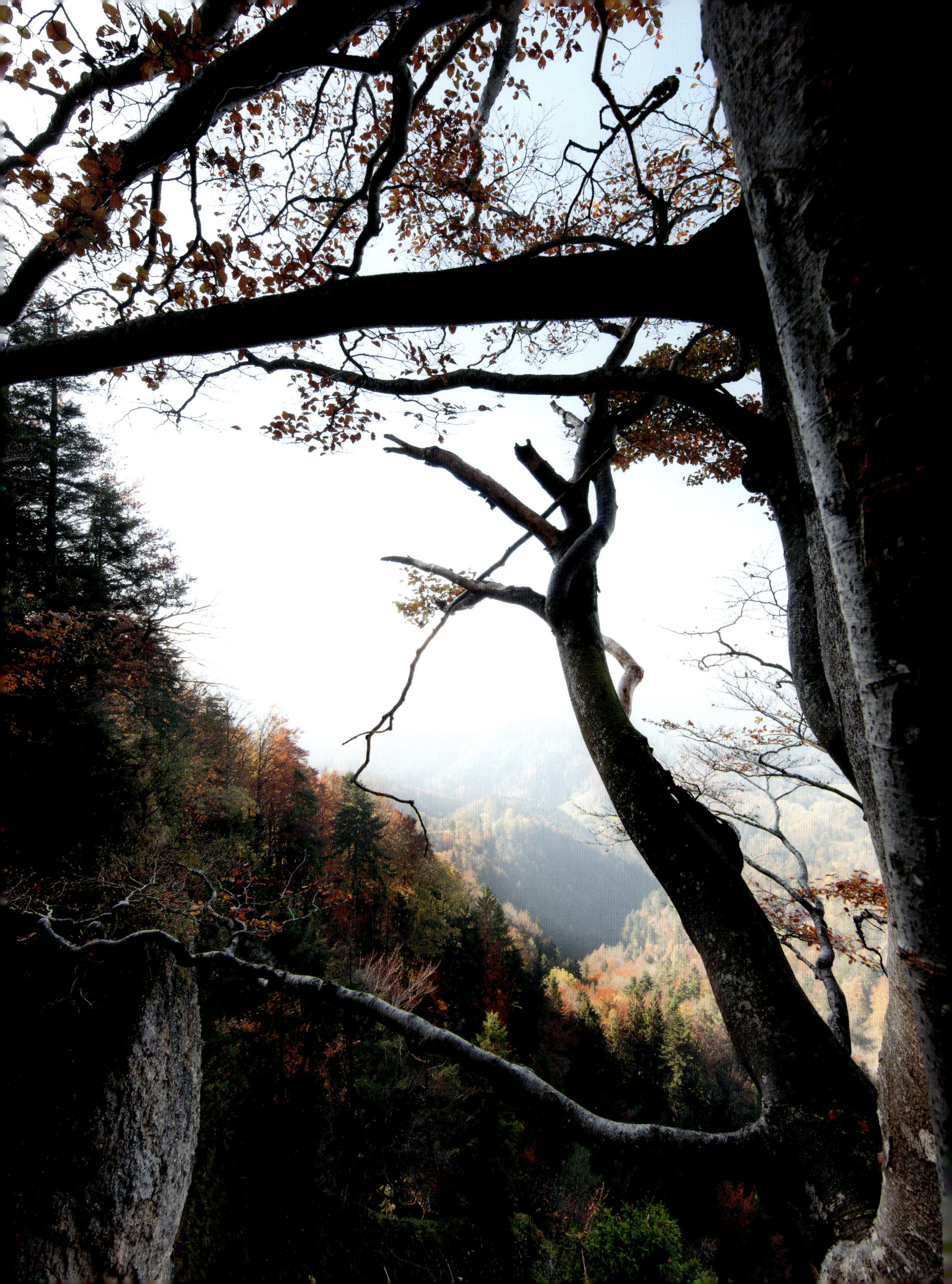

Die steilen Wälder im Quellgebiet der Hinteren und Vorderen Töss haben Schutzwaldcharakter. Hier ist ein möglichst stabiler Wald gefragt, beispielsweise ein stufiger Tannen-, Fichten- und Buchenmischwald (links).
Auch sterbende Bäume sind in ihrem «zweiten Leben» als Totholz wichtig, indem sie einem Heer von Holzpilzen, Moosen, Insekten, Spinnen, Schnecken und Vögeln Lebensraum bieten. Ein Wald kann ohne Rehe leben, aber nicht ohne Pilze (rechts).

The steep forests in the headwaters of the posterior and anterior Töss have the characteristics of a typical protected forest. In this case, the best possible stable forest is needed, for example, with a stepwise mixed forest of firs, spruces and beech trees (left).
Dying trees, in their 'second life' as deadwood, are also important because they offer a habitat to a host of wood fungi, mosses, insects, spiders, snails and birds. A forest can live without deer, but not without fungi (right).

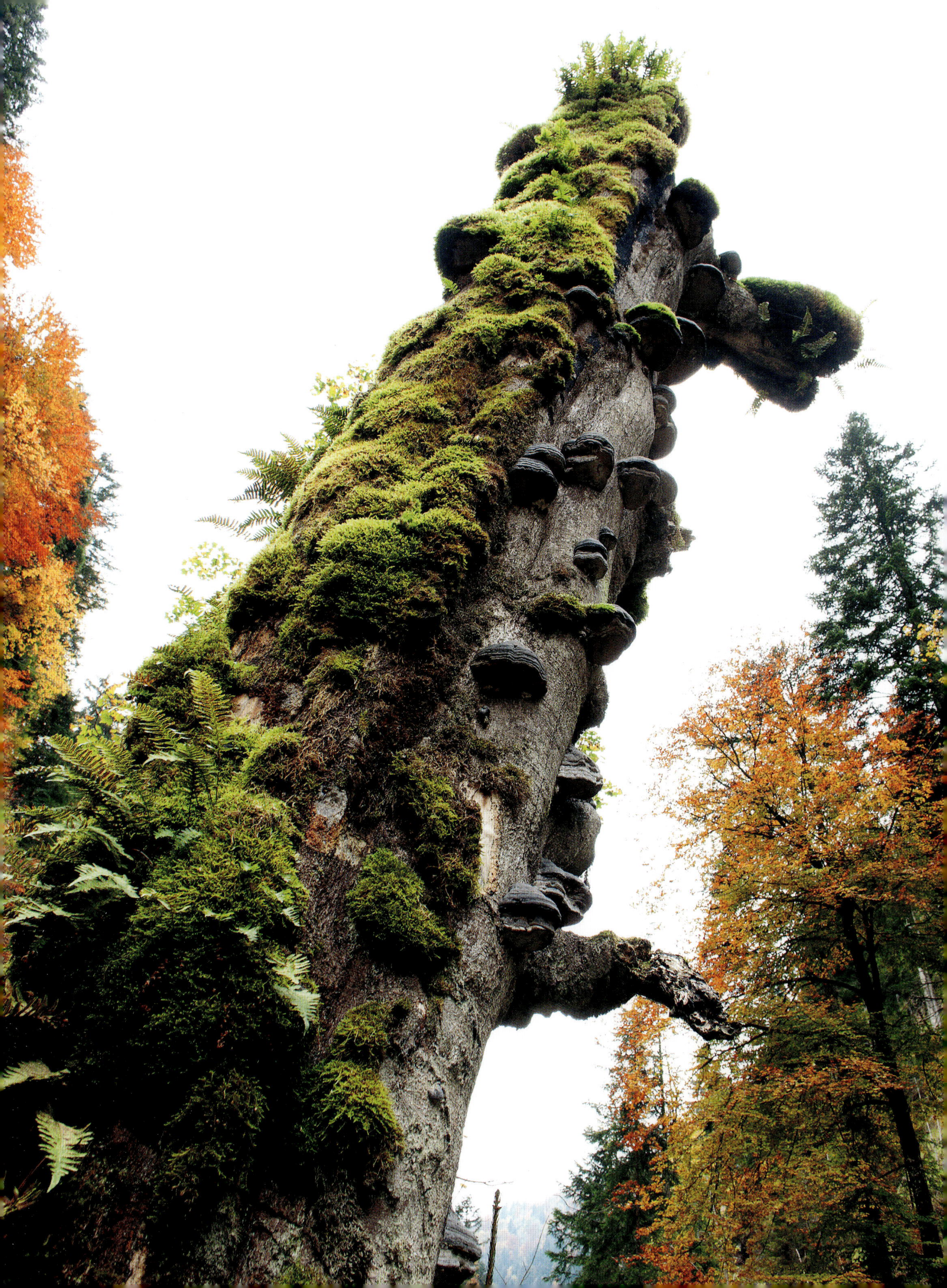

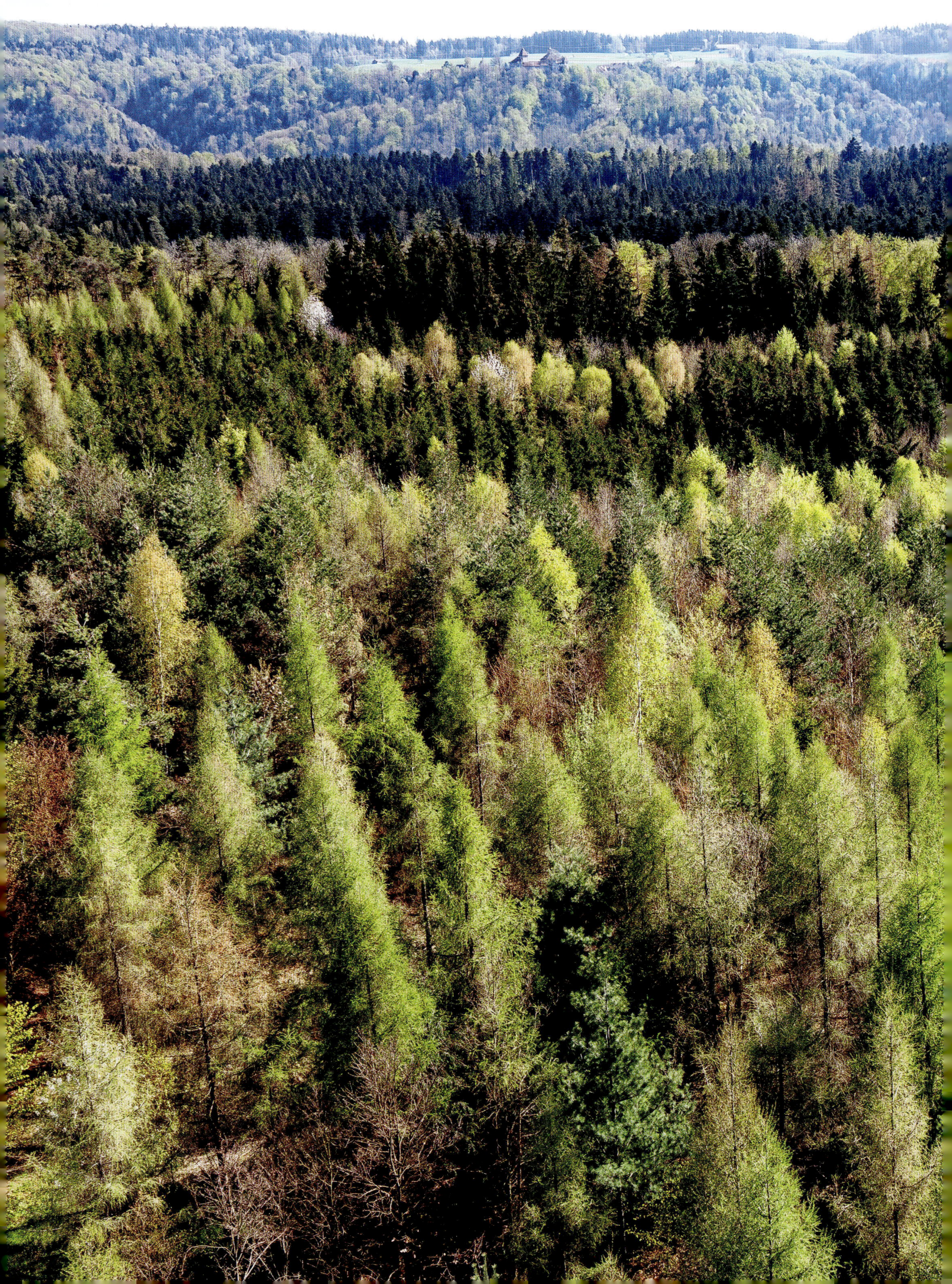

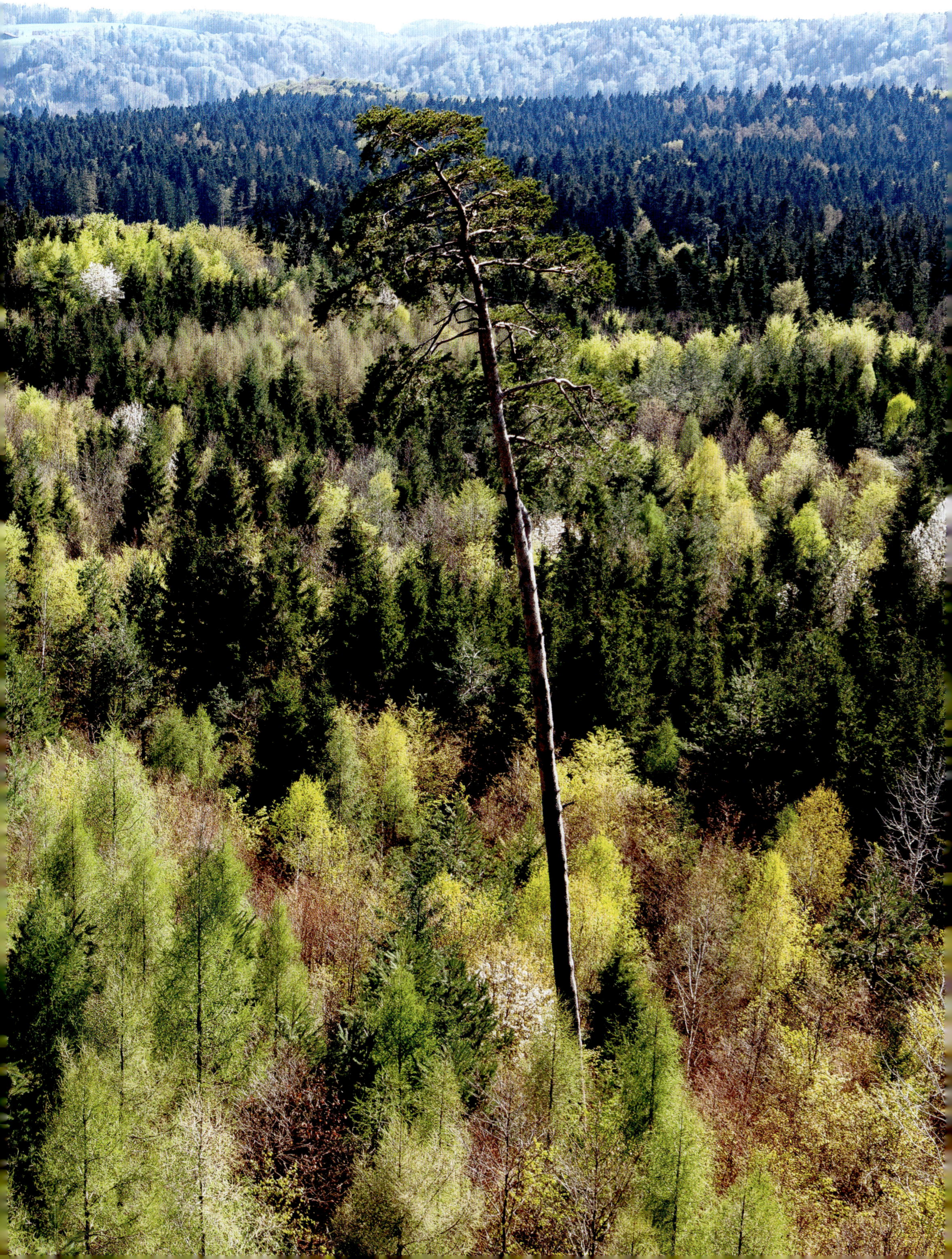

Vom Turm auf der nahezu ebenen Kuppe des Eschenbergs aus gesehen, bietet der rundum bewaldete Hügel das Bild eines schönen Mischwaldes – garniert mit einem Föhren-Überständer als Samenbaum. Auf der anderen Seite der Töss erkennt man die Kyburg vor offenen Landwirtschaftsflächen über den ebenfalls bewaldeten Hanglagen des Leisentals (vorhergehende Doppelseite).

Eichenwald in Bülach. Bäume dienen als Lebensraum und Nahrungsbasis für Hunderte von Tierarten und Pilzen, sei es lebend oder als noch stehendes oder liegendes Totholz im komplexen Verrottungsprozess. Keine andere Baumart in unsern Wäldern wird von so vielen Tieren genutzt wie die Eiche.

Looking from the tower on the nearly flat summit of the Eschenberg, the surrounding wooded hillside offers an image of a beautiful mixed forest – topped by a pine that does not grow anymore, but still serves as a seed tree. On the other side of the Töss, the Kyburg Castle is located in the open area at top left centre looking over an open agricultural landscape above the equally wooded slopes of the Leisental (previous double-page).

Oak forest in Bülach. Trees serve as a habitat and food source for hundreds of species of animals and fungi, whether the trees are alive, still standing or lying as deadwood in a complex rotting process. No other tree species in our forests is used by so many animals as the oak tree.

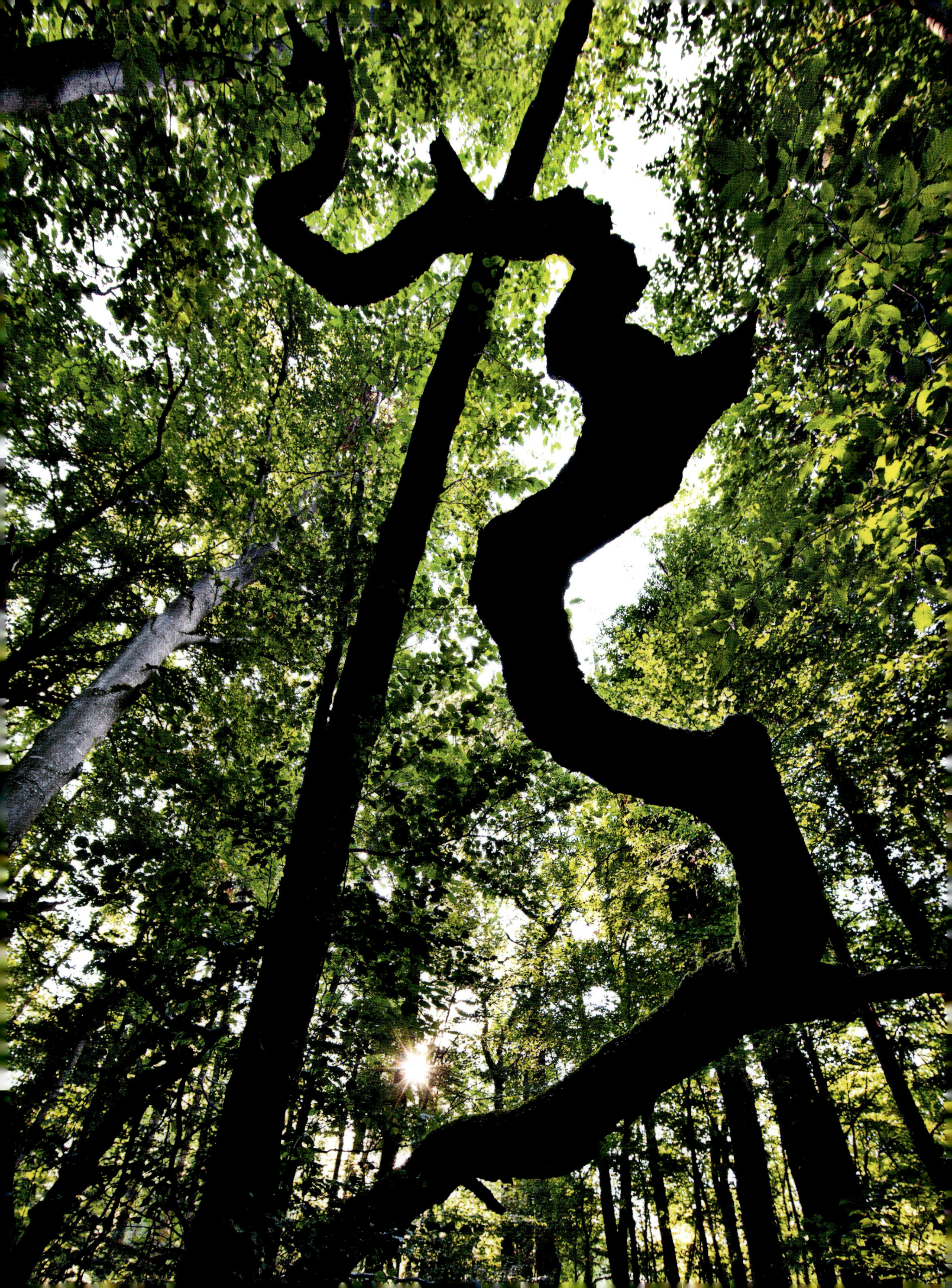

In wintermilden und sommertrockenen Lagen in den niederen nördlichen Teilen des Kantons wie im Niderholz bei Ellikon und in Bülach entwickeln sich Eichen besonders gut.
In diesem Eichenwald in Bülach wachsen die Bäume gemeinsam. Sie machen sich dabei nicht nur gegenseitig den Wurzelraum streitig, sondern auch den besonnten Kronenraum.

Oaks develop particularly well in areas of mild winters and dry summers in the lower northern parts of the canton, such as Niderholz by Ellikon and Bülach. In this oak forest in Bulach, the trees grow collectively. They are not only fighting over each other's root zone, but probably for space in the sunny canopy.

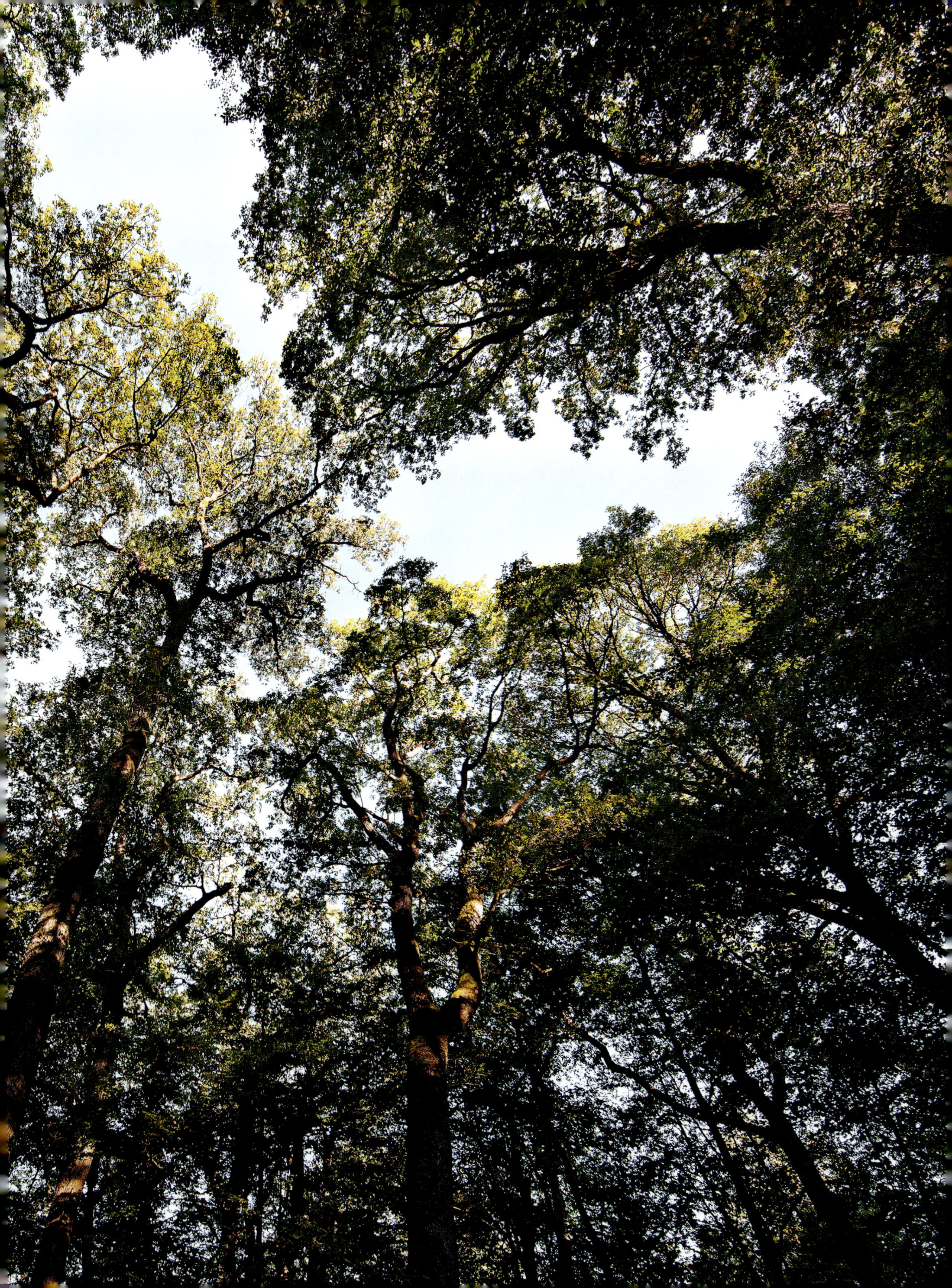

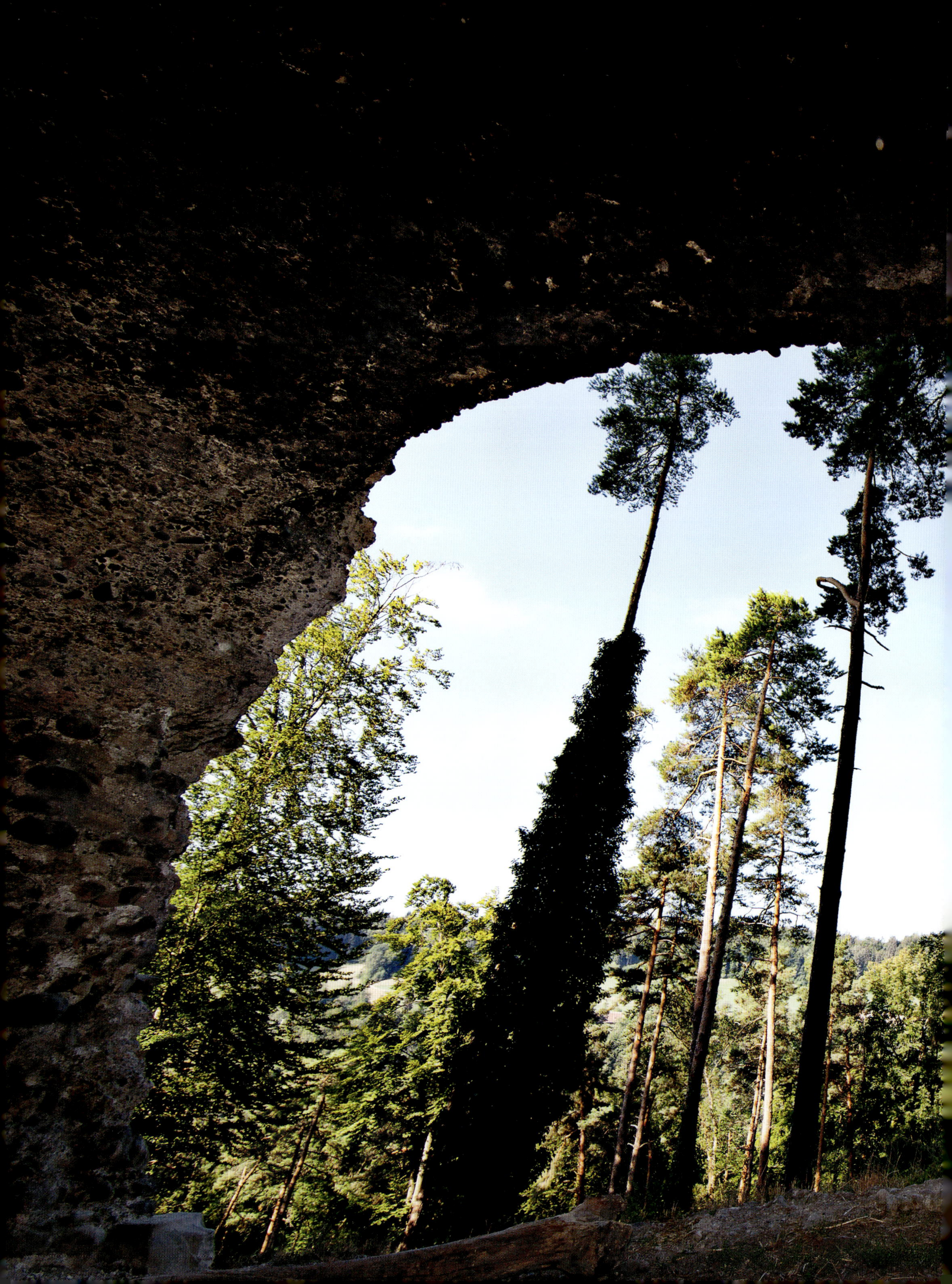

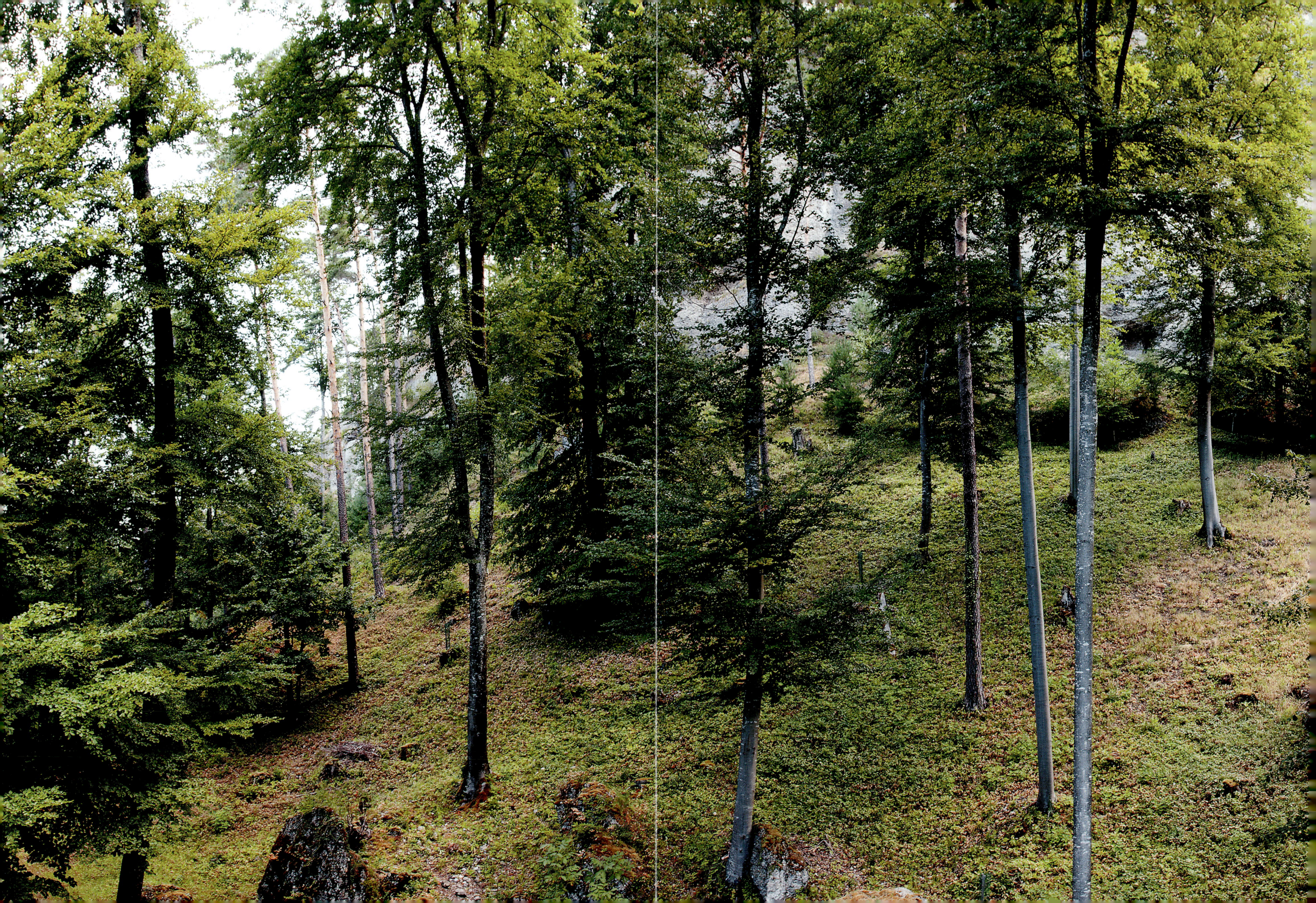

Die Höhle Hohflue bei Bachs, auch als Erdmannliloch bezeichnet, war vermutlich eine hochmittelalterliche zugemauerte Grottenburg, wie sie aus dem Bleniotal und anderen Tälern der Alpen bekannt sind. Der steile, nach Westen exponierte Hang unterhalb der Höhle ist bestockt mit aufgelichteten Waldföhren und bietet hangabwärts in einer blühenden Waldwiese eine Insekten-Weide – dank Föhrenstammen, die vom spät blühenden Efeu umrankt sind, bis in den Herbst hinein (vorhergehende Doppelseite).

The cave of Hohflue by Bach, also called the Erdmannliloch (small earthman hole), was probably a medieval walled grotto, as they are known in the Bleniotal and other valleys of the Alps. Just below the cave, the steep slope with a western exposure is timbered with Scots pine. Further downhill, a blooming forest meadow offers an insect meadow – thanks to the pine trunks that are entwined with late flowering ivy until well into the autumn (previous double-page).

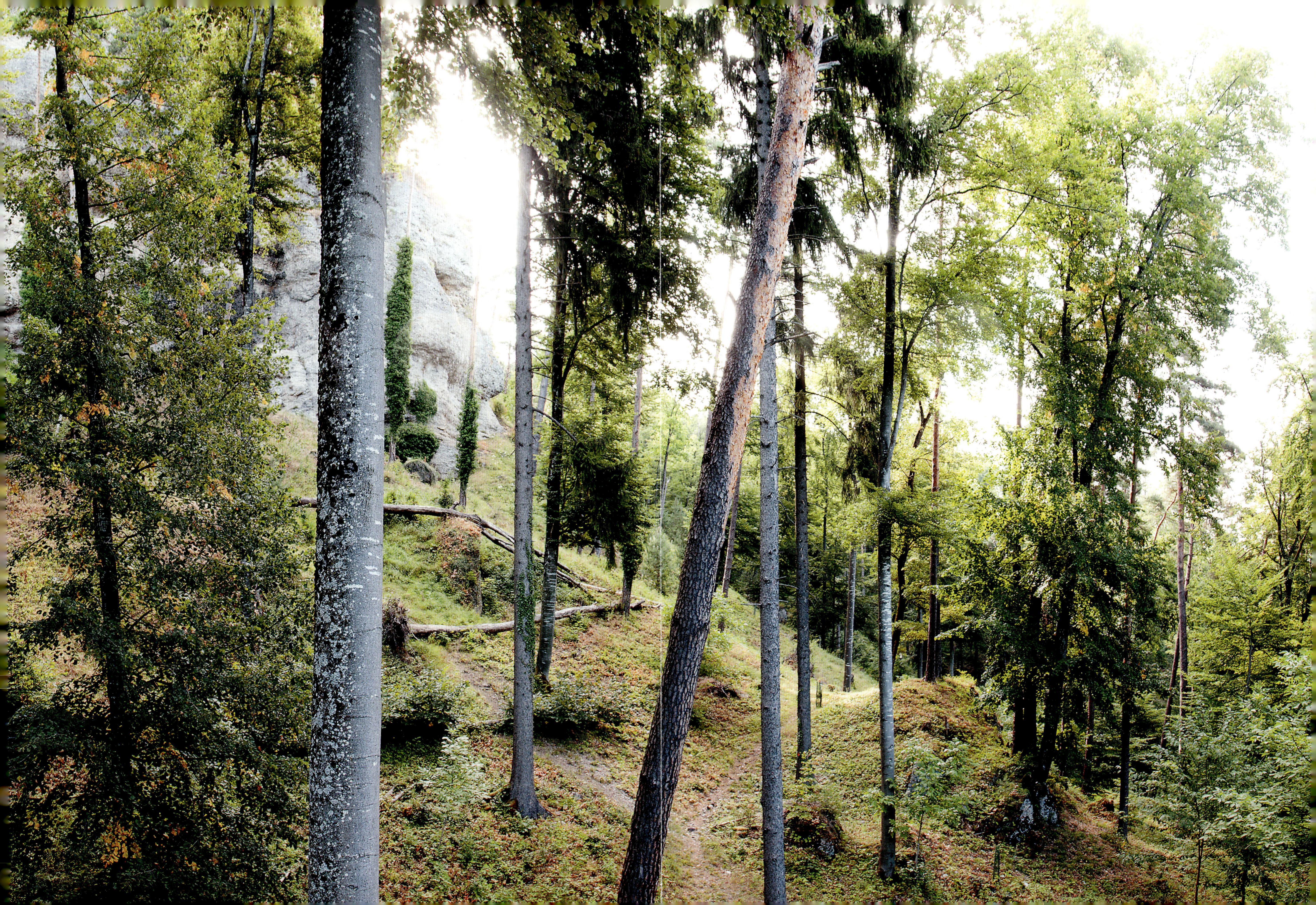

Mit dem Auflichten eines dunkel gewordenen Waldes im Bachsertal verändert sich die ganze Lebensgemeinschaft. In der Krautschicht werden lichtbedürftige Arten zulasten von schattenresistenten gefördert. Wirbellose Kleintiere nutzen reaktionsschnell das neue Lokalklima, Bäume reagieren träger.

When a dark forest in the Bachsertal was thinned out, the entire symbiotic community changed. In the herbal layer, light-demanding species were promoted, at the expense of shade-resistant species. Small invertebrate animals quickly responded to the new local climate, while the trees will respond rather more slowly.

Parkanlagen und Stadtwälder
Parks and Municipal Forests

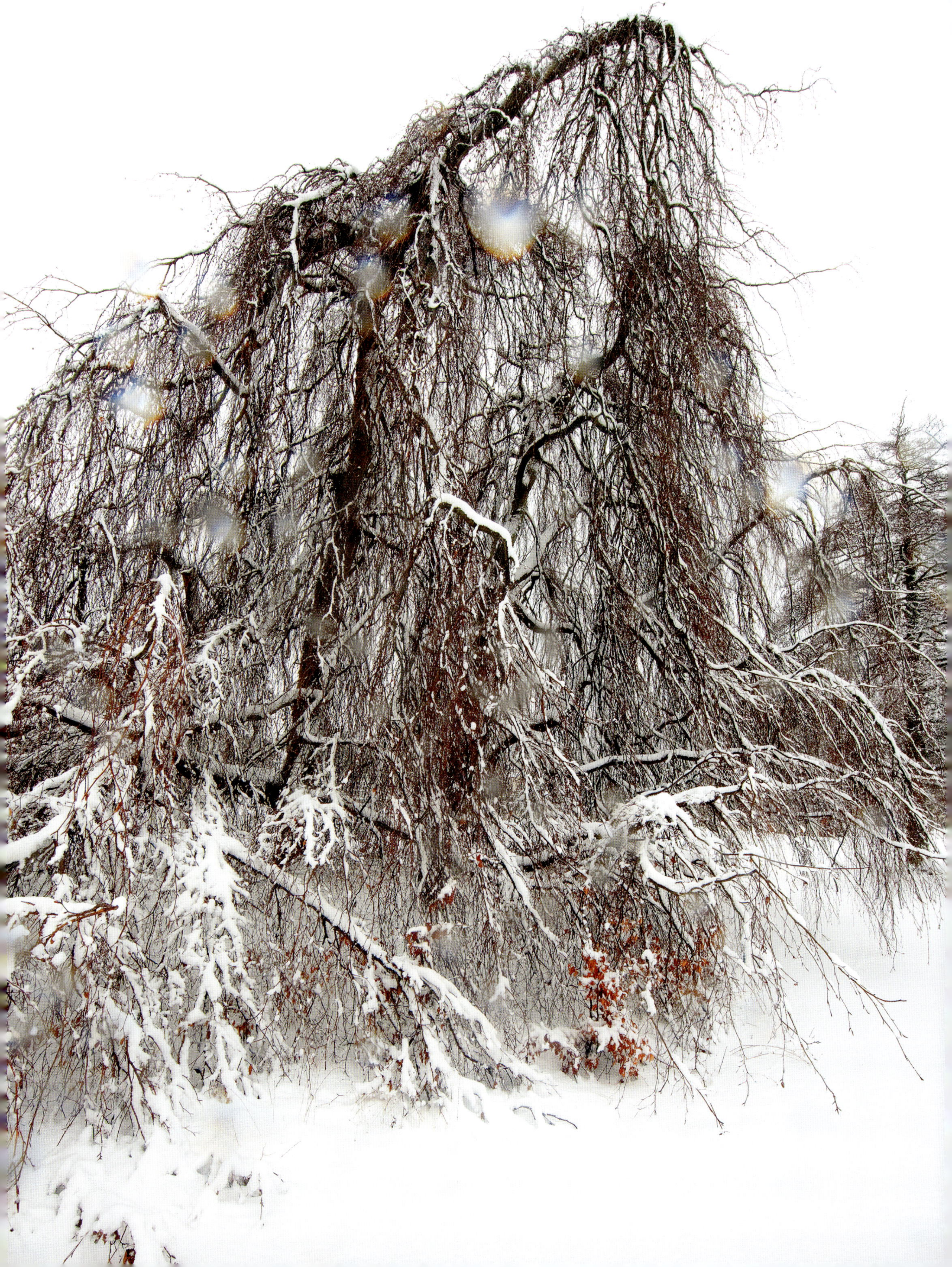

«Stadtpärke sind beschauliche Orte der Ruhe und Entspannung – auch Orientierungspunkte und gärtnerische Sehenswürdigkeiten.»

'City parks are contemplative places of quiet and relaxation – as well as orientation points and horticultural sites of interest.'

Die Hängebuche im Zürcher Allenmoosbad ist als Einzelbaum zu jeder Jahreszeit ein Blickfang.

As a single tree, the hanging beech at Zurich's Allenmoos Swimming Pool, is an eye-catcher in every season.

Die beiden grossen Städte des Kantons, Zürich und Winterthur, sind in erster Linie wichtige Zentren der Wirtschaft, von Kulturinstituten und höheren Schulen. Aber auch ihre Parkanlagen und bewaldeten Hügel sind von Bedeutung.[1] Neben dem barock restaurierten Rechberg-Garten und modern gestalteten Parkanlagen wie dem MFO-Park in Oerlikon sind in den letzten Jahren in Zürich Stadträume entstanden, in denen Naturnähe erlebbar wird. Die Werdinsel und der Wipkingerpark mit ihrem direkten Zugang zum Wasser gehören dazu, aber auch die überraschenden, im Rahmen des Bachkonzeptes ausgedolten Kleingewässer mit ihrer bachtypischen Flora und Fauna wie der Nebelbach im Stadtquartier Seefeld. In Winterthur zeugen der Eulachpark, das Reutlinger Ried und das Naturschutzgebiet Lantig von einer vergleichbaren Entwicklung: Das Bestreben, «grüne Inseln» zu vernetzen, ist Ausdruck des in den letzten Jahrzehnten in beiden Städten wachsenden ökologischen Verständnisses. Die urbane Gartenbewegung, das «Urban Gardening», holt die Natur in die Stadt. Stadtbewohnerinnen und -bewohner bauen auf Kleinflächen essbare Wildpflanzen und Gemüse an; private Gärten werden naturbewusst gestaltet und fördern die Biodiversität. Vor allem sind sich beide Städte auch der Bedeutung des Waldes als gut erreichbarem Naturwert und attraktivem Erholungsraum bewusst – mitsamt Aussichtspunkten wie Uetliberg, Waid, Rigiblick oder Lorenchopf in Zürich und Bäumli, Brüelbergturm, Eschenbergturm oder Gretelberg in Winterthur.

Die zuständigen Verwaltungseinheiten «Grün Stadt Zürich» und «Stadtgrün Winterthur» verhehlen ihren Stolz über das Erreichte nicht. Sie sorgen sich aber auch, weil die grünen Werte trotz professionellem und engagiertem Wirken verletzlich bleiben. So wurde bei einer Handänderung ein Teil des Frohbergparks in Winterthur parzelliert und überbaut, und beim Patumbah-Park in Zürich musste man zufrie-

The two largest cities in the canton, Zurich and Winterthur, are, of course, important economic centres, in part due to their cultural institutions and schools of higher education. However, their parks and forested hills also contribute to their importance.[1] In addition to the restored baroque Rechberggarten and the modern parks, such as the MFO-Park, in recent years city spaces have opened in Zurich that offer close-to-nature experiences. The Werdinsel (insel = island) and the Wipkingerpark, with their direct access to water, are part of this trend, but within the framework of the stream concept, there are also surprises, excavated small bodies of water with their typical stream flora and fauna, as in the Nebelbach (Nebel Stream) in the Seefeld section of the city. In Winterthur, the Eulach Park, the Reutlinger Ried and the nature protection area of Lantig, all show a comparable development: The effort to link 'green islands' is an expression of the growing ecological understanding that has been taking place in both cities in the last decade. The urban gardening movement is also bringing nature into the city. City dwellers now cultivate edible wild plants and vegetables on small surfaces; private gardens receive new designs that are 'aware of nature' and promote biodiversity. In particular, both of these cities are also well aware of the importance of forests as places of easily accessible 'green value' and attractive recreational spaces – including outlook points, such as the Uetliberg, Waid, Rigiblick or Lorenchopf in Zurich and the Bäumli, Brüelbergturm, Eschenbergturm or Gretelberg in Winterthur.

The departments responsible for the management of parks and green spaces, Grün Stadt Zurich (Green City Zurich) and Stadtgrün (City Green) Winterthur, do not conceal their pride in their achievements. However, they still have concerns because green values remain vulnerable, despite their best professional and dedicated efforts. For example, a change of ownership caused a part of the Frohberg Park in Winterthur to be cut into parcels and built over, while one must be

den sein, dass es wenigstens gelang, den Hauptteil zu schützen. Die Ziele des Naturschutzes sind in beiden Städten weitgehend vergleichbar – ungleich sind aber die Rahmenbedingungen, wie ein Blick auf die Zahlen zeigt:

satisfied that at least the main part of Patumbah Park in Zurich could be protected. The goals of the Nature Protection Programmes in both cities are comparable to a large extent, however, the framework conditions are dissimilar, as a glance at the numbers show:

Zürich			Winterthur
390474	Einwohner 2014	No. of residents 2014	106552
4442.3	Einwohner / km^2	Residents per km^2	1564.2
9188 ha	Fläche	Surface area	6812 ha
See, Limmat, Sihl, Glatt	Gewässer	Bodies of water	Eulach, Töss
	Flächenanteile in %	Surface use in %	
10.1	Landwirtschaft	Agriculture	24.8
26.2	Wald	Forest	40.5
14.6	Verkehrsfläche	Traffic and Transport	9
49.4	Siedlungsfläche	Settlement areas	24.5

So ist in Zürich bei einer um einen Viertel grösseren Gesamtfläche die Bewohnerdichte nahezu dreimal grösser als in Winterthur. Ausserhalb der engeren Altstadt ist in Winterthur die Besiedelung ausgesprochen locker. Unternehmer liessen für ihre Arbeiter ab der zweiten Hälfte des 19. Jahrhunderts Siedlungen errichten, in denen neben den Wohnhäusern bewusst auch Gärten eingeplant wurden. Für sich selbst bauten die Industriellen und Handelsherren Villen mit grosszügigen Gartenanlagen. So wurde Winterthur zur «Gartenstadt». Manche dieser Villengärten gingen später an die Stadt über, die sie der Öffentlichkeit zugänglich gemacht hat und bis heute pflegt: der Lindengut-Park, der Park der Villa Rychenberg, der Rosengarten oder die Parkanlage der Villa Bühler-Egg. Bereits in den 1830er-Jahren hatte der Abbruch der Stadttore und das Zuschütten der Stadtgräben Raum geschaffen für Promenaden rund um die Altstadt und Parkanlagen – aus ihnen ging Ende des 19. Jahrhunderts die grosszügige Anlage des «Stadtgartens» hervor. Auch in Zürich gibt es gepflegte Gartenanlagen wie den Irisgarten, die Rosenanlage im Muraltengut, den alten und den neuen botanischen Garten oder den mit neu geformten Hügeln und Weihern überaus reizvoll gestalteten Irchelpark. Geologen, die mit ihrem fachlichen Blick gewohnt sind, im Geländerelief die Landschaftsgeschichte zu lesen, dürften den ursprünglich vom Linth-Rhein Gletscher sauber geschliffenen Milchbuck vielleicht vermissen und das neu geschaffene, ansprechende Relief als Betrugsversuch an der Landschaftsgeschichte einstufen.

Zürich ist mit dem See, der Limmat, der Sihl und dem Schanzengraben eine Wasserstadt. Gemäss dem «Grünbuch» räumt die Stadt Zürich den Seeanlagen als Imageträger und als meistgenutzte Pärke die höchste Priorität ein. Die ausgedehnten Anlagen

In black and white, it is clear that though Zurich has 25 % more total surface area, the residential density is close to three times larger than in Winterthur. Outside the narrow Old City in Winterthur, the settlement pattern becomes notably looser. In the second half of the 19th century, entrepreneurs had settlements constructed for their workers, in which they consciously planned gardens next to the residential buildings. For themselves, the industrialists and commercial bosses built villas with generous gardens. This made Winterthur into a 'Garden City'. Some of these villa gardens were later given over to the city, which opened them to the public and has maintained them until today: The Lindengut Park, the park of the Villa Rychenberg, the Rosengarten or the park of the Villa Bühler-Egg. In the 1830s, the demolition of the city gates and filling of the city moat had already created space for promenades around the old city and parks, from which Winterthur's generous system of City Gardens emerged at the end of the 19th century. In Zurich, there are also groomed gardens, such as the Irisgarten, the Rosengarten in Muraltengut, the old and new Botanical Gardens and the extremely exciting Irchel Park with its design of newly formed hills and ponds. Geologists who are accustomed to reading a landscape's history with a single expert's glance at the terrain, could perhaps miss the original Milchbuck cleanly shaved by the Linth-Rhine Glacier and thus classify the new demanding relief as an attempt to betray the landscape's history.

With its lake, the Limmat and Sihl Rivers and the Schanzengraben, Zurich is a 'Water City'. According to the Grünbuch, which presents Zurich's strategies for sustainability, the City of Zurich acknowledges that the lake is a positive part of its image and as the most popular recreational park, has the highest

vom Zürichhorn über Utoquai, Bellevue, Bürkliplatz, General-Guisan-Quai und das Arboretum bis zum Mythenquai werden an warmen Sommerabenden und bei Fest- und Sportanlässen flächendeckend genutzt. Winterthur hingegen hat keinen See, und die Eulach fliesst über längere Strecken eingedolt oder zwischen Mauern kanalisiert durch die Stadt. Erst seit wenigen Jahren darf sie sich in Neuhegi als Teil des Eulachparks wieder freier in ihrem Bett bewegen. Der Töss wird schon länger mehr Achtung entgegengebracht: Sie zeigt sich im Leisental hinter dem Eschenberg als punktuell wiederbelebter Waldfluss, der an seinem Bett arbeiten darf.

Winterthur hatte zu seiner Eulach lange Zeit wohl ein ähnlich lockeres und unbekümmertes Verhältnis wie Zürich zu seiner Sihl. Der Bau eines doppelstöckigen Parkhauses über der Sihl beim Hauptbahnhof 1972 und der Sihlhochstrasse auf 93 Pfeilern über der Sihl 1974 zeugen von wenig Respekt vor dem Flussraum. Eine Wende zeichnete sich ab der Mitte der 1980er-Jahre ab. Im Schanzengraben erstellte die Stadt von der Gessnerbrücke an eine Fussgängerpromenade über Holzstege und Sandsteinplatten. Sie verläuft dicht am Wasser und bietet einen überraschend ruhigen Kontakt mit der Natur. Die Promenade wird viel genutzt, so wie auch die benachbarte Sigi-Feigel-Terrasse, die den Zugang zum Theaterhaus Gessnerallee und über Sitzstufen zur Sihl ermöglicht.[2] Für die unterirdische Verlängerung der Sihltal Zürich Uetliberg Bahn zum Hauptbahnhof wurde das Bett der Sihl von der Stauffacherbrücke flussabwärts verengt. Diese Massnahme war zwar nur technisch bedingt und nicht zur Revitalisierung des Flusses gedacht, hatte aber genau diese Wirkung: Das schmalere Flussbett entspricht der reduzierten Wassermenge, die seit Aufnahme der Stromproduktion im Etzelwerk 1937 durch die Sihl fliesst, was deren Geschwindigkeit erhöht. Am Sihlufer entstand so zudem ein beliebter Fusspfad durch die Ufervegetation bis zur Stauffacherbrücke. Mit dem Abbruch des Parkhauses über der Sihl wurde 2004 eine alte Sünde beseitigt, nur die Sihlhochstrasse steht bis auf weiteres als Mahnmal da.

Ein wichtiger Grünwert ist in Winterthur der grosse Anteil an landwirtschaftlich genutzten Flächen am Stadtgebiet, besonders an Wald. Es sind Grünflächen, in denen neben dem Erlebniswert die wirtschaftliche Produktion wesentlich mitzählt. Tradition haben im Winterthurer Wald Schlaglichtungen, bei denen kleine Flächen fast kahlschlagartig aufgelichtet werden. Diese Methode fördert gezielt Lichtbaumarten, und sie ermöglicht den Einsatz schwerer Maschinen, mit denen flächenweise Bäume gefällt und schon im Wald holzofengerecht geerntet werden. Diese Eingriffe verlangen lastwagentaugliche Waldstrassen, und sie

priority. The extensive grounds from the Zurichhorn to Utoquai, Bellevue, Bürkliplatz, General-Guisan-Quai and on to the Arboretum and the Mythenquai are usually abound with people on warm summer evenings and during festivals and sports events. Winterthur, in contrast, has no lake and the Eulach River is covered or flows between walled canals over long stretches through the city. It has only been a few years since it was allowed to move freely in its bed in Neuhegi as part of the Eulach Park. By then, the Töss River had already received considerably more attention: It shows in the Leisental behind the Eschenberg, where this forest river was selected for revitalisation and allowed to work on its riverbed.

Winterthur has had, no doubt, a loose, rather light-handed relationship to the Eulach River for a long time, similar to Zurich's relationship to the Sihl River. The construction of a two-storey car park on the Sihl near the Main Railway Station in 1972 and the erection of Sihlhochstrasse onto 93 pylons over the Sihl in 1974, testify to the lack of respect for the river's space. Luckily, a turnaround emerged in the middle of the 1980s. In the Schanzengraben, starting at the Gessnerbrücke (brücke = bridge), the city built a pedestrian promenade using a wooden walkway and sandstone plates. It runs close to the water and offers a surprisingly peaceful contact with nature. The promenade is much used, as is the adjacent Sigi-Feigel Terrace, which offers an approach to the Theatrehaus Gessnerallee and the river over the broad tiered seating-steps.[2] For the underground extension of the Sihltal Zurich Uetliberg Bahn (Bahn = railway) to the Main Railway Station, the riverbed of the Sihl was narrowed downstream from the Stauffacherbrücke. These measures were, in fact, only technically required and not conceived as a revitalisation of the river, but nevertheless, that is exactly what happened: The smaller riverbed correlated with the reduced amount of water that had been flowing through the Sihl since the incorporation of electricity production in the Etzelwerk in 1937, which had increased its speed. The revitalisation also led to the creation of a popular footpath through the Sihl's riverbank vegetation to the Stauffacherbrücke. With the demolition of the car park over the Sihl in 2004, one old transgression was eliminated. Now, only the Sihlhochstrasse is still standing there as a memorial – until something further comes along.

In Winterthur, an important green value is the large share of agricultural areas in the urban space, especially in the city's forests. There are green areas in which the experience value is nearly as important as the economic value. In the Winterthur municipal forests, impact clearing has a tradition by which small surfaces are opened up using a kind of clear-cutting.

sind lärmig. Nach Abzug der Maschinen fördern sie aber die natürliche Vielfalt und damit auch den Erlebnis- und Erholungswert des Waldes. Natürlich nutzt auch Zürich sein Holz. Aber der Zürcher Stadtwald ist nahezu ausschliesslich Erholungs- und Erlebniswald. Daher wird er zwischen den Wegen grosszügig dem Regime der Natur überlassen. Bäume dürfen auf natürliche Weise sterben. Das durch ein Heer von Kleintieren und Pilzen belebte Totholz bereichert die Dynamik des Waldes und schafft eigentliche Urwaldbilder: eine Grussbotschaft und Einladung des nahen Wildnisparks Zürich Sihlwald! Eine hohe Priorität hat allerdings der auf verschiedene Nutzer differenziert ausgerichtete und vor allem am Uetliberg aufwändige Unterhalt der Wege.

Für den Kulturgeographen Emil Egli waren persönlich vertraute Erlebnislandschaften «Psychotope». Er meinte damit Nährstätten der Seele, Orte, um Weite zu atmen, an die man sich aber auch zurückziehen kann und sich wohl fühlt – sei es nun der eigene Garten, die Brockmann-Eiche am Adlisberg oder die Fallätschen am Uetliberg. In Zürich wie in Winterthur verbessert der Erholungsraum Wald das durch Abgase und das Dauerrauschen des Strassenverkehrs belastete Klima. Zürich ist dabei mit seinem höheren Lärmpegel und der grösseren Häuserdichte auf die Erholungsfunktion des Waldes besonders angewiesen. Die vielen Menschen, die den Wald besuchen, zeugen vom Bedarf. Alle sind sie da: Geniesser und Erholungsuchende, aber auch Biker und Jogger, welche die sportliche Herausforderung suchen – und Wanderer, die es schätzen, auf der Albiskette und auf dem Pfannenstiel zügig voranzukommen.

These methods require targeted open-canopy species and need heavy machines to fell trees over large areas and cut them to proper lengths for wood ovens. This change required roads that could take large lorries and the lorries had a high noise level. After the retreat of the machines, the changes did promote natural diversity as well as the experiential and recreational value of the forests. Naturally, Zurich also uses its wood. But, Zurich's municipal forests are almost exclusively for recreational and nature-experience purposes and, therefore, what grows between the paths is generously left to nature's regime. Trees are allowed to die naturally. An army of small animals, insects and fungi living in the dead wood enriches the dynamics of the area and actually creates a primeval forest: a greeting and an invitation from the nearby wilderness park in Zurich Sihl Forest! A high priority is certainly directed towards the differentiated needs of various users and, mainly on the Uetliberg, the laborious maintenance of the paths.

For the cultural geographer, Emil Egli, the personal, familiar experience landscape is a 'Psychotope'. By this, he means a place of nourishment for the soul, a place one can breathe in vastness, but also a place where one can withdraw and feel well – whether it is one's own garden, the Brockmann Oak on the Adlisberg or the Fallätschen on the Uetliberg. In Zurich, as in Winterthur, the recreational forest improved a climate burdened with exhaust fumes and the continuous noise of street traffic. Zurich is especially dependent on the recreational function of the forest to help counter the higher noise levels and population density. That many people visit the forest certainly indicates a need. All types take part: from experts to cognoscente and recreational seekers, as well as bikers and joggers, athletes looking for a sports challenge – and walkers and hikers who can appreciate a quick ascent on the Albis mountain chain or the Pfannenstiel.

Der 1967 eröffnete Pavillon Le Corbusier in Zürich ist der letzte realisierte Bau des berühmten Architekten. Mit der Farbenkomposition der Wände und der Lage direkt neben der durchgehenden Freifläche vom Seefeldquai bis zur Badi Tiefenbrunnen ist ihm Aufmerksamkeit gewiss.

The Pavilion Le Corbusier in Zurich was first opened in 1967 and was the last realized work of the famous architect. The colour composition of the walls and the location right next to the continuously open area from Seefeldquai to the Tiefenbrunnen Swimming Bath, is certain to draw attention.

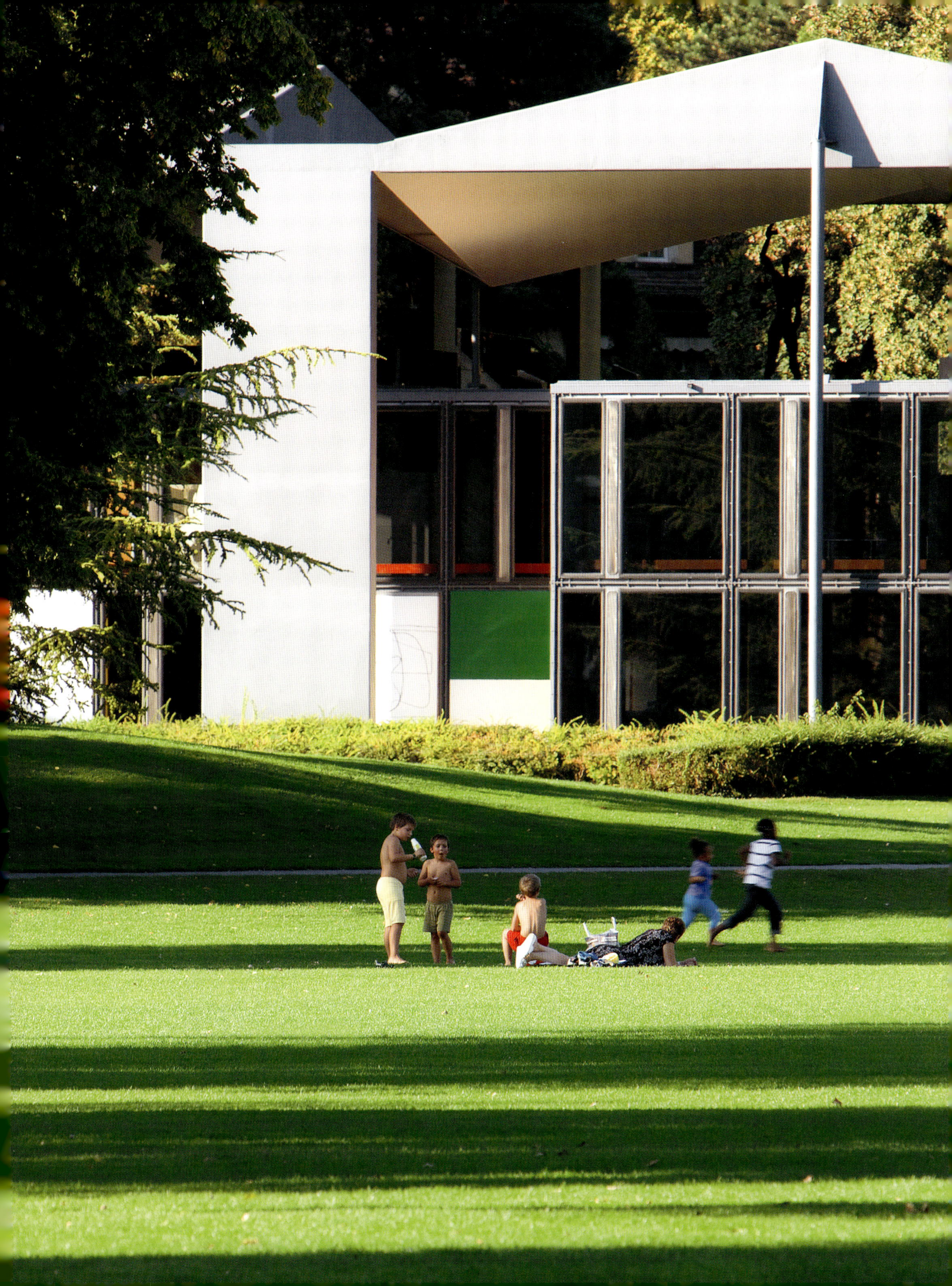

Der MFO-Park ist Teil des neuen Stadtteils Zentrum Zürich Nord, der auf dem einstigen Industrieareal nördlich des Bahnhofs Oerlikon errichtet wurde.

Mit Respekt und etwas Bescheidenheit fügt sich der urbane Grünraum in das Wohnquartier ein und schafft Begegnungs- und Erlebnisräume für die Bewohner.

The MFO-Park is part of the new urban district centre, Zurich North, which was built north of the Oerlikon Train Station on a former industrial site.

With respect and a little modesty, the green urban space fits well into the residential area and provides residents with a place to meet, rest, play or simply observe life.

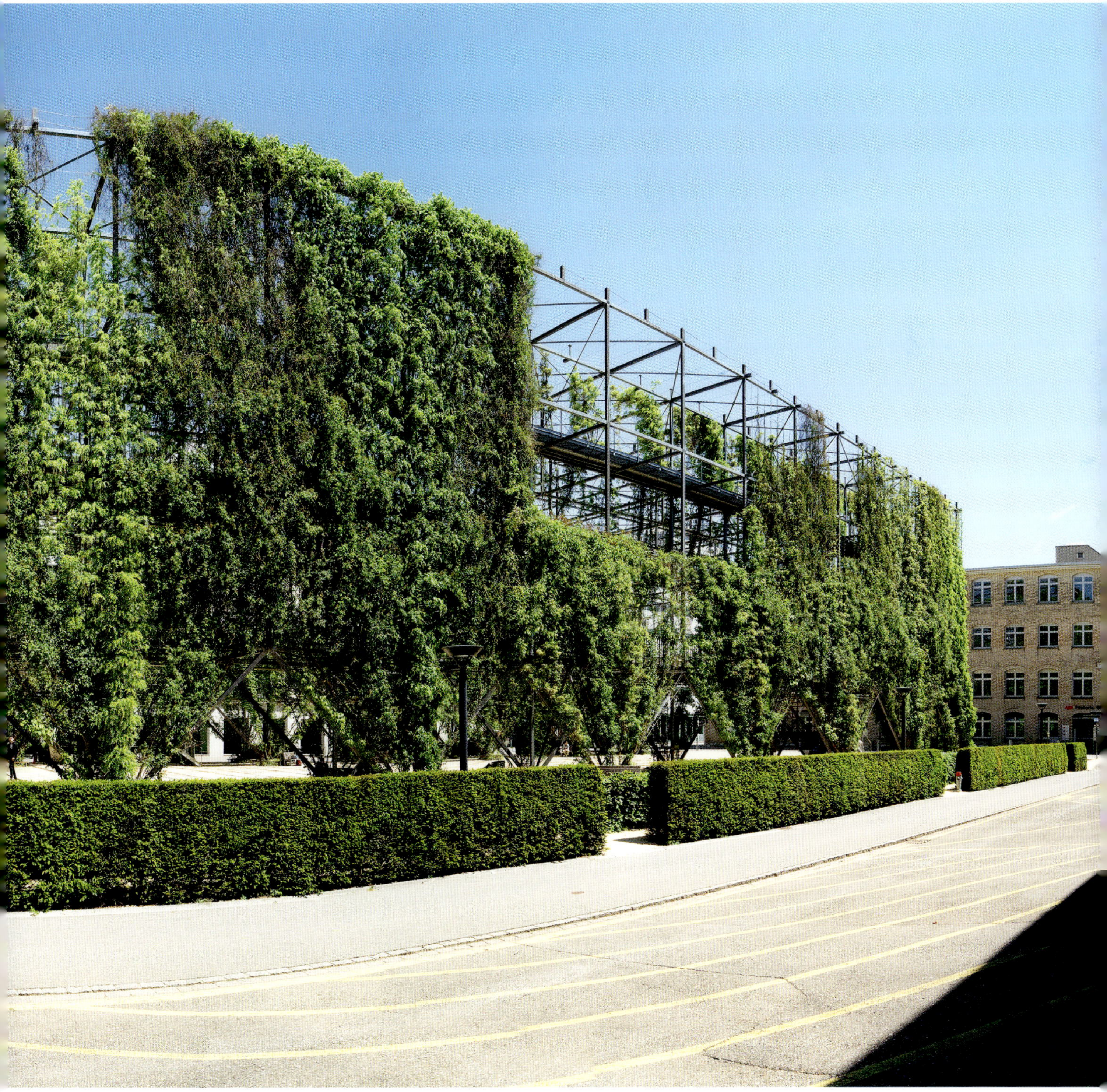

Beim grosszügigen Oerliker Park im Stadtteil Zentrum Zürich Nord war der Umgang mit dem weiten Raum für die Planer eine grosse Herausforderung. Seine Entwicklung braucht noch Zeit (links).
Der Glattpark ist ein Grossprojekt der Städte Opfikon und Zürich, des Kantons Zürich und der Grundbesitzer. Als Ausgleich für verdichtetes Bauen in den erschlossenen Teilen der grossen Gesamtparzelle wurde ein 12,8 Hektaren grosser, grosszügiger Park geschaffen. Sein auffälligstes Element ist der 550 mal 41 Meter grosse Badesee, der vor allem vom Dachwasser der Gebäude gespeist wird. Periodisch geschnittenes Schilf entzieht dem Wasser im Sinne einer biologischen Kläranlage Nährstoffe (rechts).

With the spacious Oerliker Park in the Zurich North district, the biggest challenge for the planners was how to handle the wide-open space. In fact, its full development will take still more time (left).
The Glattpark is a major project of the cities of Opfikon and Zurich, the Canton of Zurich and the landowners. To compensate for the high-density construction in the developed parts of this large parcel of land, a large, spacious park of 12.8 hectares was created. Its most striking feature is the lake; it is 550 by 41 m and fed primarily by roof water from the surrounding buildings. Cut periodically, the reeds filter out nutrients from the water, as part of a biological water treatment plant (right).

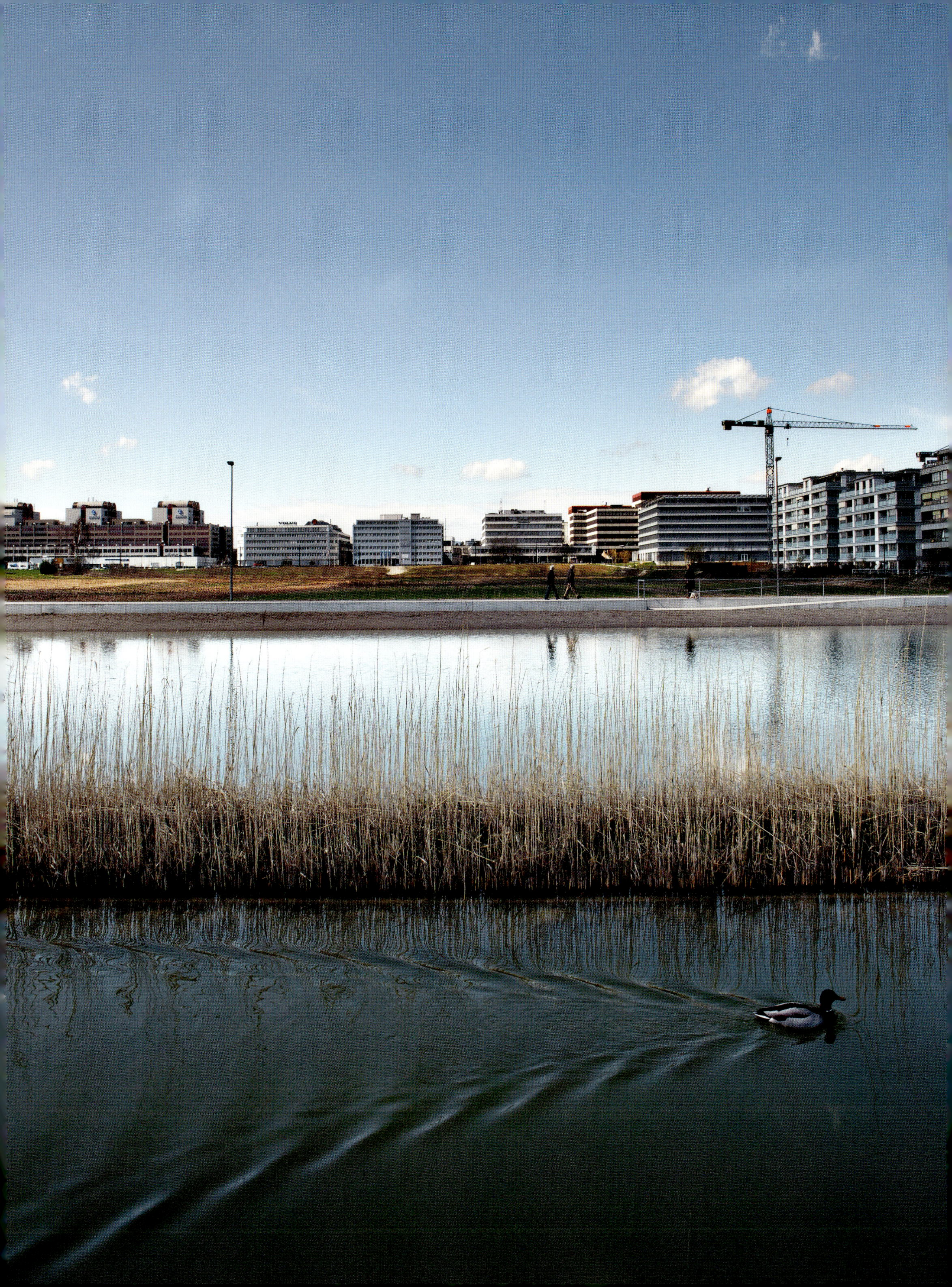

Im herbstlichen Abendlicht präsentiert sich die Sihl zusammen mit der Westflanke des Platzspitzes in Zürich vornehm zurückhaltend. Im Hintergrund ist das Landesmuseum als Pforte des Platzspitzes erkennbar. Das Regulierwehr Letten, östlich vom Platzspitz unmittelbar vor dem Zusammenfluss von Sihl und Limmat gelegen, regelt seit 1951 den Wasserstand der Limmat und des Zürichsees innerhalb einer normalen Schwankungsbreite von einem halben Meter (links).
Der im 19. Jahrhundert grosszügig angelegte Rieterpark im Zürcher Stadtquartier Enge ist zu jeder Jahreszeit prächtig. Er liegt halbwegs auf einer Seitenmoräne des Linth-Rhein-Gletschers und besticht auch durch seine landschaftliche Schönheit (rechts).

In the autumnal evening light along the western flank of the Platzspitz in Zurich, the Sihl River appears elegantly restrained. In the background is the National Museum, the recognizable gate to the Platzspitz (left). Just before the confluence of the Sihl and Limmat Rivers, a regulating dam, built in 1951 on the east side of Platzspitz, regulates the water levels of the Limmat River and Lake Zurich within a normal fluctuation range of half a metre (left).
Built in the 19th century and generously laid out, Rieterpark, near Zurich's Enge area, is magnificent in every season. It lies halfway up a lateral moraine of the Linth-Rhine Glacier and stands out for its natural beauty (right).

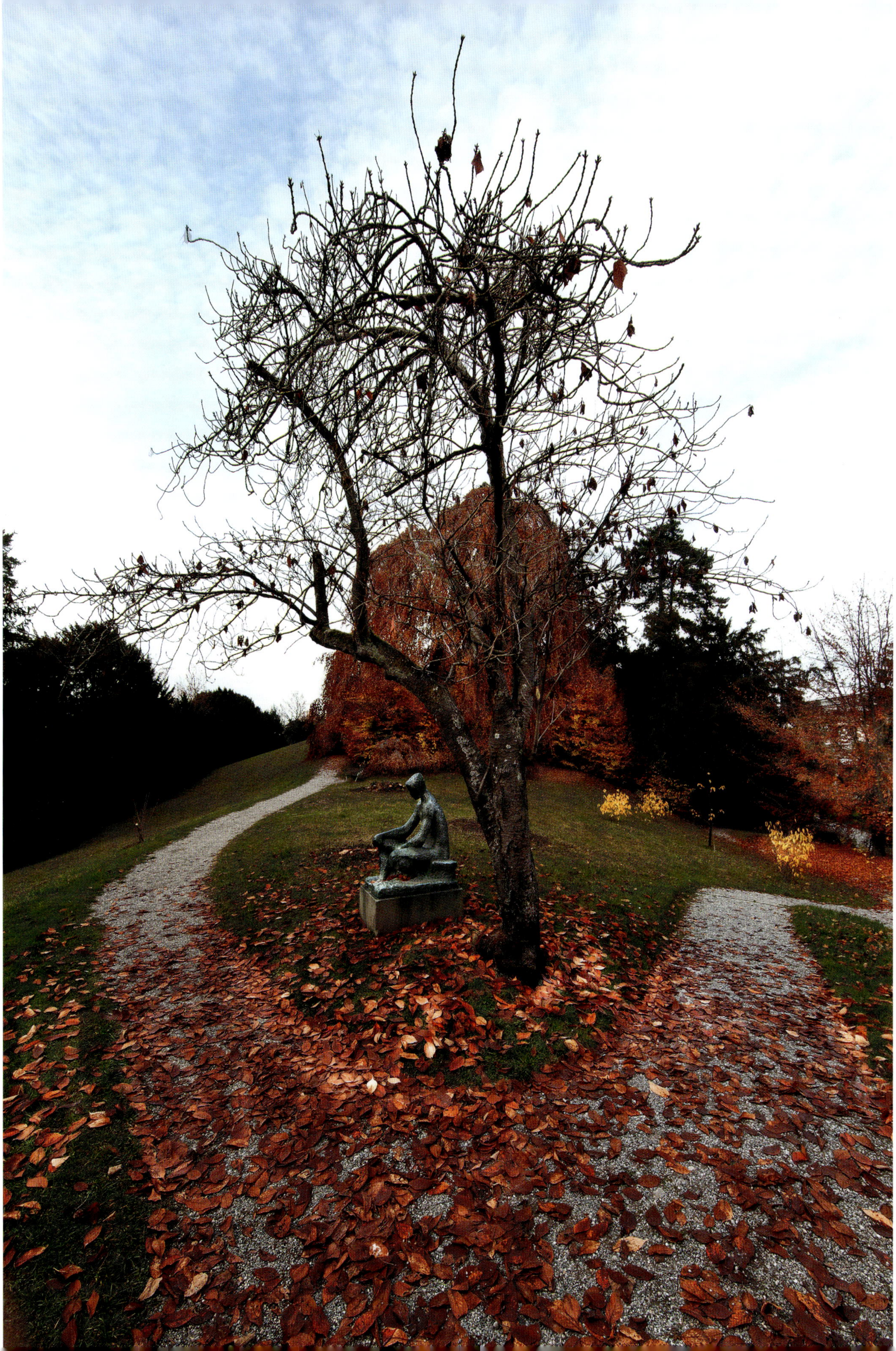

Die drei Tropenhäuser im neuen Botanischen Garten in Zürich sind ein starkes Markenzeichen (rechts). Den Eindruck einer harmonischen Landschaft aber bestimmen der einheimische Wald, die artenreichen Wiesen und der Teich. Der Garten kann eine Fülle an Besonderheiten vorweisen wie Mittelmeerflora, eine Nagelfluhwand, das Alpinum Schweiz und Himalaya sowie Medizinal- und Nutzpflanzen. Die mächtige Blutbuche (links) begünstigt mit ihrem im Sommer weit ausladenden Schattendach im nahen Umfeld schattenfeste Frühlingsblüher. Diese Landschaft ist ein offenes Lehrbuch – und ein Ort zum Geniessen.

The three tropical houses of the new Botanical Garden in Zurich are a strong landmark (right). However, the impression of a harmonious landscape is determined by the native forest, the species-rich meadows and the pond. The garden boasts a wealth of specialities, such as Mediterranean flora, a wall of molasse conglomerate, the Alpinum Schweiz and Himalaya, as well as medicinal and useful plants. The mighty copper beech (left), with its wide flaring canopy in the summer favours the shade-proof spring flowers in its immediate vicinity. This landscape is an open textbook – and a place to enjoy.

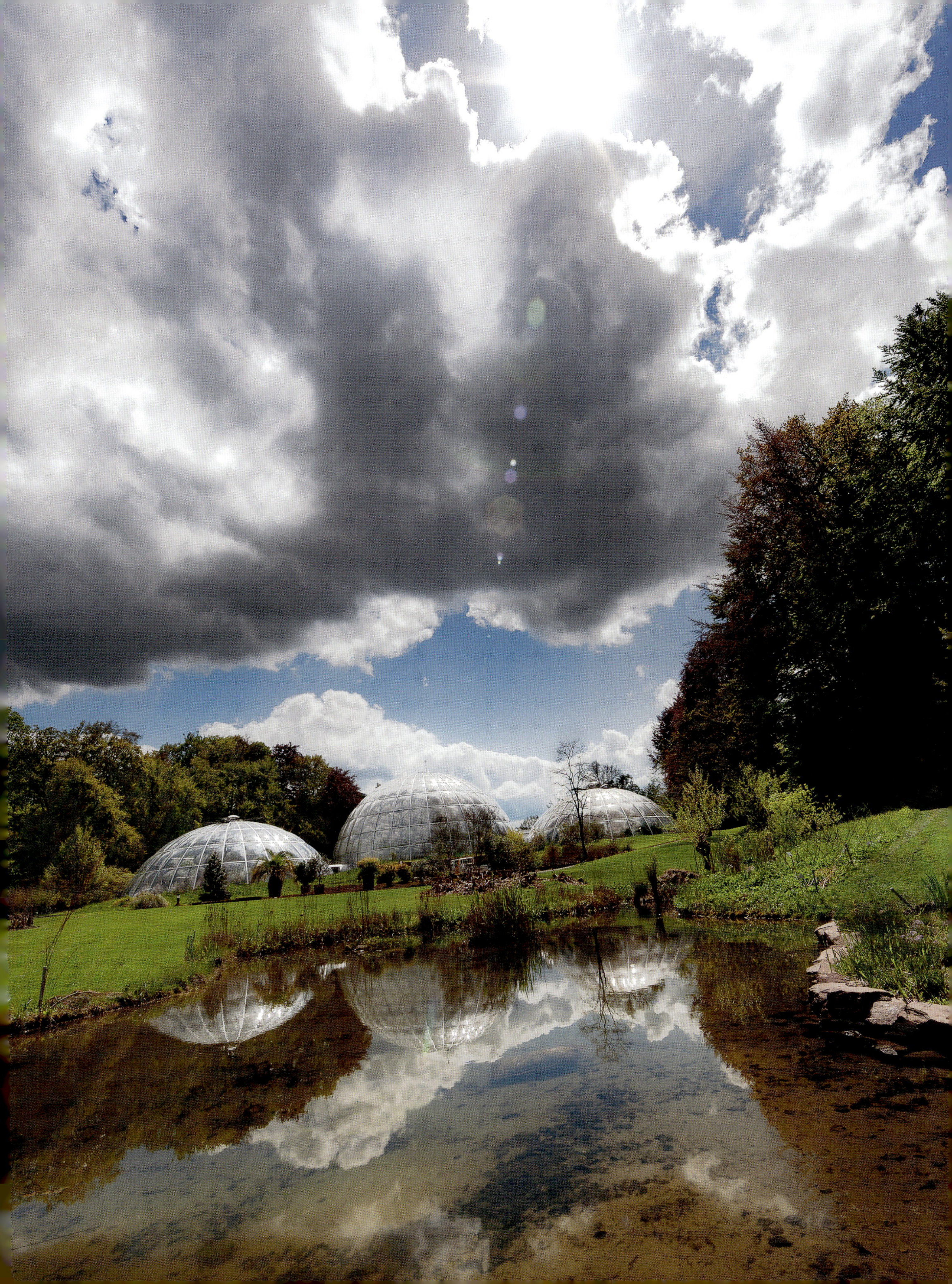

Die Sigi-Feigel-Terrasse bei der Gessnerbrücke in Zürich schafft mit Sitzstufen einen Zugang zur Sihl. Unter dem Grasstreifen verläuft der Tunnel der Sihltal Zürich Uetliberg Bahn SZU (links; siehe auch Seite 245).
Der Zellwegerpark in Uster verdankt sein Bestehen der industriellen Vergangenheit des Oberlandes: Der Aabach zwischen dem Pfäffiker- und dem Greifensee war um 1840 der bevorzugte Ort für Industriegründungen, weil mit dem Pfäffikersee ein grosses natürliches Ausgleichsbecken gegen Hoch- und Niederwasser gegeben war. Entlang dem «Millionenbach» entstanden Ensembles von Fabriken, Parks, Weihern und Arbeiterhäusern. Diese Industrielandschaft wurde im neuen Jahrtausend behutsam zur Parklandschaft umgestaltet und mit einladenden Wohnbauten ergänzt (rechts).

The 'seating steps' at the Sigi-Feigel Terrace near the Gessner Bridge in Zurich provide access to the Sihl River. Underneath the grass verge is the Sihltal Zurich Uetliberg Railway SZU Tunnel (left; see also page 245).
The Zellweger Park in Uster owes its existence to the industrial past of the Zurich Oberland: The Aabach River between the Pfäffikersee and the Greifensee was the preferred location for industry start-ups around the 1840s because the Pfäffikersee was a large natural balancing reservoir against both high- and low-water. Along this 'Millionenbach' (Millions Stream) ensembles of factories, parks, ponds and workman's houses were built. In the new millennium, this industrial landscape was carefully transformed into a park landscape and completed with inviting residential buildings (right).

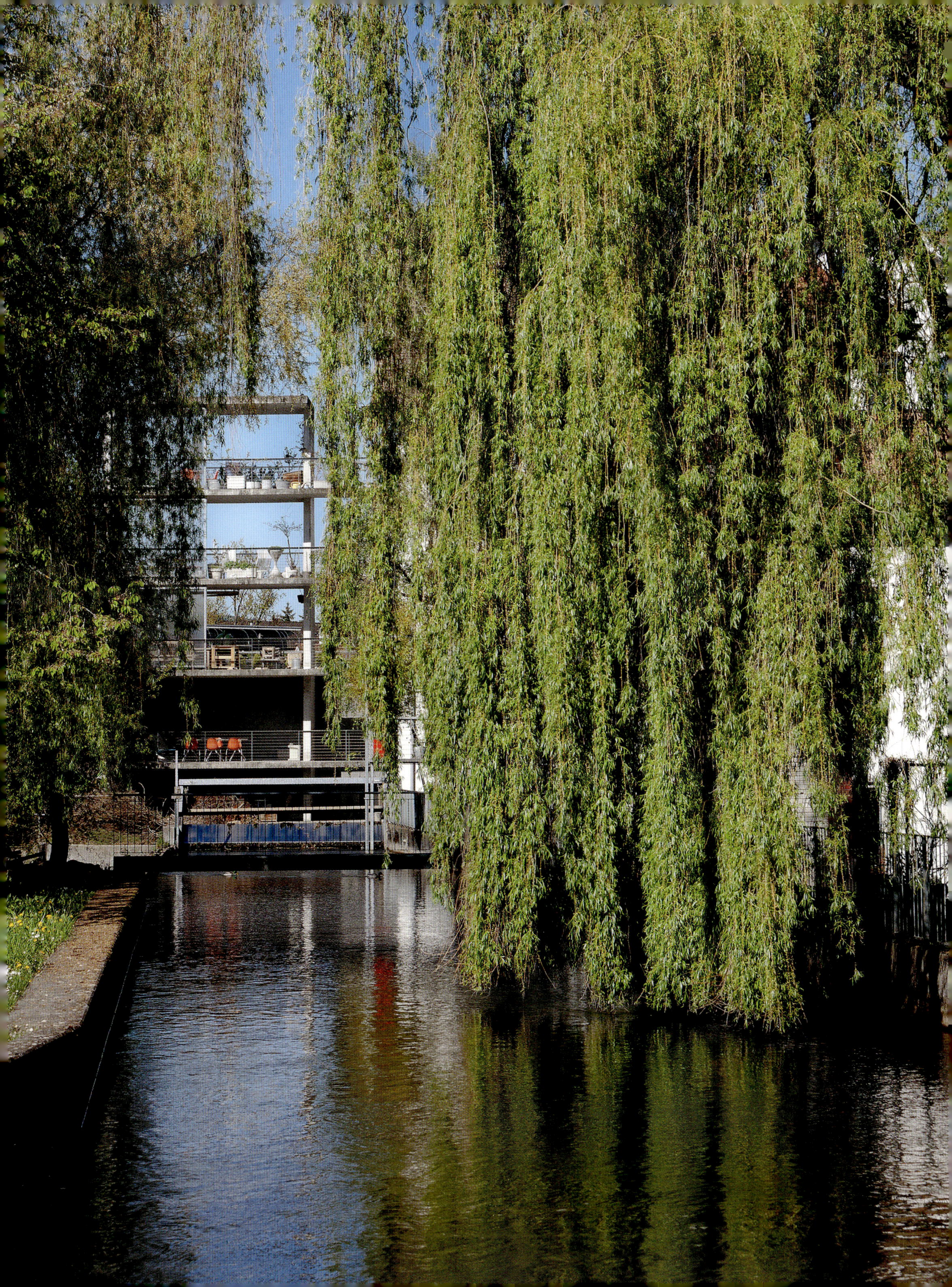

Als grosszügige Parkanlage präsentiert sich der Stadtgarten in Winterthur. Ob diese Blüten- oder Zierkirsche auch etwas japanische Frühlingsstimmung ausstrahlt? In Kyoto wird der Blühbeginn dieser Bäume seit dem Jahr 812 registriert und gefeiert – dies ist die älteste bekannte Datumsreihe zur Blüte einer Pflanze (links).
Unmittelbar nach dem Bau der neubarocken Villa Bühler-Egg an der Lindstrasse in Winterthur gestaltete der Gartenarchitekt Conrad Löwe 1870 den Park um sie herum. Mit einer Aufschüttung über das ganze Terrain, Baumgruppen und weiten Rasenflächen förderte er den stolzen Landhauscharakter. Herbstliche Blätter einer amerikanischen Roteiche geben dem Raum zusätzliche Weite (rechts).

The Stadtgarten (City Garden) in Winterthur is a spacious generously laid-out park. Do these flowering or ornamental cherry trees radiate something reminiscent of a spring mood in Japan? In Kyoto, the flowering of these trees has been registered and celebrated since the year 812; this is the oldest known range of dates to be recorded about the flowering of a plant (left).
In 1870, immediately after the construction of the new baroque Villa Bühler Egg at the Lindstrasse in Winterthur, the garden architect Conrad Lion designed the park around it. With landfill over the entire terrain, groves of trees and wide lawns, he promoted the proud country house style. The autumn leaves of an American Red Oak adds additional drama to the space (right).

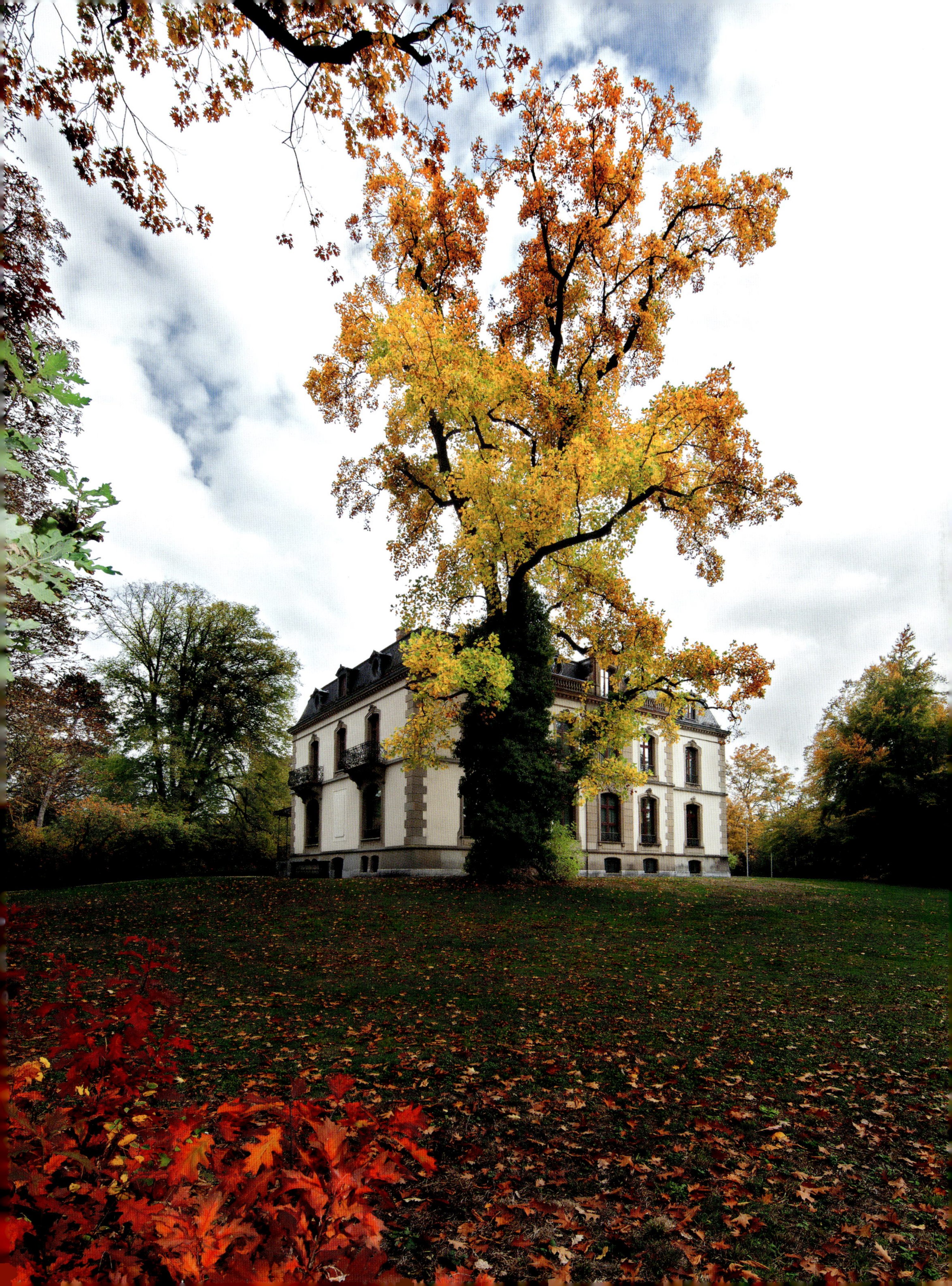

Übersichtskarte · Overview Map

Natur und Landschaft im Kanton Zürich
Nature and Landscape in the Canton of Zurich

		Seite
1	Uetliberg, Zürich	31
2	Albiskette	32/33
3	Panorama Zürichsee	34–39
4	Hirzel, Spitzen	40/41
5	Flugaufnahme Hirzel, Schönenberg	42/43
6	Frauenwinkel, Pfäffikon	44
7	Flugaufnahme Insel Ufenau	45/135
8	Flugaufnahme Zürichsee, Rapperswil	46/47
9	Gibswil	48/49
10	Neftenbach, Winterthur	50/51
11	Waltalingen, Oberstammheim	52
12	Eglisau	53
13	Truttikon	54/55
14	Unterstammheim, Waltalingen	56
15	Oberstammheim	57
16	Flugaufnahme Rheinau	58
17	Flugaufnahme Rheinfall	59
18	Bachsertal	60/61

Voralpin geprägte Landschaften
Characteristic Prealpine Landscapes

19	Scheidegg, Wald	69
20	Panorama Scheidegg	70–75
21	Flugaufnahme Roten, Mosnang	76/77
22	Schnebelhorn, Mosnang	78/79
23	Gfell, Sternenberg	80
24	Tierhag, Fischenthal	81
25	Hörnli, Fischenthal	82/83
26	Tössscheidi, Wald	84–86
27	Sagenraintobel, Wald	87–89
28	Spinnerei Neuthal, Bäretswil	90/91
29	Wissengubel, Gibswil	92/93
30	Tüfelschilen, Kollbrunn	94–97
31	Panorama Bachtel	98–103
32	Täuferhöhle, Bäretswil	104
33	Bachtelspalt, Wernetshausen	105
34	Hasenstrick, Dürnten	106/107
35	Hirzel	108/109
36	Bubikon, Grüningen	110/111
37	Fallätschen, Zürich	112–115
38	Lägern	116/117

Seen- und Flusslandschaften
Lake and River Landscapes

39	Zürichhorn, Hornbach, Heureka	126/127
40	Küsnacht	128
41	Strandbad Tiefenbrunnen, Zürich	128
42	Fähre Meilen–Horgen	129
43	Limmat, Wipkingerpark, Zürich	130
44	Limmat, Oetwil an der Limmat	131
45	Halbinsel Au, Wädenswil	132/133
46	Schirmensee, Feldbach	134
47	Sihlsprung, Hirzel	136/137
48	Reuss, Maschwanden	138/139

		Seite
49	Reppisch, Panorama Türlersee, Hausen am Albis	140–147
50	Pfäffikersee	148
51	Greifensee	2/3,149
52	Vordere und Hintere Töss, Wald	150
53	Töss, Leisental, Winterthur	151
54	Thur, Gütighausen, Uesslingen	152–154
55	Thurspitz, Flaach	155
56	Rhein, Eglisau	156/157
57	Rheinfähre, Ellikon	158
58	Rhein, Irchel, Rüdlingen	159
59	Alter Rhein, Rüdlingen	160/161

Landschaften der Auen und Moore
Water Meadows and Moor Landscapes

60	Torfriet, Pfäffikon	168–170
61	Robenhauserriet, Pfäffikersee	171
62	Greifensee, Glatt	172/173
63	Ützikerriet, Hombrechtikon	174/175
64	Chatzensee, Regensdorf	176
65	Egelsee, Bubikon	177
66	Lützelsee, Hombrechtikon	178/179
67	Rumensee, Küsnacht	180/181
68	Goldenes Tor, Flughafen Zürich, Kloten	182/183
69	Neeracherried, Neerach	184/187
70	Husemersee, Ossingen	188
71	Nussbaumersee, Hüttwilen	189
72	Bibersee, Marthalen	190–193
73	Thurauen, Flaach	194/195
74	Thur Eggrank, Andelfingen	196/197
75	Maschwander Allmend	198
76	Hagenholz, Kappel am Albis	199
77	Seleger Moor, Rifferswil	200–203

Waldlandschaften
Forest Landscapes

78	Wildnispark Sihlwald	211–219
79	Bärtobel, Bauma	220–223
80	Quellgebiet Töss	224/225
81	Eschenberg, Winterthur	226/227
82	Eichenwald, Bülach	228–231
83	Hohflue, Bachsertal	232–239

Parkanlagen und Stadtwälder
Parks and Municipal Forests

84	Seeanlage Zürichhorn	247
85	MFO-Park, Oerliker Park, Zürich	248–250
86	Glattpark, Opfikon, Zürich	251
87	Platzspitz, Zürich	252
88	Rieterpark, Zürich	253
89	Botanischer Garten, Zürich	254/255
90	Sigi-Feigel-Terrasse, Zürich	256
91	Zellwegerpark, Uster	257
92	Stadtgarten, Villa Bühler-Egg, Winterthur	258/259
93	Torfriet, Pfäffikon	266/267

17
Laufen-
Uhwiesen
Rhein
Rheinau
16
14
11
Oberstammheim
15
Truttikon
13
Marthalen
72
70
71
57
55
74
73
Thur
Andelfingen
Gütighausen
54
56
12
Eglisau
Rüdlingen
59
58
Flaach
10
Neftenbach
83
Bachs
18
82
Neerach
Bülach
Töss
92
Winterthur
Eulach
69
38
68
81
53
30
Kollbrunn
Glatt
Kloten
Regensdorf
Opfikon
Chatzensee
64
44
86
Illnau-Effretikon
85
Zürich-Oerlikon
Limmat
43
87
90
Zürich
62
Greifensee
60
Pfäffikon
93
23
Bauma
25
79
Birmensdorf
88
84
89
1
37
39
41
51
91
Uster
50
Pfäffikersee
28
21
61
Bäretswil
Fischenthal
3
Wetzikon
24
22
67
2
40
Küsnacht
32
9
29
52
80
Hinwil
19
20
26
31
33
Grüningen
36
34
27
Sihlwald
Meilen
Bubikon
Wald
Türlersee
49
78
42
Lützelsee
Reuss
Horgen
63
66
65
Zürichsee
Hombrechtikon
48
Rifferswil
77
Hausen
am Albis
45
75
Maschwanden
76
Sihl
Stäfa
Feldbach
Rapperswil
46
8
Wädenswil
4
35
Hirzel
7
5
6
47
N
0
2.5
5 km

Literaturverzeichnis · Bibliography

Natur und Landschaft im Kanton Zürich
Nature and Landscape in the Canton of Zurich
1 Tages-Anzeiger, 4. 11. 2015.
2 Eidgenössisches Departement für Umwelt, Verkehr, Energie und Kommunikation UVEK u.a. (Hrsg.): Raumkonzept Schweiz, überarbeitete Fassung 2012.
3 Bettina Jegge: Drumlins – Kompassnadeln im Kraftfeld des Gletscherstroms, in: Bernhard Nievergelt und Hansruedi Wildermuth (Hrsg.): Eine Landschaft und ihr Leben: das Zürcher Oberland, Zürich 2001, S. 36–39.
4 Oswald Heer: Die Urwelt der Schweiz, Zürich 1865.
5 Rudolf Trümpy: Abschiedsrede eines Geologen – Vom Sinn der Erdgeschichte, in: Neue Zürcher Zeitung, 8. 4. 1987.
6 Max Frisch: Tagebuch mit Marion, Zürich 1947.
7 Emil Egli: Der Kanton Zürich, Genf 1962.
8 Lucius Burckhardt, Max Frisch, Markus Kutter: Achtung die Schweiz, Frankfurt a. M. 1955.
9 Elias Landolt: Flora der Stadt Zürich, Zürich 2001.

Voralpin geprägte Landschaften
Characteristic Prealpine Landscapes
1 Max Maisch: Landschaft und Naturraum. Verständnis der Landschaftsindividualität aus der regionalen Naturgeschichte, in: Bernhard Nievergelt und Hansruedi Wildermuth (Hrsg.): Eine Landschaft und ihr Leben: das Zürcher Oberland, Zürich 2001, S. 14–64. – Dominik Jost und Max Maisch: Von der Eiszeit in die Heisszeit. Eine Zeitreise zu den Gletschern, Bern 2006, 5.Kapitel: Gletscher formen Landschaften. – Hansruedi Wildermuth: Naturschutz im Zürcher Oberland, Wetzikon 1974.
2 Emil Egli: Das Zürcher Oberland. Beitrag zur Geschichte seiner Landschaft und seiner Menschen, 6. überarb. Auflage, Wetzikon 1989. – Emil Egli: Kulturgeographische Aspekte, in: Bernhard Nievergelt und Emil Egli: Grundlagen für ein Naturschutz-Gesamtkonzept im Kanton Zürich, Projektstudie, Zoologisches Institut der Universität Zürich, Ethologie und Wildforschung, 1986, S. 79–82.
3 Hans-Peter Bärtschi: Der Industrielehrpfad Zürcher Oberland, Wetzikon 1994.
4 Heinrich Jäckli: Geologie von Zürich. Von der Entstehung der Landschaft bis zum Eingriff des Menschen, Zürich 1989.

Seen- und Flusslandschaften
Lake and River Landscapes
1 Albert Heim: Geschichte des Zürichsees (Neujahrsblatt der Naturforschenden Gesellschaft in Zürich 1891), in: Emil Egli: Erlebte Landschaft, Zürich 1943, S. 127–131.
2 Ernst F. Burckhardt: Landschaftsschutz am Zürichsee, in: Jahrbuch vom Zürichsee 1944/45, S. 3–26. – Christian Thomas: Vom Zürichsee zum Limmatsee? 200 Jahre Seeaufschüttungen, in: Tages-Anzeiger Magazin 25, 22. Juni 1974.
3 Hanspeter Rebsamen und Res Knobel: Zürichsee Landschaftsschutz 1927–2002, Stäfa 2002.
4 Christian Göldi: Das Hochwasser vom 7./8. August 1978 an der Thur; Das Buhnenfeld an der Thur bei Altikon, in: Wasserbau im Kanton Zürich, Zürich 2000, S. 32–43.

Landschaften der Auen und Moore
Water Meadows and Moor Landscapes
1 Otto Hegg, Claude Béguin, Heinrich Zoller: Atlas schutzwürdiger Vegetationstypen der Schweiz, Bern 1993, Flussufer und Auenwälder, S. 52–56. – Naturzentrum Thurauen. Nationales Auengebiet Eggrank Thurspitz. Grösstes Auengebiet im Mittelland. Flyer, Baudirektion Kanton Zürich, 2011.
2 Urs Rahm und Marco Baettig: Der Biber in der Schweiz (Schriftenreihe Umwelt 249: Wildtiere), Bern 1996.
3 Andreas Grünig, Luca Vetterli und Otto Wildi: Die Hoch- und Übergangsmoore der Schweiz (Eidg. Anstalt für das forstliche Versuchswesen, Berichte 281), Birmensdorf 1986.
4 Giuseppe Sampietro: Spät- und Postglaziale Vegetationsgeschichte anhand pollenanalytischer Untersuchungen, in: Ernst Ott und John Spillmann (Hrsg.): Der Pfäffikersee – Naturperle an Zürichs östlichem Agglomerationsrand und dauerhaft schützenswerter Lebensraum (Neujahrsblatt der Naturforschenden Gesellschaft in Zürich 218), Zürich 2016, S. 43–53.

Waldlandschaften
Forest Landscapes
1 Naturschutz-Gesamtkonzept für den Kanton Zürich, festgesetzt durch den Regierungsrat 20. Dezember 1995.
2 Zum lichten Wald: Bruno Abegg u.a.: Aktionsplan Lichte Wälder im Kanton Zürich, Zürich 2005. – Florian Suter, Christa Glauser, Schweizer Vogelschutz: Biodiversität: Vielfalt im Wald, Zürich 2011. – Heinrich Schiess und Corina Schiess-Bühler: Dominanzverminderung als ökologisches Prinzip: eine Neubewertung der ursprünglichen Waldnutzungen (Mitteilungen der Eidgenössischen Forschungsanstalt für Wald, Schnee und Landschaft 72/1), Birmensdorf 1997.
3 Zur Waldweide: Rainer Luick und Hans-Karl Schuler: Waldweide und forstrechtliche Aspekte, in: Berichte des Institutes für Landschafts- und Pflanzenökologie der Universität Hohenheim 17, Stuttgart-Hohenheim 2008, S. 149–164. – Andrea Corinna Mayer u.a.: Waldweide im Alpenraum. Neubewertung einer traditionellen Mehrfachnutzung, in: Schweizerische Zeitschrift für Forstwesen 155, Zürich 2004, S. 38–44.
4 Thomas May: Beeinflussten Grosssäuger die Waldvegetation der pleistozänen Warmzeiten Mitteleuropas? In: Natur und Museum 123/6, Frankfurt a. M. 1993, S. 157–170.
5 Peter von Matt: Verherrlichung und Schändung. Der Wald bei Gottfried Keller. Ansprache, Binding Waldpreis an die Stadt Bülach, 20. Mai 2010.

Parkanlagen und Stadtwälder
Parks and Municipal Forests
1 Bücher zum Umgang mit «grün» in Zürich und Winterthur: Grün Stadt Zürich (Hrsg): Das Grünbuch der Stadt Zürich: integral planen – wirkungsorientiert handeln, Zürich 2006. – Gartenstadt Winterthur. Ein Führer durch Winterthurs Gärten, Pärke und Grünräume, Winterthur 2010. – Michael Wiesner: Waldzeit. Wälder für Winterthur, Winterthur 2014.
2 Christian Göldi: Gewässer in der Stadt Zürich (Wege durch die Wasserwelt 1.5), Bern 2008.

Biografien der Autoren · Biographies of the Authors

Der Herausgeber:
Heinz von Arx, geboren 1945. Aufgewachsen in Adliswil. Lehre als Buchdrucker mit anschliessender Ausbildung zum Graphic Designers SGD. 1968 bis 1975 Buchgestalter im Atlantis Verlag. Ab 1975 eigenes Atelier für Werbegrafik und Buchgestaltung: Gestaltung unter anderem der Swissair Gazette (1982–1989), Corporate Design für Firmen und Verbände, Buchgestaltung für namhafte Verlage wie Orell Füssli, Artemis, Diogenes, Betty Bossi, Kein & Aber und weitere. 1991 Mitbegründer und Mitinhaber des AS Verlags, Herausgeber diverser Titel im AS Verlag.

Die Fotografen:
Marc Schmid, geboren 1963. Aufgewachsen in Bern und Zürich. Ausbildung als Fotograf an der Fachklasse für Fotografie Kunstgewerbeschule Zürich. 2000 bis 2012 freier Dozent für angewandte Fotografie an der Zürcher Hochschule der Künste, Abteilung visuelle Gestaltung.
André Roth, geboren 1961. Aufgewachsen im Aargau, in Basel und Zürich. Lehre als Fachfotograf in Basel bei Heusser und Hertig, danach verschiedene Assistentenstellen in Zürich, unter anderem bei Raymond Meier.

1984 Eröffnung des gemeinsamen Fotostudios Roth+Schmid in Zürich. Arbeiten in allen Bereichen der Fotografie, insbesondere in der Image-, Werbe-, Landschafts-, Food-, Porträt-, Auto-, Industrie- und Stillfotografie. Kunden: Kanton Zürich, Horgen Glarus, SBB, UBS, Smart, SwissRe, USM, Amac Aerospace, Axpo und weitere.

Die Autoren:
Hans Weiss, geboren 1940. Aufgewachsen in Schiers GR. Jugend und Mittelschule in Küsnacht ZH, Studium zuerst der Geologie an der Universität Zürich, dann an der ETH mit Abschluss als Kultur- und Vermessungsingenieur. 1968 bis 1972 Landschaftspfleger des Kantons Graubünden. Geschäftsleiter der Stiftung Landschaftsschutz SL ab ihrer Gründung 1970 (ab 1972 hauptamtlich) bis 1992. In derselben Zeit Lehrbeauftragter für Natur- und Landschaftsschutz an der ETH und Sekretär der parlamentarischen Gruppe für Natur- und Heimatschutz. Anschliessend Geschäftsleiter des Fonds Landschaft Schweiz FLS. Zahlreiche Publikationen, darunter zwei Bücher bei Orell Füssli: «Die friedliche Zerstörung der Landschaft und Ansätze zu ihrer Rettung in der Schweiz» (1981) und «Die unteilbare Landschaft – für ein erweitertes Umweltverständnis» (1987).

Bernhard Nievergelt, geboren 1935. Aufgewachsen in Zürich. Forscher und Lehrer auf dem Gebiet der Wildforschung und Naturschutzökologie am Zoologischen Institut der Universität Zürich, zunächst als Oberassistent und Privatdozent, 1992 bis 2001 als Professor. Schwerpunkte auf Feldstudien an Huftieren in Gebirgsregionen Eurasiens und Afrikas, unter anderem «Ibexes in an African Environment» (1981, Springer Verlag). Engagement in der anwendungsorientierten und fachübergreifenden Landschaftsforschung: Präsident der Forschungskommissionen des Schweizerischen Nationalparks und des Naturerlebnisparks Sihlwald, Präsident der Arbeitsgemeinschaft für den Wald, Projektleiter für das Naturschutz-Gesamtkonzept des Kantons Zürich. Projektstudie: Grundlagen für ein Naturschutz-Gesamtkonzept im Kanton Zürich (1986). Publikation gemeinsam mit Hansruedi Wildermuth: «Eine Landschaft und ihr Leben: das Zürcher Oberland – Vom Tierhag zum Volkiland» (2001).

The Publisher:
Heinz von Arx, born in 1945; grew up in Adliswil. Trained as a printer, followed by a diploma as a graphic designer, SGD. 1968 to 1975: Book Designer at Atlantis Verlag. From 1975: own studio for commercial art and book design. Designed, among others, the *Swissair Gazette* (1982–1989), Corporate design for companies and associations, book design for notable publishing houses: Orell Füssli, Artemis, Diogenes, Betty Bossi, Kein & Aber and others. 1991: Co-founder and co-owner of AS Verlag; publisher of diverse titles at AS Verlag.

The Photographers:
Marc Schmid, born in 1963, grew up in Bern and Zurich. Trained as a photographer in the Special Course in Photography at the Kunstgewerbeschule Zürich (merged with Zurich University of the Arts, 2007). 2000 to 2012: Lecturer in Applied Methods of Photography at the Zurich University of the Arts, Department of Visual Design.
André Roth, born in 1961, grew up in Aargau, Basel and Zurich. Trained as a Specialised Photographer in Basel at Heusser and Hertig, then held various assistant positions in Zurich, among others, at Raymond Meier.

1984: Opening of the photo studio Roth+Schmid in Zurich. Working in all areas of photography, especially in image, advertising, landscape, food, portraits, auto, industrial and still photography. Clients include: Canton of Zurich, City of Horgen, Glarus, SBB, UBS, Smart, SwissRe, USM, Amac Aerospace, Axpo and others.

The Authors:
Hans Weiss, born in 1940, grew up in Schiers GR. Studied geology at the University of Zurich, then at ETH, graduating with a degree as a Rural and Survey Engineer. 1968 to 1972: Landscape Conservator for the Canton of Graubünden. 1970 to 1992: Director of the Foundation for Landscape Protection from its founding (full-time from 1972). During the same time period: Assistant Lecturer for Nature and Landscape Protection at ETH and Secretary of the Parliamentary Group for Nature and National Protection, subsequently, Director of the Fonds Landschaft Schweiz (FLS). Has written numerous publications, including two books for Orell Füssli: *Die friedliche Zerstörung der Landschaft und Ansätze zu ihrer Rettung in der Schweiz* (The peaceful destruction of the landscape and approaches to its rescue in Switzerland) (1981) and *Die unteilbare Landschaft – für ein erweitertes Umweltverständnis* (The indivisible landscape – for an expanded understanding of the environment) (1987).

Bernhard Nievergelt, born in 1935, grew up in Zurich. Researcher and educator in the area of Wildlife Research and Nature Protection Ecology at the Zoological Institute of the University of Zurich, first as Senior Assistant and Lecturer and from 1992 to 2001 as Professor. Focus of field studies: Hoofed animals in the mountainous regions of Eurasia and Africa, including the book: *Ibexes in an African Environment* (Springer Verlag, 1981). Engagement in application-oriented and transdisciplinary landscape research: President of the Research Commission of Swiss National Parks and the Nature Experience Park Sihlwald, President of the Work Group for the Forest; and Project Leaders for the Nature Protection Master Plan of the Canton of Zurich (1986). Together with Hansruedi Wildermuth, he also published: *Eine Landschaft und ihr Leben: das Zürcher Oberland – Vom Tierhag zum Volkiland* (A Landscape and its Life: The Zurcher Oberland – From Tierhag to the Volkiland (2001).

Nachwort und Dank des Herausgebers

In meiner langjährigen Tätigkeit als Büchermacher, Herausgeber und Verleger konnte ich schon viele schöne Gegenden der Schweiz zwischen zwei Buchdeckeln verpacken. Die Vielfalt der Landschaften der Schweiz auf engem Raum ist einmalig. Und warum denn in die Ferne schweifen? Warum nicht einmal ein Buch über die Landschaften des Kantons Zürich – praktisch vor der Haustüre – publizieren?

Die naturräumliche Vielfalt des Kantons Zürich mit seinen Seen-, Fluss-, Wald-, Auen- und Moorlandschaften ist gross. Beachtlich ist auch der Reichtum an topografischen Varianten mit dem Zürcher Oberland, dem Bachtel und Pfannenstiel, der Albiskette und der Lägern. Natürlich kann man das Zürcher Oberland mit der höchsten Erhebung des Kantons – dem Schnebelhorn mit 1292 Meter Höhe – nicht mit den Berner oder Walliser Alpen und ihren Viertausendern vergleichen. Aber das zerklüftete Oberland mit seinen unzähligen Wasserfällen bietet einen ganz besonderen Reiz, und der Blick über die Kantonsgrenze bei Föhnstimmung bringt uns die verschneiten Alpen zum Greifen nah in unsere Wohnstuben. Auch das gehört zum Kanton Zürich.

Zusammen mit dem Fotografen André Roth bin ich aufgebrochen, um für dieses Buch eine Bestandesaufnahme der Landschaftstypen in unserem Kanton vorzunehmen – und auch mit dem Ziel, den Bewohnerinnen und Bewohnern die noch intakten Landschaften unseres Kantons aufzuzeigen. Über ein Jahr lang waren wir auf Fotoexkursionen im ganzen Kanton unterwegs. Wir haben keinen Aufwand gescheut: Wir kletterten im Bärtobel in der steilen Westwand am Hörnli und stiegen auf der Direttissima durch die Fallätschen. Wir begaben uns frühmorgens auf die Pirsch, marschierten in der brütenden Sommerhitze, wateten durch Sümpfe und Flüsse. Nichts konnte uns aufhalten, unseren Kanton von der schönsten Seite zu zeigen. Und selbst die kleine Ausbeute von zwei Fotos nach einer Tagesexkursion, bei der das Wetter nicht mitspielte, hat uns nicht entmutigt. Mein grösster Dank gilt darum den Fotografen Roth+Schmid für ihren unermesslichen Einsatz und die gelungenen Fotos.

Den bekannten Landschaftsschützer Hans Weiss habe ich schon in früheren Jahren kennen und schätzen gelernt. Gerne gestaltete ich als Grafiker seine Bücher. Für dieses Buch hat er spontan sein profundes Wissen über den Naturschutz zur Verfügung gestellt. Von seinem einleitenden Text über unseren Kanton bin ich begeistert; vor allem seine ausführlichen Beschreibungen – Was ist eine Landschaft? – haben meinen persönlichen Blick geschärft.

Ein Glücksfall ist der Wildforscher und Naturschutzökologe Bernhard Nievergelt, der durch die Vermittlung von Hans Weiss zum Autorenteam gestossen ist. Er kennt den Kanton Zürich wie kaum ein anderer und hat uns viele Standorttipps mit auf den Weg gegeben. Sein enormes Wissen über die ökologischen Zusammenhänge in der Natur hat uns bei der Arbeit begleitet und inspiriert. Für den grossen Einsatz und die schöne Zusammenarbeit danke ich den beiden Autoren, Bernhard Nievergelt und Hans Weiss, ganz herzlich.

Das Buch konnte nur dank der finanziellen Unterstützung durch den Lotteriefonds des Kantons Zürich und der Mithilfe vieler Personen realisiert werden. Ich möchte allen Beteiligten für ihr grosses Engagement danken:

Förster Rolf Stricker, Sternenberg Gfell; Stadtforstmeister Beat Hildebrandt, Bülach; Karin Hindenlang, Wildnispark Zürich; Stefan Heller, BirdLife-Naturzentrum Neeracherried; Werner Loosli, Flughafen Zürich; Manfred Blum und Silvan Fluder, Park Seleger Moor; Lorenz Hurni, Institut für Kartografie und Geoinformation, ETH Zürich; Beverly Zumbühl, WordsWork Zürich (Übersetzungen); Andres Betschart, bürobetschart Winterthur (Lektorat); Aurel Feher und Peter Enz (Piloten bei den Flugaufnahmen); Ferdinand Pfister, Olten.

Im Weiteren danke ich meiner Frau Susanne Jahn von Arx und meinem Bruder Jakob von Arx sowie meinen Mitarbeitern im Verlag Urs Bolz, Matthias Weber und Claudia Neff, die mich tatkräftig in meiner Arbeit unterstützt haben.

Für die Grafik Seite 66 danke ich Max Maisch vom Geographischen Institut der Universität Zürich. Folgenden Spendern danke ich: Severin Coninx, Thomas Diem, Siegfried Baumgartner, Peter Endress, Elsbeth und Matthias Steinbrüchel, Elisabeth Studer Weiss. Die Fotografen Roth+Schmid danken Daniela Eggs vom Sportamt der Stadt Zürich für die Verwendung folgender Bilder: Seite 128 unten, Seite 176 und Seite 242. Die Autoren Hans Weiss und Bernhard Nievergelt danken Christian Göldi, Wasserbauingenieur, Schaffhausen; Max Maisch, Geograf und Gletscherforscher, Gockhausen/ZH; Siegfried Baumgartner, Geologe, Küsnacht/ZH.

Heinz von Arx, Herausgeber und Verleger
Juni 2016

Epilogue and Acknowledgements

In my many years as a book-maker, editor and publisher, I have managed to pack many beautiful aspects of Switzerland between two covers. The diversity of the landscapes in Switzerland in such a small area is unique. So then, why go so far afield? Why not publish a book about the landscapes in the Canton of Zurich; it's practically at my door!

In the Canton of Zurich, with its lakes, rivers, forests, fens and moor landscapes, the natural spatial diversity is great. Also remarkable is the richness of topographical variations in the Zurich Oberland, the Bachtel and Pfannenstiel, the Albis mountain range and the Lägern Mountains. Of course, even with highest elevation in the canton, the Schnebelhorn at 1292 metres, the Zurich Oberland cannot compare with the Bernese or Wallis Alps and their four-thousand-metre mountains. However, the ragged Oberland with its countless waterfalls has a very special appeal, and the view beyond the canton's border on a Föhn day (a warm wind that brings good weather for a short time) brings the snow-covered Alps right into our living rooms. That is also part of the Canton of Zurich.

Together with the photographer, André Roth, I set out to make an inventory of the landscape types in our canton for this book, and, with the goal to present the still intact landscapes to the residents of our canton. It took one year for us to complete our photo excursion of the entire canton. We did not shy away from any effort: We climbed the Bärtobel on the steep west wall of the Hörnli and ascended the Direttissima through the Fallätschen on the Uetliberg. We launched ourselves early mornings on the pursuit of interesting landscapes, marched on in the brutal summer heat and waded through bogs and marshes and rivers. Nothing could stop us from showing the stunning side of our canton. Even after a day's excursion when the weather did not cooperate, the small trophy of two photographs did not discourage us. My greatest appreciation therefore goes to the Fotografen Roth+Schmid for their immeasurable commitment and successful photographs.

In earlier years, I met the well-known landscape protection advocate, Hans Weiss, and have appreciated him ever since. I felt lucky to work on his books as a graphic designer. For this book, he spontaneously offered his profound knowledge about nature protection and wrote the introduction. His knowledge about our canton excited me, in particular, his detailed description in 'What Is a Landscape?' has sharpened my personal view. Through a stroke of luck, the wildlife researcher and nature protection ecologist, Bernhard Nievergelt was persuaded to join the author team through the influence of Hans Weiss. He knows the Canton of Zurich like no one else and gave us many tips about various locations and sites along the way. His incredible knowledge about ecological relationships and contexts in nature has supported and inspired us in our work. For their major contributions and wonderful collaboration, I offer my heartfelt thanks to our two authors: Bernhard Nievergelt and Hans Weiss.

The book was only possible thanks to the financial support of the Lottery Fund of the Canton of Zurich and the assistance of many people. I want to thank all of the participants for their generous commitment to this project:

Forest Warden Rolf Stricker, Sternenberg Gfell; City Forest Manager Beat Hildebrandt, Bülach; Karin Hindenlang, Wildnispark Zürich; Stefan Heller, BirdLife-Naturzentrum Neeracherried; Werner Loosli, Zurich Airport; Manfred Blum and Silvan Fluder, Park Seleger Moor; Lorenz Hurni, Institute of Cartography and Geoinformation, ETH Zurich; Beverly Zumbühl, WordsWork Zurich (translations); Andres Betschart, bürobetschart Winterthur (editing); Aurel Feher and Peter Enz (pilots for aerial photographs); Ferdinand Pfister, Olten.

A further thank-you goes to my wife, Susanne Jahn von Arx, and my brother, Jakob von Arx, as well as team at AS Verlag: Urs Bolz, Matthias Weber and Claudia Neff, who actively supported me in my project.

Thanks go to Max Maisch of the Geography Institute, University of Zurich for the graphic on page 66. I also want to thank the following contributors: Severin Coninx, Thomas Diem, Siegfried Baumgartner, Peter Endress, Elsbeth and Matthias Steinbrüchel, Elisabeth Studer Weiss. The Fotografen Roth+Schmid thank Daniela Eggs of the Sports Department of the City of Zurich for the use of the following photographs: page 128 below, page 176 and page 242.

The authors, Hans Weiss and Bernhard Nievergelt, want to thank Christian Göldi, Hydraulic Engineer, Schaffhausen; Max Maisch, Geographer and Glaciologist, Gockhausen/ZH; and Siegfried Baumgartner, Geologist, Küsnacht/ZH.

Heinz von Arx, Editor and Publisher
June 2016

Das Autorenteam
von links nach rechts:

The team of authors
from left to right:

Heinz von Arx
Hans Weiss
Bernhard Nievergelt
André Roth